ULFA

Praise for the Book

'This is a careful, granular and informative study of the origins and evolution of the United Liberation Front of Asom. The work provides suitable political context, is nuanced in its judgement and avoids making sweeping claims. Those interested in the emergence and role of this critical political movement in a vital state in India's long-troubled northeast will benefit much from a careful perusal of this volume.'

—**Prof. Sumit Ganguly**, Rabindranath Tagore Chair in Indian Cultures and Civilizations, Indiana University, Bloomington, USA

'[This book contains] gripping details about the rise and fall of ULFA, intertwined with the roles (at telling moments) of Pakistan, China, Myanmar, Bhutan and Bangladesh.'

—**Veena Sikri**, former High Commissioner of India to Bangladesh

ULFA

The Mirage of Dawn

RAJEEV BHATTACHARYYA

HarperCollins *Publishers* India

First published in India by HarperCollins *Publishers* 2023
4th Floor, Tower A, Building No. 10, DLF Cyber City,
DLF Phase II, Gurugram, Haryana – 122002
www.harpercollins.co.in

2 4 6 8 10 9 7 5 3

P-ISBN: 978-93-5699-308-2
E-ISBN: 978-93-5699-304-4

Typeset in 10.5/14.4 Sabon LT Std at
Manipal Technologies Limited, Manipal

Printed and bound at
Replika Press Pvt. Ltd.

CONTENTS

The detailed notes and appendices pertaining to this book are available on the HarperCollins website. Scan this QR code to access the same.

AUTHOR'S NOTE

THE RICKETY MOTORBOAT roared in the swirling waters of the Dibang river en route to a remote village in Sadiya, along Assam's border with Arunachal Pradesh. It tilted perilously at regular intervals, giving goosebumps to the dozen-odd journalists who had been eagerly waiting for over a month to attend the press conference they were heading to now. Senior functionaries of the outlawed United Liberation Front of Asom (ULFA) had raised the banner of revolt against the leadership, in a development unprecedented in ULFA's history. And they belonged to the outfit's dreaded 28 Battalion, which had struck terror continually in the eastern districts of the state for over a decade. When the boat finally reached the remote village of Amarpur, the commanders (the senior functionaries who had struck out on their own) were excitedly waiting to disclose astonishing aspects of the organization's internal conditions and decision-making process that had prompted them to chart a different route.

That was on 26 June 2008. During the many months before this, ULFA was being gradually cornered as a result of the intensified counter-insurgency operations of the security forces in Assam. It was not the first time that the rebel group had been on the backfoot in its separatist campaign seeking independence for Assam from India. But on those earlier occasions it had been able to recover and regroup in an unexpectedly quick span of time. However, it was clear that the situation had become vastly different when the majority of the functionaries of 28 Battalion decided to come overground for talks with the government in 2008. Serious doubts were cast over whether ULFA would be able to bounce back with the same vigour as earlier. Whatever might have been the actual situation, the press conference served the purpose of enhancing my curiosity, making me delve deeper into the issue and fine-tune my research into ULFA.

My interest in the subject had been kindled years ago when I was working with *The Telegraph* in New Delhi. Surrendered rebel functionaries, with whom I had developed a rapport, had repeatedly underscored the dire need for a book on ULFA that would be objective and based on facts. One incident, in particular, which they recounted and later confirmed, left an indelible imprint on my mind, prompting me all the more to focus upon the subject. Sometime in the late 1990s, ULFA publicity secretary Ruby Bhuyan, who doubled up as secretary to chairman Arabinda Rajkhowa, was tasked by the ULFA leaders in Dhaka to write the history of the outfit. He took the plunge with earnestness, only to abandon it six months later. There was no consensus on the origin of the movement and on some incidents that happened in the 1980s! Every leader wanted only his version to be given primacy, whereas the birth of ULFA was the outcome of several factors and efforts put in by many people at many different places.

So, a book detailing the roles of all the functionaries in the different events in the life of ULFA was essential for an objective appreciation of the organization which had marked a watershed moment in the history of modern Assam. The book also assumes importance as many ULFA leaders have decided to pen their own narratives of the movement. Certainly, these books would be replete with exclusive snippets blended with the unique flavour of an insider's account. Such accounts are bound to have great appeal among readers. But at the same time, the outsider's perspective on a movement like ULFA is no less important, given the conflicting accounts of its history and activities, the internecine squabbles within the outfit and the wide range of its clandestine activities in neighbouring countries, not all of which were known to all of its own leadership.

The research took me on an investigative trail to remote places in Assam, to the rebel camps in Myanmar, to Bangladesh, Bhutan and New Delhi, over a long period stretching to more than a decade. I soon realized that extracting information on ULFA was not as easy as I had thought, for a variety of reasons. Sometimes the missions ended in abject failure, as was the case with my efforts to contact a Rohingya leader of an erstwhile militant group in Bangladesh's Cox's Bazar or my journey to Samdrup Jongkhar in Bhutan to interview a Nepalese resident who was a crucial link in the supply chain to the rebel camps. Documents published by the outfit were hardly available; many overground and surrendered rebel functionaries who were willing to be interviewed were unable to recollect many important episodes in full detail, and there were difficulties occasionally in cross-checking their accounts. In this regard, the diaries maintained by a few of them in the camps, some of which were converted into books (in Assamese), and the memoirs of former police and army officers who had served in Assam, helped expand the narrative.

I also learned with incredible pleasure that surrendered, apprehended and overground rebels usually do not reveal their entire story to their captors. The rebels often deceive them by concocting tales whose veracity the interrogators are unable to ascertain. And, invariably, the latter would be in a hurry to frame the charge sheet and move on to the next case. Still, there were no details about a few incidents, nor could some information on them be confirmed for inclusion in the narrative. Similar to other militancy-ravaged zones, Assam saw many heinous acts committed by the rebels and the security forces, and both sides engaged in many secret assignments. But not everybody was willing to admit their involvement. I knew some people whose accounts would have added more punch to the book, but to prod them further would have been to invite danger. Like the universe of intelligence agencies, the world of insurgency is murky and many truths get buried, never to be retrieved.

So, *ULFA: The Mirage of Dawn* is not an encyclopaedia, listing every incident at all places, although all the major events associated with it have been included, with a greater focus on its foreign bases and operations. It is a narration in a journalistic style, containing a plethora of facts that were unknown earlier, as well as unpublished photographs. The account does not fit into any 'framework', nor is it overloaded with data and statistical tables, except where necessary to acquaint the reader with the developing trends. References have been cited and titles of all the relevant books and articles have been provided for the interested reader to probe further into the episodes covered. The details I gathered on many events did not match with the accounts of them that had gained currency over the years. The assassination of eminent editor Parag Das, who was an ideologue of ULFA, and Operation Golden Bird, are two examples in this regard. As such, I cannot rule out sharp reactions to some chapters, as some of the revelations there could prompt the reader to rethink his or her opinions on many aspects of the movement and the government efforts to stem it. Connecting the dots helped discern the linkages between the developments in Assam and in the neighbouring countries, where ULFA and other rebel groups had pitched tent. The changing situation in the outfit's foreign bases had a decisive impact on the trajectory of the separatist campaign in Assam.

Besides having substantial knowledge about ULFA, I also obtained considerable insights from my research into the counter-insurgency operations by the security forces, their bewildering range of tactics, their limitations and the differences in approach between the police and the army. It was astounding to unearth how some officers dovetailed their personal ambitions with the demand for producing immediate results. The success of the counter-insurgency operations was frequently proportional to the amount of actionable intelligence made available by the security agencies. And actionable intelligence was not always available, owing to multifarious factors. At times, the intense rivalry among the agencies and units engaged in the combat precluded sharing of information. There had been instances when the agencies were groping for information because of lack of sources, which was particularly true in the case of certain developments in ULFA's foreign bases. There were many episodes in ULFA's history that remained unknown to the intelligence agencies.

The research enriched me with a better understanding of society and politics in Assam. The continuing turmoil resulting from the unresolved issues created the conditions and the space for the emergence of militant movements among many communities in the state. While some fizzled out in no time, outfits like ULFA and the National Democratic Front of Bodoland (NDFB) survived longer, as internal and external factors were conducive for their sustenance. My field visits enabled a peek into the different layers of conflict that pervade Assam, their comparison with the conflicts in the neighbouring states and countries, and the reasons hindering conflict resolution. Undoubtedly, Assam's situation is the most complex in the entire region, where the issues raised by the myriad armed outfits in the state will have to be addressed sooner than later for lasting peace.

On the flip side of my endeavour to dig out the details of the phenomenon and present them in the book were the accusations hurled at me from certain sections on both sides of the fence. The allegations came from people who have meagre knowledge of the functioning of media and how professional journalists operate in conflict situations. I know many fellow journalists covering other conflict areas who have had to face the same allegations—of either being a sympathizer of the rebels or agent of the government. This is because insurgency and efforts by the government to stem it also entail a war of information, where journalists are vital cogs in the apparatus. Reporting on conflict can be like skating on thin ice, and quite often a minor glitch can lead to lethal consequences. No wonder many journalists get caught in the crossfire and sometimes get killed in conflict situations. The challenge is always to know where to draw the line and remain at a safe distance from all the actors. It is never easy, though, to maintain one's balance in all situations.

Finally, I nurture the fondest hope that *ULFA: The Mirage of Dawn* will contribute to a better understanding of ULFA and the conflicts in Assam. The book comes at a critical juncture, when uncertainty looms large on the state's horizon, throwing up a host of unanswered questions. There is an all-pervading optimism that an accord with the outfit will be clinched by the government, one which is also expected to redress the decades-old grievances of the people in the state. This book will have served its purpose if it enables lessons to be drawn for attainment of enduring peace in the troubled state.

PROLOGUE

ASSAM AND THE hill states of India's frontier zone, collectively known as the Northeast, had existed as independent principalities before the onset of British colonial rule in a long process that began from the early nineteenth century. Concurrent with the sovereign existence of the region were active cultural and trade links between the principalities and other kingdoms, especially between Assam and the Indian mainland, as evidenced from the numerous references to 'Pragjyotishpura' and 'Kamrupa', ancient names for the region, in several ancient Sanskrit texts.[1] The status quo somewhat changed when invasions began after the establishment of the Delhi Sultanate in the thirteenth century and subsequently during the Mughal regime, when its generals ventured deep towards the east to bring more territories under its control.[2] But the local kings, aided by a combination of valour, a humid climate, and the jungles, successfully thwarted the incursions every time.

A landmark event in this tug-of-war for territory was the Battle of Saraighat, fought near Guwahati in 1671, in what was arguably the greatest naval battle in the country. The numerically superior Mughal army under the celebrated Rajput general, Ram Singh, was routed and forced to retreat by the Assamese forces led by Lachit Barphukan. The end of external aggressions meant peace and stability for around a hundred years in the Brahmaputra valley. The Ahom rule was consolidated; the neo-Vaishnavaite movement spread its wings to include more communities within its fold, and the Assamese language, which was already equipped with a script, began to be spoken by more people.[3] Assamese nationality, whose foundation had been laid much earlier, began to assume a definite character.

The Ahom kingdom continued well until the end of the eighteenth century when the Moamoria rebellion, a series of peasant uprisings, shook the empire. The incapable rulers sought the help of the British, who reinstated Gaurinath Singha on the throne and then withdrew, as the East India Company was not interested in extending its empire further to the east. The rebellions were crushed but the king's position hardly improved as internal strife triggered one crisis after another. In 1817, forces from Myanmar landed in Assam in response to a request from a group of royalists who wanted to clip the wings of the powerful prime minister, Purnananda Buragohain. The troops returned home after confirming Ahom King Chandrakanta as the ruler, but they arrived again after two years after the king was toppled.

For five years, all that the Myanmar forces did was to loot and murder, resulting in the depopulation of a large tract on the southern bank of the Brahmaputra. They committed the error of foraying into the neighbouring British territory, sending alarms bells ringing at the headquarters of the East India Company in Kolkata. Meanwhile, the Ahom king who had been restored to the throne made an appeal to the British to drive out the Burmese forces from Assam. In a series of battles, the invaders were defeated and, after the Treaty of Yandaboo was inked with Myanmar in 1826, Assam became a part of British India. Myanmar also relinquished its claims over the contiguous states of Cachar and Manipur.[4]

British rule came as a huge relief to the people after the barbaric regime of the Myanmarese, but the jubilation dissipated when the British unleashed their new policies. A large area in upper Assam was allowed to be retained by the king on payment of an annual tribute of Rs 50,000. When he failed to make this payment, the whole Brahmaputra valley was annexed by the British in 1838. Focused efforts were made by the new administration to erect a structure for optimizing land revenue by discarding the earlier systems that had been in vogue for hundreds of years. This entailed immigration of people from neighbouring Bengal to fill up official positions, followed by the imposition of Bengali as the official language of the province.

A major consequence of these policies was the growth of political consciousness in Assam in the second half of the nineteenth century. The trailblazer was a young entrepreneur, Maniram Dewan, who was hanged in 1857 for his efforts to stage a revolt, with the goal of restoring Ahom rule in Assam. The nascent middle class joined hands with the peasantry at Phulaguri and Patharughat to organize uprisings against the excessively high revenue rates. Denial of recognition to Assamese as a separate language provoked a fierce campaign by a few Assamese scholars and American missionaries active in the province.

Finally, after three and a half decades, Assamese replaced Bengali as the official language of Assam in 1873, but the change came with new policies aimed at consolidating colonial rule in the province. Assam was attached with the district of Sylhet, which was separated from Bengal and converted into a chief commissioner's province. This apart, new laws were enacted, introducing an 'Inner Line', segregating the hills from the plains of Assam. The laws were aimed at making the inhabitants of the hills dependent on the government and to prevent European entrepreneurs from venturing into the terrain. The age-old ties between the hills and the plains werc ruptured.

These policies coincided with what some scholars have termed as an 'economic revolution' in the state—proliferation of tea gardens, discovery of coal and oil fields, construction of roads and railways and rapid growth of the timber industry resulting from large-scale clearance of forests.[5] The logical corollary of all this activity was the continuing influx of outsiders, either in search of jobs, as indentured labour for the tea gardens, or to reap the benefits of the economic boom. The policy of encouraging immigration to Assam was extended to include Muslim peasants from erstwhile East Bengal, with the goal of increasing the revenue yield by bringing more land under cultivation. Under normal circumstances, the local Assamese ought to have reaped immense benefits from the thriving economy. But they faced stiff competition as the British continued with the earlier policy of preferring Bengali officials to man the bureaucracy. Laws were biased in favour of Europeans, which was most apparent in the tea sector.[6]

It was against the backdrop of rapidly changing circumstances that organized efforts were made by the Assamese intelligentsia and students in Kolkata to further the cause of Assamese nationalism. The new organizations that came into being, such as the Assam Association, and literature in the form of books and journals, mostly underscored the economic exploitation of Assam by the colonial state, its changing demographic composition and the need to establish a separate cultural identity for the Assamese people. This was also the time when the first rumblings of Assam as a separate nation were heard from some scholars like Kamala Kanta Bhattacharyya. The heightened awareness of Assamese identity among the people found expression in sporadic protests when a massive agitation erupted in Bengal in 1905 against the government's decision to partition the province and club Assam with East Bengal. There were also reports of efforts being made to motivate students to engage in terrorist activities in Assam.[7]

Clearly, the political landscape of Assam was undergoing a transformation with the emergence of the two parallel streams of regionalism and pan-Indian nationalism. The drift towards the latter was more conspicuous after the launch of the Assam chapter of the Congress in 1921. This was also the trigger for an unprecedented mobilization for the Non-Cooperation Movement at different places in the valley.[8] Never before had Assam witnessed such large-scale participation of people in a movement, consisting of all age groups and including women and students. Thousands courted arrest, lawyers stopped going to the courts and students quit school. The movement was halted by the Congress after two years, but its echo continued to reverberate in Assam over the issues that had remained unresolved.

The Assamese were overwhelmingly disturbed over the continuing immigration from the neighbouring provinces, which showed no signs of waning. The danger was underscored by none other than Census Commissioner C.S. Mullan, who warned that the time was not far off when the Assamese homeland would be confined only to Sivasagar in eastern Assam.[9] Mullan's alarming statements came on the heels of the shrill demands from some immigrant leaders like Maulana Abdul Hamid Khan Bhasani for abolition of the 'Line System', which was implemented from 1920 to protect the land rights of the indigenous communities. The immigrant leaders' demands were accepted when grazing and forest reserves were thrown open in central Assam for settling more immigrants in the land in the 1930s and early 1940s. Predictably, as a result of immigration, Assam's population grew at an astonishing rate of 103.5 per cent between 1901 and 1941, while the country's population grew by much less—33.6 per cent—during the same period.[10]

The outcome of the massive migration into Assam was the heightening of the refrain of protecting the Assamese homeland against immigrants, coupled with the idea of a 'swadhin Asom' or independent Assam, reflected in the writings of Ambikagiri Roychoudhury and Jnananath Bora, which began to be articulated by more people and organizations as the British prepared a roadmap for granting independence to India.[11] Most of the leaders were disillusioned with the apathetic attitude of the Congress towards Assam, which was starkly evidenced by Assam's place in the Cabinet Mission Plan of 1946, of the colonial government, to transfer power to the Indian leadership. Assam was grouped with Bengal in the plan, and it would have been merged with Pakistan if Mahatma Gandhi had not intervened.[12] Protests swept the entire state, even as the Assam assembly resolved, in an unprecedented move, that a provincial constitution would be framed only by the state's own representatives.

Assam had a narrow escape from being included in East Pakistan, but its ordeals did not end with the extinction of colonial rule. The twin evils of immigration and economic exploitation during the colonial regime continued unabated after Independence, triggering regular bouts of unrest, beginning with a fleeting armed rebellion by the cultural icon Bishnu Prasad Rabha under the banner of the Revolutionary Communist Party of India (RCPI).[13] The first major cause of friction between Assam and New Delhi in the post-Independence era was over the settling of Hindu refugees from the newly created East Pakistan. By 1950, Assam had already provided shelter to around 3 lakh displaced people from the region. Nehru threatened to halt financial aid to Assam if it continued to oppose the settlement of more refugees.[14] He seemed to not be concerned that Assam was already reeling under a severe economic crisis after Partition.

After Independence, Assam had been transformed into a landlocked state after the closure of the centuries-old commercial arteries through land and river that linked it with East Bengal. The tea sector could hardly be expected to contribute to the local economy, since it continued to remain the garden of resource extraction, as in the colonial days. The state's leaders appropriately perceived that Assam would continue to remain backward without industrialization. For them, establishment of oil refineries in the state was part of the answer to revive the flagging regional economy.

But it was too late. The Centre had already made up its mind to divert the crude oil from Assam to a refinery in Barauni in the state of Bihar. The decision sparked the first popular agitation in Assam in 1957 in the post-Independence period, which was supported by all parties. The Centre was compelled to sanction a mini-refinery with a much reduced capacity in Guwahati.

The tremors from the agitation had hardly diminished when the People's Liberation Army (China) marched through Arunachal Pradesh and knocked at the doors of Assam. Prime minister Nehru delivered an emotional speech, which was misinterpreted to mean that he had resolved to leave the region to the mercy of the Chinese invaders. Fortunately, the PLA withdrew, but the episode was followed by greater turbulence in the state on issues ranging from language, price rise to economic underdevelopment, reinforcing the assumption that agitations were a precondition for wresting concessions from the Centre or for securing any legitimate right. And, as if this was not enough, the Bangladesh War of Liberation (1971) brought in continuous waves of Hindu refugees from East Pakistan, aggravating the indigenous communities' insecurity about being outnumbered by the immigrants. According to one estimate, over 100 lakh refugees crossed over to Assam during the war, out of which about 10 lakh never returned. Vast tracts of land continued to be occupied, reducing the per capita agricultural holding by 26 per cent in Assam, which was much higher than the national average decline of 16.7 per cent during 1961–71.[15]

Nor were there any signs of improvement in the state's economy, despite the flourishing condition of the tea, plywood and oil sectors and the huge revenue garnered from them by the Centre. Not surprisingly, unemployment soared in Assam in the absence of adequate opportunities. Between 1971 and 1980, the number of educated unemployed persons rose by 343 per cent, comprising almost 40 per cent of job seekers registered at the Employment Exchange in the state.[16] Predictably, there was a drift again towards extremist ideas, which found expression in the birth of the Lachit

Sena in the late 1960s and the attacks on Marwari traders in Guwahati. In some meetings, the refrain of 'Assam for the Assamese' and occasional outbursts justifying sovereign status for the state were also heard.[17]

So, by the mid-1970s, conditions were ripe in Assam for a full-blown agitation again. The trigger came in 1978, with the Election Commission's notification for revision of the electoral rolls after the demise of member of Parliament Hiralal Patowary, who represented Mangaldoi. In the process, as many as 36,780 foreign nationals were deleted from the rolls, which not only came as a surprise but also prompted the state government to extend the operation to eighty-one assembly constituencies.[18] However, the Election Commission issued orders halting the exercise after elections to the Lok Sabha were announced, which meant that lakhs of foreign nationals were being allowed to cast their votes as Indian citizens.[19] Civil society groups swung into action, constituting the All Assam Gana Sangram Parishad (AAGSP) to oppose the Commission's order. The bugle was sounded for a movement that eventually turned out to be the biggest mass upsurge in India in the post-Independence period.

The historic agitation erupted against the backdrop of almost two centuries of crises in Assam, which stemmed as much from colonial policies as their continuation in the post-Independence era. Although the movement's primary demand was identification and expulsion of foreign nationals, the yearning of the masses was also for resolution of the issues that had festered since time immemorial. There was a large section that participated with utmost passion in the movement but was also convinced that an alternative path beyond agitations was imperative to coerce New Delhi to redress Assam's grievances. They drew inspiration from the burgeoning secessionist movements in the neighbouring states of Nagaland, Mizoram and Manipur, where government security forces were engaged in a bitter combat with them and were employing aggressive tactics to bring the situation under control.[20]

CHAPTER 1

THE RISING SUN

Sowing the Seeds

ON A HOT summer morning sometime in mid-1978, the historic coal hub of Margherita on the eastern tip of Assam was greeted with an unusual spectacle. Two dozen teenaged boys and girls, dressed neatly in white, began to march on a playground in the small town that had also served as a military base of the Allied Forces during the World War II. They returned to do it again the next week, and the next, and then so often that it became a daily affair, with an expanded curriculum that included freehand exercises and martial arts. They identified themselves as cadres of 'Jatiyo Rakshi Bahini (JRB)', or National Guards, whose goal was to establish a disciplined society in Assam. Discipline, they assumed, could be the first step towards creating greater awareness among the people of the dangers looming large over Assam.[1]

JRB was conceived by Biraja Nanda Chowdhury, a former senior instructor with the Special Service Bureau (SSB), a defence unit formed after the Chinese aggression of 1962 to train the border populace to resist further incursions by the Chinese army. Known for his expertise in guerrilla warfare, Chowdhury was among the many officers in Assam involved in training some batches of the

Mukti Bahini at Haflong to take on the Pakistani army during the War of Liberation (1971) in East Pakistan (Bangladesh). Prior to that, he had been engaged, as a political officer for many years, in implementing the SSB's mandate of preparing the border villages in Arunachal Pradesh to resist Chinese incursions. He became the guiding force of the JRB, which his daughter Rita, who was later to become famous as a litterateur, had formed by training the first batch of teenagers and appointing Binu Chetia, a well-known young man in the town, as the commander.[2]

The JRB became the rallying point for a section of the Assamese who were convinced that only an armed campaign could remedy the deteriorating situation in the state. In 1978, two more developments unfolded to lay the foundation of the armed campaign in Assam. A student organization named Asom Jatiyatabadi Yuva Chatra Parishad (AJYCP) was founded; its ideology was a blend of communism and nationalism, and its goals ranged from securing dual citizenship and constitutional safeguards for the indigenous communities to self-determination for Assam and acknowledgement of the rights of the tribal groups.[3] Towards the end of 1978, AJYCP and JRB joined hands with other prominent groups to organize a 'Jatiyo Abhibartan' (National Convention) at Namrup on the current situation in Assam. All the prominent leaders of the day from the intelligentsia and civil society groups attended the event, their voices reflecting their diverse views on the issues afflicting the state. They unanimously accepted that the existing situation could not be allowed to drag on indefinitely. But there was no clear answer on the strategy to be adopted for achieving the desired results.[4]

Among the participants was also a small clique not in favour of adopting the earlier tactics of agitations and hunger strikes, but preferring an armed movement, which would compel New Delhi to take immediate attention. This group included some men who were to be actively associated with the launch of ULFA a couple of years later. After the conclave, this group began to assemble like-minded people at different venues in the state, with the result that more outfits were formed as the 1970s drew to a close.[5]

The AJYCP organized 'shakhas' or training sessions at Jeraigaon in Dibrugarh, which was also Anup's native village, after floating an armed wing called Samaj Seva Bibhag, in which some members of the JRB were also office bearers.[6] In Namrup, a section of government officials led by Someswar Gogoi, a stenographer at the local unit of Hindustan Fertilizer Corporation Ltd, took the lead in organizing meetings; the squad in Moran, led by a schoolteacher, Budheswar Gogoi, went a step further by sacrificing a duck at the historic Talatal Ghar in Sivasagar and naming themselves 'Saptarishi', with the avowed aim of putting an end to the economic exploitation of the state. [7]And at Lakua, prominent student leader Jiten Rajkonwar was engaging in similar activities but with the greater ambition of forging a wider platform. Attached to this group was Arabinda Rajkhowa, AJYCP general secretary of Sivasagar and the son of a renowned freedom fighter, who would later assume the role of ULFA chairman. Rajkhowa had already organized a squad of over fifty boys for a month-long training session of the JRB at Sivasagar.[8]

Within a year, these erratic endeavours were merged to create a common platform after a slew of meetings at Salapathar and Moran. The new outfit was named United Liberation Front of Asom (ULFA), whose goal was to check the influx of and expel foreign nationals and control the domination of outsiders in the state.[9] Weapons were to be acquired from separatist groups in neighbouring Manipur and Nagaland, and efforts made to reach their bases in Myanmar for training the cadres. The driving force behind these efforts was the soft-spoken AJYCP general secretary of Dibrugarh Anup Chetia, who began to take the lead in forging ties with rebel outfits in the neighbouring states.[10]

The quest for an armed revolt also gathered steam from 1979 onwards, with the historic Assam Movement against foreign nationals sweeping the state. A section of participants in the agitation eager to adopt the cult of the gun had founded many secret groups and were exploring sources of weapons. So, in a brief span of time, several organizations agitating for the same goals emerged, such as the United Liberation Front, Matri Mukti Bahini, Assam People's Liberation Army and Seswa Sevak Samiti. These outfits engaged in acts of violence at regular intervals.[11] A desperate AJYCP functionary, Hari Barkakoty, even hurled a grenade at the vehicle of state home minister Hiteswar Saikia in 1980, only to be killed himself.[12] The lessons on bomb-making learnt at Margherita were put to use early in 1981 by ULFA when a pipeline carrying motor spirit from Digboi to Tinsukia was ripped apart by an explosion, followed by another blast at Sivasagar. The twin explosions, considered among the first acts by ULFA, spurred other radicals to trigger more blasts as the agitation surged ahead in the early 1980s.[13]

Amid these developments, ULFA resolved to try its luck in the commercial hub of Dimapur in Nagaland for contacts with the newly founded National Socialist Council of Nagaland (NSCN), which had established camps in Myanmar. As many as four trips to Dimapur between 1980 and 1982 yielded no results, primarily because of the lack of genuine contacts. These failures notwithstanding, some weapons were procured by the squad through other sources. Anup's cousin Paresh Baruah, who went on to become the chief of the armed wing of ULFA, succeeded in purchasing a .25 pistol in Nagaland with some rounds of ammunition. He also persuaded a sergeant of the Central Reserve Police Force (CRPF) to bring a couple of country-made revolvers from his native village in Bihar.[14] Another close associate of the group, Robin Handique, had already amassed grenades and ammunition from his contacts in Dimapur.[15]

Certainly, a few pistols and grenades were not sufficient to raise an armed outfit. The lack of adequate weapons continued for months, with Paresh missing a terrific opportunity to forge ties with a new group named People's Liberation Army (PLA) of Manipur, which was keen to establish its footprint in Assam.

The PLA gave him documents and a magazine called *Dawn* at a meeting in Churachandpur in Manipur, but the link with the organization could not be sustained.[16] The PLA knew that Paresh could be their point person for spreading its network in Assam. Besides being a promising football goalkeeper, Paresh was already a well-known figure in Dibrugarh for his run-ins with the Hindi- and Bengali-speaking residents of Tinsukia. He had already shot dead a businessman known for his anti-Assamese activities.[17] In another incident involving a group clash, he was arrested for slashing a Bengali leader with a machete, but had to be released when a large crowd assembled at the police station.[18] All these activities notwithstanding, for various reasons Paresh could neither be convicted nor dismissed from his job as a porter with the North East Frontier Railway in Tinsukia.

Some progress was achieved by ULFA in mid-1982 when a trip by a three-member squad to Manipur's Ukhrul resulted in a brief meeting with Angelus Shimray, the flamboyant, soft-spoken foreign secretary of the NSCN. He suggested that the group frame a constitution and a manifesto before proceeding to meet the NSCN leaders in Myanmar. He told them the safest and shortest route to the camps in Myanmar was through the border district of Changlang in Arunachal Pradesh, where the NSCN had already recruited cadres. He handed a letter of recommendation with his signature, which was to be given to the Naga leadership. It was agreed that two Naga functionaries, including Anthony Shimray—who went on to become the chief of the armed wing of the Isak-Muivah faction of the NSCN—would accompany the group to Namrup for exploring potential sources of income for the group.[19] This triggered an unexpected episode, which closely attached Paresh with the group.

In a style reminiscent of Western movies, the two Naga functionaries barged into a small branch of State Bank of India at Namrup with pistols, assembled all the employees and the few customers at the branch into a corner, ordered them to put their hands up and quickly gathered some cash in two bags. The rebels managed to run some distance, but their luck ran out as they were surrounded by a mob. Anthony was nabbed and handed over to the police, but his associate managed to flee to a hideout in Jeraigaon. Paresh shifted him to different locations to avoid him being nabbed before helping him escape to Dimapur, from where he reached Ukhrul in Manipur. Anthony scaled the high walls of Dibrugarh jail to freedom after a few months.[20] The NSCN duo's sojourn in Tinsukia was hardly of any help to ULFA in locating the route to Myanmar's rebel base.

Nonetheless, the failure this time around had a positive outcome—a committee was formed by ULFA towards the end of 1982 with Budheswar Gogoi, who had taken the lead to organize meetings in Moran as the chairman, and Suren Dihingia, a stenographer at the Namrup unit of HFCL, as the vice chairman. The other members in the central committee were Bhupen Borgohain, who was the finance secretary, Someswar Gogoi, the defence secretary, and a few other members, including Anup Chetia, who assumed the role of organizing secretary. [21] But there was neither a constitution nor explicitly defined goals. Only a fictitious name, 'Doi Kao Rong', was chosen for the mobile headquarters of the outfit, meaning 'valley surrounded by mountains' in the Tai language, which was spoken by the Ahoms when they arrived in Assam from China's Yuanan province in the thirteenth century.[22] For the majority of the members, the objective was the same that had been spelt out during the Namrup convention four years ago. Till then, sovereignty as its goal had not been pronounced and was discussed only among a few functionaries.[23]

Within weeks of the committee's formation, Paresh gathered information about a chief, Negurtang, at a Tsingpho-inhabited village in Arunachal Pradesh's border district of Changlang, who had intimate ties with NSCN's vice president S.S. Khaplang. When Negurtang was contacted by Paresh, the latter was informed that the former was willing to assist a 'small group' across the border for a hefty sum of money. In addition, for reasons of safety, Paresh was asked for some 'credentials' of the ULFA group that was to be taken to the NSCN camp.[24]

Paresh was given the green signal by the other leaders to arrange funds for the assignment. It was also decided that the group would approach Bhim Kanta Buragohain—a bachelor leading a secluded life at Dhola, later to become famous as 'Mama' in ULFA—who would stand guarantee for the group before Negurtang. The message spread like wildfire in the group. Not less than thirty functionaries willing to undertake the journey turned up at Namrup, but only fourteen were selected for the visit to Negurtang's village. But there was hardly any money among them to meet the expenses of the journey ahead.[25]

Paresh came to the rescue with a daring robbery at a tea garden with the assistance of some locals. All the necessary items, including medicines and clothes, were purchased, but departure was stalled owing to the turbulent situation that had enveloped Assam early in 1983.[26] The Election Commission was hell-bent on holding the assembly polls against the wishes of all the organizations engaged in the popular agitation against foreign nationals. They demanded that the names of foreigners be deleted from the electoral rolls before the elections were held. A call for boycott of the polls was issued by the organizations, and it was accepted as almost a bounden duty among the majority of the Assamese to thwart the government's efforts at holding the elections.

What happened thereafter was one of the goriest chapters in post-Independent India as large-scale riots engulfed many regions in the Brahmaputra valley. Apart from the massacres were the numerous bomb blasts targeting the polling stations, government offices and residences of Congress politicians who were in favour of the elections. In the end, at least 7,000 people from different communities lost their lives in the most blood-spattered elections ever to be held in the country.[27] And yet, the Centre was in no mood to accept the demands of the movement in Assam for identification and expulsion of foreign nationals.

Quite expectedly, the Congress won the polls, but it rolled out a lethal plan that seemed to further justify ULFA's plan for an armed insurrection. Preparations were made to enact a new law called the Illegal Migrants (Determination by Tribunals) Act, which would effectively make it impossible to detect and expel foreign nationals from the state. In sharp contrast with other laws applicable in the rest of the country for detecting foreign nationals, the new law placed the onus of providing proof against the accused on the government. The message was clear once again to ULFA that the government would have to be coerced into accepting the demands of the people. Within weeks of the Congress government assuming charge, Chief Minister Hiteswar Saikia's nephew was shot dead by ULFA in Duliajan to deliver a stern message.

With the polls over, the fourteen-member ULFA team went into a huddle for the last time near Tinsukia in May before hitting the trail to Arunachal Pradesh.[28] They were enthusiastic but puzzled as well about the uncertain journey ahead. Nobody had the faintest idea as to whether the NSCN would actually welcome them or turn them back, nor did they have any knowledge of the Naga domain in Myanmar. Their only hope was the letter of recommendation from NSCN foreign secretary Angelus Shimray, which they had received more than a year ago in Manipur. If the reception was positive, the Naga leadership would have to be convinced to offer training to subsequent batches of ULFA too. There would be no better place than Myanmar's Naga region to set up a base, since the Myanmar government did not exercise effective control over the region.

Stepping into Myanmar

The NSCN's zone of influence was the sparsely populated Naga-inhabited area in Myanmar's northern Sagaing Division, west of the Chindwin river and contiguous with Nagaland and the eastern districts of Arunachal Pradesh. The outfit was struggling to establish unity among the myriad Naga tribes in the area since the age-old isolation that marked the Naga culture was still partially discernible in the region. Each village continued to be a 'little republic', a world unto itself, whose interaction was limited to a few hamlets with whose people it had kinship ties or shared the same language.[29] In addition, village wars were not uncommon, sparked by disputes over boundaries or competition to literally claim more heads as victors' trophies, in a custom called 'head-hunting'.

The NSCN had already clamped a complete ban on head-hunting as it was a stumbling block towards unity among the Nagas, but mobilization against this was a slow process owing to low political consciousness among the people.[30] The World War II and India's Independence fuelled a degree of political activity, but it was confined to a small section of people. During the war, the Nagas assisted the British against the Japanese, only to have their dominion sliced and shared between India and Myanmar in 1947. In Nagaland, this heralded the birth of the Naga National Council (NNC) and the separatist movement. In Myanmar also, an organization called the Naga National Convention had declared the independence of the Naga-inhabited areas on 14 August 1947, although it did not have links with the NNC of Nagaland. In a separate development, Naga delegates from the southern region of Myanmar's Sagaing Division submitted a memoranda to the government expressing their reservations about joining the Union of Myanmar, but their pleas were ignored.[31]

It was not until the early 1960s when, galvanized by a couple of episodes, more Nagas plunged into the action in Myanmar. In 1962, general Ne Win staged a coup, putting an end to civilian rule in Myanmar. Formation of new political groups was banned, Buddhism promoted as the state religion and campaigns launched against the warring hill tribes, who were mostly Christian. To make matters worse for the Nagas, thc junta (the military government in Myanmar) attached a part of their homeland to Kachin State.

The decision to create an autonomous region for the Nagas hardly improved their situation as it excluded some townships and mineral-rich areas like Hkamti and Homalin.

Sensing the danger, a young Naga in his early twenties, S.S. Khaplang, who had attended school in Assam's Margherita, began the onerous task of forming an armed squad for the Nagas in Myanmar to ward off further dangers. He set up a training camp at Kungkitu, the Naga-inhabited region of Myanmar, which was destroyed within a few weeks by the Kachin Independence Army (KIA), adding greater urgency for the Nagas' need have an armed group.[32] But the Nagas had an advantage over the Kachin—a huge cache of weapons and ammunition left behind by the Japanese fell into the hands of the National Defence Force, which was constituted as the armed wing of the Naga National Convention.[33] Within months the Nagas retaliated, preventing further inroads by the KIA. On one occasion, the severed heads of KIA soldiers were brought to a Naga village and mounted on bamboo poles.[34] The conflict also had the effect of unleashing an aggressive campaign by the rebels for unity among the Nagas. They also began to emphasize conversion to Christianity as a tool for fostering a common identity among the tribes.[35]

Khaplang's organizational and leadership capabilities were recognized when he was appointed vice-chairman of the Eastern Naga Revolutionary Council (ENRC) in 1965, which succeeded in enlisting membership of the Nagas from the Somra Tract, located south of the region where Khaplang lived. Three years later, hostilities with the KIA drew to a close and the ENRC, which had been rechristened as the Eastern Naga National Council (ENNC), also began to assist batches of rebels from Nagaland marching through Myanmar for training in China.[36]

For Khaplang, however, it was more important to counteract the damaging impact of the Shillong Accord, which was a turning point for the separatist movement in the Naga domain. This was hastily inked in 1975 between a section of the NNC leaders and the Indian government after only four rounds of closed-door negotiations lasting a month. The agreement stipulated that the signatories would lay down weapons and abide by the Indian Constitution in lieu of suspension of operations by the security forces. Further, representatives of the underground groups would be given time to formulate 'other issues' for a final settlement. However, the subsequent developments were contrary to the expectations of the government and signatories of the accord. Only 150 weapons were deposited, and the outfit was split into two rival camps of supporters and opponents of the accord.[37] Thus, the stage was set for a bloody turf war.

Khaplang was also opposed to the accord, but he decided to conceal his views for the time being. He had already firmed up a plan to gain a foothold in Nagaland and obtain a position of eminence. After he assumed the role of chairman in the ENNC, he decided to merge the outfit with the NNC to strengthen the Naga nationalist movement. His plea that Nagas on both sides of the border should be united under a single banner found wide acceptance among both factions of the NNC. His popularity soared as a neutral leader, catapulting him to the post of NNC president in 1979. He then began to implement his next plan of action.[38]

Among the first tasks identified by Khaplang was to join hands with all the senior functionaries of NNC who were opposed to the Shillong Accord. He played a key role in the release of two senior leaders—general secretary Thuingaleng Muivah and vice-chairman Isak Chisi Swu—who had been placed under house arrest by the NNC's armed wing for denouncing the accord, whose plan was also to award capital punishment to them. After their release, the two headed straight to Myanmar with almost all the senior functionaries opposed to the Shillong Accord.[39] The retaliation by the Khaplang group and NNC leaders began within a few weeks—all the areas in Myanmar with pockets of NNC support were identified and raided. The most gruesome raid was the one on the villages in the Khiamniungan region where not even women and children were spared.[40] The blood-letting continued sporadically, with the NNC eventually losing its support base in Myanmar.

With a stronghold established, all the hardliners converged at Thengpa in Myanmar's Naga-inhabited region to establish the NSCN, which was formed on 31 January 1980 with the goal of securing independence for the entire Naga-inhabited region spanning India and Myanmar. The leaders on both sides of the border now stood on a common platform, led by the 'triad' of Swu, who was declared the chairman; Khaplang, the deputy chairman; and Muivah, the general secretary. It decided to set up the Government of the People's Republic of Nagaland (GPRN) with kilonsers (ministers) as the heads of different departments. However, even as efforts were being made to expand the base of the new organization, some of its policies triggered severe resentment among the local populace.

The NSCN issued orders for forced conversion to Christianity, which also meant the renouncing of certain customs. In the Lainong Naga region, wine jars were smashed by NSCN cadres, males compelled to trim their long hair and a village burnt down when its residents showed reluctance to accept the new religion. Then, the villages were all warned not to assist the Myanmar army by carrying their loads or ration, which was a common practice of forced labour resorted to by the rebel group as well. Heavy fines were imposed on the villages found flouting these orders. Unable to withstand the exactions any longer, a section of leaders among the Lainong Naga obtained weapons from the Myanmar army. In the revolt, as many as forty-two cadres of the NSCN were killed in eight villages. It was not until 1984 that the hostilities ended, after delegations were sent by the NSCN with a message of friendship to the village chiefs.[41]

These operations resulted in a huge scarcity of weapons and ammunition for the NSCN. A vast quantity fell into the hands of the Myanmar army when it raided the NSCN camp at Janlam, which also left ten cadres and a colonel of the NSCN dead.[42] The consignments that had been brought from China were almost exhausted, with no other source for replenishment. So, when the Meitei rebel groups from Manipur—the People's Liberation Army (PLA), United National Liberation Front (UNLF) and People's Republican Party of Kangelipak (PREPAK)—approached the Nagas for shelter, they were allowed to pitch tents at select locations in Myanmar. Naturally, there were many advantages to be reaped from the alliance. The resources of all the groups could be marshalled in times of danger and their networks utilized for access to sources of weapons, medicines and other items essential for the sustenance of the camps.[43]

As such, the situation was tricky and complicated in Myanmar when the ULFA squad boarded the bus at Tinsukia en route to Jagun on the Assam–Arunachal Pradesh early morning in mid-May. The fourteen men were received by a local businessman and an old accomplice of Mama's who was tasked to lead the group to the destination on the border. He instructed the group members to identify themselves as timber merchants were they to be accosted by the Indian security forces, which was unlikely since deployment of government troops was thin in the eastern districts of Arunachal Pradesh bordering Myanmar.[44] These districts were still calm and devoid of any activity on the part of the Naga rebel group.

After a quick meal at Jagun, the group began to trek along a narrow path a couple of miles from the township. The path meandered through densely forested hillocks to the hills above. Two villages were crossed before noon, and the group stopped at each for a few minutes as its guide paid a courtesy visit to the chiefs and informed them about their mission to meet Negurtang. This was a norm that had to be followed as no outsider could pass through these villages without the permission of the village chiefs. It was late in the afternoon, after hours of trotting in the humid weather, that the destination came into view from a distance. It was not long before they were face to face with chief Negurtang, a man with piercing eyes, who was reserved and spoke little. He grew cagey upon seeing the fourteen-member squad that had come prepared for its mission.[45]

Negurtang narrated to them his long association with NSCN vice-president Khaplang over the past several decades. The chief revealed that a large group crossing the border was a recipe for disaster. There was constant danger of ambush by the Myanmar army; the terrain was hilly and hostile; and food was in extreme shortage. The economy in the region was still subsistence-oriented, with hardly any surplus production in the villages. The mantra was to move fast, stealthily and duck for cover whenever the need arose. Chairman Swu and general secretary Muivah were at the NSCN general headquarters deep in the mountains, in a place that would require as long as two weeks of continuous trekking to reach. Before reaching the headquarters, it was imperative to call on vice-president Khaplang, who was based at a village called Waktham. He would have to be requested to send a messenger to the headquarters informing the other leaders about the group from Assam. The journey could be resumed only after the green signal had been received from them, which might take several days.[46]

Negurtang was willing to settle for a group of only six; the others would have to return home. He was eager to send the squad across the border at the earliest after arranging essential items like rice and tarpaulin sheets for the journey, and four porters who would also double up as guides.[47] Later in the evening, the entire group went into a huddle to decide which six among them would go ahead to Myanmar. Four were selected without debate—Anup, Paresh, Budheswar Gogoi (not the chairman) and Pradip Gogoi—but there was a contest for the remaining two. Finally, Robin Neog and Pabitra Gogoi were included. The rest of the men were to return, taking the trail that had brought them to the Tsinghpo tribe's village. Negurtang informed the group that the journey to Myanmar would commence after two days.[48]

Pact with NSCN

It was still dark when the ULFA squad was woken up for the journey ahead. They assembled at Negurtang's hut with the four porters. A dish of rice, boiled vegetables and dried fish was served. The chief offered them the final tips for the journey—the group would have to abide by all the instructions of the guides and nothing was to be done without their knowledge. And, most importantly, it was necessary to remain alert against mosquito bites, which could prove fatal.[49] On day one, the destination was a village called Thahoo-3, high up in the Patkai Range in Myanmar, which had branched off from its parent village of Thahoo located further east in the hills.[50]

Everybody was loaded with over-packed rucksacks filled with rice, utensils, medicines, clothes and tarpaulin. The porters were carrying even heavier baskets. The hamlet was draped in a thin layer of mist at the break of dawn when the march began on a narrow pathway that steadily passed the village halfway up the hill. It was not long before the path steered upwards into the dense forest of an adjoining hill on a moist track strewn with leaves. It was the rainy season and there had been a heavy downpour only three days ago. Every step had to be taken with caution to prevent mishaps, which was common in such terrain.[51]

The track had bypassed a small deserted village after a couple of hours in a sharp turn to the south when the guide leading the group finally announced that the border was only a few metres away. It was just an imaginary line running across the mountain peaks in a north–south direction. But the group's trekking pace left much to be desired, from the perspective of the guides who would often advance to a distance and wait for the entire group to catch up. With the exception of Paresh, who was used to regular exercise as a footballer, everybody else struggled to cope with the rigours of the terrain, which not only called for a great deal of energy but also deftness in negotiating the slender path. [52]

Thahoo-3 was a Tsingpho-inhabited village of barely 200-odd people. The group was accommodated in three huts arranged by the village chief. Almost everybody was groaning with pain, most of them from soreness of the neck and back after their roller-coaster march, which had necessitated bending backwards and forwards all the time. The subsequent destination was another village, called Thahoo-2, which too had branched off from its parent village. It was expected to be reached in the afternoon, but two hours into the journey the next morning came the information from a local inhabitant passing by that the Myanmar army had pitched tent at a spot only 2 kilometres from the village. There was a high possibility of the neighbouring villages being raided and burned. So the guides decided to head to Papong further east, the expectation being that it was beyond the range of the army. From Papong, a letter was dispatched to Khaplang at Waktham, which was only a day's walk from the village.[53]

A week later, Khaplang himself appeared at Papong to take the group to Waktham. But before that a volley of questions was fired by the Naga leader at the wannabe rebels, who were astonished at his knowledge about Assam.[54] Khaplang had become well versed with Assam at an early age while attending school at Margherita. Satisfied with the group's commitment, Khaplang decided to take them to his village after a couple of days.[55]

At Waktham, a grand party was thrown by the Naga leader in honour of the guests. A buffalo was slaughtered early in the morning, the village cleaned and a bamboo gate erected to receive other guests from the neighbouring villages. It was a long stay for a couple of weeks at the village, but each day was unforgettable for the visitors. The village was a world to explore and it never failed to throw up surprises. The ULFA members taught the Nagas the art of using the ploughshare for cultivation on the flat terrain contiguous to the settlement. There was more to learn and to offer, but it was also time to leave. Khaplang finally announced that the next destination was the central headquarters (CHQ) of the NSCN at Tonu, between the villages of Rokhu and Challam Basti, where the other leaders resided.[56]

The group was enlarged to more than a hundred, including the porters carrying rice and other items, and two dozen armed Naga cadres to provide security. The first night was spent in the jungle in makeshift camps, but the Myanmar army had received inputs about the movement of the large group. It transpired later that the army had been waiting for the perfect opportunity to strike. But the group dodged all possibilities of ambush by marching at an incredible speed for the next twelve days till it reached the central headquarters of the NSCN at Tonu atop a hill.[57]

Trouble came knocking at the door only a couple of days after the ULFA team had settled down. Khaplang summoned all of them to his hut and informed them that the army was advancing at lightning speed for a raid. He ordered that the base be evacuated immediately and flight taken to a safer place in the hills. The army fired the first shot even before he could finish briefing them. Then there was silence for a few seconds. Everybody rushed out towards their huts, preparing to abandon the camp even as mortar shells began to explode at the periphery of the settlement.[58]

All the guests, women and children were assembled at one place with whatever belongings they could carry. About a dozen armed cadres were assigned to escort them to a location in the jungles, where they would be shielded from the assault. The evacuation began even as the cadres positioned themselves at different spots around the village. Fighting raged on till late afternoon, and in the end both sides suffered losses. Around five or six rebel cadres, including the camp adjutant, and some army personnel presumably lay dead at the end of the day. The NSCN's arsenal included LMG, rocket launchers and G-3 rifles, but it was crippled by the scarcity of ammunition, preventing a successful counter-offensive. So there was no option for the combatants but to withdraw to the jungles to join the rest who were preparing to halt for the night.[59]

The army ransacked and burnt the camp, although the fire was doused by a downpour late that evening. At night, the ULFA group huddled with the NSCN cadres under shelters made of bamboo and leaves. Their food stock was exhausted in just a day, as not a great quantity of rice could be carried from the camp. Wild edible leaves, bamboo shoots and yam came to their rescue during the next three days, until it was considered safe to return to the camp. The army had withdrawn, but not before looting everything, including the foodstuff. So the same diet continued for the next couple of days till some rice arrived from a neighbouring village, which had not been raided by the army.[60]

At a meeting of the senior NSCN functionaries it was unanimously agreed that the current location was vulnerable to more raids by the army. It was resolved to march to the general headquarters (GHQ) at Suyang, which was reached after a week. However, as the possibility of a raid by the army here was also high, the senior functionaries ordered their relocation to another spot further up in the hills where makeshift camps were erected. With no stocks of rice, the entire group subsisted on herbs and leaves in the mosquito-infested jungle for close to two weeks before it was decided to return to Tonu. The CHQ was reconstructed from the ruins. [61]

Soon it was time for the ULFA team to engage in discussions with general secretary Muivah on a host of issues. Like Khaplang, he wanted to assess the sincerity of the group before committing to offer them training and entering into a pact with them. A week later, Muivah dropped hints that he was keen on an agreement, but there was a hitch—an agreement could only be inked with the chairman of the organization. Muivah was reluctant to conclude the pact with commander-in-chief Budheswar Gogoi, who had been hurriedly selected for the post at the camp by the rest of the ULFA members. [62]

Faced with this dilemma, the ULFA group resolved to send Anup to Assam, who would return to the central headquarters with chairman Budheswar Gogoi in Assam and another senior functionary of the committee for signing the agreement. Anup decided to hit the trail back since he was suffering from severe stomach ailments. So, within a week, Anup was marching home, escorted by a senior Naga cadre, albeit on a different route which was safer and easier to negotiate.[63] The rest of the ULFA members settled down to a dreary schedule of getting up early, fetching the rations and water, preparing food, watching the NSCN cadres perform drills and sometimes playing cards. There was scarcity of food occasionally, which sometimes required dividing the day's ration for lunch and dinner.[64]

Even after two months, there was no information, either from Anup or any senior functionary from Assam. The NSCN leadership was persuaded to allow Paresh to return to Assam, but on the condition that he would take a dozen Naga functionaries to Assam for treatment for malaria.[65] Two more months elapsed, with the rest of the four ULFA members continuing with the same routine at the camp, until one evening when a Naga officer informed them that three ULFA delegates were headed for the camp. Everybody jumped with excitement, as it meant that the ordeal at the camp was drawing to a close.[66]

A day later, vice chairman Suren Dihingia and defence secretary Someswar Gogoi arrived at the camp with Paresh. The joy among the ULFA members was short-lived as the Nagas sprang another surprise—a pact was possible only after a constitution had been compiled by ULFA, spelling out the goals and structure of the organization. So, ten points were hastily written, listing sovereignty for Assam as one of ULFA's goals. A structure for the organization was envisaged, mandating a minimum service of three years for every functionary before he or she could be recommended for enrolment in the organization by the district committee.[67] The

NSCN leadership was still reluctant to ink a pact, but eventually it consented to sign one with the two senior leaders who had arrived from Assam. The agreement focused on mutual assistance. The NSCN expected all kinds of support from ULFA if its cadres were to land up in Assam for any reason in the future. ULFA was also assured cooperation in Myanmar, but the group was still not imparted any training for a couple of weeks more, until one morning when they were handed dummy rifles and instructed to assemble in the small parade ground.[68]

Thus began a session of three months consisting of early morning drills, lessons on ambush and bomb-making. But there was no scope for the trainees to handle the real weapons, which everybody had been eagerly waiting for. ULFA was advised to streamline the organization for an advanced course some months later. After completion of the training, the Nagas would not allow the group to leave the camp, on the plea that the situation in Assam was unfavourable for their return. It was not until mid-1984 that the group was permitted to embark on the return trail to Assam, following Dihingia's relentless efforts at convincing the NSCN leadership.[69] Two AK-47 rifles with some rounds of ammunition were gifted by the Nagas to the ULFA members as a mark of friendship between the two groups.[70]

None of the ULFA members had enjoyed the experience at the Naga camps, but invaluable lessons had been learned and insights gained into how a rebel outfit operated. First, leading an armed campaign and sustaining a rebel outfit was a more serious affair than had been envisaged by ULFA. The task called for dedicated and full-time efforts, preparation, sacrifice and commitment to undergo the hardships and perils that could surface from time to time. Second, the Myanmar experience underscored the importance of establishing bases in the neighbouring countries and alliances with like-minded organizations in the region. And third, people's support had been the most crucial factor sustaining the NSCN camps in Myanmar.[71] At the camps were members of the United National

Liberation Front (UNLF) from Manipur's Imphal valley, which was even older than the NSCN. It was founded in 1964 but it had not yet launched an armed campaign, as its primary focus was on creating a support base. A rapport was developed with this outfit which prompted a decision by ULFA to send a delegation to Manipur after a few months for a peek into the UNLF's organizational structure and the nature of its activities. A similar agreement on cooperation and support as with the NSCN was concluded with the UNLF.[72]

Spreading Its Roots

In Assam, the situation had taken an unexpected turn, precluding Anup's early return to the NSCN camp in Myanmar. He had dashed straight to Namrup, hoping to break the news to the other ULFA members who he presumed would be waiting with bated breath to hear about the developments at the Naga base. But he was startled to find the three groups at Namrup, Sivasagar and Moran working at cross purposes, with hardly any coordination among them. Worse, the relationship among some members was strained, preventing the conduct of regular meetings to chart out the future roadmap of the organization. The conduct of a senior functionary who sought to portray ULFA as an organization of and for the Ahoms had fuelled conflict, compelling the other members to bar him from attending further meetings.[73] But that did not put an end to the problems in the group.

Anup's proposal before the other members for admitting Arabinda Rajkhowa, who had been an active member of the Sivasagar faction as a member of the committee, was spiked by defence secretary Someswar Gogoi. Anup then broached the topic of deputing two senior dignitaries to Myanmar for the agreement with the NSCN. There was no response from anybody to this, with chairman Budheswar Gogoi expressing his reluctance to undertake the arduous trek. Weeks rolled into months, until Paresh's arrival from Myanmar, which imparted greater urgency for dispatch of a delegation to the NSCN camp. The stalemate was finally broken with the constitution of a two-member team comprising Suren Dihingia and Someswar Gogoi, who departed with Paresh within a month of signing the agreement.[74]

However, even as they crossed the border, the police launched a crackdown on the group in Assam. Its activities were being tracked ever since the first batch had landed at Jagun en route to the border village in Arunachal Pradesh. Mama was arrested for facilitating the group's meeting with the Tsingpho chief. He was the first ULFA functionary to be arrested by the police, and he spilled valuable details about the group's activities. A couple of days later, chairman Budheswar Gogoi was nabbed, and both he and Mama gave an undertaking that they would not associate with ULFA in future.[75] A leadership crisis gripped ULFA, with none of the senior functionaries willing to assume greater responsibilities. Suren Dihingia grudgingly agreed to remain the chairman for a few more months, covertly and without an active role, after returning from Myanmar.[76]

No senior position in the organization could be left vacant as it would convey the wrong message not only to the NSCN but also to all new members. Anup's gaze fell on Rajkhowa again for the post of vice chairman since there was nobody else to take it on. Rajkhowa was disconnected with the latest developments, but the offer from Anup spurred him into action again. He knew that it was only a matter of time before he would be vested as the chairman after Anup explained to him the reluctance of the senior members to assume greater responsibilities. Rajkhowa's new role in ULFA had the immediate effect of expanding the outfit's network to neighbouring Sivasagar and Jorhat. Soon Anup, Paresh and Rajkhowa went into a huddle to hammer out a strategy to accomplish a few immediate tasks.[77]

A list of eighteen persons for the second batch who would undergo training in Myanmar was compiled, and it included some members rejected in the first batch. Unlike the route taken by the earlier group, this group's journey began from the Assam–Nagaland border at Sivasagar and crossed the border at Mon, a district in eastern Nagaland, with Paresh as the guide.[78] Two months later, after Paresh's return to Assam, the first general council was convened near Nalbari towards the end of 1984. It bade farewell to the old guard and confirmed the appointment of new members in the six top positions—Rajkhowa was appointed as chairman, Pradip Gogoi as vice-chairman, Anup as general secretary, Asanta Bagh Phukan as organizing secretary, Chitraban Hazarika as finance secretary and Paresh as commander-in-chief. The conclave resolved to enlist members in all the districts of Brahmaputra valley and also to prepare the next list of functionaries to undergo training in Myanmar.[79] It also accepted the necessity of funds, without which none of the plans could be implemented. NSCN never charged anything for the food and training it had offered, but the trainees had to be properly equipped with clothes, shoes and medicines.[80]

The responsibility to replenish ULFA's coffers fell on Paresh, whose attention was drawn to the treasury of a tea garden near Chabua. It was looted, although the booty was less than expected.[81] A daring attempt made at a branch of United Commercial Bank in Guwahati ended in a disaster due to faulty planning, and the entire squad engaged in the operation fell into the police net. Better results were achieved at a coal depot on the outskirts of Guwahati when a team led by Paresh forced its manager to part with the cash collected over the week.[82] Other functionaries launched business ventures such as restaurants and grabbed government contracts for supply of the locally brewed liquor.[83] ULFA's finances were shored up, enabling the fulfilment of its immediate errands. An enlarged batch of thirty-five cadres selected from different districts in the valley crossed over to Myanmar within a month of the previous group's return.[84]

Availability of funds enabled Anup to travel across the valley on his Enfield motorbike, convening meetings and identifying eligible men for senior positions in the districts. In the meantime, the ULFA flag, which was given final shape by Atul Barua, depicted a rising sun with seven rays, indicating the seven states of the Northeast in muga silk, symbolizing Assamese culture.[85] The outline of the constitution was compiled, although 'independence' was not mentioned as a goal since it would have invited retaliation from the Indian government. Instead, the word 'freedom' featured a lot in the leaflets distributed across the towns in the valley.[86] For gaining publicity, a bomb blast was triggered at a cinema hall in Guwahati, resulting in the death of one person and injuries to several, which was followed by hoisting of the ULFA flag at Tezpur on 26 January 1985 and distribution of promotional leaflets.[87]

These episodes made ULFA a household name in the Brahmaputra valley. And they could not have happened at a more appropriate time, as events in the state in mid-1985 further catapulted it to new heights of popularity. The 'historic' Assam Accord, which brought to an end the six-year agitation against foreign nationals, failed to satisfy the hardliners, who interpreted it as an 'absolute surrender' to New Delhi. In particular, the cut-off date of 24 March 1971 for determining citizenship in Assam was unacceptable to many leaders who had actively participated in the agitation.[88] In December 1985, a new regional party called Asom Gana Parishad (AGP) swept the assembly polls in the state, with the mandate to implement the Assam Accord. High expectations were raised, but ULFA's stock also soared at the same time after it denounced the accord. ULFA was viewed as an alternative by all the radicals opposed to the agreement. Functionaries from a small rebel group called Assam People's Liberation Army (APLA), which included some former members of All Assam Students' Union (AASU), also joined ULFA to strengthen the armed campaign.[89]

The quantum leap in ULFA's support base was least expected by the leadership, but it was an incentive to expedite the implementation of its earlier plans. It was also time to declare the organization's goals and policies. In a pamphlet released late in 1985, ULFA proclaimed that its objective was to 'liberate' Assam from India's 'illegal occupation' by means of an armed campaign. The movement for a sovereign, independent Assam was not secessionist, since Assam had never been a part of India, and so the campaign was not a conspiracy to break the Indian union, it explained. The brochure accused India of encouraging the influx of foreigners from East Pakistan into Assam and of economically exploiting the state, resulting in poverty among the people and threat to their identity.[90]

With the declaration came the need to explore the possibility of alliances with like-minded groups in other regions for weapons and links in the neighbouring countries. The NSCN could not be expected to gain access to a large quantity of weapons owing to its paucity of funds and contacts. China topped the list among the countries to be approached for assistance—the training and weapons offered to the Naga National Council (NNC), Mizo National Front (MNF) and People's Liberation Army (PLA) in the 1960s and 1970s were still fresh in the public memory. In January 1986, a ten-member ULFA delegation landed at Tatopani in Nepal for a mission to China. They left a memorandum for the chairman of the Chinese Communist Party, asking for support with the customs office at the border after being barred from proceeding further.[91]

Bangladesh was presumed to be an easier destination to reach as there were multiple routes by which to sneak into the country through the porous India-Bangladesh border. An added advantage was the PLA's offer to assist ULFA in its endeavours and give shelter to the team at its hideout in Sylhet among the Meitei population. Chitraban Hazarika, who was hardly known in the organization and who would later be appointed as finance secretary, was assigned to lead a three-member team to Bangladesh. His first task was to get in touch with a rebel leader from Tripura, Bijoy Hrangkhawl, who headed the Tripura National Volunteers (TNV). The outfit could be willing to sell a part of its arsenal since it had already begun talks with the Indian government for a negotiated settlement.[92] The ULFA squad reached Bangladesh, but none of its efforts was successful. The mission failed and the team retraced its journey to Assam.[93]

Inside the country, ULFA's gaze fell on Punjab, where militancy had registered an upswing after the infamous Operation Bluestar at the Golden Temple in Amritsar. Actively supported by Pakistan, several outfits had surfaced to campaign for the independence of Punjab. An ULFA delegation led by Anup landed thrice in Punjab in a span of five months with the hope of procuring weapons. Meetings were held at different locations with rebel groups, including a location close to India's border with Pakistan. Close associates of Jarnail Singh Bhindranwale, who had assumed an iconic image at the time, were keen to know about ULFA's objectives. But they neither showed any interest in maintaining links with ULFA nor any willingness to part with weapons. Among the other groups, functionaries of the Khalistan Commando Force went a step further by dispatching a delegation to Guwahati, which was lodged at a gurudwara in the outskirts of the city, near Beltola. The links were not sustained as it became increasingly clear to the Punjab groups that there was hardly any benefit to be derived from an alliance with ULFA.[94]

The ULFA leadership understood that a better option was to contact the Kachin Independence Army (KIA) in northern Myanmar, which had been waging war against the Myanmar government since its emergence in 1961. Reaching Kachin might open the door to China as well, and to sources of weapons. The Nagas, especially Khaplang, already knew the KIA over the past two and a half decades when there was a brief period of hostility between them and raids on each other's camps. Thereafter, the ties between the two sides had by and large remained cordial, which also resulted in occasional cooperation while fetching weapons.[95]

There was another reason for ULFA to actively explore the possibility of reaching Kachin. The PLA of Manipur had established a presence in Kachin, with one of its batches already having completed training under the KIA, possibly at China's behest.[96]

Beijing's commitment to New Delhi to stop aiding separatist rebels from the Northeast following the visit of former external affairs minister Atal Bihari Vajpayee to China in 1979 was not meant to be actually followed.[97] Efforts made by ULFA in early 1986 to contact the KIA through the Nagas yielded results sooner than expected. The KIA replied saying it was willing to train a batch of about 100 ULFA youths. What about the duration? And the expenses? There was no further information. Weapons and ammunition could be expensive and ULFA might also have to shell out money at the KIA base for food. So a plan was hurriedly conceived to screen 300 youths at the NSCN camps in Myanmar, select the eligible among them and enroll the rest in different capacities in the organization.[98]

Again, the problem was one of funds, which had to be gathered within a short span of time. A few sensational killings in 1986—of former Congress minister Tonkeswar Dihingia, former chief councillor of Golaghat Debojit Choudhury, president of the United Minorities Front Kalipada Sen and two relatives of the wife of former Congress chief minister Hiteswar Saikia—made ULFA's task of gathering funds from a select group of traders easier. Two successful bank robberies were pulled off in quick succession at Tangla and Namrup, which yielded more than Rs 40 lakh.[99] Two ministers of the ruling Asom Gana Parishad (AGP) government opened their purse strings to contribute to ULFA's kitty for the assignment to Kachin.[100]

A few trusted aides at ULFA were sent to metropolises for conversion of a large amount of the funds into dollars, since rupee payments were not accepted beyond the Naga villages in Myanmar. Trunks filled with dollars were innocuously loaded onto trains at Kolkata and New Delhi and safely reached Guwahati and Tinsukia.[101] All the leaders in the districts were instructed to select as many eligible young men as possible. They had to appear sturdy enough to withstand the rigours of the assignment in Kachin. In the end, a large group of about 180 young men hit the trail to the

NSCN camps in Myanmar in mid-1986. Paresh was already there to receive the batches and help them acclimatize at the camps.[102]

In Assam, Anup continued to focus on the task of fortifying the organization, which was yet to develop roots in all parts of the Brahmaputra valley. He toured the valley again, recruited more members and explained the organization's goals and policies. But his activities were also under the surveillance of the police. The involvement of ULFA in killings and extortion was well known, but a crackdown was not feasible since several AGP ministers, including home minister Bhrigu Kumar Phukan, were active sympathizers of the outfit.[103] Still, the police managed to send Anup to jail for a few months after nabbing him from the house of a professor on the outskirts of Guwahati.[104]

CHAPTER 2

THE KACHIN EXPERIENCE

Operation Lachit

IN MYANMAR THE situation continued to be explosive, with the army launching yet another devastating raid on the NSCN general headquarters at Challam Basti in December 1985, causing extensive damage and casualties. The Nagas knew that the army was marching towards the camp for a raid. But they failed to respond in time owing to their preoccupation with Christmas celebrations. As the attack began, the inmates scurried to reach the safe zone at the periphery of the camps, but not before a few senior functionaries and cadres were killed. A young captain of the Kachin Independence Army (KIA) who had arrived at the NSCN camp a few days earlier with a small group to escort journalist Bertil Lintner, his wife and daughter to Kachin, also lay dead with a bullet in his head, along with two of his colleagues.[1]

In the evening, at a spot in the flanking hill where everybody had assembled, a decision was taken by the NSCN leadership to evacuate Challam Basti and march to Noknu along a circuitous path while halting briefly at the villages Doknyu, Roku and Sungsa. Even if the army had plans to pursue the rebels, it would be confused and compelled to give up the operation. The journey lasted a week before it terminated at the new destination located further up in the hills. Orders were issued by the NSCN leadership to erect a new central headquarters, as returning to Challam Basti was unreasonable and fraught with danger.[2]

So, it was at Noknu and the neighbouring hamlet of Thengpa that the ULFA batches began to converge from mid-1986, on a route passing through Nagaland and the Konyak Naga tribe region across the border.[3] The daily curriculum of the Naga cadres was replicated by the ULFA lads to prepare for the tougher task ahead at Kachin. The training of three months imparted lessons on laying ambushes, survival in inhospitable terrain, raids on enemy camps, conducting operations at night and handling rifles, although no firing was allowed due to the paucity of ammunition. In the afternoon, NSCN general secretary Thuingaleng Muivah delivered lectures on the current situation in the Northeast, on the Indian Constitution and the rationale for the campaign for independence for Assam. By late 1986, the entire ULFA group had undergone the refresher's course, where their performance was evaluated for selection to the final squad to Kachin. Those who failed the test were to be stationed at the camp for some time and then sent to Assam for organizational work.[4]

Similar to the earlier training experiences, there were periods when rice was in tremendous scarcity during the seven months the ULFA group stayed at the NSCN camp. There were intermittent phases when their diet consisted only of pumpkin, squash and herbs. Sometimes, rice had to be carried over from distant villages. Salt was a scarce item and was purchased at exorbitant rates—unlike rice, for which the NSCN never charged anything from the rebel groups. Water was in short supply as well, and was fetched in bamboo trunks from a waterfall located about a kilometer away.[5]

Even as the final list was being drawn for the assignment to Kachin, something unusual was noticed—NSCN general secretary Muivah was nowhere to be seen at the camp. His absence at the camp was a riddle for many days, even to the senior functionaries, until it became known that he was en route to Kachin with a mission to cross over to China to seek assistance. The ULFA leaders were astonished, as it shattered a tripartite pact arrived at only three months ago between three outfits, including the NSCN and the UNLF. The pact had stipulated that a joint delegation would be sent to China with a request for training and weapons. ULFA chose not to express its displeasure since it was imperative to sustain its rapport with the NSCN. But it could not fathom the rationale that had prompted Muivah to embark upon the ambitious mission alone.[6]

Perhaps Muivah had the accelerating tension between India and China, following a row along the border in Arunachal Pradesh, in mind when he decided to head for Kachin. He also had reasons to be confident about making the trip as he had been to China twice earlier. He had led two batches of the Naga National Council (NNC) to Yunnan in 1966 and 1975 and was chosen to visit Vietnam for exposure to revolutionary tactics.[7] But much had changed by 1986 and the Chinese were unwilling to offer the same treatment to Muivah as they had earlier, and he had to return from the Sino-Myanmar border in Kachin. Incidentally, UNLF general secretary Sana Yaima was also denied entry into China a year ago at the same spot.[8]

This setback notwithstanding, preparations were in full-swing at ULFA for the mission to Kachin. On 14 January 1987, which coincided with the popular Assamese festival Magh Bihu, Rajkhowa read out the final list of eighty-seven cadres selected for the mission, including himself and Paresh.[9] At night, Paresh briefed them once again about the historic mission whose outcome would have a profound bearing on the political landscape of Assam in the future. The young men were reminded to follow all the norms laid down for the Naga region. All commands from the seniors must be executed without any objection, even if it meant facing the greatest of dangers; village elders and women were to be treated with utmost reverence and comradeship was to be maintained everywhere. The case of an ULFA youth who was spanked ten times every day for a month for misbehaving with a Naga girl was cited to warn them and get them to refrain from such activities, which might invite harsher punishment in Kachin. This apart, training and living with the KIA would also mean accepting the new rules and customs in their camps.[10]

So, the long march codenamed 'Operation Lachit' began early morning on the next day in an eastward direction to the Hukawng valley on the banks of the Chindwin river in Myanmar. Guiding them were two young Naga cadres who had earlier travelled to the KIA camps on the same route. Marching through the valley that was reached after about a week of trekking in the hills was easier, less chilly and less prone to attacks by the Myanmar army.[11] It was the same region through which the Japanese troops had both entered Manipur and Nagaland and retreated during the World War II, after a series of battles.

The group pitched tent at Taga in the valley, a place which had begun to be colonized by Nagas from the hills. Near the camp was the Tanai river, where TNT packed into small bamboo jars were lit with a fuse and thrown into the waters several times in the evening. The result was an abundance of fish for a feast that continued late into the night. The trek continued in the morning along the banks of the Tanai, which merged with the Chindwin further ahead in the valley. The route to Kachin turned north on the banks of the river when the marching speed drastically dropped, owing to the swamps in the area, which often saw the party stepping into the waters intermittently. They continued along this vexing terrain for four days, breaking journey only in the evenings, when the camps were erected. Equally irritating for the marching cadres was the silent attack by leeches on their bodies, which sometimes left gaping holes in their skin and caused severe loss of blood.[12]

In Kachin, the first destination was Nampiu, the site of 13 Battalion of the KIA under the Second Brigade, which was reached after about two weeks. Similar to the arrangement at the NSCN camps, spots were allocated to ULFA near the battalion headquarters where bamboo huts covered with tarpaulin sheets were erected. The daily schedule and training had more components, like obstacle jumping, crossing of rivers and crawling. Sometimes the sessions would stretch into many hours. Some senior functionaries were allowed to fire from the M-21 (Chinese variant of the AK-47) for the first time, although nobody could hit the target.[13]

The serenity at the site of 13 Battalion seemed to conceal the dangers from the army that lay ahead in the cadres' journey. ULFA's plan was to stay for about a month at Nampiu before proceeding to the next KIA centre, but it was disrupted three weeks later, on receipt of information that a large contingent of the Myanmar army was proceeding towards the camp. KIA was prepared for such eventualities since raids by the army were quite frequent in Kachin state. Alternative spots where the supply chain would remain intact had already been selected in advance by the KIA as a contingency measure. So the headquarters was vacated within an hour as the inmates began to march to a location deep in the hills where new structures were built.[14]

The entire old base was occupied and demolished the next morning. Three ULFA youths were found missing in the evening at the new site after the roll call.[15] Kachin had begun to take its toll on the ULFA youths. And there was a calamity again in a brief span of time. Neither the ULFA nor the KIA had any inkling that the army had kept a close tab on their movements and had already hatched a plan for another assault, albeit differently this time around.

After a week of their settling down in the new camp, a group of ULFA and KIA cadres who had gone to fetch rice from a godown in the hills came under fire by army snipers who had positioned themselves on the trees around. Two ULFA cadres and one from the KIA died on the spot, while the rest frantically dived to the ground, falling on a descending slope that took them rolling to the stream below. They escaped the ambush, but a KIA cadre's head was severed after he stepped on a landmine on the bank of the stream. The other three ULFA cadres began to trudge along the shallow stream aimlessly till afternoon when they came across a dilapidated hut, where they stayed the night. Climbing up and reaching the camp was not an option since the army could be stationed along the route, waiting to fire more shots.[16]

Next morning, another ULFA cadre reached the hut after wading through the stream the entire night. The group resumed their walk till they bumped into two local fishermen to whom they explained their predicament using gestures, telling them they needed to reach the camp. The fishermen offered them some rice they were carrying and advised the ULFA youths to remain hidden at a spot till they returned. It was only after dark that a young boy turned up and gestured to them to follow him. Did he belong to the KIA? Or to the army? The group was in a fix, but decided to follow him anyway. Around midnight, they arrived at a makeshift camp of the KIA, where they halted for the night. They were taken to the ULFA camp the next day.[17]

A sombre mood was discernible at the camp. Five ULFA cadres were already dead and a dozen more were showing symptoms of weakness. They were unable to get up from bed and participate in the daily chores of the training and do other errands. It was surmised that they had contracted 'mokhlong' from mosquito bites, which was apparent from their other symptoms, like vomiting and high fever. KIA kept sufficient stocks of quinine, but supply had not yet been established at the new camp. The other treatment for the disease, which required scratching the body of the patient with a grenade or a sharp-edged object and then piercing the fingers with a needle to draw out blood, did not yield any results. Only three cadres recovered from the ailment while nine were dead within a week.[18]

Nonetheless, the daily routine of drills was continued at the camp for two weeks more when the ULFA leadership was summoned to the council headquarters of the KIA at Pa Jau along the Sino-Myanmar border. The trek to the KIA headquarters was tougher than the previous journeys. At many places, the route was just a few inches wide on the hilly ridges. The safer tracks had been abandoned for fear of sniping by the army. Still, the track had to be changed twice to avoid ambushes in the long journey to Pa Jau that stretched close to two months. But before that, the marching group halted briefly at KIA's Second Brigade headquarters at Tanai Yang and its military headquarters at Na Hpaw. It suffered two more deadly ambushes by the army, resulting in the death of at least a dozen functionaries from both the KIA and ULFA.[19]

The council headquarters at Pa Jau was spread over a sprawling area of both flat and hilly terrain. It consisted of big and small huts that housed the cadres' barracks and the different departments of the organization.[20] The ULFA leadership had just began to settle down when an alert was sounded after three days that a raid by the army was imminent. The information was received a bit too late. There was no time to duck for cover as mortar shells began pounding the establishment at multiple locations within a few minutes. Three ULFA cadres were blown up after a shell landed at their barrack. As the operation intensified, orders were issued to the cadres to vacate the site and shift to another location called Laisen Bum, also along the border with China, where the KIA established its new council headquarters.[21]

Split of NSCN

The KIA and its political wing, Kachin Independent Organisation (KIO), were larger organizations than the NSCN and was well equipped and prepared to offset the damages inflicted by the continual army raids on its camps. Since its emergence in 1961, KIA's goal has changed from sovereignty for the Kachin-inhabited territory in Myanmar to autonomy, but that has not diminished its conflict with the government. Sensing that it would be a long-drawn war, KIA erected as many as four brigades, stationed not only in

Kachin but also in northern Shan State, where almost 12,000 troops were stationed. Its intelligence wing was considered extremely efficient and could anticipate the plans of the Myanmar army in advance. However, the raid on and capture of Pa Jau in May 1987 came as a surprise. It had resulted from information leaked by a KIA functionary to the army. The turncoat was later arrested and executed.[22]

The reverses notwithstanding, the KIA still retained control over vast swathes of territory in Kachin, and this could be attributed to two factors—the ethnic cohesiveness of the region and the consistent sources of income from the export of jade and timber to China and Southeast Asia. Like the Nagas, the Kachins consisted of a number of tribes, like the Jingphaw, Maru, Lashi, Atzi, Lisu and Rawang, but the divisions were more along linguistic lines. Unlike the Nagas, these tribes are interlinked in a web of clans which cuts across tribal barriers. The only tribe that chose to remain detached from the KIA movement was the Rawang inhabiting the Putao region, which was among the few strongholds of the Myanmar army in Kachin state; and there was also the countryside around Myitkina and some towns along the railway to Mandalay not attached to it.[23]

At Laisen Bum, for the first time, senior leaders of the KIA interacted closely with the ULFA functionaries. Discussions sometimes dragged on for hours, often focusing on the reasons for ULFA's revolt against the Indian government and its requirements of training and weapons. Conversation was difficult and slow as it had to be carried out in the local Jingphaw language, which the ULFA leaders had started to pick up, and in the scrambled English they could speak.[24] The KIA's warm gestures gave the impression that it was extremely delighted with ULFA's presence and its courteous conduct at the camps.[25] ULFA's functionaries soon began to be dispatched for operations with the KIA against the Myanmar army, including an attack on a train carrying army personnel and an ambush in the hills on a platoon. Around the same time, two ULFA functionaries were selected to undergo a course in wireless transmission at Laisen Bum following the purchase of radio sets by the outfit. Another three members were sent for training in medicine, surgery and anaesthetics to a hospital of the KIA located between Laiza and Pa Jau, straddling the border with China. After these episodes lasting for over six months, the ULFA team was instructed to march to Pa Jau and join a bigger KIA group.[26]

So, the ULFA functionaries gathered valuable experience on the battlefield almost a year after their arrival in Kachin. But so far, only one of the three objectives of the mission to Kachin had been fulfilled. The means by which to engage with Chinese government officials for assistance was not yet discernible. Nor were any sources for procuring weapons traced, although the KIA had been assuring ULFA about the arrival of a large consignment. The ULFA leadership had other reasons to be worried too. On 5 September 1987, the Junta demonetized the 25, 35, and 75 kyat notes to check black-marketeering and proliferation of counterfeit currency. There was no provision for any exchange of the scrapped notes. The lakhs of dollars that ULFA converted into kyat in Kachin were rendered worthless.[27]

News also trickled into the ULFA camp at Laisen Bum about the widespread rumours in Assam that Operation Lachit had ended in a disaster. According to the rumours, Paresh had been killed in action along with a large number of cadres and the early return of the rest of the functionaries who survived was uncertain. There were unconfirmed reports that some senior members of ULFA in Assam had already begun talks with the government for an agreement. The chain of command had been ruptured in several districts in the state as it was becoming difficult for Anup to tackle the crisis single-handedly. So it was decided that Paresh would leave within a month for Assam with select cadres to put an end to the chaos in Assam and streamline the organization.[28]

When the KIA leadership was informed about the plan, it decided to part with some grenades and about thirty rifles of G-2, G-3 and M-21 varieties from its arsenal. The weapons had already been used for many years. ULFA had to shell out money only for purchase of ammunition, which had become scarce after the raid on Pa Jau. The quantities of all the items amounted to very little, but ULFA had no choice in the matter. A better deal could be expected only after the arrival of the consignment that KIA had been bragging about for a long time, or after tracing new sources for procurement. These failures notwithstanding, there was something else for ULFA to rejoice about. KIA gave it the nod for another large group to be trained at different centres under the organization.[29]

So, Paresh hit the return trail to Nampiu in a group of fifteen, accompanied by KIA cadres. The journey picked up pace till they reached a spot four weeks later, when KIA sounded an alarm about the possibility of an ambush by the army. A safe option was to cross the region at night, which would also require traversing a route near a rail line on a flat stretch of land for some hours. The group descended on the track when a yell from the middle of the marching column scattered the group in different directions. One group, which decided to sprint along the rail line, was later compelled to cut out deep in to the adjacent jungle and lie there the whole night. In the morning, they resumed their march. They came upon a woman and two men sitting near a rice field who agreed to take them to the nearest village where some KIA cadres were stationed. In the village they found that all the dispersed cadres had already regrouped and were ready to resume the trek.[30]

The danger zone had been crossed without any casualties, but a bigger surprise was in store at the KIA camp in Nampiu. The commander informed ULFA that the NSCN had split into the Isak-Muivah and Khaplang factions following a bloody feud that had killed at least a hundred of its cadres! The ULFA squad was speechless upon hearing the news. They had heard murmurs about the growing tension between the two factions, but they could not have imagined that a deadly clash would unfold between them.[31]

ULFA was in a quandary—it was unable to gauge the situation in the Naga region and to arrive at a decision as to whether to join hands with the Isak-Muivah or Khaplang clique. The majority view favoured the continuation of ties with Khaplang since Myanmar would be extremely crucial to sustain the movement in Assam, and a neutral relationship with the Isak-Muivah faction, which was likely to consolidate in a greater part of the Naga-inhabited areas in the Northeast.[32] The group proceeded to Taga, where it learnt that Muivah and his wife had narrowly escaped from the marauding squads unleashed by Khaplang. The couple were able to flee unscathed only after some ULFA cadres who were stationed in the Naga region agreed to rescue them and take them to Assam. They were able to pass off as ULFA functionaries in the villages that were loyal to Khaplang. So the NSCN general headquarters and the big camps were all but abandoned, with Khaplang and his coterie also shifting to secured places northwards, near the border in Arunachal Pradesh.[33]

There are conflicting versions about the causes that precipitated the clash, but it is undeniable that the conflict was the outcome of differences among the leadership over vital issues and its inability to resolve them amicably. Isak and Muivah were suspected by Khaplang and his coterie of exploring the possibility of talks with the Indian government for a negotiated settlement on the basis of a proposal forwarded by Rungsung Suisa during the late 1960s.[34] Suisa, a former Member of Parliament from Manipur, had been associated with the NNC for a while before he forwarded a proposal to resolve the deadlock in the peace process in Nagaland after the formation of the Nagaland Peace Mission. He favoured a confederation with shared responsibilities between India and Nagaland in foreign and military affairs, but full Naga sovereignty when it came to internal affairs. The proposal, which was placed by the mission before the Naga rebel leaders, was rejected as the solution envisaged an arrangement for Nagaland within the Indian Union.

Subsequently, Suisa discussed the plan with prime minister Indira Gandhi, who was agreeable to it. But the plan met with a dead end after Angami Zapu Phizo's (the president of the Naga National Council) refusal to give the green signal. Khaplang alleged that Muivah's objective was to carry forward Suisa's plan, which would mean an agreement with the Indian government, entailing acceptance of greater autonomy instead of sovereignty.[35] Some former rebel leaders in Nagaland are of the view that Muivah projected it as a two-step formula for ultimately achieving sovereignty, which was misinterpreted by the NSCN functionaries in Myanmar and in the eastern districts of Nagaland.[36] Khaplang claimed that Muivah had placed the proposal for talks with the Indian government at a meeting towards the end of 1987 and had decided to go ahead with the plan without fetching approval from all the senior functionaries. This was a breaking point, as Khaplang was determined not to settle for anything less than sovereignty for all of the Naga-inhabited territories.[37]

The distrust among the factions was deep rooted and had its origins in the immediate aftermath of the founding of the outfit in 1980. The conduct of some of the Tankhul Naga functionaries from Manipur caused widespread disenchantment among the cadres in Myanmar and eastern Nagaland. The forced conversion to Christianity in areas inhabited by the Konyak, Pangmi and Lainong Nagas was widely resented. Differences of opinion among the leaders in the NSCN were aggravated when orders were issued to the cadres by a section of the top functionaries hailing from Nagaland and Manipur to conduct raids on the strongholds of the Naga National Council (NNC).[38]

Years later, another version of the conflict underscored the 'grave charges' made against the NSCN vice president, S.S. Khaplang, for financial irregularities and immoral behaviour. According to this version, he distanced himself from the council meetings and fell a prey to the machinations of Choumai, the commander of the Kachin Independence Army (KIA), who provoked him to take over NSCN and expel the leaders from India's Northeast. A large quantity of arms and ammunition was made available to Khaplang for staging the coup on 30 April 1988 at Hanseng, in which more than sixty functionaries were killed on the spot. This version further says that Khaplang's followers killed another hundred loyalists of Isak-Muivah in the weeks that followed with the assistance of the Indian and Myanmarese armies.[39]

It is possible that a few Kachin leaders might have encouraged Khaplang to evict the Indian Nagas from Myanmar.[40] But this must have been at a later stage, and months after the clash following the inroads made by India's external intelligence agency Research & Analysis Wing (R&AW) in Kachin. The Isak-Muivah faction continued to be supported in the eastern districts of Nagaland and Arunachal Pradesh and in some pockets in Myanmar. However, the involvement of Indian or Myanmarese troops in the killings can be safely ruled out.

At the heart of the conflict was the difficult task of framing a common minimum programme for the entire stretch of Naga-inhabited territories in India and Myanmar. Not only were the social, economic and political conditions vastly different in these countries, but even the government responses were dissimilar to the separatist movements. The Indian government employs a range of strategies to come to grips with insurgent movements while always keeping a window open for suspension of operations, talks and a negotiated settlement. In Myanmar, it was always a scorched-earth policy by the army, entailing barbaric raids and destruction of all resources that could be useful to the rebels. As such, diverse strategies were needed for sustenance and consolidation of rebel movements in these different zones.

The ULFA squad reached Taga, from where it trekked to Waktham near the border with India for a meeting with Khaplang and other leaders from the Konyak and Pangmi tribes that had revolted against Isak and Muivah. ULFA was categorical in delivering the message that it valued more its ties with Khaplang than with the other faction.[41] Khaplang already knew that Muivah had been able to escape to Assam because of the assistance of a few ULFA functionaries. But that was irrelevant to him for the time being. For the chief, it was imperative to station more cadres in Myanmar, streamline the sources of funds and gather weapons for erecting a new outfit. Even more important was the immediate need to tide over the food crisis in the village. Funds were donated by Paresh, enabling the transportation of rice and other essential commodities from a far-off village. After a week or so, the ULFA group resumed its journey to Assam after assuring all kinds of assistance to the Naga chief.[42]

Framing the Structure

Within a week of his release from jail, Anup plunged headlong into consolidating ULFA's base across Brahmaputra valley with the assistance of committed functionaries. The absence of Paresh and Rajkhowa in Assam made his task challenging since the organization was yet to be moulded along a structure raised from the grassroots. Recruitment had continued at a steady pace after the departure of the batch to Kachin, and the outfit could boast of 1,000 cadres by mid-1988.[43] The bulk of them were drawn from Jorhat, Sivasagar, Dibrugarh, Lakhimpur, Tinsukia and Nalbari, which was also the Assamese heartland in the Brahmaputra valley. So, the focus was entirely on the region inhabited by the mainstream communities, with the result that people in the tribal-dominated hill districts of Karbi Anglong and Dima Hasao and communities such as the tea tribes were neglected.

The formation given shape by ULFA consisted of the political and armed wings headed by the president and commander, respectively, but it was the former who exercised more powers as the head of the district committees. No major operation could be executed without his approval, and he also had the authority to overrule any decision of the armed wing. The general impression was that the structure would be similar to those of other outfits such as the NSCN, PLA and UNLF, where the armed wing was one among the many departments of the organization. These district committees incorporated lower units, called sakha parishads, going all the way down to the villages. In the plan there was also provision for regional committees, comprising district committee members, and for a central committee positioned above the regional committees.[44]

During his incarceration in jail at Guwahati, Anup had also compiled a constitution with the assistance of other functionaries who had been convicted earlier. Among them were Sunil Nath, who would be appointed ULFA's publicity secretary, and Munin Nabis, the fiery student leader who was among the first AASU activists to denounce the Assam Accord. While still in jail, they were able to gather four documents—a single-page preamble compiled by the Moran group after the Namrup convention in 1978, the constitutions of the erstwhile United Liberation Front and the United National Liberation Front (of Manipur), and ULFA's brief compilation of its objectives, which had been given to the NSCN leadership in Myanmar—that were examined, and sections selected for the new constitution. The motto of '*Liberation, Unification and Emancipation*' was coined by Nath after weeks of debate that often dragged late into the night.[45]

In brief, the constitution laid down that ULFA was a 'revolutionary political party' with the military wing working under the supervision of the party. The revolution, which was envisaged in two stages, had the distinctive influence of the Asom Jatiyatabadi Yuba Chatra Parishad manifesto combining communism and nationalism. For ULFA, Assam's liberation or independence would be followed by the implementation of 'scientific socialism' to put an end to inequitable distribution of wealth and to create equal opportunities to all sections of society.[46] The general assembly or council was the highest decision-making body with the power to amend the constitution, lay down norms for the organization and change the composition of the executive council. However, in effect, the greatest powers would be exercised by the permanent council, where the chairman, vice-chairman, general secretary, commander-in-chief and a senior member from the executive council were members. It was also mentioned that all decisions by the permanent council would have to be ratified by the executive council of fifteen senior members of the organization.[47]

With the expansion of the network and formation of a structure came the inevitable necessity to replenish the coffers to meet the increasing expenses. A list of prospective donors was compiled, consisting of tea estates, business establishments owned by non-Assamese persons and corrupt government officials and contractors. Coercive tactics were employed with those who were reluctant to loosen their purse strings.[48] At least three businessmen were gunned down in 1987–88, including the president of the influential Kamrup Chambers of Commerce, Giridharlal Harlalka. A joint operation was successfully carried out with PLA at the commercial hub of Fancy Bazar in Guwahati when a van carrying cash deposits from a bank was waylaid and the cash looted. The ULFA functionaries involved in the heist were apprehended after a week, but only after the booty had been transferred to a safe destination.[49] The funds crunch was resolved for the time being.

So, Paresh's arrival in Assam offered the perfect occasion to convene a meeting for fine-tuning ULFA's future roadmap. Sometime in mid-1988, senior district functionaries converged at Jeraigaon for a week-long meeting that began with Paresh furnishing a detailed account of the assignment in Kachin, the reasons for the deaths of so many cadres and the meagre quantity of arms and ammunition that could be procured. His plea to take another, larger group of cadres for training to Kachin was endorsed, as also the need for more funds and essential items for success in the mission, codenamed Operation Chilarai.[50]

That Kachin was beginning to have an indelible impact on the leaders, especially on Paresh and his associates who had returned, was quite evident when he made a case for all ULFA functionaries to undergo military training and for establishment of camps and training centres at convenient locations in the jungles across the valley. The plan was also to station the armed wing at these centres, where new recruits would be trained by the group that had arrived from Kachin.[51] The proposals were sanctioned, but a suggestion to trigger blasts in cinema halls screening Bengali movies for gaining publicity elicited diverse opinions. It was opposed by the Kamrup unit, whose plea for a focused approach to publicity through a separate department was accepted.[52] The meeting approved the constitution and the organizational structure that had been erected, with the suggestion to bring the civil departments under the central headquarters and the army under the general headquarters.[53]

The participants deliberated at length on the failed mission to Bangladesh and the scope of repeating the endeavour with a different strategy and team. Bangladesh, called B-2 or Base-2, after B-1 for Myanmar, was considered too crucial not to have a footprint in as it could provide the easiest route to linkages with foreign agencies and countries. It was also much easier to sneak into Bangladesh through the multiple routes along the porous border with India. NSCN(K)'s domain was not only remote but vulnerable to raids by the Myanmar army, necessitating frequent change of camp location. So there was a dire need for a base in another neighbouring country from where the leadership would be able to operate if the need arose.[54]

Earlier, almost all the major rebel groups from the Northeast had more or less met with success in Bangladesh. The trend began in the late 1950s when Pakistan allowed the Naga National Council (NNC) to set up office in Dhaka and training camps in Sylhet.[55] A splinter group of the UNLF led by its foreign secretary Oinam Sudhir Kumar was in East Pakistan a decade later, exploring the scope of assistance around the same time that the Mizo National Front (MNF) had pitched tent in the country's Chittagong Hill Tracts.[56] A little-known outfit called Sengkrak, which was the first organized armed tribal movement in Tripura, had also established links in the country with MNF's assistance.[57] The Pakistani authorities expected them to rake up disturbances in the Northeast, which was ample reason for the strengthening of ties within a brief span of time.

The camps and other facilities in East Pakistan came to an abrupt end after the creation of Bangladesh in 1971. MNF transferred all its assets to the camps in Myanmar's Arakan region contiguous to the Chittagong Hill Tracts.[58] It was not until the late 1970s that rebels from the Northeast were able to set foot in the country again, when the MNF and Tribal National Volunteers (from Tripura) established camps and hideouts in the Chittagong Hill Tracts. They were dismantled after both outfits inked agreements with the Indian government in the late 1980s.[59] So, when ULFA began to mull a similar endeavour, only a few outfits from Manipur, such as the PLA and UNLF, had hideouts in Bangladesh among the Meitei community at Chotodemai, Ramnagar, Kamalpur and Dhaka.[60]

Bangladesh had been discussed and a plan already firmed up by Anup and Nabis at the Guwahati jail after the constitution was compiled. They huddled together for hours to give shape to a plan that had brighter chances of success than the previous assignment led by Chitraban. The two realized that cultivating contacts in foreign countries could be time consuming, but that it might be rendered easier through local sources in Dhaka. Nabis agreed to embark on the assignment with another ULFA functionary who had relatives in Bangladesh among the few Assamese Muslim families that had migrated to East Pakistan after Partition in 1947.[61] Those at the meeting in Jeraigaon had no qualms about approving Anup's plan when he informed the gathering that a two-member team selected for the assignment was preparing for departure. In addition, it was resolved to send a team led by Gajen Bharali to the US for garnering support from Assamese expatriates.[62]

ULFA extended whole-hearted support to a new organization, Jatiya Unnayan Parishad (JUP), founded in 1987 under the leadership of Ram Rajkonwar and Diganta Konwar with the avowed objective of making the Assamese economically self-reliant. The leadership viewed JUP as a tool that could further many of its objectives as an overground organization of the outfit.[63] There were people across all the districts who did not join ULFA but were active sympathizers who could be roped in by the JUP for its activities. The JUP's agenda included increasing the agricultural output through multiple-cropping, bringing fallow land under cultivation, establishing cooperative societies and breaking the monopoly of non-Assamese businessmen on trade. After it was launched, the venture began to spread fast in the Assamese-dominated districts of the valley. In particular, the cooperative farms that were established and JUP's philanthropic activities had begun to strike a chord among people in the rural areas of eastern and central Assam.[64]

With all these issues having been deliberated upon, the meeting provided the tempo for implementation of the next phase of ULFA's agenda. Anup was to continue focusing on consolidating the outfit in Assam and in recruiting and firming up consistent sources of funds for the organization. He also had a plan to go to Bangladesh to supervise organizational work in that country, which would depend on the feedback received from the squad led by Nabis.[65] The leadership was most concerned about locating sources for procurement of weapons. ULFA was hopeful of receiving a large quantity from the consignment that KIA had been hoping to receive. But what was to be done if it did not arrive? Waiting indefinitely at the KIA headquarters was not a feasible proposition. The alternative would be to request the KIA again to provide weapons from its armoury, but the quantity would be too little and that would certainly hinder the ULFA plan to provide weapons to all the district units.[66]

Even as the matter was being discussed there came a suggestion from some middle-rung functionaries which the leadership found appealing. It was a known fact that the KIA leaders had a liking for 12-bore double-barrel shotguns, which were not easily available in the grey market for weapons in Southeast Asia. They proposed that the KIA leaders could be gifted with these guns in exchange for assault rifles. This apart, an excess of guns was always desirable, at a time when procurement of assault rifles was still uncertain. The guns could be utilized for a variety of purposes, including for training and in operations if more weapons were unavailable in the future.[67]

Orders were issued to gather firearms from licence holders in all the districts, causing tremendous disenchantment among a large section of the populace. The police stepped in at some places and ordered submission of all weapons by licence holders at the police stations to preempt ULFA from grabbing them, but not before a huge quantity had already been amassed by the outfit. It can be safely concluded that some 2,000–3,000 single- and double-barrel shotguns were grabbed, never to be returned to the owners.[68] They were distributed in the training camps set up in the valley, and a small quantity was taken to Kachin by the subsequent batches heading there for training.[69]

Sufficient funds had also been gathered from different sources, which again included donations from some AGP ministers.[70] Select groups were dispatched to the metropolises to convert rupees into dollars, albeit in larger quantities.[71] By mid-September, the final list of around 160 youths was compiled after interviews at different centres by the district committees, with Dibrugarh and Nalbari contributing the highest numbers.[72] The rationale of the decision to adopt two routes to cross the border, one through Nagaland and the other through Arunachal Pradesh, was to minimize the unpredictable hardships that would surface in the Naga region. There were frequent periods of food scarcity in the villages and the Myanmar army continued to be hostile. The plan was to depart for Myanmar at a convenient time towards the end of 1988, after the rainy season, when the chances of contracting mokhlong were less in the hills.[73]

Operation Chilarai

Early in December, the second batch began to march to Kachin, with Paresh at the front leading a group of about a dozen cadres. All of them were overloaded with rucksacks filled with clothes, medicines and dollars. They safely crossed the border into Myanmar at the border village of Longwa after sunset, and were followed by other groups in a trail that began near Tizit along the Assam-Nagaland border.[74] The movement of so many cadres alerted the Assam Rifles—a central paramilitary force deployed in the states bordering Myanmar—which swung into action with additional deployments at certain locations. But it hardly had the numbers to choke all the clandestine hilly arteries criss-crossing the eastern districts of Nagaland. Only one group from Nalbari consisting of less than ten youths was apprehended, and a lone cadre was injured following a shoot-out after he alighted from a vehicle near Sonari, which is contiguous to Tizit.[75]

The destination for the second batch in Myanmar's Naga region was the council headquarters of the NSCN(K) at Sungnu. The camp had a thin presence of Naga functionaries following the eviction of the Isak-Muivah faction from Myanmar. It began to bustle with greater activity after the arrival of the ULFA cadres from Assam, some of whom were also stationed at the neighbouring settlement of Sumsa. A large patch of the jungle in the hills adjacent to the headquarters was cleared, the shrubbery burned down and rows of thatches erected. The same itinerary of basic training was introduced for the cadres, with the objective of also weeding out the unfit youths for the onward journey to Kachin.[76]

However, within a week, adversity came knocking on the door of the camps again, but it was not the army this time around. A Naga officer informed the ULFA team that the rice supplies would be exhausted after a week as the supply chain from the villages had been snapped. The precise reason was not known; perhaps it was the movement of the Myanmar army in the region again or the engagement of manpower from the villages by the army. The officer explained that cadres had been dispatched to other settlements to scout for rice and whatever other foodstuff was available. As during similar previous occasions, only one meal was served every day, in the afternoon, the camp making do with boiled bamboo shoots and edible leaves and herbs gathered from the jungle. The crisis was over two weeks later when the supply lines with the villages were restored.[77]

With the customary routine established again at the camp, ULFA prepared the final list of around 140 functionaries for Kachin.[78] The rejected cadres were to be stationed for a few months at Sungnu and then dispatched to the camps in Assam. Similar to the first batch, the plan was to reach KIA's 13 Battalion under the Second Brigade at Nampiu and then to firm up the subsequent itinerary, which would depend on the instructions received from KIA's leadership. ULFA yearned to reach the KIA headquarters along the Sino-Myanmar border at the earliest, since weapons could be obtained only from these centres.[79]

So, after almost two months at the NSCN(K) headquarters, the journey to Kachin began. The cadres traversed on the same route the earlier batches had, touching Taga in Hukawng Valley and going onward to Nampiu. The difference was that this time around the trek along the banks of the Tanai took longer as they moved over the boulders and clammy earth further away from the banks to avoid the commonly used path. The fear was of landmines that were frequently planted by the army on the tracks used often by the rebel cadres. The journey lasted for over a week before the group finally set foot in and settled down at Nampiu.[80]

A squad from the previous batch that had completed its training in Kachin was already in Nampiu en route to Assam. Even as they departed, a group of Manipuri rebels also arrived from Kachin, but they belonged to the UNLF and not the PLA that had undergone training under KIA. Leading the group was its chairman, Rajkumar Meghen, alias Sana Yaima, who looked crestfallen and tired, and spoke very little. Soon it emerged that the UNLF was unable to cross over to China and that its plans to procure weapons had ended in failure.[81] The KIA leadership had also refused to impart training to the UNLF as it was not considered a rebel organization along the lines of the PLA or ULFA.[82] After a week or so, the squad resumed its journey to the central headquarters of the NSCN(K).[83]

At Nampiu, the ambience was unusually relaxed with less worries than usual about the possibility of army raids. The army columns had withdrawn to the north for a sustained offensive against others establishments of the KIA. So, the supply lines were intact and the evenings were enlivened by the volleyball matches played among the outfits. The same daily curriculum was repeated, with early morning drills and exercises, which were of longer duration than earlier, followed by political classes. The schedule dragged on for three months till the nod to proceed further came from the KIA leadership. While a smaller ULFA group was left behind at Nampiu, the rest began the march with Paresh to the KIA headquarters at Pa Jau along the border with China, which had been rebuilt after the raid by the army.[84] The plan was to halt at KIA's Second Brigade headquarters at Tanai Yang on the way before embarking on the trek to the final destination. The route was changed a bit by the two young KIA guides to avoid skirmishes with the army. It went zigzagging along the border over narrow mountain passes that went into and came out of China at several places. The KIA cadres would always conceal their weapons in their rucksacks at such places, as a mark of respect for the neighbouring country.[85]

A month later, the second group also reached Tanai Yang from Nampiu. They had taken a different route, skirting a railway line on a stretch of flat terrain. They settled down in the barracks and new camps erected on the slopes of the adjacent hills. Soon all the ULFA cadres, having been attached to different combat units of the KIA, plunged into action. The first assignment was at a village that had been reluctant to send its youths for recruitment to the KIA. All the able-bodied males and females were rounded up and assembled near the church after the village was surrounded. Barring a few who were let off, the rest were compelled to march to the nearest KIA establishment for training. Hardly had the training begun for the recruits when two teenaged boys in the group were apprehended for trying to escape from the camp. Both were tried and awarded the death penalty.[86] What followed next remained etched in the memory of the ULFA youths.

The hands of the accused were tied with rope and they were taken to a spot deep in the hills by a few KIA officers. Following them was the entire squad of new recruits from the village and the ULFA functionaries. The pair was told to dig graves, after which they were beaten with sticks and hacked with machetes by the KIA officers until they collapsed in a pool of blood. It did not matter whether they were dead or alive; they were simply buried in the graves. The episode was meant to serve as a deterrent against future offences by recruits and a reminder that there was no mercy for certain offences, like desertion and spying. No wonder such incidents were extremely rare with the KIA.[87]

From Tanai Yang, another ULFA squad engaged in an operation against the Myanmar army in what was the most prolonged and extensive exercise, at a spot not far from the jade town of Hpakant. Close to fifty cadres of the KIA and a second lieutenant were selected. It took the team almost a month to march to the region from Tanai Yang. An ULFA squad comprising two dozen youths was tagged with the supply and combat units. Even as they reached the destination, news poured in that a large column of the army was advancing to ensnare them. Orders were immediately issued to fall back on a ridge through which the army would pass. The spots chosen were vulnerable to mortar shelling. Realizing the flaw in the plan, a couple of ULFA youths suggested another location to the KIA officer, but to no avail. Nothing would convince him to shift to a vantage position. Refusal to carry out orders could mean instant death penalty.[88]

Sensing that an ambush was being staged, the advancing column of the army positioned itself at the top of an adjoining hill with better cover and space for manoeuvre than the KIA and ULFA had. The exchange of fire that began continued for almost a week, with interruptions. An ULFA functionary engaged in the episode recalled that the task was just to empty the magazines from the Kalashnikov assault rifles that were being continuously delivered at the trenches through an efficient supply line. Both sides suffered casualties, including at least half a dozen of the KIA and one from ULFA. The KIA was forced to retreat on the same route to the Second Brigade. There were at least a dozen injured KIA cadres who were carried on bamboo poles to a makeshift hospital located north of the conflict spot. Another operation that was planned at a far-off location had to be aborted at the eleventh hour after receipt of information that the army had amassed greater resources in terms of men and weapons.[89]

Amid these operations was the scourge of mokhlong again and some unexpected incidents which took a heavy toll on the ULFA cadres. The rains brought mosquitoes and the occasional disruption of the channels supplying medicines from China. Most of the youths who were down with this ailment could not be administered the essential medicines at Tanai Yang, as it is located farther from the border. The local treatment of scratching the body with a sharp-edged object and piercing the fingers with a needle to suck out the blood was resorted to, but only a few who contracted the disease could be saved. In the end, the tally of the dead among ULFA crossed twenty in a brief span of three months.[90]

Besides mokhlong, other unexpected reasons led to the death of some ULFA functionaries. A young cadre in his early twenties was bitten by a leech in the leg when he had gone to fetch rice from a godown in the hills. He returned and soon fell asleep in the evening, never to wake up again. Another cadre shot himself dead after it was decided that he would be put on trial for misbehaving with a young woman from the KIA. He presumed he would meet with the same fate as the cadre who was caught escaping the camp.[91] The most dreadful episode came weeks later, at the KIA central headquarters in Laisen Bum, where a squad of ULFA functionaries had settled down.

Another young cadre, named Abani Dutta, alias 'Cassette', who hailed from Jorhat, was suspected of gathering information to be passed on to an Indian intelligence agency after his return to Assam. He had already become unpopular in the camp for his drinking binges. A sketch showing the camps in the Second Brigade, with descriptions, was found in his bag. He was awarded the death sentence after being put on trial. And since the crime happened in Kachin, some leaders surmised that the style of execution had to conform to the local norms. A few senior functionaries had made a case for him to be put before the firing squad, which was turned down. Ten cadres were instructed to grab machetes and hack him to pieces. Those who felt opposed to his killing were of the unflinching view that he had become the target of some senior functionaries for being close to another senior leader, Ratul Kotoky, who was suspected of making efforts to talk to the government for a negotiated settlement.[92]

At Laisen Bum, there was no danger from the army as it had begun to focus on operations at far-off locations. Functionaries from ULFA were selected to undergo training in commando tactics, while a few who were able to converse in the local language taught the children at schools in the neighbouring villages.[93] It was from this location that Paresh began his forays into China and eventually came in touch with some officials of a Chinese intelligence agency. Paresh asked for assistance, but they were categorical in rejecting his overtures, which also explained Muivah and Sana Yaima's failure to reestablish links in the country. Nonetheless, Paresh succeeded in cultivating contacts at a few places like Ruili in the Yunnan province of China, contiguous to Kachin, which were hubs of business activity and were frequented by merchants and arms dealers.[94] Rajkhowa engaged in a long discussion with a senior member of the Chinese Communist Party and requested for assistance. The functionary, who was based in Yunnan, dropped a bombshell when he advised him that ULFA should opt for the Gandhian model of non-violent agitation for redressal of its grievances against the Indian government.[95]

The wait for weapons from the KIA had been too long and without any certainty of their arrival. A consignment would have to be procured by ULFA at any cost as the organization was expanding in Assam, training was on at many of the jungle camps and there would be greater chances of a confrontation with government forces in the months ahead. So it made sense for the outfit to be proactive in exploring sources of weapons and firming up deals wherever the opportunity arose. ULFA was permitted by the KIA to explore avenues for procurement of weapons, on the condition that 40–50 per cent of the consignment would have to be delivered at the KIA armoury if a deal were to materialize.[96]

Coup in Kachin

The hope of procuring weapons had prompted the ULFA leadership to summon two more small groups from Assam, comprising around sixty cadres, four months after the batch led by Paresh reached Kachin.[97] They were led by two senior functionaries, Bhaskar Barua and Ramu Mech, who also carried with them a huge quantity of dollars in gunny bags. After being trained for a few months, separately, at a camp of the NSCN(K), both the ULFA groups converged at KIA's 13 Battalion at Nampiu for the journey ahead to Kachin.[98]

Before reaching Nampiu, Mech's team had a miraculous escape from a mishap that almost jeopardized the assignment. Mech had divided his group of forty-odd youths into three squads. He was marching behind them with seven cadres from Hukawng Valley en route to the Chindwin river. Reaching the opposite bank of the river, already in full spate due to the rains, was possible only by means of the wobbly rafts of banana trunks and bamboo assembled weeks ago by the villagers. While the earlier groups were somehow able to cross the river, one of the rafts ferrying Mech and his squad was ripped apart when it hit a floating log in the middle of the river. A large bag containing dollars fell into the waves and two youths dived in to retrieve it. While one was able to grab the bag and swim to the bank, the other was sucked into a whirlpool, never to be seen again. The group decided to erect tents on the banks of the Chindwin, hoping to retrieve the body of the youth for burial. A long stretch downstream of the river was scanned, but there was no trace of the body.[99]

Early next morning, the journey to Nampiu was resumed. There the dollars were dried and then packed into bags again. In a couple of weeks, after the arrival of Bhaskar's group, with a young KIA functionary serving as the guide, the march to KIA's Second Brigade headquarters at Tanai Yang began. The route was the same as the previous group's, but they were not as lucky as the previous group to escape the Myanmar army ambush. At one spot, there was an unexpected hail of fire from the army as the group was negotiating a steep hilly track. Fortunately for the group, the army unit was stationed at a far-off ridge and the cadres were able to dive to safety.[100]

More perilous was mokhlong again, which devoured four youths, all in their early twenties, during the journey. Whenever somebody grew weak or exhibited symptoms of disease, he would usually keep mum about it as it could mean a break or delay in the journey. So, two boys collapsed while on the march, while the other two went to bed never to wake up again. The anti-malarial medicines did not have any effect; there were no injections for the disease, nor the time to take recourse to the local treatment. The dead bodies were buried and the march continued, albeit with greater caution against mosquito bites and about drinking water from waterfalls and streams. The group was able to relax only a month later, after reaching Tanai Yang, where it caught up with an ULFA squad from the second batch undergoing training.[101]

Meanwhile, at Laisen Bum there was still no indication of weapons for procurement. Paresh grew jittery at the lack of any positive response from the KIA leadership. All-out efforts were made to contact agents at different places, including those with networks at Laos, which had been the source of weapons for many rebel outfits in the past. The search extended to Kambaiti in Kachin, on the border with China, which was an area controlled by the Communist Party of Burma (CPB) and known to be flush with weapons. But the former CPB functionaries were reluctant to sell them to the KIA or its allies.[102]

Towards the end of 1989, another potent source emerged in Myanmar's Shan State, which was contiguous to Kachin and where the CPB had battled the government forces for the past several decades. The CPB, an erstwhile ally of the KIA, had splintered into five groups following the revolt by the Wa tribesmen against the Myanmarese leaders in the outfit. Predictably, KIA was dismayed with the news of CPB's break-up, but it suggested that a team ought to be sent to the neighbouring Shan State to explore the possibility of purchasing weapons. With the CPB cadres returning home from a life in the jungles, it was assumed that they would sell their weapons at concessional rates. Within no time a joint team of ULFA and KIA was dispatched to the region, where they held meetings with the leadership of Shan State Progress Party and Restoration Council of Shan State. A small consignment of fourteen assault rifles was procured from the first outfit, but the transaction also came with the rider that some of its functionaries would accompany them on the return journey to KIA headquarters to sell heroin! It was in need of immediate funds to tide over a crisis, and there can be no quicker means than selling an item that had a huge market.[103]

On the return journey, the squad was compelled to halt after a week at KIA's Fourth Brigade at Mong Ko. The route ahead was blocked following the army's deployment of additional forces. The rebels from Shan State returned without being able to sell the heroin. The ULFA group was permitted to resume its journey after three weeks, despite the uncertainties along the route, but was instructed by KIA to leave its share of weapons behind with the brigade. KIA promised the rifles from Shan State would be delivered soon at Pa Jau, which never happened.[104]

The uncertain situation prompted Paresh to arrive at a slew of decisions. He resolved to return to Assam and explore other sources of weapons. And as if this was not bad enough, there came another devastating development that stunned ULFA. Nobody suspected anything when Paresh was summoned by the KIA leadership for a day-long meeting at the office of a top functionary at the headquarters. After the meeting, he assembled his senior functionaries to inform them that ULFA has been asked to pack up and leave Kachin![105]

Had any blunder been committed by ULFA? What drove KIA to take such an extreme step? The reason lay somewhere else. It was startling for the entire group as it was most unexpected. KIA had finalized a deal with the Research & Analysis Wing (R&AW), India's external intelligence agency, which entailed commitments from both sides. R&AW would supply arms and ammunition to KIA on the condition that no rebel group from the Northeast would be allowed to set foot in Kachin. KIA agreed, as it was a relief to receive weapons at a time when war was on with the Junta and most of the other sources had either dried up or remained uncertain.[106]

The Indian government had been concerned about the likelihood of ULFA and PLA enrolling as members of the larger alliance of ethnic insurgent outfits in Myanmar, called the National Democratic Front (NDF), formed in 1986. Besides the KIA and the CPB, rebel armies of the Karen and Palaung had also joined the front. The members had agreed to enter into a defence pact, with the goal of adding greater punch to their demand for regional autonomy in Myanmar. If the groups from India's Northeast were to join the coalition, it could ensure their access to not only sources of weapons but also to the establishments and training facilities of these outfits in Myanmar. It could also lure other rebel groups from the Northeast to land in Kachin and derive similar benefits from there.[107]

R&AW had been receiving information about the activities of ULFA and PLA in Kachin since 1986, and this information was confirmed by a detailed report compiled by the Special Branch of the Manipur police a year later.[108] R&AW's station chief in Thailand, B.B. Nandy, had met with Kachin Independence Organization (KIO) chairman Maran Brang Seng and facilitated his travel to New Delhi. A deal, which got KIO to agree to expel the ULFA and PLA from its territory in return for some concessions by the Indian government, was struck. KIO was allowed to open the Representative Office of Kachin Affairs (ROKA) in New Delhi and avail of weapons, financial assistance and diplomatic training from India.[109]

R&AW insisted that it must have evidence of the rebel outfits vacating Kachin. KIA agreed to take two officials of the agency to its headquarters at Pa Jau, where they were accommodated at a hut some 300 metres away from the barracks of the ULFA functionaries.[110] But, the pact with R&AW notwithstanding, KIA was unwilling to sever all ties with the rebel outfits from the Northeast.[111] There were benefits to be derived from cordial relations with them and with the Nagas. KIA could always take refuge in and recoup the Naga domain if the pressure from the Myanmar army operations became excruciating—a possibility that could not be ruled out in the future. In all likelihood, there would be more deployment of the army in Kachin after the end of the CPB in Shan State.

Secondly, schools in India's Northeast could be utilized to educate children from Kachin, in a manner that had already been done in Thailand and China. Over a dozen children from Kachin had already been taken to Assam by a previous batch of ULFA for enrolment in schools. According to the plan, they would live in the households of ULFA sympathizers across the different districts of the state and be admitted in schools. The expenses would be borne by ULFA. After finishing their studies, the children were to return and set up schools in Kachin.[112]

Finally, KIA knew that the locals selling jade and timber had always received a raw deal from the Chinese merchants. Timber could not be carried to India, but it was possible to ferry jade if a market was available. The topic was broached many a time by KIA officers and samples of jade were shown to ULFA members on at least two occasions. ULFA was requested to explore if better rates were available in India than those offered by the Chinese merchants in Kachin. The organization assured KIA that efforts would be made and they would be informed if the endeavours were successful.[113]

KIA also gave its consent for a new camp at a convenient location in Hukawng Valley bordering the Naga domain, where other rebel groups could also station their cadres. But the spot had to be remote so that it remained shielded from the Indian intelligence agencies. It was decided that KIA functionaries would be sent to select the location and assist in the erection of the camp, but essential aspects like supply of food would have to be arranged by the Northeast outfits themselves. ULFA agreed after getting the green signal from Paresh, who discussed the matter with other senior functionaries.[114]

So, unknown to R&AW, KIA struck a deal with ULFA to fulfil multiple objectives. Paresh left Kachin with a heavy heart, but not before convincing the KIA to part with some weapons from its arsenal again. So, KIA gifted some weapons to ULFA, including a few old pieces of different brands like the G-3, G-4 and M-21 rifles, besides 9 mm pistols, land mines and bottle grenades. There was more ammunition for the G-3 rifle, besides new radio sets, for which ULFA had to make a payment.[115]

Paresh's urge to set foot in Assam at the earliest was hindered owing to mokhlong that he contracted at the KIA Second Brigade headquarters at Tanai Yang. He lay in bed for two weeks even as he instructed the group under Bhaskar and Mech to march ahead to Laisen Bum and make efforts to obtain more weapons from the KIA.[116] The duo's task was also to assemble all ULFA cadres undergoing medical and wireless training and those who were attached with the KIA battalions at different locations ahead of the return journey. They accomplished the mission successfully, and during the same time, the KIA leadership was persuaded yet again to release around thirty assault rifles from its armoury. So, in all, only about 100–120 weapons, comprising assault rifles and pistols, besides grenades and landmines, could be obtained in Kachin by the three ULFA batches trained there.[117]

Sometime in mid-1990, around four months after Paresh reached Assam, the ULFA group departed from Laisen Bum through a longer and meandering route devoid of army presence. The safety of the weapons they carried was their primary concern. The weapons were loaded on two elephants with other items and taken all the way through the hilly trail as far as Nampiu near the Chindwin river. An incident during the journey that stretched everybody's limits occurred after KIA guides received information on the movement of the army. The march was discontinued for almost a day as the danger of being trapped in an ambush would have to be avoided. A further message on the radio carried by the guides instructed the group to reach a certain location without halting anywhere for food. The plan was to reach a safe zone and then divert to a route less traversed by the army. The plan worked, but entailed a continuous march of almost thirty hours, punctuated by breaks of only fifteen minutes every two hours. Functionaries held on to each other as the trek continued at a slow pace throughout the night. The saving grace was the reduced elevation of the hills and the broadly chiselled paths, which prevented mishaps. From Nampiu, the group took several days to transport the consignment to the NSCN(K) council headquarters at Sungnu, and further north to another location in the

Pangmi Naga region. They were instructed by the ULFA leadership to settle down at these camps until further orders.[118]

Camp of Doom

After the pact was clinched between R&AW and KIA, another batch of about 100 ULFA youths, led by Bilu Saikia, which had already set foot in Kachin and was on its way to Tanai Yang, was instructed by Paresh to withdraw to Taga in Hukawng Valley. They were to await the arrival of two KIA officers who would guide them to a spot identified for a new camp, where cadres of ULFA, UNLF and NSCN(K) were to be trained jointly. The leaders of these three outfits had decided to form an alliance called Indo-Burma Revolutionary Front (IBRF) for mutual assistance, although no date was fixed for the agreement. The camp was envisaged to lay the foundation of the pact, which could be expanded later to include more outfits from the Northeast with similar objectives.[119]

As per the plan chalked out, two middle-rung KIA officers turned up at Taga, accompanied by two senior ULFA functionaries who had already completed their training in Kachin. Dukum across the Chindwin river on the border of Kachin and Sagaing Division, was to be the location of the camp, where about 100 cadres from the Naga and Manipuri outfits would also assemble for training. It was an expanse of plain land sandwiched between three mountains with an abundance of creeks. It was considered safe since the army hardly forayed into this region.[120]

Still, something was amiss at Dukum—there were only a few settlements inhabited by the Tsinghpo near the site, whose residents could not speak Nagamese. The youths from Assam could not follow their language at all. Where would the food come from? It could take days to ferry bags of rice and other edible stuff from the handful of villages in the valley on the western bank of the Chindwin. A few cadres of the UNLF group that reached the spot were able to speak the language. They managed to purchase a few quintals of rice and vegetables, but that would not last for more than three weeks. It was also agreed that the three outfits would manage their own food but participate in the training together. Essential medicines for the treatment of common diseases were also almost out of stock.[121]

Nonetheless, the training commenced with the same zest seen at all new camps. The module combined the syllabi in the Naga region and Kachin with physical exercises, drills, political classes, mock raids and other components. However, within a week, the curriculum had to be revamped with a slash in the duration of all the sessions. It was summer, hot and humid, and Hukawng Valley was sizzling under the sun.[122]

The weather notwithstanding, everything seemed to settle down for a while until murmurs began in the ULFA barracks about an impending shortage of food. There was evidence of this in the form of reduced quantities of food at the two meals served every day. The other two outfits were less concerned as they had established their supply channels with the villages. They introduced a few suppliers to ULFA, but it had no money to pay the hefty sums demanded. As much as Rs 300 was quoted for sixty cups of rice, but ULFA was left with only Rs 15,000, which meant food for only one week.[123]

An SOS was flashed over radio to the ULFA camp in the Pangmi Naga region up in the hills, but that camp was also reeling under the shortage of money. So, only Rs 3,000 could be sent, which was hardly enough to tide over the crisis. Nor did the NSCN(K) or UNLF have surplus funds to help the ULFA cadres. Only one meal was served for a whole week at the ULFA camp, and then recourse was taken to herbs and leaves from the jungle. Weakness drove many to lie in bed for endless hours, unable to complete their day's schedule. The option to withdraw to a safer location did not exist when there was no money or approval from the leaders. The situation was gradually spinning out of control.[124]

The first death occurred after a cadre was administered an injection on the assumption that he was suffering from malaria. But his condition only grew worse as he became dehydrated following continuous urination. He died the next day. After a day's gap, another cadre was found dead in bed early morning, ahead of the drill. It then became a regular affair at the camp—the dragging out of dead bodies to the jungle for burial. On one occasion, a cadre who was digging a grave collapsed after the task was completed. He opened his eyes for a few seconds after water was sprinkled on his face. He muttered a few words and then closed his eyes forever. He was buried in the grave he was digging for the dead body. As many as seven youths died over the next ten days, and within a month the toll reached twenty-eight.[125]

Anybody who complained of dizziness was relieved from his daily assignments as it was a clear signal that his days could be numbered. The daily errands of fetching water, firewood and herbs were entrusted to the few who were still active, among whom some were tasked with the round-the-clock duty of attending to the sick. The morning drills, political classes and other ingredients of the training module, like lessons on ambush and night marches, were all but halted. Another message was sent to the ULFA leadership in Assam explaining the dire conditions in the camps.[126]

Hope stirred several functionaries to fight for survival. Mrinal Hazarika, the future commander of the dreaded 28 Battalion, fought his way back to life after he was assumed dead.[127] Another cadre had a miraculous tale of survival to tell after attempting suicide. Many functionaries were woken up one night to a weird sound emanating continuously from a corner of the barrack, resembling that of a saw gnawing at a piece of wood. Their blazing torches focused on a cadre who was slitting his throat with a khukri! He uttered a sound every time the blade cut into his throat. His colleagues snatched the machete from him. His bed was drenched with the blood trickling from the gashes in the throat. A medic rushed to wrap the wound and stitched it up for the healing to start. He lost his voice but survived to resume the journey to Assam.[128]

Meanwhile, crisis had also gripped the NSCN(K) camp where the death toll was almost the same as at ULFA's. The reason for the calamity in their camp was also paucity of funds, which was not surprising given the outfit's scant sources of revenue generation.[129] The split in the group a year ago had dealt a body blow to the Myanmar faction as funds were arranged mostly from India's Northeast through imposition of 'taxes'. Most of the functionaries in charge of the finances decided to join the Isak-Muivah faction, leaving the coffers with Khaplang almost empty. Myanmar's northern Sagaing Division, where NSCN(K) exercised control, was sparsely populated. Nor was money an established mode of exchange, since all the villages here were almost self-sufficient. Collection of tax was more in kind from these hamlets than in cash.

UNLF was an exception at the camp, with only two of its youths falling ill, contracting malaria and typhoid. The group was small, with only about forty cadres, which made the task of managing food and other items easier. The commander of the camp had trained many batches earlier in Myanmar. He knew the local language and the intricacies of managing a camp in the region. He was able to gauge that the situation could turn hazardous, which had prompted him to arrange for funds and medicines in advance and also to firm up a contingency plan if things turned really bad. But the group did not have enough stocks to share with the others.[130]

The decision to pack up from Dukum came only after ULFA general secretary Anup Chetia rushed from Assam to meet Khaplang in Myanmar. Before that, the ULFA commander had also petitioned the Naga chief for a quick decision on abandoning the camp, but Khaplang was reluctant to issue permission for some time, since a camp at the location also conveyed the message that it was Naga territory. But he finally agreed to abandon the site after the meeting with Anup. He issued instructions to the villages to offer assistance to the returning squads who were told to arrive at the NSCN(K) headquarters at Sungsa across the Chindwin river.[131]

The ULFA plan was to evacuate from Dukum in stages, jointly with the other groups, and head for Sungsa at the earliest. There were over a dozen cadres who were not bedridden but who were too weak to carry extra loads for the long march ahead. It was a gruelling journey of three weeks, and some cadres had to be caned many a time by the senior functionaries to continue the march.[132] Three sick cadres of ULFA, who were carried on bamboo stretchers on the trek, died before the destination in the hills was reached. The Nagas fared better, with no casualties; only one cadre had to be carried during the last three days of the journey after he became unconscious. There were no casualties among the UNLF on the return journey.[133]

Finally, at Sungsa, the ULFA cadres were instructed to settle down until further orders from the high command in Assam. The order came as a tremendous relief to everybody after weeks of hunger, hardship and insecurity at Dukum, resulting in the death of at least thirty cadres, almost one-third of the entire group. There was no shortage of food at the camp for the time being and so recovery was fast. The relaxed schedule continued for two months more, when it was interrupted by a warning from the Naga functionaries that the Myanmar army was planning another raid on the camp.[134]

The information was correct. The army swooped down after four days and burnt the headquarters without engaging in a gun fight as all the rebel cadres had already withdrawn to a location deep in the hills. After having been being battered several times, NSCN(K) was better prepared to offset the damage this time around. All the inmates dispersed to four locations, including a place called Jakhya, where all the senior Naga functionaries assembled.[135] The army raid hastened the formation of the Indo-Burma Revolutionary Front (IBRF), which was in abeyance following the debacle at Dukum. The thrust came from the NSCN(K), as it was concerned over the rapid advances made by the Isak-Muivah faction (NSCN-IM) to extend its influence over large parts of Nagaland.[136]

In a series of meetings at Jakhya, senior functionaries from the three outfits compiled a tentative agreement, which was forwarded to the leadership of all the groups for their approval.[137] It was resolved to send a joint delegation without delay to Zunheboto in Nagaland for expanding the base of the Khaplang group. Large numbers from the Sumi tribe in the district, which had been at the vanguard of the separatist movement in Nagaland, were uninclined to support the Isak-Muivah faction. But as the delegation crossed the border at Tuensang, it was greeted with a hail of bullets in an ambush laid by the Isak-Muivah group. Information had been leaked that a squad was on its way from Myanmar to Zunheboto.[138]

There were no casualties as the encounter was brief, lasting for only a few seconds, but the damage was done. Why did the attackers withdraw when they had the upper hand in the attack? Suspicion fell on the five-member ULFA squad for two reasons. It was well-known that the NSCN(IM) leaders could not have escaped from Myanmar without ULFA's assistance after the clashes in 1988. So, it was surmised by the other members that it was from ULFA that information about the assignment had spilled out. Further, they surmised that the attackers backed out because they did not want to kill the youths from Assam.[139]

There was now a distinct change in the attitude of the others towards the ULFA cadres, who soon complained about it to the Naga commander heading the squad. But it hardly helped salvage the situation. It was a risky proposition to issue a command to a group that lacked unity. The group reached Zunheboto, but the operation was called off without completion of the task. The group retraced its journey to the camp in Myanmar along with the ULFA cadres. It was resolved by all the groups to halt joint operations until a formal structure was evolved for the alliance, with explicit guidelines.[140] The agreement for launching the Indo-Burma Revolutionary Front (IBRF) came months later, on 22 May 1990, after several rounds of negotiations between the top leaders at the NSCN(K) headquarters in Myanmar. Khaplang assumed the role of chairman, Rajkhowa was appointed the vice chairman and UNLF's Sana Yaima the general secretary of the coalition, which also declared independence for India's Northeast and the contiguous Naga domain in Myanmar as its primary goal.[141]

The importance of an alliance with like-minded organizations was a fundamental lesson learned again by ULFA in Kachin. There were many benefits to be reaped from a united front when the enemy was unyielding and endowed with greater resources to continue the battle. For KIA, the open-door policy of joining hands with other outfits was combined with active diplomacy, which was evident in its pact with R&AW and its secret understanding with ULFA, both of which fulfilled a range of objectives.

Above all, the most important takeaway from Kachin for the trained ULFA cadres was the need for multiple and consistent sources of funds to sustain the campaign. The trajectory of the war in Kachin would have been different without the vast reservoirs of jade and timber with a ready market in China and Southeast Asia, ensuring a continuous flow of funds to the KIA for meeting all its expenses.

CHAPTER 3

MISSION ROBIN HOOD

A State within a State

IN ASSAM, ULFA was galloping on an escalating graph of support and expansion, aided greatly by the general disenchantment with the ruling AGP. It was becoming increasingly apparent that the government had no intention of fulfilling its mandate of identifying and expelling illegal migrants, let alone implementing long-term measures to deter infiltration. Not only did the promise of a corruption-free administration turn out to be a damp squib but there were also allegations galore against several ministers, most of whom became drunk with power, gratification and ill-gotten wealth. A sizeable chunk among them were unscrupulous country bumpkins, hailing from humble backgrounds, who never imagined they would be catapulted into such positions so fast. Resentment against the government soared in 1988 as it was unable to offer timely relief when the state was ravaged by one of the worst floods it had experienced, which killed over 200 and disrupted the lives of 80 lakh people.[1]

ULFA began to be viewed as an alternative to the AGP, with its support base eventually extending to the intelligentsia and the middle class. In real terms, its popularity was not so much for its plans of staging a 'two-stage revolution' or independence from the Indian Union, which were still not widely known, but mostly on the presumption that it would expel the lakhs of Bangladeshi immigrants who had settled in the state, seek redressal of the Assam's grievances against New Delhi and assert the domination of all the indigenous communities in the state. For the people, the contrast between the AGP and ULFA was easily evident. ULFA had appeal because it appeared different—the youths with the gun did not indulge in loose talk; they were highly disciplined and committed; they meant business and they appeared determined to achieve their goals.

ULFA's mounting trajectory was aided in no small measure by the government's inability to crack the whip on the outfit. It was already on the back foot for non-performance; a crackdown on the rebels would have fuelled greater bitterness against the government and the party. Many AGP legislators and ministers were active supporters of ULFA, which was another reason why the government chose to be silent. Home minister Bhrigu Kumar Phukan participated in several meetings with ULFA leaders at his residence in Guwahati ahead of the departure of the second batch to Kachin. He found support among several party functionaries and legislators, some of whom were of the view that ULFA could serve as a pressure group, with beneficial long-term results for the party. [2]

An offshoot of the situation was the complete paralysis of the police, which remained a mute spectator to ULFA's activities. It was groping for intelligence on the group's plans following the near-total collapse of the information gathering machinery of the Special Branch.[3] Some top officials were convinced that a sizeable chunk of the police had developed a soft corner for ULFA, which also explained the absence of timely reports and filing of cases against rebel functionaries involved in crimes and extortion. A few police officials who chose to take on ULFA were either threatened or shot dead.[4]

As 1987 drew to a close, ULFA's parallel government began to take shape, gradually consolidating in the subsequent months with a slew of other activities. Its operations extended to more areas with a greater number of people falling prey to its squads of assassins. According to one estimate, ULFA had been responsible for as many as 113 killings between 1986 and 1990, including those of Congress activists and government employees. The killings kept increasing until the fag end of 1990.[5] Chairman Rajkhowa thundered at a public meeting that a sovereign independent Assam was ULFA's primary goal, which was underscored in a press release on the outfit's tenth raising day on 7 April 1989.[6] The examples of Vietnam, Mozambique and Angola were profusely cited to justify the path of armed struggle for an end to New Delhi's 'colonial rule' in Assam.[7] The United Nations was petitioned with a detailed memorandum underscoring the ethnic distinctiveness of the Assamese, the circumstances in which Assam was merged with the Indian Union and a justification of the community's right to 'self-determination'.[8]

As many as twenty big and small camps and training centres mushroomed across the valley, with the biggest at Lakhipathar in Dibrugarh, designated as the general headquarters (GHQ). The ULFA leadership was convinced that these camps could fulfil multiple roles, as had the camps in the Kachin and Naga regions in Myanmar. Living in the camps would segregate the cadres from public life, get them to adhere to a military discipline and remain in a state of preparedness to take on the enemy. These centres would also help identify the cadres who were likely to drop out or deviate from the ideals of the group.[9]

The training manual for these centres combined the modules at the different camps in Myanmar, except that the constant preparedness to shift to safer locations at short notice was absent. There was no danger yet in Assam of raids by the army or police. The dearth of weapons and munition meant no handling of firearms and shooting, except on occasion at Saraipung in

Dibrugarh, which registered the largest congregation of new recruits undergoing training.[10]

With training camps established all over the state, it was also time to enrol women into a separate wing. All the district units were instructed to recruit promising young women, but only Sivasagar, Lakhimpur, Dibrugarh and Nalbari were able to fulfil this directive. Apparently, large numbers of women had assembled at the meetings in the districts, but only a few decided to leave home for full-time work with ULFA. The first batch of eighteen women was trained for forty-five days at two centres in Sivasagar and Tinsukia alongside the men and on the same manual.[11] They were then divided into three groups for specialized training as nurses, medics and propaganda workers.[12] By mid-1990, some 300-odd women were actively engaged with the outfit at its different centres under the wing headed by a lecturer from Nalbari College, Pranati Deka, who was the president, and her deputy, Rinku Bhuyan, who assumed the role of general secretary.[13]

The role of women was further channelized into an overground organization called Mahila Kalyan Parishad, whose members were new recruits as well as some functionaries who had already completed their training. The leadership envisaged that overground groups would be needed to mobilize people for protests if the government were to unleash repressive measures against the outfit.[14] With the AGP government's dismal performance, the possibility of the Congress winning the next assembly polls was not ruled out by the ULFA leadership. And if that were to happen, counter-insurgency operations similar to those in Nagaland and Manipur would commence in Assam with the promulgation of special laws and deployment of the army.

But for now, ULFA's writ ran large in all nooks and corners of the valley. Its word was law; there was nothing that escaped the attention of the outfit's functionaries. So it was also time to unleash moral policing as a strategy to enlarge its support base. Sale of liquor was banned, along with gambling dens and brothels;

the mekhela-chador, the traditional Assamese dress, was enforced as a dress code for women; culprits found indulging in criminal activities were apprehended and punished. Those who harassed women, corrupt government officials, bootleggers and petty drug peddlers were given mild punishments, like kneeling down for a few hours at public places, and let off with a warning to desist from such activities in future.[15]

No mercy was shown to history sheeters with a record of crimes like human and drug trafficking, spying and rape, or for impersonation as ULFA cadres. While some of these suspected criminals were abducted, some were declared guilty by the kangaroo courts that surfaced in the remote villages. Jails were created at some centres like Lakhipathar, where some abductees were tortured for days in the most inhuman ways before being killed.[16] Many of these acts had the tacit approval and support of large sections of the people in the valley, who believed that the criminals would have gone unpunished under the existing judicial system.

The fallout of these policies was startling—officials reported in time to office; harassment of women, eve-teasing, human trafficking, poaching, sale of liquor and embezzlement of funds in government offices drastically reduced. The idleness that typically marked the rural landscape in the valley was transformed at many places. All these efforts had a tremendous social impact, which boosted ULFA's image and strengthened its parallel government that was already operating in most parts of the valley. Certainly, the late eighties were the 'golden phase' of ULFA, which, although brief, was never to be replicated again in the future. The euphoria prompted a person no less than the cultural icon Bhupen Hazarika to sing a couple of songs on ULFA, titled '*Udit suruj*' ('*The rising sun*') and '*Dekhisa ne sei tumi sonali pua*' ('*Have you seen that golden morning*'), which were often played out loud in some strongholds of the outfit in the valley.[17]

With the social reforms came a slew of welfare activities, mostly implemented by the ULFA-backed Jatiya Unnayan Parishad (JUP).

The thrust of the programmes was to promote collective farming, which was practised on plots of fallow and government land in Nagaoan, Lakhimpur, Goalpara, Sivasagar and Goalpara. Groups of unemployed youth were organized to cultivate vegetables and rice, set up fisheries, poultry farms, goateries and piggeries, and sell the produce in the local markets. The profits were distributed equitably and a percentage diverted for sponsoring the education of children from poor families or invested in establishing schools. A few development schemes sanctioned by the government, which had remained incomplete for years, were expedited. Entire villages were mobilized for repair of roads and embankments on river banks at several places that had been neglected by the government. Participation was wholesome, with the women also pitching in in many of these ventures.[18]

Among these initiatives were two unique endeavours by JUP-ULFA to divert rivers to prevent the twin dangers of floods and soil erosion. A scheme was implemented under the leadership of Mama at Sadiya to divert the Kundil river to check river bank erosion. The JUP's plan was not only welcomed by the residents of Sadiya but also struck a chord with the neighbouring villages in Arunachal Pradesh too. No wonder that thousands of people from all communities were engaged in the project for three months before it was abandoned two weeks ahead of the army's deployment when Operation Bajrang was launched in November 1990. It might have been completed if the project had been launched a few months earlier.[19]

More ambitious was the attempt to divert the Dikrong river in Lakhimpur, where the intensity of erosion at some villages like Bihpuria and Narayanpur was even greater than at Sadiya. The plan was to construct a one-and-a-half-kilometer-long channel to divert the river from its usual meandering route. The embankments built by the government as a protection against overflowing river water had outlived their utility because of the rising river bed.

Almost every household in Bihpuria, cutting across all communities, participated in the project, which went on for about two weeks.[20]

Only a small portion was left to be completed when the scheme had to be halted a week ahead of Bohag Bihu, which is the most popular festival in Assam. Nonetheless, it was successful in getting the river flow through the canal that was constructed, giving respite to a large number of villages on the brink of being wiped out. ULFA perceived this as a triumph and as a valid reason to declare the Hawajan-Bandardewa-Bangalmara region in Lakhimpur as a 'muktanchal' (liberated zone), where a centre was also set up to train new cadres.[21] However, its plan to resume work after the festival could not materialize due to opposition from a section of the locals. Certainly, something had gone wrong somewhere in the project, which the ULFA-JUP could not gauge.

Resentment had been brewing among some villages against the domineering attitude of the ULFA cadres entrusted with the project, many of whom were too inexperienced for such endeavours. There were instances of misbehaviour on their part with the elderly residents, punishments, forcible collection of rice from households as well as allegations that they swindled funds that were donated. As it turned out, the canal was conceived and executed wholly on the plan submitted by the villages inhabited by the upper castes among the Assamese. The Mising tribals, who constitute a large chunk of the population in the district, had reasons to be offended—not only were their views not considered but they were also compelled to extend their support and services to the project. They were already disillusioned with the ULFA ban on their traditional brew, which was a livelihood for many families. Many leaders from the community were not in favour of the 'liberated zone', thinking it would harm their interests and make them subservient to the mainstream Assamese, but dared not oppose it for fear of retribution.[22] The zone had already become a no-go region for the police; all crimes were reported to ULFA, which investigated the cases and dispensed justice. All government activities in the area were also carried out with the approval of the rebel leaders.

The reaction among the Mising in Lakhimpur was indicative of a trend discernible in some other places in the valley, where a silent resistance was brewing against ULFA among certain sections of the populace. This was the outcome of an interplay of many factors, which the leadership knew but failed to address. Only a few dared to speak out occasionally against the outfit, while the vast majority chose not to voice their grievances. However, in Lakhimpur and neighbouring Dhemaji, the situation took a more serious turn as the resentment against ULFA sparked a bigger movement, engaging people from other communities and places. This was the first major organized opposition to ULFA in Assam in which the CPI (Marxist-Leninist) had a major role to play.

Squaring Off with 'Enemies'

CPI(ML)'s tryst with Assam can be traced to the late 1960s when its functionaries landed in the state to escape persecution in West Bengal. There were reports of squads led by Kanu Sanyal taking shelter in Assam's Goalpara town for brief spans, prompting the police to nab him. Years later, Bhaskar Nandy toured the state to expand the outfit's base, but his efforts did not yield any results.[23] Fresh attempts were made since mid-1985 when the party held a series of meetings with representatives from marginalized groups in Assam. The goal was to organize them on a platform for a crusade against the long-standing issues neglected by the government.[24] The leaders also held the view that a pact with ULFA could help to spread the roots of the outfit faster in the absence of dedicated cadres.[25]

CPI(ML) activists led by Kamal Das huddled in meetings with ULFA delegates with the goal of evolving a common minimum programme. Although Anup was keen to examine the scope of a joint venture, other ULFA functionaries were reluctant, since focusing on class struggle would mean digressing from the outfit's envisaged objectives.[26] CPI(ML) was upset and compelled to join hands with other local groups under a banner called the United Reservation Minorities Council of Assam (URMCA) on 21 February the next year, but expansion of the movement was tardy owing to financial constraints. Three years later, Lakhimpur, where a hushed resistance had been brewing against ULFA, emerged as the focal point for the launch of the movement. URMCA's cause was helped by the fact that its general secretary Ranoj Pegu was a Mising with political ambitions.

URMCA received a warm response in the entire belt inhabited by the Mising in the Lakhimpur-Dhemaji region. Locals were recruited in large numbers and a series of programmes was organized to oppose ULFA. Entry of the rebel group was banned in many of the villages in this region. At some places, ULFA cadres were even beaten up as a retaliation against the atrocities they had committed earlier in the Lakhimpur-Dhemaji region.[27] The situation turned worse when URMCA leaders hurled allegations against ULFA saying it was an organization of men addicted to a lifestyle of luxury and that it was a militant manifestation of Assamese chauvinism. In a series of press conferences, it also cited specific instances of ULFA cadres snatching motorbikes and extorting funds from the locals. ULFA retaliated by asserting that URMCA was a creation of the central home ministry with the sole objective of checking the ULFA's expansion in Assam.[28]

Even as the war of words continued, ULFA decided to train its guns on its adversaries. More than ten senior leaders of URMCA were gunned down in a span of three months, triggering a reaction among prominent citizens of the state, who issued statements urging both groups to bury their differences. Finally, a meeting between the senior functionaries of both outfits at Lakhimpur resulted in a truce that drastically reduced the conflict. The killings drew to a close, but not the hostility of the Mising-inhabited areas towards ULFA. Nonetheless, the ban on ULFA was lifted. However, its activities were still curtailed, with the result that the outfit's expansion in the region was halted.[29] ULFA did not have an alternative plan to make fresh inroads here either, as it was grappling with graver issues.

More funds were required to sustain the elaborate structure and the camps that had been set up in Assam. The list of donors among the non-Assamese business communities, especially the Marwari community, was expanded to include petty traders across the valley. ULFA's decision to target these trading communities also stemmed from other factors. There were frequent complaints by local businessmen about the domination of Marwaris and their propensity to promote only members from their own community. The rebels saw it as a perfect opportunity to intervene as it would only create goodwill among the locals. An overwhelming majority of the Marwari traders who were served with demand notices fell in line and opened their purse strings. But there were a few who were reluctant until they were showed the gun. Whatever opposition existed was eliminated by early 1990 after a spate of assassinations, which included the killing of another president of Kamrup Chambers of Commerce, Sankar Birmiwal, who was also suspected to have made a case for President's Rule in Assam before influential politicians in New Delhi.[30]

These killings not only provoked widespread condemnation across the country but also led to hectic lobbying in the capital for deployment of the army against the rebel group in Assam. The Bharatiya Janata Party (BJP), a Right-wing party supporting the non-Congress National Front government at the Centre, was vocal in demanding an outright ban and crackdown on ULFA. The demand had the support of deputy prime minister Devi Lal, who began to lobby with prime minister V.P. Singh for dismissal of the AGP government in Assam. But the National Front government had its own compulsions, which inhibited tough action against ULFA. Deployment of additional troops could not be done without the concurrence of the ruling AGP, which was a constituent of the National Front government. The Centre was in a fix and unable to find an answer to the situation in Assam. A meeting convened by Singh with law minister Dinesh Goswami, who belonged to the AGP, and home minister Mufti Mohammad Sayeed decided to summon chief minister Mahanta to the capital for a review of the situation in Assam.[31]

Held early in August 1990, the meeting was also attended by state governor D.D. Thakur and top intelligence officials.[32] The home ministry was armed with all the details about the outfit's expanding activities—video footage of a documentary filmed by Newstrack on the camps in Assam, which had already been telecast, the press briefing by senior ULFA functionaries at a hideout in Nalbari, and the frequent meetings between Assam home minister Phukan and the rebel leaders. Earlier, photographs and video filmed by R&AW operatives in Kachin on ULFA had already been in circulation among the security agencies.[33] Mahanta was told in categorical terms to take all possible measures to prevent further killings and extortion of funds by ULFA.[34]

Of course, the chief minister did not admit that the situation in Assam was veering out of control with no possibility of a crackdown against the rebel group. There was no way the police could swing into action as it was further demoralized following the assassination of senior superintendent of police Daulat Singh Negi by ULFA in a meticulously planned operation. Apparently, as he was being tortured in police custody in Guwahati, deputy commander-in-chief Hirak Jyoti Mahanta had told Negi that he would be killed within forty-eight hours of his release.[35] Mahanta was set free by the government in return for the release of a general manager of the Guwahati refinery, H.K.L. Das, who had been abducted by ULFA. Another officer, S.P. Mullick, escaped an ambush in Dibrugarh, but his wife and children were killed.

Nonetheless, the danger of army deployment was looming large, which prompted some AGP ministers to summon ULFA leaders to their residences in Guwahati for a briefing on the Centre's concerns. The ULFA leadership agreed to desist from killing, bank robbery and abduction of government officials.[36] But for how long? The warning had hardly any effect. So the situation continued to deteriorate, with the tea sector also stepping up its campaign for deployment of the army. Like the Marwari traders, the tea gardens were at the receiving end of ULFA's exactions, which only grew after the return of the trained batches from Kachin. ULFA had an axe to grind with the tea estates, and its demands for funds and welfare measures from them found wide support among the local populace.

In the late 1980s, the annual turnover of the 850-odd gardens, which were owned mostly by Indian firms, was around Rs 2,500 crore.[37] Their role in the state's economy was crucial, given the state's low agricultural productivity and lack of industries. The long-standing demand by local groups and civil society organizations to the tea companies to shift their head offices from Kolkata to Guwahati had fallen on deaf ears, which gave credence to the grievance that these companies were hardly bothered about developing the local economy. A common grievance across the state was the gardens' sourcing of all the commodities required for production as well as labour from other states. This could have been done locally, according to ULFA. The workers' wages continued to be abysmally low and the bulk of the managerial staff too was recruited from other regions of the country. The gardens continued to be clusters where the planters lived the same extravagant lifestyle as their predecessors did during the colonial era. So, ULFA's justification for funds from the gardens was simple—they must reimburse to the people of the state a part of the colossal profits they had minted over more than a hundred years. The demands varied from Rs 5 lakh to Rs 30 lakh at a time, depending upon the size and turnover of the estates. Sometimes, a rate of Rs 2,000 was fixed for every hectare of land under plantation.[38]

ULFA's demand notes elicited a mixed response from the tea gardens' head offices in Kolkata.[39] The management of most of these companies could not believe ULFA's growing clout in Assam, but the Assam chapter of the Indian Tea Association (ABITA) knew that the sector was headed for trouble. Sensing the danger, it drew up a slew of welfare measures for investment.[40] But it was too little too late. Not convinced about the tea companies' commitment, ULFA persisted with its demand for funds, only to be greeted with a dismal response from the general managers of the gardens. Finally, with no indication of a positive response, ULFA felt that drastic measures were called for to compel the gardens to open their purse strings.

Opportunity came knocking when information was received from an employee of a garden owned by the Apeejay Group that its vice chairman Surendra Paul was on his way to its estates for the annual inspection. Paul was known to have high-level connections in the Central government, besides being the brother of British member of Parliament Swraj Paul. After the dates were confirmed, a meeting at ULFA's Lakhipathar camp deliberated on whether he ought to be abducted and released after acceptance of the demands or gunned down to deliver a message to the entire sector. The decision was overwhelmingly in favour of the latter proposal.[41] On 9 April 1990, Paul lay dead in his vehicle near Lahowal with multiple bullet injuries after being shot by motorcycle-borne assassins.

The killing sent alarm bells ringing at many places. In New Delhi, security agencies furnished the latest reports on ULFA's activities to the home ministry, which painted a worrying scenario of the deteriorating law and order situation in Assam. Prime minister V.P. Singh was briefed, but there was precious little he could do except to speak to chief minister Prafulla Mahanta, who responded saying that an action plan to tackle the crisis would be submitted to the home ministry at the earliest.[42] Mahanta plunged into action by convening a series of meetings with his top officials where a plan was put in place for the deployment of paramilitary forces in some zones in the eastern districts of the state where ULFA was most active.[43]

More serious efforts were made in London as many of the tea companies were from the UK. The companies began hectic lobbying with the Indian High Commission for dismissal of the AGP government, imposition of President's Rule in the state and army deployment to flush out the rebels. A month later, the British government summoned high-ranking officials from the High Commission to make a case for stringent action against the rebel group.[44] To stave off the crisis, top tea industry executives met in Dibrugarh, where a decision was taken to raise a special fund for welfare schemes in sports, education, health, agriculture and mitigation of floods in the regions where the estates were located. But there was no consensus on ULFA's demand for hard cash. Eventually, most of the companies decided to pay up, in the absence of viable options. By July, ULFA was flush with funds again, and had such large amounts that its leadership even lost track of the total amount it had extorted from the estates.[45]

President's Rule in Assam

Meanwhile, the rift between the Centre and the state government kept widening as there was no consensus on the policy to be implemented for improving law and order in Assam. The state government's demand for paramilitary forces was accepted by the home ministry, but with the rider that a few districts would have to be declared as 'disturbed' ahead of the deployment, which would give extraordinary powers to the security forces to carry out counter-insurgency operations, as in the case of neighbouring Nagaland and Manipur.[46] Mahanta agreed and prepared a cabinet memorandum for approval, but met with stiff opposition from his colleagues, who went a step further to get the AGP to adopt a resolution demanding the removal of governor D.D. Thakur as he was perceived to be a hardliner in favour of dismissal of the state government and imposition of President's Rule.

Extremely upset over the development, chief minister Mahanta transferred the political wing in the State Home Department to his own office, on the plea that ULFA was more a political rather than a law and order issue. Home minister Phukan was left fuming, but there was nothing he could do to retrieve the portfolio. Governor Thakur sought to bridge the gap between the two senior leaders, but to no avail. His suggestions for improvement of law and order in the state, such as appointment of a single sessions judge with adequate security in Guwahati for the trial of all ULFA-related cases, fell on deaf ears.[47]

With hardly any scope for improvement in the situation, the governor and the Intelligence Bureau were convinced that dismissal of the government was the only option before the Centre. Two developments in quick succession hastened the downfall of the AGP government. Among the tea companies that had refused to give in to ULFA's demands was Hindustan Lever, which owned Doom Dooma India Ltd. It was clear that an offensive against the officials of the estate by the rebels was imminent. The company decided to withdraw from Assam and its representatives in London requested the Indian High Commission to rescue all the officials and their families from Doom Dooma. Responsibility for the operation was vested with the Research & Analysis Wing (R&AW), since it already had an establishment in the town.[48]

So, early on 8 November 1990, sixty people were airlifted from Doom Dooma to the airport in Guwahati, from where they took scheduled flights to different destinations. It was only in the afternoon that the news began to spread, much to the disenchantment of the government and the ULFA leadership. Meanwhile, the political scenario in the New Delhi took a different turn after the collapse of the National Front government following the BJP's decision to withdraw support. Chandra Sekhar was sworn in as prime minister on 10 November with the support of the Congress. He was never in doubt about the future course of action to be adopted in Assam. His thoughts resonated that of the Congress, which was also keen to dismiss the AGP government. The Congress's target was the assembly polls scheduled in Assam for December. Anti-incumbency sentiment was high in the state, but the regional party could still end up winning the elections with ULFA's support. As such, for the Congress, it was imperative for the polls to be held under President's Rule and with the deployment of the army.

A week later, home secretary Naresh Chandra called up the governor to inform him that the prime minister had decided to impose President's Rule in Assam.[49] But for that, the governor must submit a report to the President justifying the dismissal of the government in the state. The Intelligence Bureau had already prepared a report, which was placed before the governor, but he preferred to compile his own recommending President's Rule in the state.[50] With the receipt of the report by the home ministry, the decks were cleared for banning ULFA and for declaring Assam as a 'disturbed state', which would also mean promulgation of the Armed Forces (Special Powers) Act 1958 and deployment of the army.

The army had gauged the shape of things to come in Assam as early as July, when a discussion was held among the top brass at the headquarters in Delhi.[51] The topic was broached again at a conference at the Kolkata-based Eastern Command headquarters on 10–11 September, where the commander, Lt Gen. K.S. Brar, had outlined the long- and short-term plan to tackle insurgency in Assam.[52] The army plunged into action in the second week of November by convening a series of meetings again at the headquarters in the capital for fine-tuning the counter-insurgency tactics against ULFA. Lt Gen. Ajai Singh was summoned from the Western Command to head the exercise as the general-officer-commanding of the Tezpur-based 4 Corps.[53] A proposal to launch the exercise, code-named *Operation Cyclone,* on 18 November was postponed as the army was unprepared.[54] As many as 20,000 troops were mobilized from different regions of the Northeast, to be deployed in two phases.[55] According to the plan, simultaneous raids on ULFA camps in eastern Assam in the first phase were to be followed by the establishment of a counter-insurgency grid covering the entire valley in the next.[56] Finally, a notice was issued by the

Eastern Command specifying 28 November as the date for the start of the exercise, which had been renamed as *Operation Bajrang*.

At the same time, the army knew that dearth of intelligence and unfamiliarity with the terrain could prove to be their biggest handicaps in the operation. Eastern Assam had no hills, a feature that had been a great advantage for rebels in the neighbouring states, but there were dense forests suited for guerrilla warfare. Thick bamboo clusters, vegetation and the creeks scattered across the countryside could make the task of apprehending militants no less challenging than in the hills. The Intelligence Bureau and R&AW briefed the army, but these agencies could not fulfil their commitment to provide the army guides, as assured earlier.[57] Nor had the military acquired any intelligence on its own, despite the fact that the army knew it would be deployed in Assam. The state police were not taken into confidence since it was assumed that ULFA had deeply penetrated the organization. So there was no detailed information about the camps in the jungles. Whatever information had been gathered was from news clippings in the dailies and magazines, which were sometimes exaggerated and speculative.[58]

By the third week of November, the Second Mountain Division at Dinjan in Dibrugarh was bustling with a greater presence of the army and their increased movement at night in vehicles for familiarity with the terrain. Helicopters hovered over the dense jungles at Lakhipathar and Saraipung for a peek into the landscape where the operation was to be launched. The camps' inmates at Lakhipathar went into a tizzy, prompting some among them to fire a few shots into the air.[59] The helicopters stopped the survey after two days, but nobody was in doubt that the days of the AGP government were numbered.

On 27 November, chief minister Mahanta and his police chief, B.D. Kharkwal, dashed to New Delhi for last-minute efforts at salvaging the situation. By the time they landed in the capital, the cabinet had already passed a slew of resolutions for the dismissal of the state government, imposition of President's Rule, declaring the state as a 'disturbed area', promulgation of the Armed Forces (Special Powers) Act 1958, banning the ULFA, and deployment of the army. Neither prime minister Chandra Sekhar nor any senior minister was willing to meet Mahanta. The proclamation of President's Rule was made late in the evening on All India Radio. Mahanta returned to Guwahati the next day, only to be informed by his colleagues that the Secretariat had been locked and made a no-go zone for the ministers. There were widespread rumours that their residences would be raided, but Mahanta was assured by the governor that there were no such plans by the government.[60]

The entire top brass of ULFA had gathered at Lakhipathar for a general council meeting to chart the future roadmap of the organization and to firm up a plan to counteract the impact of the operation.[61] The meeting was disrupted when information came in about the army's deployment in Assam. ULFA had been briefed on a regular basis on the ongoing developments by some ministers of the AGP government. The ULFA high command had already issued orders for vacation of the camp ahead of the operation.[62] Prudence demanded prompt withdrawal, in the typical guerrilla style. It would have been suicidal to confront the army with only the small quantity of assault rifles, pistols and grenades at the camp.

Most of the senior functionaries decided to shift to the training centre at Saraipung, located about 20 kms north of Lakhipathar, near the border with Arunachal Pradesh in the dense jungles of Dehing Patkai. The leadership aptly inferred that the army would take at least a week or even more to reach Saraipung, where the general council could be resumed. The narrow, winding tracks leading to the camp were dug up at some points, trees felled and a couple of mines planted on the road to there from Tingrai.[63]

The jungle was denser at Saraipung, where the meeting commenced on 28 November. The constitution was accepted as well as 'independence, sovereignty and socialism' as the goals of the outfit.[64] Paresh underscored the need for more funds and weapons to take on the Indian army, which was contrary to the suggestion of the senior functionaries, who were of the view that creating a support base among the people ought to be on ULFA's immediate agenda rather than retaliation against the Indian army. Anup focused on the loopholes in the organization and on ways and means to eliminate them. Many were hoping for a session to discuss streamlining of the procedure for collection of funds, punishments and recruitment, but there was hardly any time to delve into these issues. There was also no detailed discussion on how to cope with the army's offensive, which was expected to continue for some months. It could stretch for a longer duration if the Congress were to win the forthcoming assembly polls in the state. The only orders issued to all the functionaries were to disperse, settle down in safe locations and evade arrest until further orders from the high command.[65]

Weapons, munitions and all valuable items were bundled in bags and divided among the several groups geared up to scatter in different directions. A squad with chairman Rajkhowa proceeded to a hideout in Sivasagar along the border with Nagaland, where most of the women cadres and a few top leaders also made a beeline for them. Another squad began to walk all the way through the Kaziranga National Park to Lumding, a place considered safe as it was inhabited mostly by Bengalis working in the railways.[66] Chetia limped all the way to Panitola with his bruised ankle before heading to a safe hideout in the hills of Karbi Anglong, where the general headquarters was subsequently erected for a few months.[67] Paresh, who was suffering from malaria, retreated to a remote location on the banks of the Dirak river bordering Arunachal Pradesh with a large group of cadres armed to the teeth.[68]

Empty camps were waiting to greet the army!

Chinks in the Armour

Early in 1990, there was an unusual visitor at ULFA's general headquarters in Lakhipathar. Moderately built and dark complexioned, he spoke little, and only in English to the two functionaries from Guwahati who were attached to him. He strolled all around the large camp and ventured deep into the jungle occasionally. Sometimes he would also scribble into a small diary tucked in the pocket of his full-sleeved shirt. In the evening, he engaged in long discussions with his two associates, posed queries and listened attentively to their replies.[69]

He was Rajan and an emissary of the Liberation Tigers of Tamil Ealam (LTTE) from Sri Lanka. A long journey by boat, train, bus and elephant with two ULFA functionaries had brought him to Lakhipathar all the way from Jaffna, which was an LTTE stronghold on the island.[70] ULFA's plan was to forge an alliance with the LTTE, similar to its earlier efforts to ally with the rebel groups in Punjab. The journey of a two-member squad selected for the journey to Sri Lanka took an unpredictable turn when a contact failed to turn up at Chennai. An option emerged only a couple of weeks later, when another contact was established with a person who facilitated their travel by boat to the island nation.[71]

After reaching Sri Lanka, they were taken to a Tamil village where they stayed for a week before being able to meet a middle-rung LTTE officer. The two could not reach the LTTE citadels like Kilinochchi, but they managed an appointment with senior leader Yogaratnam Yogi, who was non-committal about a pact. But he agreed to send an envoy with the group to Assam after obtaining the high command's approval.[72]

After a week at Lakhipathar, Rajan departed by train from Tinsukia, but not before sounding a note of caution to ULFA. He was never in doubt that the Lakhipathar camp could be blown up very easily. There was no adequate defence, nor enough cadres, guns and ammunition to hold back an assault for very long. He was clearly unimpressed with ULFA. It did not take long for him to realize that ULFA was at a nascent stage and did not have any long- and short-term strategies to achieve its goals. He was at a loss to understand how a pact with the LTTE could be of benefit to it, given the huge distance that separated the groups.[73]

The link with the LTTE could not be revived again. But Rajan's premonitions were spot on. Months later, ULFA decided to vacate the camp without confronting the army. ULFA's retreat evoked a mix of opinions in the valley. Nobody, not even its functionaries, was certain about the future strategy of the outfit since there had hardly been any deliberation on the topic at the general council at Lakhipathar and Saraipung. For some people, the move was a clever stratagem which offered the scope to regroup and then launch attacks on the army. At the same time, it came as a surprise to many people who expected relentless resistance from the Kachin-trained guerrillas.

The truth was something else, concealed, and far removed from the public domain. ULFA's larger-than-life image exceeded its actual strength and capability to engage in a sustained campaign against the Indian state. Its inability to evolve an immediate plan for counteracting the army offensive was due to some fundamental drawbacks, which were often interrelated. The leadership was not totally unaware about the fault lines in the organization, but they were never considered perilous enough to be eradicated soon. So, they lingered, proliferated and began gnawing at the very edifice of the organization.

What went wrong?

By the late 1980s, most of the founder-members of ULFA had dissociated themselves from it, either intentionally or out of fear of being prosecuted by the government. The mantle fell upon the triumvirate—Paresh, Rajkhowa and Chetia—to steer the ship, but they were inexperienced and young, all in their early or mid-thirties. None possessed the wisdom and experience to lead an armed rebellion against a mighty state like India. The top leaders had no time to discuss important matters; they were indulging in a game of one-upmanship to carve out their own niches in the organization.[74] The result was confusion cutting across every level of ULFA's activity, and from the district upwards to the high command.[75]

The strife between Rajkhowa and Paresh had started soon after the return of the first batch from Kachin.[76] The new rule mandating military training for everybody was perceived by the political wing headed by Rajkhowa as an attempt by the general headquarters to concentrate all powers in its own hands. All cadres of the armed wing were instructed to take orders from the general headquarters and avoid sharing information with the political wing, which flew in the face of the plans chalked out earlier, entailing collective decision on all matters in the districts after mutual consultation between the twin departments. The established practice followed by the bigger rebel outfits was of the gun following the party and not the other way round, as envisaged by ULFA's general headquarters.[77]

Before long, a section of ULFA functionaries also began to cast doubts on the role of the JUP, which had begun to usher in a revolution of sorts in the rural areas. ULFA grew anxious about the possibility of its functionaries shifting allegiance to the JUP and enrolling in it as full-time members.[78] Meetings between the two organizations not only failed to resolve the impasse but they fuelled fierce debates, with each side trying to justify its opinions in the matter. In Nalbari, for instance, the JUP was compelled by ULFA to put a halt to its activities after a meeting at a remote village.[79] The JUP did not survive long to sustain its movement, following the army's crackdown during Operation Bajrang. But there is no gainsaying that ULFA's campaign would have taken a different turn if JUP had been encouraged to spread its wings further, as it would have enabled the organization to strike deeper roots among the masses.

The list of blunders was long and traced their origins to the founder-members themselves. They had focused more on establishing contacts across the border than in firming up a few basics, like the constitution, which is usually given shape after a lot of discussion and debate. ULFA realized the need for a constitution only at the NSCN camp in Myanmar, when a few pages were hurriedly compiled. It was not until 1987 during Chetia's incarceration in jail that one was finally compiled, but it was endorsed only three years later, at the general council at Lakhipathar, coinciding with the launch of Operation Bajrang. Still, the rank and file in the organization remained unsure about the goals, the organization's long- and short-term tactics and the strategy for the proposed revolution.[80]

A section of functionaries was baffled when a bomb blast was triggered at a cinema hall in Barpeta, leaving many people injured. For many it was an act of terrorism unrelated to the revolutionary ideals of ULFA so assiduously espoused by the leaders. The irregular political classes at the camps delved only into the history of Assam, the 'colonial policies' unleashed by New Delhi and the rationale for an armed struggle, without any effort to indoctrinate the cadres. Not even the batches trained in Kachin were adequately briefed about the objectives of their assignment, except for some 'dos' and 'don'ts'.[81]

ULFA's pact with the NSCN in Myanmar opened the route to Kachin, giving it scope to fulfil some immediate requirements, like training and acquisition of weapons. Their experience in Myanmar's Naga region and Kachin left a deep impression upon the minds of the leaders, and especially upon Paresh. Both the regions were at war with the Myanmar Junta, which necessitated a state of readiness to survive and offset the damage from the army raids that sometimes continued for many days. In the given circumstances, it was only typical for the army to gain the upper hand over the political wing among the rebel organizations in both regions. In Myanmar, the government was yet to establish its authority over vast areas along the border, which facilitated the establishment of zones under the control of the rebel groups.

ULFA sought to replicate these Myanmar models in Assam without realizing that there were vast differences in the social, economic and political milieu of the two regions. The momentous step of carving out a 'muktanchal', or liberated zone, in Lakhimpur was arrived at without mulling over the implications of it, which only fuelled unrest and the birth of another outfit opposed to ULFA. Complaints from the local people in other areas about the raucous behaviour of some of the ULFA functionaries kept pouring in, but there was no effort made either to redress their grievances or to plug the loopholes in the organization.[82]

The root of the problem lay in the disorderly recruitment of cadres, without adherence to any norm, in sharp contrast to the practice followed by the bigger rebel outfits in the Northeast. The system of checking recruits for their background remained in vogue at ULFA only till the mid-1980s when small squads were sent to the NSCN camp in Myanmar. Sometime in the late 1980s, ULFA evolved guidelines for recruitment, which ran into thirteen points, but they remained only on paper as hundreds were enrolled when the organization's network swelled to cover more areas in the valley.[83] Only a few who could grasp the rationale for the movement or its consequences had joined out of conviction.[84] And they were also the ones who refused to surrender or come overground for a long period of time.

Further harm to the organization was caused by the AGP government, which was compelled to remain silent about ULFA's mounting activities. Sometime before the departure of the second batch to Kachin, an unwritten agreement was arrived at between ULFA and a section of AGP leaders led by home minister Bhrigu Phukan for 'mutual assistance', following a meeting at Numaligarh.[85] Functionaries came to be groomed in peace and comfort, and even those who returned from Kachin were sucked into a life of sloth and corruption. Their word became law; none dared to oppose them for fear of being identified as an enemy of the jati. There was no consistency in the standard operating procedures among the districts, and the procedures in place were twisted by senior functionaries to suit their interests.[86]

One of the best examples of such discrepancies in the rules came from the punishment meted out to a senior leader of Nalbari, Upen Deka, who was among the first to join ULFA and who had taken a lead role in several operations, including the bank robbery at Tangla. A norm was supposedly laid down that no cadre could marry as long as he remained associated with the outfit. Deka was summoned to the general headquarters at Lakhipathar soon after news reached the high command about his wedding. He was compelled to face a trial before a panel of judges at the camp and was punished with hard manual labour for a week.[87] But only a few months into Operation Bajrang, cadres were baffled to hear of all their three top leaders tying the knot! The bar on marriage for ULFA cadres was suddenly gone.

An episode that created ripples in the organization was the award of capital punishment to deputy commander-in-chief Ratul Kotoky. Kotoky, who hailed from Bokakhat, could never actually get along with the top leaders. The rift between them widened further when the high command was informed that Kotoky never deposited the funds he had extorted from a corrupt official at Kaziranga National Park with ULFA.[88] The leaders were also rattled over rumours that Kotoky was in touch with former Assam chief minister and Mizoram governor Hiteswar Saikia for exploring the possibility of talks with the government, which could cause a split in the outfit. The matter reached a flashpoint after Kotoky rebuffed an order from the high command asking him to submit a reply on the allegations against him. Soon, he was summoned to Sivasagar on the pretext of a meeting. He was hacked to death and his body was thrown into a river.[89] The incident triggered the emergence of an anti-ULFA group in the Bokakhat region, led by a former ULFA functionary, Jiten Gogoi. Kotoky's execution was carried out on the orders of a few senior leaders, but there were several killings in the districts made without the approval of the high command, in contravention of ULFA norms.

The list of such incidents was long, and horrendous tales were heard about them. On several occasions, the dead bodies were dumped into rivers or in jungles and never recovered. The cruellest treatment was meted out to the victims lodged in the jail at the Lakhipathar camp on charges of being informers, poachers, smugglers and human traffickers. Many victims with proven crimes were tortured to death through a variety of methods—some were starved, some hung on trees for days, some used as targets to be shot at with air guns; a few were buried alive, some had boiling water poured over them while some were lined up in a column and a shotgun fired into the stomach of the person right in front so that an average of four persons would die on the spot with their stomachs ripped open.[90]

Equally appalling was the muddle in the collection of funds, which escalated from early 1989. There is no precise estimate of the quantum extorted by ULFA, but it may be assumed that something between Rs 200–300 crore was extorted from tea estates, business establishments, traders and government officials.[91] Kamrup and Dibrugarh yielded bigger amounts, as business establishments and tea gardens were more concentrated in these two districts.[92] There were no strict guidelines for the gathering of funds, except that district commanders and senior functionaries were instructed to focus on business establishments owned by the non-Assamese and the tea gardens.

There was too much money all of a sudden, far exceeding the expenses at the camps.[93] There was no effective auditing system, nor any monitoring to keep tabs on the funds gathered by the middle- or lower-rung cadres. This was a boon to some functionaries and middlemen looking for opportunities to earn a quick buck. Years later, some cadres suspected of diverting funds would be asked to return the money; a few were shot dead while some groups from Dibrugarh and Guwahati were successfully able to duck for cover and divert the funds into business ventures after they surrendered before the government.[94]

The late 1980s was the golden phase of ULFA, resulting from the political situation in Assam when the ruling AGP fell into disgrace.[95] No other rebel outfit in the Northeast, or perhaps in the entire country, had it so easy in the formative years as did ULFA, which even established a parallel government with the support of large sections of the populace. A huge advantage for the outfit was the absence of any competitor in the Brahmaputra valley, unlike the situations faced by the rebel groups in neighbouring Nagaland and Manipur. But the fragility of the organization was apparent in the months after Operation Bajrang when the leaders were found to be totally disconnected from each other and from the cadres. ULFA's weak fundamentals were to reverberate through every facet of its activity in the future.

Reign of Terror

On 27 November 1990, the army was deployed in large numbers on the 25 km highway between Duliajan and Digboi hours before the proclamation of Operation Bajrang on the radio. A convoy of vehicles and armoured personnel carriers was stationed at Tingrai, which was the starting point of a narrow non-concrete track that led straight to ULFA's general headquarters at Lakhipathar.[96] It was the most common route used by the rebels to reach the camp, located some 10 km from the highway. A fierce resistance from the rebels—similar to the opposition put up by the Sikh militants before Operation Blue Star—was expected by the army.[97] The jungle was dense and visibility low, compelling the army to decide on advancing cautiously, at a snail's pace.[98]

The operation commenced with the break of dawn the next day as the trucks and armoured personnel carriers embarked on the path to Lakhipathar. About a couple of hours later, the convoy was jolted by a landmine blast which damaged a truck.[99] The army presumed that the entire area would be covered with mines and booby traps to cause maximum damage to the advancing troops. The soldiers began to proceed further on foot at a sluggish pace after the vehicles were withdrawn. They hacked their trail through the forest, sending off volleys of fire from their machine guns and assault rifles to prevent ambushes. The operation was halted in the afternoon and resumed early morning on the next day, with the advancing column reaching a point about 5 km ahead of the headquarters. The army expected to see defence camps and bunkers around the camps, as is usually the case with rebel establishments.[100]

The operation was extended deeper into the forest a day later without any encounters, which left the army awfully baffled. Were they being lured into a trap? Were all the cadres ensconced at the camp for the final battle? Perhaps—and that was reason enough to intensify mortar shelling as the army advanced on the last lap of the operation.[101] The outskirts of the sprawling camp came into view by late afternoon. The camp was incessantly sprayed with gunfire to drive out the inmates. As the army inched closer, it became apparent that the camp had been abandoned, belying all expectations of a stiff resistance. Items like blankets, utensils and trunks were strewn all over camp, which had undergone substantial damage from the shelling. It was occupied by the army and plans were finalized to storm the training centre at Saraipung and ULFA hideouts in the other districts of the valley.[102]

As many as ten spots where camps had been established by ULFA had been identified by the army on the north bank of the Brahmaputra across Lakhimpur, Nalbari, Darrang and Kamrup, based on inputs provided by the Intelligence Bureau.It was decided to storm five among them with smaller units of the army and to conduct a heliborne operation from Lilabari airfield. As the troops reached within 5–6 km of the camps and were moving in, they discovered that they too were all deserted.[103] Unlike in Lakhipathar, the rebels in the other camps had planned their evacuation days in advance and no items were left behind. The army decided to withdraw from these areas and focus on Dibrugarh, where all the top rebel leaders were believed to be holed up.[104]

The march to Saraipung was no less treacherous, with the hillocks and creeks retarding the pace of the operation. The same strategy of bombardment with mortars and gunfire was adopted to eliminate chances of retaliation by the rebels. The camp could be raided only after a week or so, but it too was found abandoned, as expected by the army.[105] The mopping-up operations carried out in the two camps between 2 and 4 December yielded a large pile of documents, which proved valuable to the army, giving it a peek into ULFA's strategies. What it did not expect was a mass grave of decomposed bodies at Lakhipathar; the corpses were of people who had been killed weeks ago after being tortured for many days.[106] The empty camps confirmed the army's suspicion that ULFA was tipped off in advance about the operation by its sources in the government.[107]

By 8 December, the counter-insurgency grid was erected in the valley with the arrival of additional troops. The entire valley was divided into nine sectors, but the army continued to be hamstrung by the dearth of actionable intelligence, so vital for counter-insurgency operations in Assam.[108] Language continued to be a hurdle in the absence of interpreters and guides. So the army deployment in the other districts resulted only in massive cordon-and-search operations, blockades on the highways and random raids on residences of suspects. Nobody was above suspicion, as pressure was exerted on the commanders by the 4 Corps headquarters in Tezpur to produce quick results.[109] The demands sparked blunders and atrocities, including a serious confrontation with the police at Sivasagar, resulting in the detention of the superintendent of police by the army on the suspicion that he had links with ULFA! Extremely embarrassed by the incident, the army ordered the transfer of the brigade commander. [110] The civil administration continued to be hostile towards and non-cooperative with the army.

For a while, the army focused on executing operations using smaller squads, which too failed to yield the desired results.[111]

Frustrated with its failure to nab the leaders and eliminate them, the army reportedly unleashed a reign of terror in all the neighbouring villages of Lakhipathar and Saraipung, considered the strongholds of ULFA. It was presumed that many rebel functionaries had vacated the camps at least a week ahead of the army operation and were hiding in the adjoining settlements. At least twenty-five villages were identified as hot spots and were reportedly kept surrounded for many days.[112] Combing operations were launched in all the villages along the Digboi-Duliajan highway and at Makum in Dibrugarh, mostly inhabited by the Moran-Motok communities that inhabit the eastern zone of the state.[113] There were allegations of atrocities by the army on the women; severe restrictions were imposed on the movement of the people, many of whom fled and took refuge at a school in Digboi.[114]

The army knew it would never be indicted for atrocities committed on civilians. It was shielded by the Armed Forces (Special Powers) Act 1958, which vested not only extraordinary powers with the army in its operations but also impunity from being prosecuted for criminal acts. The Act allows the army to prohibit gatherings of five or more persons in an area, to use force or even to open fire against any person contravening the law or for carrying arms and ammunition. It gives it powers to arrest individuals without warrants, on the basis of 'reasonable suspicion', and also to search premises without warrants. There can be no prosecution or legal proceedings against army members without the prior approval of the Centre. But while the Act gives powers to security forces to open fire on people, this cannot be done without prior warning given to the suspects. The Act also says a suspect must be handed over to the local police station within twenty-four hours of being apprehended. It also lays down that the armed forces must act in cooperation with the district administration and not as an independent body. Needless to mention, adherence by the army to these safety clauses has been more an exception than the rule, as army exercises conducted in other states reveal.

It was not surprising that no one dared to report the abuses of the army during Operation Bajrang, which was gradually extended to more villages in Dibrugarh. The public call offices in the villages and small towns were shut down to prevent the locals from relaying information to the media. The barricades on the highways and at other places prevented journalists from reaching the affected zones. Weeks later, senior media persons were allowed to accompany a few politicians to some areas, but not to the villages where the operation was being conducted by the army.[115]

The limited success of these exercises can be gauged from the fact that out of the total of 2,204 suspects picked up by the army, only 204 were identified as belonging to the hardcore category. It is likely that most of them were middle-ranking functionaries since none of the top leaders could be nabbed.[116] The army's estimate that there were 1,200 hardcore rebels is extremely doubtful, as only around 350 cadres were able to gain experience and training in Kachin, including at the session in Dukum, where the UNLF and NSCN(K) were also present.[117] The bulk of the weapons seized consisted of 12 bore guns, which the ULFA had snatched from many households two years ago.[118] And all this was achieved at a heavy cost, which caused further alienation from and disaffection for the government among the local populace. The seeds were sown for more militancy in Dibrugarh and other areas in the years to come, which the army did not realize.

Some of the barbarities perpetrated by the army during the operation were detailed in a report released by Amnesty International on 26 March 1992 covering all the states in the country where counter-insurgency operations were going on.[119] On Assam, it begins by quoting a report from *The Times of India*, which read, 'Every single day reports pour in from different parts of the state about army atrocities, including killings, torture, rape and harassment. The local newspapers are full of heart-rending reports of ordinary people being picked up by the army for no reason, women being raped and houses raided at uncanny hours.'[120]

According to another report in the *North East Times,* which was also quoted from, the army arrested 1,846 people in their search for ULFA militants between 28 November 1990 and 10 April 1991 during Operation Bajrang. A further 1,000 were arrested by the police. Many were detained at random during the mass raids on their villages; others were arrested at the army check posts or because they had broken curfew. They included peasants, labourers, academics, political and social activists, doctors and businessmen. Youths and students were a particular target. Many of those arrested are believed to have been tortured. In December 1990, the army denied allegations of torture and rape during Operation Bajrang and claimed they were fabricated by 'political leaders with vested interests'.[121]

The Amnesty report went on to state that,

> Over 100 habeas corpus petitions were filed in the Guwahati High Court between 27 November 1990 and March 1991 on behalf of people illegally detained and tortured during army operations in Assam. The High Court has upheld many petitions and ordered that the detainees be brought before it. Two brothers, Rituraj and Padmaraj Barua, who were detained by the army on 1 and 2 December 1990, both claimed they had been severely tortured for 20 days when the army produced them on the order of the court. The court ordered that they be taken to the Guwahati Medical College hospital for treatment, and transferred them to judicial custody. It awarded the brothers compensation for the torture they had suffered and eventually, on 4 April, released them on bail.
>
> However, the security forces have defied some High Court rulings. In January 1991 the Guwahati High Court acquitted student Rajumoni Bezbarooah and ordered that he not be taken into custody without the permission of the university hostel

warden. Rajumoni Bezbarooah was detained again some two months later and reportedly severely tortured at an army camp at Golaghat. He alleged that soldiers had destroyed the court's order when he showed it to them.

In February 1991 a team from the CPDR visited six districts in Assam. They gathered information on 49 cases of torture, 13 of rape, eight extrajudicial executions and one 'disappearance'. The PUDR also published a report on Assam, in May 1991. It concluded: 'Most of the persons detained by the army were tortured. We have interviewed many torture victims, visited three hospitals, met concerned doctors and gone through a number of court documents. Beating, stripping and hanging them upside down and then beating on head and chest, thumping on chests with boots, pouring ice cold water, burying them up to chest and then beating or keeping a bucket over the head, squeezing testicles with clamps, dipping in cold water drums, forcefully keeping them awake for days together, denial of food or water are some of the forms of torture used. But the most common form is electric shocks. Sensitive parts of the body including ears, tongue, armpits, genitals and head were repeatedly given electric shocks sometimes in progressively higher voltages. With electrodes at each temple the brain was subjected to electric waves.[122]

Besides eastern Assam, the Bodo-inhabited districts in the western zone of the state were undergoing the same ordeal, which too the report highlighted. But these were perpetrated by the police, and especially after the state government got wind of a sinister design by the previous Congress government at the Centre to motivate a section of Bodo youths to embark upon militancy for a separate state. A senior IPS officer who hailed from the state was supposedly assigned the job of training a few batches at a unit of the Special Service Bureau (SSB) near Tezpur. The rumour was that R&AW was also involved in the operation since it worked in close coordination with the SSB, and both the departments were under the administrative control of the Union Cabinet Secretariat. And there were names of some senior Congress politicians doing the rounds as the conspirators who were apprehensive of an erosion in the party's support base in the state after the AGP swept to power in 1985.[123]

Prelude to Polls

Even as the army continued with its operation, governor Thakur scampered to fill the vacuum in the state administration created by President's Rule. H.N. Das, who had been shunted out to an insipid post by the AGP government, was reappointed as the chief secretary. Thakur undertook a whistle-stop tour of the most affected districts, held meetings with district officials and impressed upon them the need to crack the whip on ULFA while making provisions to equip the officials with greater manpower and security. Realizing that bridging the gap between the army and civil administration could yield dividends, a coordination plan was implemented, entailing exchange of information on raids and operations.[124] For many government officials, and especially the police, the confusion over lack of a clear policy on ULFA seemed to have been laid to rest. They swung into action, producing some results in a brief span of time.

Crores of rupees were seized from ULFA hideouts, both by the army and police, weapons confiscated, hundreds of functionaries arrested and some eliminated in encounters.[125] Amid these episodes were shady deals and pilferage of funds, safely hidden from the prying eyes of the media and the higher authorities.[126] News items published in the dailies were replete with such incidents for almost two months after the launch of Operation Bajrang. For instance, on 10 January 1991, one such item mentioned the recovery of Rs 32 lakh by the police and army at a newly constructed building of the Assam Medical College in Dibrugarh.[127] Among the persons who were picked up in connection with the incident and interned at the army camp at Grahambazar was a state government official. The official claimed that during his internment at the camp he heard sounds of gunshots in the night coming from the office of the commanding officer.[128]

Most of the collective farms set up by the JUP were dismantled and the protagonists nabbed.[129] Security for the vulnerable tea gardens and the oil installations at Digboi, Duliajan and Guwahati was beefed up. All cases related to ULFA were transferred to Guwahati since the judges in the districts were not provided with adequate security. An effective media campaign was chalked out to counter ULFA propaganda after mass graves were unearthed by the army from the camps. The fifteen decomposed bodies at Lakhipathar prompted the army to look for more graves at the other camps. By 12 January 1991, a total of thirty-five bodies were dug out of the camps, of which only eighteen could be identified, including those of Congress and URMCA activists, businessmen and local criminals.[130] The unknown chapter of the terror perpetrated in the ULFA camps was beginning to get unravelled, drawing condemnation from all over the country.

All these actions against ULFA notwithstanding, its leaders managed to remain ensconced in their safe hideouts, waiting for an opportunity to regroup. Paresh decided it was time to strike against the army. He quietly stole out of his hideout on the banks of the Dirak river with a squad of thirty cadres to a location near Kuarigaon in Naharkatiya in the dead of night. They knew the army had been moving in the area with convoys for operations in villages suspected to be ULFA hideouts. A spot was selected for laying a landmine; it was on a narrow road surrounded by jungles. The mine was triggered early morning the next day, resulting in damage to an army vehicle.[131]

The army allegedly ran amok again, rounding up all the residents of Kuarigaon and torturing them to disclose information about ULFA.[132] In reality, the operation was executed by the ULFA group in absolute stealth in a few hours' time, and without the knowledge of any resident of the village. After the blast, the squad quietly slipped away to the same hideout on the banks of the Dirak, which was still outside the army's radar. Across the river was Namsai in Arunachal Pradesh, which did not have army presence. It was safe enough for a new general headquarters, which was established by ULFA at Tengapani in the same location after a couple of weeks.[133]

Soon the camp swelled with new recruits and Kachin-trained commanders who descended from the hills in Myanmar. A meeting of the executive council was summoned after Anup's arrival from Karbi Anglong by a circuitous route to avoid detection.[134] The conclave focused on the issues that could not be deliberated on at length in the previous session at Saraipung due to the army operation. All the participants unanimously approved the plan to establish new camps in areas still outside the ambit of the army operation. The leaders' gaze fell on inaccessible areas in western Assam along the inter-state and international borders, where all the cadres who were in hiding could be instructed to assemble and more batches trained to take on the army. Further, new sources of weapons and funds were to be explored; the existing base in Myanmar's Naga region to be sustained for as long as possible; and efforts to be made to talk with the Indian government to halt the army operation. Some actions were also called for to dispel doubts about ULFA's commitment and fighting capabilities. So, a call was given for boycott of Republic Day celebrations on 26 January and orders issued to the cadres to target Congress activists, police and army informers, businessmen who were opposed to ULFA and tea gardens that had refused to shell out money.[135]

Meanwhile, in New Delhi, senior Congress leaders impressed upon prime minister Chandra Shekhar the need to explore the possibility of talks with ULFA. The party's goal was to clear all roadblocks for holding assembly polls in the state.[136] The prime minister informed the Rajya Sabha that the government was willing to engage with the outfit in a peace process, which was relayed to a delegation of the AGP led by Dinesh Goswami.[137]

The government's gesture prompted ULFA to declare a unilateral ceasefire on 28 February, with the hope that the army operation would be suspended. But it was not, probably because the roadmap for the peace process was not yet ready. ULFA continued to regroup in most of the districts, unaffected by the army operation.[138]

By the end of March 1991, it was increasingly clear that Operation Bajrang had failed in its objective of neutralizing ULFA.[139] Most of the senior functionaries of ULFA were still at large, shifting from place to place, moving around with ease through networks that could not be dismantled. Information disclosed by the arrested functionaries indicated that a large group was camping in Myanmar and waiting for orders to cross the border. The governor and his team went into a tizzy, harbouring serious doubts as to whether the polls could be held soon. Their assessment was definitely not music to the ears of the Congress in New Delhi, which was pitching for assembly polls to be held at the earliest.

At the same time, it was increasingly dawning on the government that the police would have to play an effective role for better results and for creating a situation conducive for the assembly polls.[140] The home ministry surmised that a quick answer to rejuvenate the police would be to make changes at the top by appointing officers who had experience in counter-insurgency operations. So, senior police officer Prakash Singh was transferred from Uttar Pradesh to Assam as the police chief, while E.N. Rammohan, who had served for many years earlier in the state, was appointed as the inspector general of operations. Within a month, the two were greeted by an episode which revealed ULFA's capacity to survive and wriggle out of tricky situations.

After ULFA's executive council meeting concluded at Tengapani, Paresh decided to visit Naharkatiya again, but information had somehow reached the army about his plan. A day after he landed at a village called Kaliapani ahead of Naharkatiya, the entire area was cordoned off and combing operations to nab him began. Escape was possible only through the route leading to Duliajan, a township east of Naharkatiya, which too was blocked by the army. Confident that a senior leader would be finally nabbed, additional troops were hurriedly deployed in the operation, named Sher-e-Dil.[141]

Left with no option, Paresh decided to reach out to the government with an offer for talks and a commitment not to interfere in the assembly polls. His old buddy from Jeraigaon, Rebati Phukan, managed to slip through the cordon to meet him and to deliver a message from him to Congress leader Hiteswar Saikia. A letter written by Rajkhowa to the governor underlined the same message, but with the condition that the army must call off its operation at the earliest.[142] It was too tempting an offer for the Congress to spurn as its stock would further soar, ahead of the assembly polls. The party high command in New Delhi pulled strings, triggering a flurry of actions. Topping its agenda was removal of Governor Thakur since he had developed serious differences with Hiteswar Saikia.[143]

Thakur had been refusing to play ball with the caretaker government in New Delhi and was not heeding its instructions. His tiff started with minister of state for home affairs Subodh Kant Sahay, which offered scope to Saikia to step up the campaign for his removal. Congress president Rajiv Gandhi even delivered a speech before the Congress Parliamentary Party declaring Thakur's continuation as governor as a hurdle in effectively tackling insurgency in Assam.[144] Thakur was replaced by a former Congress functionary and Rajya Sabha member Lok Nath Mishra following a recommendation from Gandhi, which the caretaker government could not turn down. The stage was set for implementing the next plan of action for the assembly polls.

The army was prevailed upon to withdraw from Naharkatiya, allowing Paresh to escape to Tengapani again.[145] The ten-day operation managed to nab only sixteen Kachin-trained functionaries, besides confiscation of a small quantity of weapons and ammunition.[146] A week later, on 20 April, the government halted Operation Bajrang, with the justification that the situation was conducive for elections. The opinion of army and police officers, that ULFA's gestures were no more than hogwash, was brushed aside. The officers were of the firm opinion that its objective was to disrupt the polls, as evidenced by the intelligence reports.[147] And the police was further convinced about ULFA's motives when information was received about the camp in Tengapani on the banks of the Dirak.[148]

Rammohan plunged into action with a combined contingent of the CRPF and the Border Security Force (BSF), which marched all the way to a remote village on the banks of the river that it then cordoned and searched. Even as the operation was on, ULFA functionaries resorted to firing from the opposite bank. Two functionaries managed to snatch a rifle from a CRPF personnel before escaping by plunging into the river. Even as the exchange of fire continued, some blasts were triggered by ULFA from the other bank, but all the senior functionaries fled in time before the troops raided the camp after crossing the river. Only a junior ULFA functionary was apprehended and later handed over to the police.[149]

After the operation, ULFA again declared that it would neither interfere in the elections nor support any political party contesting the polls. The motive was to put a brake on the operations by the police and paramilitary forces, which would have put a spanner in the works for its plans of regrouping—plans that had started in remote locations in western Assam.[150] A proposal by a few senior functionaries to field candidates in the elections was disapproved by the senior leaders, some of whom still harboured the optimism of the AGP returning to power.[151] But chances of the party winning the polls were slim. Besides anti-incumbency, AGP was battling internecine squabbles as well, which had led to a split that saw former home minister Bhrigu Kumar Phukan walking out to form the Natun Asom Gana Parishad (NAGP). ULFA made feeble efforts to bridge the gulf between the warring factions, but there was hardly any possibility of a rapprochement.[152] Separate candidates were announced by factions for the parliamentary and assembly polls.

For ULFA, a pressing concern was the continued incarceration of its senior leaders and cadres. How could their release be accomplished without a general amnesty or a cabinet decision by the government? And there would be no reason for the Congress to do either, when many of its activists had been shot dead by ULFA or were forced to resign from the party. Some drastic action would be needed. The consensus was to abduct as many government officials as possible after the elections at an opportune moment and demand the release of the jailed cadres in exchange for the abductees.[153] The army was back in its barracks, and the police was still not geared to fight ULFA. All that would be necessary for ULFA was to get efficient squads to choose high-profile targets. A list of the probable abductees would be compiled from all the districts, and hideouts selected and safe routes firmed up to shift them frequently to avoid detection. And, if this operation were to be accomplished, the army in all likelihood would be redeployed again.

CHAPTER 4

CRESCENT AND THE DRAGON

Trail to Pakistan

THE SITUATION IN Bangladesh had undergone a sweeping change two years after the ULFA duo landed in the country. In December 1990, president Hossain Mohammad Ershad of Jatiya Party, who had been in office since 1983, resigned after months of an anti-government campaign by the Opposition parties and student organizations. The Bangladesh Nationalist Party (BNP) won in the general elections held in February and formed the government by securing the support of smaller parties, including the fundamentalist Jamaat-e-Islami (JeI). BNP and JeI were distinctly pro-Pakistan, which was also an indication that the government would turn a blind eye to the presence of Indian separatist groups in its territory. ULFA's chances of carving out a base in Bangladesh seemed to have been brightened.

Munin Nabis had crossed over to Bangladesh from Dhubri in 1988 and was joined a month later by another ULFA functionary from Guwahati who knew some Assamese Muslim families in Rangpur that had migrated to East Pakistan after Independence. Some of their relatives in Dhaka helped them to acquire a rented house in the city's Mirpur locality and gave them valuable suggestions as to how to fulfil their objectives. First, and most importantly, they had to eliminate all traces of their Indian origin, which they did by assuming fake identities. Their fluency in Bengali was an added advantage, which served to remove doubts as to their origin.[1]

To ensure a steady source of income, they invested the money brought from Assam in opening a restaurant at Mirpur, a travel agency and a motor-driving school, and also began purchase and sale of second-hand Japanese trucks from a construction firm named Oasis. The third step was the most crucial—building a network among the local politicians who could assist them in establishing contacts with the foreign embassies. The waiting period was brief for the ULFA duo after they got in touch with some influential politicians, including Ghulam Farooq Abhi of the Jatiyo Party, who had extensive links with the underworld. Some among the politicians had relatives in Assam, which was a reason why their friendship strengthened in a brief span of time.[2]

With the first phase of the operation successful, Nabis's associate decided to leave for Assam and brief the ULFA leadership about the success they had achieved so far; this happened almost a year ahead of Operation Bajrang. The high command was elated to receive a report from him detailing all the developments and the scope for making further progress in Bangladesh. The ULFA high command decided to send Anup and publicity secretary Sidhartha Phukan to Dhaka with funds to boost their efforts at cultivating links with foreign governments.[3]

Soon the ULFA delegates were knocking on the doors of several embassies in Dhaka. Their focus was Europe, and they requested support for the outfit's campaign in Assam and permission to open offices in the countries there. The most extensive briefing was offered to British diplomats with an indirect hint that the tea companies from their country would not be harassed in Assam with demands for funds if their proposals were accepted. The diplomats assured them that their proposals would be examined, but they were reluctant to entertain the ULFA delegation again.[4]

The topmost priority was accorded to Pakistan for seeking assistance. Early in 1991, Nabis took up a job as a manager at a glass-making factory, which was a joint venture between two firms, one in Bangladesh and the other in Pakistan. His first contact with officials of Pakistan's external intelligence wing, Inter Services Intelligence (ISI), was in Hyderabad (Pakistan), where the firm's top executives had gathered to fine-tune a plan for manufacturing bangles. In a brief meeting, Nabis succeeded in convincing the ISI about ULFA's goals and the dire need for training and weapons. Subsequently, a series of meetings with the ISI officials in Bangladesh followed, at different locations. It was not until six months later that the agency finally agreed to take a small team of about a dozen cadres to Pakistan for training.[5]

The message from Nabis to the ULFA leadership could not have come at a more opportune moment, as Operation Bajrang had already dismantled the big camps in Assam. The ULFA leaders hurriedly compiled a list of functionaries for the journey to Pakistan within a week of its decision not to interfere in the assembly polls in the state. The group was to include all the top functionaries, except Paresh, who decided to join the subsequent batch only if there was positive feedback after the Pakistan visit of the group and indications of a long-term association with the ISI.[6]

In Dhaka, in 1991, passports were easily procured with the assistance of the politicians whom ULFA had developed a close rapport with. After they had obtained the visas, two officials from the Pakistan High Commission briefed the squad about the 'dos and don'ts' of the journey. They were to identify themselves as businessmen if quizzed by the immigration officials at any airport. In Karachi, the group boarded a domestic flight to Islamabad, where an official briefed them about their onward journey by road to a camp at a remote location. They would be taken to the camp of Mujahideen leader Gulbuddin Hekmatyar, who had supposedly agreed to impart training to the ULFA squad. He headed a militia called Hezb-e-Islami, which was actively engaged in the war against the Soviet occupation of Afghanistan during 1979–89.[7] In such operations, it is not uncommon for intelligence agencies to use proxies to fulfil their goals. Pakistan was engaged with the war in Afghanistan and the ISI continued to have a rapport with most of the Afghan warlords opposed to the Soviet occupation.

ULFA was categorically instructed not to gather details of the camp or the location where the session would be held, and it would have to abide by all the norms laid down by the trainers. After a quick dinner at a safe house in Islamabad, the squad sat in a large army truck equipped with a thick curtain at the rear, which was pulled down. It was dark and stuffy, with only a few holes at the top for air to pour in. There was no way the ULFA cadres could gauge the route, although it was apparent that the destination was somewhere along Pakistan's border with Afghanistan and possibly in North West Frontier Province, which was a base of the Mujahideen guerrillas during the war.[8]

Early in the morning, after alighting from the truck, the ULFA functionaries saw a chain of big and small denuded mountains with patches of vegetation here and there. There was a row of barracks at some distance on a stretch of flat land below. The officer who was seated with the driver in the front seat of the vehicle asked the ULFA squad to follow him on a descending path leading to quarters that resembled a small army establishment. This was where the training would be conducted, but only after a meeting with Hekmatyar on the next day at his camp, which was about a couple of kilometers away, further deep in the hills. The weather was hot and dry, unlike the humid conditions in Assam.[9]

At the camp next day, the ULFA functionaries sat in two rows inside a colourful tent, in front of the rebel chief who was flanked by two aides. The discussion began with a briefing to the chief about ULFA's objectives, the current state of the movement and the dire need for training and weapons. Speaking in both English and

Urdu, Hekmatyar posed several questions on Assam before speaking his mind, which served as an absolute dampener to the guests. He explained his inability to offer assistance to ULFA as they were located a great distance away and also because of the differences in the nature of his movement and ULFA's. Nonetheless, Hekmatyar agreed to train the batch since ULFA was also a revolutionary group and they should not return empty-handed. Two experienced commanders were assigned to the task, which was expected to be completed within two months.[10]

The day began early with exercises, followed by breakfast and sessions of firing, which sometimes dragged on till afternoon, and finally games like volleyball in the evening. In the afternoon, the mercury peaked, converting the region into a furnace almost. Unlike in Myanmar, there was no scarcity of guns, ammunition or explosives, which were delivered at regular intervals to the camp. But after a couple of weeks, if anybody missed a target, then push-ups were awarded as punishment, which was made harsher when the target was missed with rocket launchers. After the training was over, the batch was further divided into three groups for specialized training in espionage, wireless communication and bomb-making. The three members selected for intelligence gathering were also taken to far-off destinations in Afghanistan for practical lessons.[11]

So, by early-1992, three batches comprising about forty cadres passed out from these training facilities. They went on to train more cadres at the camps in Assam, Bangladesh and Myanmar. All the batches followed the same route, from Karachi to Islamabad and beyond to Afghanistan, and curriculum, although the training centres were different for each of the groups. To the subsequent batches that went to Pakistan, the trainers introduced themselves as Mujahideen commanders who had been instructed by the ISI to impart them training. Clearly, they could not have been Hekmatyar's men as the chief had already spelt out his reluctance to continue his group's association with ULFA. Members of the second batch were taken to a spot in Kandahar by other trainers for a few days and then shifted to another location, where they spotted tiny lights in the evening from the mountains at a far-off distance, which they assumed was the capital city of Peshawar in Pakistan's North West Frontier Province.[12]

All these sessions were peppered with some spectacular incidents. Paresh and publicity secretary Sidhartha Phukan were in the second batch to Pakistan, but the two decided to engage in meetings with the ISI rather than proceed to the training camp. Perhaps the ISI expected ULFA to be totally submissive, which irked Baruah no end. He was not willing to bow down before the agency and accept all its diktats, such as taking regular commands for operations to be conducted in Assam. At some point, he was convinced that their association with the ISI had reached a dead end. He abruptly stood up in the last meeting and left the venue with a 'goodbye'.[13]

However, the ISI knew that Baruah was a prize catch who could not be allowed to get offended. It knew that many benefits could be reaped from ULFA, including access to other separatist outfits from India's Northeast who could be trained in Pakistan. So, the agency not only allowed the second batch to complete its training but also soon instructed its officials at the embassy in Dhaka to request Baruah to dispatch the next batch. This he did, and also landed at the ISI headquarters in Rawalpandi again after three months. The spat was not only over but it had sealed a deal that was to endure for many years.[14] And, true to the expectations of ISI, ULFA would soon facilitate the training of other separatist outfits from the Northeast in the region.

There were some scrapes that other ULFA functionaries got into during these sessions. Lohit Deuri, who was in the second batch, was taken to the army headquarters in Rawalpindi for an extensive briefing on intelligence gathering and then asked to stay at a rented room in the city. He was given assignments, but he ran into trouble while taking photographs of a cinema hall, arrested by the police and locked up till he gave them the phone number of his ISI handler, who soon rescued him from the police station. Deuri landed in trouble again after he refused to drink tea at a restaurant as it had milk in it. ISI was ignorant about the widespread habit of drinking 'lal cha' or tea without milk in India's Northeast. Deuri came under suspicion of being a spy, was confined in a room for several hours and interrogated by senior ISI officers. A heated exchange ensued until one Colonel Baba arrived and spoke to the other officers. The spat was extinguished, enabling Deuri to continue with his spying assignments for a week more before boarding the flight to Karachi. He was joined by two ULFA functionaries who had been taken to the arms bazaar at Darra Adam Khel in the foothills of the Safed Koh mountains after completion of their training.[15]

That ULFA had blazed a trail to Pakistan became known to the Indian government only after some trainees spilled the beans months after being apprehended in Assam. Some details were disclosed by them to inspector general of operations E.N. Rammohan during their interrogation, and the officer informed R&AW about it. A top R&AW official who landed in Guwahati the next day to quiz the detainees gathered the lurid details of ULFA's activities in Bangladesh and Pakistan. He was astonished that no report on any of this had been sent by the agency's officers in Bangladesh.[16]

The fast-paced sequence of events in Bangladesh and Pakistan was paralleled by another momentous development in neighbouring Bhutan, where another team of ULFA functionaries led by Shashadhar Choudhury had launched a survey for establishing camps. After training in Pakistan, Shashadhar had returned to Nalbari, where he hailed from, and began a recce for favourable spots to set up camps. The first camp in Samdrup Jongkhar was abandoned after a month for a better location along the border at Uttarkuchi, where a camp was erected towards the end of 1991.[17] Some of them were correct in their evaluation that sustenance of camps in the kingdom would neither be tough nor hazardous, as assumed by a few other senior functionaries. There were ample reasons justifying their optimistic appraisal of the location.

Two years earlier, in 1989, militants belonging to the Bodo Security Force (later rechristened as the National Democratic Front of Bodoland) had already established a sprawling camp at Kaurong-Dwifam in Bhutan across Udalguri in Assam, about 60 km east of Uttarkuchi. The Bodo group's decision to explore the possibility of setting up camps in the kingdom was arrived at soon after its efforts in Myanmar's Naga region was turned down by the NSCN. The Bhutanese authorities were aware of the presence of the Bodo rebels on their land, but they preferred to turn a blind eye to their activities.[18] Perhaps they assumed that the rebels' presence would be a safeguard against the Nepalese migrants who had encroached on a vast region in the southern districts.

Bhutan's southern districts were still in a flux after the devastating riots of the late 1980s resulting in the eviction of around 1 lakh Nepalese migrants who were rehabilitated at refugee camps in eastern Nepal. The migration of the Nepalese, or Lhotsampa, as they were known in Bhutan, can be traced to the nineteenth century, and it picked up after the Anglo-Bhutanese war of 1865. They were formally granted citizenship and tenure of land by the Bhutanese government in 1958, but the Drukpa elite continued to remain apprehensive about the growing numbers of the migrants, who they felt could soon dominate the economy and politics. In 1985, the Bhutan National Assembly approved a revision of the existing laws, restricting citizenship to those who could prove residence before 31 December 1958. The law was implemented three years later, after a census conducted in the districts of southern Bhutan inhabited by the Lhotshampa.[19]

Within weeks, the government identified a large section of the Lhotshampa who were unable to establish their citizenship. They were termed as '*ngolops*', or 'anti-nationals', who could be expelled from Bhutan. Further, in 1989, the king of Bhutan declared that the country would adopt the 'One Nation, One People' policy, which almost banned the Nepali language, the Hindu religion and any dress other than the traditional Gho and Khira. Soon, security forces resorted to mass confiscation of citizenship certificates, torture and imprisonment of those who protested. The Ngolops were compelled to sign voluntary migration certificates. This sparked the beginning of the forced expulsion of the Lhotshampa population to Nepal; they were estimated at one-sixth of Bhutan's population.[20]

Similar with the case of the Bodo rebels, the Bhutan government was aware about ULFA's presence in the country but chose to ignore it, which only emboldened the rebel outfits. Another ULFA group led by Lohit Deuri landed in Bhutan to set up another camp at Sukhuni Basti, about 30 km east of the previous camp.[21] As a former top Indian intelligence official recalled, 'It was a policy of live and let live for them (Bhutan government). There was no reason to oppose the presence of the rebels in their territory.'

Election, Abductions and Operation Rhino

The Congress's victory in the assembly polls was along expected lines in Assam. Many of its candidates were returned from eastern Assam, considered the bastion of ULFA and which the AGP had swept only five years ago. ULFA's decision not to interfere in the elections was a message that there was no bar to participation in the polls. The tranquillity that marked the elections flew in the face of the intelligence reports that predicted large-scale violence by ULFA.[22] A triumphant Hiteswar Saikia was sworn in as chief minister on 30 June 1991 along with his council of ministers, only to be jolted on the very next day.

As per the plan chalked out earlier, at least twenty small teams were unleashed by ULFA to choose the targets for abduction. Finally, after having been on the prowl for several weeks, on 1 July 1991 they managed to abduct fourteen senior government officials from different regions of the state, including an IAS officer, a Russian engineer, Gritchenko Sergei, employed with Coal India Limited, and senior employees of Oil and Natural Gas Corporation Ltd. Three days later, ULFA demanded the release of six senior detainees in exchange for the release of the chief physicist of ONGC, Bhola Nath Jaiswal, and Sergei. ULFA warned they would be killed if its demand was not accepted by the government within six days.

The government was rattled, prompting Saikia to summon a meeting of top government officials, but there was no consensus on the strategy to be adopted. Police chief Prakash Singh and his deputy, E.N. Rammohan, were opposed to the chief minister's plan to not only accept the demand but also to grant general amnesty to all ULFA detenus. Instead, they proposed that the government ought to insist on unconditional release of all the abductees by ULFA, and only those ULFA functionaries in jail without criminal charges would be set free.[23] There were a total of 594 ULFA detainees in jail, out of whom there were specific charges against 251. But Saikia had already made up his mind to follow a policy of moderation, knowing full well that ULFA still had the potential to cause disturbances in the state.[24]

On 9 July, 324 functionaries were released from jail, but the government's expectations were belied when it was known that the Russian engineer was dead. ULFA's press release did not reveal the details, but Sergei was shot dead when he attempted to snatch a weapon from the abductors only two days after he was picked up.[25] ULFA knew that the government was relenting under pressure. Two days later, its demand for the release of another twenty-four functionaries from jail was accepted by the government, in return for which four abductees were released. Next, a demand for the release of two senior functionaries was placed, but that could not be accepted since they were at a jail in neighbouring Meghalaya. ULFA responded by killing ONGC's mineral expert, T.S. Raju, which drew sharp criticism of the outfit's activities from all over the country.

The message was clear for the government—the detainees would have to be set free from jail for securing the release of the abductees. And ULFA was in no mood for talks with the government. Rattled by the developments, the Hiteswar Saikia government ordered the resumption of army operations against ULFA. So, on 15 September

1991, the army took position once again in Assam, in an exercise codenamed Operation Rhino, but in more areas where the NDFB was also active.[26] The deployment plans were similar to those of Operation Bajrang, except that more troops were pressed into action from eleven brigades in the nine sectors that made up the counterinsurgency grid. More quick-response teams and squads for heliborne operations were created for surprise raids across the valley.[27]

The army and the top brass of the police were never in doubt that ULFA would step up its campaign after the polls.[28] The army was also convinced that sooner rather than later, it would be tasked to take on the rebels again, which meant that its strategy must be revamped to circumvent its earlier mistakes.[29] The army had learned valuable lessons from Operation Bajrang. It was now equipped with more information about ULFA and the terrain, which pointed to the inescapable conclusion that the nature of insurgency in Assam was different from those in other states. It would be a long-drawn battle, to be fought on several fronts and with different weapons besides the gun.[30]

An essential ingredient in the new strategy was an intelligence apparatus not dependent on the civilian agencies. The army had created its own network of informers in several districts after Operation Bajrang was shelved.[31] It realized that whenever necessary, the police would have to be involved in the operation, given its knowledge of the terrain. Further, the army decided that a potent tactic against ULFA would be to target the middle-rung leaders who served as the vital link between the top echelons scattered in different places and the functionaries on the ground.[32] And, finally, the media would also have to be co-opted and journalists who could be engaged in psychological operations and churning out news reports against ULFA had to be identified.[33]

The police were still struggling to get its act together, with the chief Prakash Singh tendering his resignation over the government's decision to release the ULFA detenus from jail. His forceful plea that general amnesty must be given only if ULFA agreed to accept the Indian Constitution, abjured violence and surrendered all weapons did not have too many takers. He was at daggers drawn with several senior bureaucrats who saw greater wisdom in implementing the chief minister's proposal. In a strongly worded letter to the home secretary, he warned:

> ... the coming days are going to be extremely difficult. Whatever was achieved by the police, paramilitary forces and the army during the last nearly five years has been nullified with one stroke. On the other hand, all the losses which ULFA suffered during the period have been restored to them. I may be permitted to say that the (state) government made some very basic mistakes in handling the problem arising out of kidnappings.[34]

Singh's exit from Assam notwithstanding, the cooperation between the army and police yielded quick results. By December, several top- and middle-rung functionaries of ULFA were either apprehended or shot dead. The links between the foot soldiers and the leadership were snapped at many places.[35] Anup was nabbed in Kolkata with two accomplices; vice president Pradip Gogoi was arrested in Sivasagar after being trailed for close to two weeks; deputy commander-in-chief Hirak Jyoti Mahanta, who was known to be a hardliner, was picked up from a house and shot to death in the outskirts of Guwahati, barely a month after he had returned from Pakistan; and Javed Bora, who headed the committee to liaison with the foreign embassies in Dhaka, was gunned down by unidentified assailants in Dibrugarh within a couple of days of his release from jail. Many lower-level cadres were persuaded to join hands with the army and police for identification of the overground functionaries and sympathizers of ULFA.[36] A unified command was set up, with the chief secretary as the chairman, where the army, police and paramilitary were represented. But on most occasions, it was the army that bulldozed its way in the meetings on counter-insurgency operations.[37]

ULFA was feeling the heat again after a gap of six months, with the situation turning more perilous than a year ago when Operation Bajrang was on. There was no communication between chairman Rajkhowa, who was putting up in Shillong, and Paresh, who had crossed over to Bangladesh months ago. Not only were the rest of the six abductees released, but Rajkhowa also dashed off a letter towards the end of 1991 to prime minister P.V. Narasimha Rao declaring a unilateral ceasefire and signalling his intention for talks with the government, although he also underscored that the final decision would have to be ratified by ULFA's general council.[38]

The rumour among the hardliners was that the chairman had been apprehended by the security forces and compelled to sue for peace after being lodged at a safe house in Shillong.[39] They were further convinced about this when they came to know of the letter underlining his willingness for a negotiated settlement within the framework of the Constitution, renouncement of violence and surrender of weapons—the three preconditions that the government had insisted on during talks with other rebel outfits in the Northeast. Rajkhowa also urged prime minister Rao to create an ambience conducive for the peace process by repealing the ban on ULFA, putting an end to the army operation and removing the 'disturbed' tag for Assam, which would also mean an end to the sweeping powers given to the security forces under the Armed Forces (Special Powers) Act 1958.[40]

The Assam government was unsure if Rajkhowa's appeal had the support of the entire top brass of ULFA. Chief minister Saikia harboured doubts as to whether the hardliners would agree to sit for talks with the government. Nonetheless, he decided to take it forward by convening a series of meetings with the central ministries of home and defence.[41] The decision was on implementing a strategy to explore the possibility of talks with ULFA. Anup and ULFA vice president Pradip Gogoi constituted a six-member team of senior ULFA functionaries after being released from jail for a meeting with prime minister Rao in New Delhi.[42]

On 12 January 1992, the ULFA delegates reiterated the salient points of the letter from chairman Rajkhowa to the prime minister at a brief meeting in the capital, which was also attended by top officials from the intelligence agencies, the home ministry and the chief minister. The team was told categorically that the government was willing to accept ULFA's demands of halting the army operation, removing the 'disturbed' tag on Assam and the other demands, but an agreement could be inked only if ULFA accepted the Indian Constitution, surrendered all weapons and dropped the demand for talks on Assam's sovereignty. The delegates agreed to this but refused to sign a declaration, on the excuse that the peace process must be approved by all the top leaders and the general council of ULFA. They were presented with pens by the prime minister as a gesture of goodwill and to drive home the message that the government was sincere about the talks.[43]

Home minister S.B. Chavan and the intelligence agencies were not so optimistic about ULFA's gestures to smoke the peace pipe. Still, it made sense to support the Assam government's efforts, as it could trigger a split in the ULFA ranks. There were intelligence reports suggesting that a large number of its lower- and middle-rung functionaries were confused and willing to come overground.[44] For the security agencies, police and the army, surrendered rebel cadres would also mean an extra pool of resources for gathering intelligence and conducting covert operations, which were already beginning to yield encouraging results. So, a decision was taken to prepare a lucrative peace package for UFLA with the help of bank loans and to suspend the army operation again, if necessary, as a confidence-building step.

However, unknown to the government, a section of ULFA hardliners had managed to escape the army operations and was determined to carry on with the armed movement for independence.

They were actively implementing Paresh's instruction to set up camps at remote locations in the western districts of the state. So, by the end of 1991, big and small camps came up in Kamrup, Nalbari, Darrang, Karbi Anglong, Bongaigaon, Goalpara in Assam, and in Namsai in Arunachal Pradesh.[45] Some of these camps, such as the one in Namsai, were raided by the army within a few weeks. The rest of the camps sustained for a longer duration without discovery by the security forces. Training was imparted to small batches of new recruits, despite the scarcity of funds and weapons.[46]

All these district units devised ingenious tactics on their own to survive, explored sources of weapons and gathered funds for the expenses at the camps. Functionaries in charge of the training centre in the jungles of Rani near Guwahati went on an abduction spree to gather funds.[47] The Darrang unit went a step further by investing a small amount in the lucrative coal trade, which fetched quick returns within a few months. It also sent a team to Dimapur for the purchase of four revolvers with ammunition for a price of Rs 1 lakh.[48] Funds were also transferred to Bangladesh, where a hideout had been established by ULFA. An important episode was surreptitiously unfolding in the neighbouring country, far from the prying eyes of the Indian security agencies. It was to have a decisive impact on the trajectory of the separatist campaign in Assam.[49]

The First Split

Its string of successes in networking and establishing camps in the neighbouring countries was a windfall for ULFA, beyond the expectation of the leadership. Paresh had no qualms about revealing the support ULFA had got from the ISI in an interview to *India Today* at a Southeast Asian capital, where he had gone to purchase radio sets and explore sources of weapons.[50] The experience of ULFA in Bangladesh seemed to suggest that the ambience was congenial for them to pitch tent there. ULFA was encouraged by the camp that had already been set up by the All-Tripura Tigers Force (of Tripura) at Satcherri. The PLA continued to fortify its presence among the Meitei residents of Sylhet, an activity that had begun in the early 1980s. Not to be left behind, the NSCN(IM) had also begun to make forays into the country's Chittagong Hill Tracts (CHT) after the clash with the Khaplang faction in Myanmar. And, so far, there had been no incident of rebels from the Northeast being apprehended by the Bangladesh government.[51]

So, the hardliners in ULFA, led by Paresh, were convinced that the campaign for independence could be continued in spite of the reverses suffered in Assam. The peace offer from the government must be spurned, even if it meant a split in the organization. There was no indication of an 'honourable settlement' from the government, which appeared to be obsessed with the surrender of weapons by ULFA and its return to the mainstream.[52]

Nonetheless, the peace process in Assam gathered steam, with army operations suspended intermittently between January and April 1992 and a financial package called the '100 per cent Margin Money Scheme' announced, which was to consist of two categories of loans for the surrendered militants, preferential treatment for them in government contracts, permission for them to operate trade syndicates in certain items like fish and coal and to carry their own guns and avail of police escort for their security.

The peace deal was lucrative enough to lure many ULFA functionaries, but with them also came many unemployed youths, whom the Hiteswar Saikia government in Assam had deliberately targeted to prevent their recruitment into ULFA. In the final count, the list consisted of more than 3,000 surrendered persons, which was actually more than the cadre strength of ULFA! The intelligence agencies compiled reports raising an alarm about this, but that hardly mattered since Saikia had the blessings of the prime minister in working out the peace deal.[53] The exercise enriched quite a number of government officials and overground ULFA cadres who played a key role in the disbursal of the corpus of Rs 110 crore received from the Centre.[54]

Still, a large chunk of the ULFA functionaries refused to be enticed by the offer, which was evident at the Pratinidhi Sabha convened by Anup in 1992 near Tezpur to gather their opinion on the proposed talks with the government. In particular, the district units of Dibrugarh, Darrang and Nalbari struck a defiant chord by spurning the government offer and pitching for continuation of the armed campaign.[55] Chetia surmised that a clearer picture would emerge from the general council, which he decided to summon at the outskirts of Nagaon. However, the meeting hardly made any difference to the existing mood as Paresh refused to attend and most of the functionaries from the armed wing endorsed his uncompromising posture.[56]

With no sign of the deadlock being resolved, the meeting was disbanded on the second day without ratification of the peace process with the government. Anup and Rajkhowa convinced the government to allow them more time to evolve a consensus among the ULFA functionaries, which would also necessitate a meeting with Paresh, who was still in Bangladesh. Anup and Rajkhowa slipped out quietly to Dhubri, where Baruah had also crossed over from Bangladesh to meet them.[57] Two days later, the triumvirate arrived at a unanimous decision to reject the offer of talks. They resolved to convene an executive council in Bangladesh at the earliest, to hammer out a strategy to offset the government policy and surrenders and to strengthen the outfit for a renewed campaign. Anup and Rajkhowa snapped all communication with the government.[58]

So, on 31 March 1992, the chief minister held a meeting with the pro-talks ULFA leaders from the five districts of Kamrup, Barpeta, Jorhat, Lakhimpur and Sonitpur to deliver the message that the peace process must surge ahead without the participation of the hardliners. Subsequently, a resolution adopted by the pro-talks group outlined its rationale for engaging in the peace process with the government while alleging that the ULFA leaders had not only failed to give directions to the people of Assam but had also ensconced themselves in secured zones far from the atrocities perpetrated by the army on the common man.[59] The talks, it explained, would be held in an open atmosphere with the full confidence of the people. Further, it said that all illegal weapons would be collected and their accumulation opposed since they had been misused in the name of a 'people's revolution'. What was more important was an appropriate platform in a 'non-violent democratic ambience' for the venting of grievances by the people, which could result in the resolution of the long-standing issues. The statement condemned the atrocities committed by both the government and non-government groups. A central committee consisting of eight members was formed to supervise the peace process; it included four senior functionaries from Guwahati.[60]

The ULFA high command responded with a series of virulent press releases issued over the next whole week, even as the government ordered resumption of the army operation in all the districts where its cadres had refused to surrender. The press releases reiterated the leadership's commitment to strive for an independent, sovereign Assam, condemned the pro-talks leaders as traitors and the government for perpetrating atrocities against its members and for creating a division in the ranks of the outfit. They also accused the government of hypocrisy, which they said was manifest in the manner in which the peace process was conducted. The outfit's demand for the release of fourteen jailed leaders ahead of the general council at Nagaon was also rejected; neither did the government honour its commitment to release all the detainees booked under the Terrorist and Disruptive Activities Act (TADA). Further, ULFA alleged that operations against it had continued in spite of a solemn assurance by the government that they would be halted by the army till 1 April.[61]

Many allegations levelled by ULFA against the government were accurate, and this prompted the release of 245 detainees arrested under TADA early in May as no evidence could be gathered against them on their involvement with ULFA.[62] Simultaneously, efforts were intensified to weaken the ULFA formations in the districts that had turned down the peace package. Resumption of army operations again paid rich dividends, with as many as 113 cadres considered hardliners deciding to come overground within a couple of weeks.[63] Most of them were middle- and lower-rung cadres, and with only a few pistols and G-2 rifles to surrender as the bulk of the weapons in ULFA's possession had been successfully diverted to safe locations by the hardliners.[64]

An underlying feature of the split was the lead taken by the functionaries who were former activists of the All-Assam Students' Union (AASU) in Guwahati belonging to the Kamrup unit. They were groomed in a democratic tradition of debate and discussion, which was not only missing in ULFA but also considered blasphemous. Nabis had more reason to be upset after he was instructed by Paresh to blow up the oil refinery in Guwahati at the behest of ISI after returning from Pakistan. He refused to do it and returned to Guwahati from Bangladesh a week later.[65] More importantly, the Kamrup unit was opposed to ULFA's senseless killings which had continued even after the camps were busted during Operation Bajrang.[66]

In 1991, there were four killings by ULFA that rattled Assam, inviting widespread condemnation. The young daughter of Congress leader Lachit Kalita was accidentally killed in Guwahati when a grenade was lobbed into the car in which she was travelling. Journalist Kamala Saikia was gunned down following his scathing articles on the ULFA cadres' extravagant lifestyles and immoral conduct, on the orders of a functionary who surrendered only a year later. A senior leader of the AJYCP, Bipul Mahanta, met with the same fate as Saikia after he began efforts to facilitate talks between ULFA and the government. Congress general secretary Manabendra Sarma was shot dead without justification after orders were issued by the high command to target as many functionaries of the party as possible for its role in the army operations.

With the division of ULFA complete, the stage was set for a bloody round of conflict between the ULFA and the surrendered functionaries—or SULFA, as they came to be known. The ULFA leadership was most offended by the decision of a section of SULFA to join hands with the police and army in the counter-insurgency operations, resulting in the busting of ULFA hideouts and its sources of funds.[67] A stern message also had to be delivered to all ULFA functionaries that neither desertion of the organization nor collusion with the enemy would be tolerated. All district units were instructed to make optimum use of the available resources and train their guns at surrendered functionaries and the security forces whenever the opportunity arose.[68]

ULFA's first major retaliation was a landmine blast at Sankuriya in Nalbari on 12 April 1993, when the lessons learnt in Pakistan were first put to use. Gelatin explosives and detonators were improvised to make a landmine that ripped apart an army truck.[69] At least six army personnel were reportedly killed and an equal number injured, prompting an intensification of operations by the security forces at all the strongholds of ULFA in remote locations.[70] ULFA followed up the blast with the killing of three SULFA activists within a week in Tezpur. SULFA retaliated by gunning down some ULFA cadres in meticulously planned encounters, which only provoked more reprisals. The clashes continued sporadically for almost two years till the end of 1994, with both groups suffering losses. The most chilling episode was at Naipam in mid-1994, after the ULFA district commander summoned nine SULFA youths to a secluded spot, supposedly for a discussion, and shot them dead.

Naipam had the effect of further alienating the middle class and intellectuals who had supported the armed campaign of ULFA. Like the rest, the middle class in the Brahmaputra valley had glossed over the organization's deficiencies despite the indications that had surfaced from time to time. The leadership's decision to shift to

Bangladesh came as a shock; this was unexpected of an organization that had adopted an alternative path to redress the state's grievances, including the influx of foreign nationals. A distinct change was also noticeable in the stance adopted by the media, with some houses becoming overtly critical of the organization's strategies and its capabilities to deliver what it had promised.[71]

There were also editors and intellectuals, such as Parag Kumar Das, Ajit Bhuyan and Nibaran Bora, whose columns were as critical of ULFA as they were appreciative. Their writings contributed in no small measure in swaying large numbers in the rural areas in ULFA's favour. Das and Bhuyan also joined hands with a lawyer, Niloy Dutta, to form the Manab Adhikar Sangram Samiti (MASS), to highlight the untold atrocities perpetrated by the security forces on the people. Between 1992–95, they organized meetings, awareness programmes and mass protests across the state, established a network with human rights organizations in other states and even produced evidence at a press conference in New Delhi on the terror perpetrated by the forces in Assam that had not spared women and the elderly.[72]

The campaign had a negligible impact on government policies. The blatant misuse of TADA continued unabated, with close to 7,000 people being booked under the law until the end of the Congress regime in the mid-1990s. Not more than 5 per cent of those put behind bars were actually ULFA functionaries. And less than a dozen persons apprehended under the Act could be convicted on trial.[73] In one episode early in 1994, the 18 Punjab Regiment army men shot and killed four persons, including a former AASU activist, at Dibru-Saikhowa Reserve Forest on the suspicion that they had a role in the abduction and murder of a general manager of a tea estate by ULFA. The case would have been buried but for the habeas corpus petition filed by AASU vice president Jagadish Bhuyan in 1994 at the Gauhati High Court, which eventually resulted in a charge sheet against the killers by the Central Bureau of Investigation (CBI). Justice was delivered twenty-four years later, in 2018, when seven army personnel, including a major general and two colonels, were sentenced to life imprisonment by a general court martial for the fake encounter killings.[74]

No wonder the activists at the vanguard of MASS were also booked under the National Security Act (NSA), but the movement continued to expand into most of the districts in the state. MASS demanded release of the detainees booked under TADA, repeal of all repressive laws, including the AFSPA, lifting of the ban on ULFA for facilitating dialogue and a negotiated settlement, and recognition of the right to self-determination by all ethnic groups in the state. These issues were taken up at the UN Sub-Commission on the Promotion and Protection of Human Rights at Geneva where the human rights abuses by the government in Assam were vehemently condemned by organizations from other countries. The movement soon invited widespread allegations that MASS was a frontal organization of ULFA's, provoking further government crackdowns.

Were the allegations against MASS true? The movement engaged people from all nooks and corners of the state and from different age groups, not all of whom were associated with ULFA. However, in course of time, some MASS leaders developed a close rapport with the outfit, entailing regular communication and exchange of ideas.[75] There were widespread rumours that some activists of MASS were planning to cross over to Bangladesh and join ULFA at the proposed general council meeting at Narayanganj.[76] The security agencies were also armed with reports that a few MASS activists were actively involved in extortion for the rebel group.[77] Years later, Anup would claim that ULFA had a role in the foundation of MASS.[78]

The continuing atrocities by the security forces had the effect of diminishing whatever success the government might have achieved against ULFA. The surrenders notwithstanding, there was always a queue of wannabe rebels waiting to take the plunge and join the outfit. Their motives were multifarious, but the predominant factors were undoubtedly unemployment and poverty. In 1993–94, an estimated 45 per cent of Assam's population was below the poverty line in the rural areas, which was much higher than the all-India average of 37 per cent.[79] Efforts by SULFA to kick-start talks with the government also came to naught, driving home the message that New Delhi was focused only on a military solution to the conflict in Assam.[80]

Stunning Volte-face

ULFA's general council in Bangladesh's Narayanganj resulted in a slew of resolutions to meet the emerging challenges in Assam. But ahead of the meeting, Baruah dropped a bombshell, saying that he would distance himself from the proceedings and would be actively engaged only after he had been successful in achieving a goal he had set for himself.[81] He did not spell out what this goal was, but it was apparent that he was aiming to procure a consignment of weapons to help the organization tide over the weapons crisis it was in. He watched in silence, locked horns for a while with Asanta Bagh Phukan, who again made a case for adoption of Marxist doctrines as a goal and reminded all the participants at the meeting to desist from one-upmanship and conspiracies that would weaken the organiztion.[82]

Most of the sessions focused on the dire need for revamp of the organization, for regrouping and filling up of the positions left vacant after the surrenders by a section of its functionaries. Resolutions were passed accepting 'scientific socialism' as a primary goal for the organization and for an elaborate organizational structure, with the general, executive and permanent councils as the three principal organs of the outfit. Although the general council was envisaged as the highest decision-making body, in effect it was the five-member permanent council of the five top functionaries that would take all decisions. Shashadhar Choudhury was appointed as foreign secretary, a post which was created for the first time, Chitraban Hazarika as finance sccretary, Mithinga Daimary and

Pranati Deka as secretaries in charge of publicity and culture, and Asanta Bagh Phukan as organizing secretary. The two senior members—Mama and Robin Handique—were to be advisers who would operate out of the camp in Bhutan. Anchalik Parishads, or regional councils, replaced the district committees, while three zones were planned to be created to cover the entire state with 'meeting points' to facilitate coordination among the functionaries.[83]

The meeting accepted that the anti-Bangladesh and anti-Muslim image of ULFA must be discarded if the base in Bangladesh were to be consolidated. The leaders realized that it was more important to curry favour with the ruling BNP and its allies in Bangladesh, which were fundamentalist, anti-India and pro-Pakistan. So, a fifteen-page booklet in Assamese, addressed to '*The People of Assam of East Bengal Origin*' was issued. It began with a denunciation of the historic movement against foreign nationals in the state as being based on 'emotion', and the explicit acceptance that the migrants had become an inseparable part of the national life of Assam, whose contribution to the state's economic output had been 'noteworthy'. It went on to declare that the freedom struggle would never yield results without the support of the migrants who earned their livelihood by hard physical labour.[84]

Two more decisions were arrived at before the week-long meetings drew to a close at Narayanganj. Instructions were issued to all senior functionaries to explore permanent sources of funds using a mechanism different from the earlier ad-hoc policies adopted ahead of Operation Bajrang. More money was now required for the expenses of the two camps in Bhutan, where new recruits had landed for training. This apart, a small training centre was functional at Goalpara and two sites had been selected for camps at Srimangal and Satchari in Bangladesh, near the existing establishments of the All-Tripura Tiger Force.[85] These camps alone were expected to call for a monthly expenditure of over Rs 1 lakh.[86]

Finally, district commanders were to be instructed to put in efforts to procure weapons in small quantities from wherever possible till a bigger consignment was available. It was resolved that the top three leaders would be based at different locations to strengthen the organization. Paresh was to continue to stay in Bangladesh while Anup would be based in Assam's Karbi Anglong to supervise the regrouping in the valley.[87] A tougher role was earmarked for Rajkhowa, who would head for the Naga hills in Myanmar, where another chapter was unfolding for ULFA, albeit with greater difficulties than either in Bangladesh or Bhutan.[88] The trigger for setting up this camp was the intensified army operations in Dibrugarh, necessitating a search for safer places to set up camps and training facilities.[89]

Towards the end of 1991, a group of ULFA cadres, led by Mrinal Hazarika and Rontu Neog who had managed to dodge the army, had begun to reestablish the dismantled network in Dibrugarh. The search for a place to establish camps had begun soon after the district had turned down the proposal for talks with the government at the general council in Nagaon. A small team led by Anirban Gohain landed at the council headquarters of NSCN(K) near Lunglung, opposite Changlang in Arunachal Pradesh, to meet Khaplang, who was still struggling to streamline his outfit after the factional clashes of 1988. The Naga chief accepted ULFA's proposal to set up a new camp and agreed to station one of his own battalions in the new establishment, named First Battalion. Within six months, Manipuri groups such as the PLA, UNLF and PREPAK had also established their own camps near First Battalion.[90]

The location was considered safer than the zone inhabited by the Konyak Naga, where the previous NSCN centres had been raided occasionally by the Myanmar army. Lunglung was in the Pangmi Naga region, more remote, and any attempt to launch an assault on it would be known in advance. But unlike the Konyak areas, there were difficulties in ensuring an uninterrupted flow of rice and other essential commodities at Lunglung. The saving grace was that the Dibrugarh unit of ULFA was able to tap some traders and businessmen for a regular supply of funds, facilitating the transportation of food from distant villages, though at exorbitant prices.[91]

Even as the new centre became functional, Khaplang grew cagey about security at the camp. He knew that the Myanmar army would retaliate after the offensive launched by the Nagas, called 'Operation Dao' at the fag end of 1991. In this offensive, the small Myanmar army camps at Pengnyu and Lachan were destroyed, all the soldiers either shot dead or decapitated and their arms and ammunition looted.[92] The Naga chief was correct in his judgement about a counter-attack, although the reason for the army's attack was later found to be different. Early in 1994, a column of the army began marching towards the First Battalion in a clear indication of a raid, prompting the commanders to prepare for vacation of the camp.[93] The first mortar shell landed on top of a thatch in the ULFA camp early the next morning. A hail of fire from light machine guns continued for the next ten minutes, followed again by a round of mortar shelling, which left the ULFA and NSCN(K) camps almost entirely shattered. There were no casualties and all the rebel cadres moved, in time, to a location 3 km west, where a new camp was erected over the next couple of days. The army decided to withdraw after burning the establishment.[94]

A month later, Khaplang informed ULFA that there was no order from the Myanmar army headquarters to its unit at Namjung, the army establishment closest to the new camp, to raid the camp. In all probability, the commanding officer, who happened to be a Nepalese, was allegedly bribed by the Indian army to launch the offensive in a deal that covered all expenses of the operation, including the porters'.[95] There was interrupted calm for a long time in Myanmar's Naga region after the raid. The Myanmar army was more interested in combating insurgent outfits in other parts of the country than the Nagas.[96]

Activity was stepped up by ULFA at another location further south, in the Konyak Naga region, where another camp called the Second Battalion was established. Chairman Rajkhowa arrived at the site from Bangladesh in 1993 with his wife Kaberi Kachari, who had earlier played a crucial role in the foundation of the women's wing (Mahila Kalyan Parishad), ahead of Operation Bajrang in Assam.[97] Jungles were cleared, barracks built for the trainees and a network established with several neighbouring villages for supply of food. The task was rendered somewhat easier since the three Manipuri outfits had already established their camps in the vicinity a year ago.[98]

With the Second Battalion camp firmly established, two new batches, comprising about 300 cadres, were trained here till mid-1995. Like the situation at the other bases, the trained cadres continued to remain at the camp after the end of their training sessions as large-scale operations were still not possible in the absence of weapons.[99] The Dibrugarh unit had managed to establish contacts in Punjab for the purchase of assault rifles, but only two Kalashnikov rifles with six magazines could be transported, hidden in a truck. There were militants in Punjab who were willing to sell more, but there was no truck driver who would undertake the risk of carrying the items over such a long distance. Four Self-Loading Rifles (SLRs) were also seized from the constables of a paramilitary outfit guarding an oil-collecting station near Lakhipathar. An Assamese constable was killed in the operation, resulting in a public uproar, and there were subsequent orders from the ULFA high command to the cadre to refrain from such acts without prior approval.[100]

There were many issues to be sorted out between the district units and the high command, but there was no sign that another general council meeting would be held any time soon. The demand for one was getting shriller, with a clique led by Asanta Bagh Phukan even issuing a deadline for the meeting.[101] Rajkhowa was in favour of a meeting, but Paresh would not give the nod till he had been successful in grabbing a consignment of weapons.[102] His objective was to make the armed wing stronger and usher in changes in the organizational structure, much beyond what had been approved at the executive council meeting. This, in effect, would also strengthen his position in the organization. Many senior functionaries had begun to allege that he was deliberately postponing the meeting for vested interests.[103]

More importantly, and unknown to most of the senior functionaries, a grave crisis had gripped ULFA in Bangladesh for a few months towards the end of 1993, which made Paresh more averse towards accepting the demand for convening the general council. ULFA's history would have taken a different course altogether if Bangladesh's external intelligence wing, the Directorate General of Forces Intelligence (DGFI), had not chosen to keep the momentous episode under wraps. Anup dashed from the camp in Karbi Anglong to Dhaka after being informed about the episode. It had been almost three weeks since Paresh and a small group of ULFA functionaries had gone to the port city of Chittagong, but they had not returned home![104]

Paresh Imprisoned by the DGFI!

By mid-1993, Paresh was convinced that the only way to grab a large quantity of weapons was through the seas and by landing them either at Cox's Bazar or Chittagong port in Bangladesh on the Karnaphuli river. He knew that the NSCN(IM) had been successful only a year ago with a consignment that had been offloaded at Cox's Bazar following a deal with gun merchants in Thailand. The weapons were carried to Nagaland through Mizoram and Manipur on a perilous route to avoid the Indian paramilitary forces along the border.[105] But the Nagas would not easily reveal their contacts to ULFA because of the latter's alliance with its bête noire, the NSCN(K). The NSCN(IM) was apprehensive that the weapons would also find their way to the camps in Myanmar and eventually to the eastern districts of Nagaland, where its rival still held sway.[106]

After months of trying to hook up a contact, Baruah succeeded in gathering details about an agent in Singapore whose parents had migrated from Tamil Nadu several decades ago. He was closely associated with the Israeli spy agency Mossad, and also doubled up as a gun merchant occasionally to earn a quick buck.[107] Paresh boarded the flight to Singapore with another ULFA functionary to finalize the deal. However, what the agent disclosed unnerved the duo—if a consignment was needed soon, then the deal must be clinched not with gun dealers in Thailand but with the Romanian government as it was looking for buyers of small arms.[108]

The agent agreed to be present in Romania during the negotiations for clinching the deal.[109] Sometime towards the end of 1993, Paresh and two ULFA functionaries were headed to Romania's capital of Bucharest where the agent from Singapore had already fixed appointments with officials of the defence ministry and the secretary of the foreign ministry in Romania.[110] But there was an unexpected glitch in London, where the trio had landed for a connecting flight to Bucharest. Some officials at Heathrow airport began to get suspicious about the authenticity of the passports shown by Paresh and his associates. They were interned and extensively interrogated by highly placed officials from other departments. It was only after two days that they were allowed to proceed to Romania.[111]

In Bucharest, the task of finalizing a deal was easier for ULFA than what was envisaged earlier. The foreign secretary engaged in a long conversation with Paresh on ULFA's armed campaign against the Indian government. He wanted to know more about the Northeast, which had been reeling under disturbed conditions after India's Independence.[112] Satisfied with Paresh's answers, the secretary facilitated the display of a wide range of weapons before the ULFA team. An order for about 600 weapons, consisting of AK-47 rifles, light machine guns, pistols, ammunition and explosives, was placed. The payment was made and details of the delivery spot off Chittagong port in Bangladesh were submitted. A ship would arrive there after a month with the consignment. From Romania, Paresh headed to Ukraine with the agent for a brief sojourn, where they also explored the possibility of purchasing weapons in the future. [113]

After returning to Bangladesh, Baruah hired four trawlers from Chittagong to receive the consignment, which was expected to arrive after a month. The plan was to ferry the weapons to the camps at Satcherri and Srimangal before distributing them among different destinations.[114] The agent from Singapore landed in the country to accompany Paresh and two other ULFA functionaries for receiving the weapons, but the ship could not be traced. For two nights the squad scouted the waters for hours on end, but without success. It was resolved that the agent would make efforts to contact his sources in Bucharest to ensure the ship's arrival at the chosen location. But something unexpected happened before he could embark on the task. The ship arrived at Chittagong and moored at a location brimming with police personnel![115]

The ship charted a different route from the one the receiving group had expected it to take, which is why it could not be spotted by the group on board the trawlers. The ULFA squad was alarmed when it heard about the development. Loading the weapons on to trucks without the knowledge of the port authority and the police looked like an impossible task. The ship could not remain moored for an indefinite period either. But before any decision could be arrived at, the consignment had been seized. Within hours, the police were knocking on the doors of the hotel in Chittagong where Paresh, Shashadhar and other functionaries were putting up. They were taken to a police station and transferred to the headquarters of Bangladesh's external intelligence wing, the Directorate General of Forces Intelligence (DGFI), at Mirpur in Dhaka. Paresh continued to be detained with another functionary while the rest were released within a couple of days.[116]

DGFI was fully aware about the activities of ULFA and other rebel groups from India's Northeast in Bangladesh. But it never expected the outfit to be so brazen as to secretly import a large consignment of weapons into the country! So, Paresh and the other

ULFA functionary were lodged in separate cells of the DGFI, but none was subjected to physical abuse, unlike what usually happens at such places.[117] It was at this point that Anup was able to establish contact with a senior DGFI officer to make a case for the release of the Paresh and his associate, and also of the weapons seized at Chittagong. The officer was upfront about the impossibility of releasing the weapons, since highly placed government functionaries and a large section of the police at Chittagong were aware about the episode. Instead, Anup was advised by him to get in touch with the Rohingya leaders settled in Cox's Bazar for future consignments, as they were experienced and adept at such operations.[118]

At Mirpur, at the end of two months, Paresh decided to go on a hunger strike in the cell to break the stalemate. This was enough for the officers to take the matter more seriously and listen to his version of the episode. He was quizzed for over an hour by senior officers who were eager to identify the source of the weapons and the middlemen who had fixed the deal. In all probability, DGFI was reeling under the impression that Rohingya militants were involved in the consignment, which might have been sourced from Southeast Asia. Paresh denied any role of the Rohingya leaders in the deal but decided to mention Bangkok as the place where the deal was firmed up. The sources in Europe had to be kept a secret as there was a possibility of acquiring more weapons from them in the future. At the end of the discussions, the officer informed Paresh and his associate that they would be released in the evening. Paresh abandoned the strike, ate a hearty meal and prepared to step out of the cell with the other functionary after nearly two and a half months in custody.[119]

It is not known what caused the change of mind on the part of the DGFI, leading to release the ULFA squad, but it might have made more sense to them not to throw a spanner in the outfit's efforts to wage war against the Indian government from Bangladesh. There was no reason to crack the whip on the outfit when no action had been initiated against other rebel groups from the Northeast that had pitched tent in the country much earlier. Some ULFA functionaries were of the opinion that the top positions in the agency were manned by officers who were loyal to the BNP-led government. It is also likely that the ISI might have pulled strings to ensure the ULFA men's discharge from the cantonment.[120]

In the end, the episode turned out to be a mixed bag for ULFA. It was the beginning of a process that contributed to intimate links between the rebel group and a section of the DGFI which was were closely attached to Pakistan's ISI. ISI was further convinced about the rebel group's commitment to wage war against India. The connection with Singapore was snapped as nothing further was heard from the agent, who had flown out of Bangladesh a couple of days after the arrival of the consignment at Chittagong. Soon he went missing, never to be traced again. He was believed to have been killed by Mossad after the agency unearthed his role in firming the arms deal for ULFA. Above all, the failed mission entailed a huge financial loss for ULFA, at a time when funds were scarce, and the payment to Bucharest was made out of the contributions from several districts in the valley and possibly from the ISI.[121]

Auspiciously for ULFA, the crisis ended without the media in Bangladesh getting wind of it, which would have alerted New Delhi. After returning to Dhaka, Paresh decided to lie low for a couple of months and shun the usual errands of networking and searching for weapons. Anup dropped his plan to return to Assam and opted instead to make a representation to the US, the Netherlands and Swiss embassies, explaining ULFA's movement. He also decided on a trip to Thailand to connect with the Karen National Liberation Army that had been engaged in an armed campaign against the government in Myanmar for over four decades and was known to sell weapons occasionally. If the journey to Thailand were to be successful, then the subsequent step would be to strike a deal with the Rohingya leaders in Cox's Bazar for ferrying the weapons from the sea.[122] Funds must be arranged in advance and kept ready ahead of the meeting with the Karen leaders. ULFA's coffers were beginning to see regular flows since mid-1994, after a long period of slump.[123]

In Assam, most of the tea companies and business houses realized that neither the police nor the army could provide fool-proof security to them against the militants. There was a brief respite from ULFA for a couple of years after the launch of Operation Bajrang, but there was no indication of the outfit having been wiped out. No less terrifying for the tea estates were the increasing demand for funds by NDFB rebels on the north bank of the Brahmaputra, who operated out of camps in Bhutan. Failure to fulfil the demands invited retaliation, similar to the events that had unfolded with ULFA.[124]

In 1990, a tea garden employee, Jawahar Jain, was shot and killed by the NDFB near Tezpur; this was followed by a couple of successful abductions of managers working for the tea companies Williamson Magor and Goodricke. In 1993 came the famous abduction of a deputy general manager of Tata Tea Limited, Bolin Bordoloi from Guwahati, which punched holes in the government's claims of an improved situation in Assam. Bordoloi was taken to Bhutan by the rebels and set free after 330 days in captivity. Although the tea company had maintained that no money was paid as ransom, Paresh spilled the beans two years later in an interview to a news portal about Rs 1 crore having been paid to NDFB to secure Bordoloi's release![125]

By late 1993, a battalion called the Assam Tea Plantations Security Force (ATPSF) was deployed in sixty-six vulnerable gardens across the state. The Indian Tea Association agreed to shell out Rs 10 crore for raising the force and equipping it with weapons and communication devices, besides paying the monthly salaries. But the situation hardly improved, with ULFA adopting the tactics that had already paid rich dividends to the other rebel outfits in the different regions of the Northeast, which meant targeting the gardens, business houses and contractors individually and compelling them to make a fixed annual payment at secured locations.[126]

Payments by the gardens were made in the metropolises to agents tasked by ULFA to collect the money. These agents would then disburse the funds to different destinations using the hawala route. An estimate of the quantum of funds gathered by the rebel groups from the estates came to light after a functionary of the NDFB was nabbed by the army. Two account books found with him revealed that Williamson Magor had paid over Rs 1 crore to the outfit during 1994–96, and smaller gardens had shelled out amounts ranging between Rs 10 lakh and Rs 25 lakh during the same period.[127] Evidently, the tea companies had firmed up a deal for peace with the rebel groups, and the same tactics were adopted by them in the case of other business houses, contractors and corrupt government officials. Incidentally, after the mid-nineties, there was only one instance of abduction by ULFA—of two tea garden employees working for Tata Tea Limited, who were released on the very next day.[128]

Anup did not have to wait for long for funds to pour into Dhaka. Soon he was headed for Bangkok with Shashadhar, while Paresh renewed his search for new sources of weapons. From Bangkok, the duo headed to Mae Sot in north Thailand, where functionaries of the Karen National Liberation Army took them across the Myanmar border to Manerplaw in south-east Myanmar for a meeting with senior leaders of the outfit.[129] The functionaries revealed that weapons could be delivered at Cox's Bazar by ship, but the full payment would have to be made to them in advance for the consignment. Anup and Shashadhar insisted on paying half of the total bill in advance and the rest after receipt of the weapons. To pay the entire amount in advance was too high a risk, which the two were unwilling to undertake. The negotiations came to a dead end, with the Karen leaders unwilling to budge from their position. The ULFA pair returned to Dhaka and decided to explore other avenues of weapons.[130]

Weapons at Last

Concurrent with the failed endeavour to acquire weapons in Bangkok were efforts by Paresh with other sources that eventually yielded results. He was assisted by some senior members of two political parties in Bangladesh—the Jasod and Awami League—to establish contact with arms dealers in China and Thailand. In the entire episode, the involvement of officials of a Chinese intelligence agency cannot be ruled out, as some later developments were to indicate.[131] Convinced that the agents were genuine, Baruah got on with the equally vital task of firming up a deal with Rohingya leaders in Cox's Bazar before placing the order in Thailand.[132] They would have to be roped in for ferrying the weapons over from the sea and storing them at a secured place before their dispatch to other destinations.

Befriending a Rohingya group turned out to be easier, with some people in Dhaka lending a helping hand to ULFA.[133] The Rohingya group comprised former rebel leaders who had high hopes of waging war against the Junta in Myanmar for its repeated persecution of their community. Going on an offensive was tougher than imagined. They hardly had any money to buy weapons or to organize training modules. They were just managing to make both ends meet through some petty business in Bangladesh. Paresh instantly developed a rapport with them, and they revealed the 'dos and don'ts' to be followed during the operation and the safer spots where the weapons could be received on the sea. It was decided that the consignment would be carried inland by trawlers and then transported to a hideout at Bandarban in the Chittagong Hill Tracts contiguous to Cox's Bazar. The Rohingya leaders were reluctant to go out on the seas, for reasons that were not spelt out, but they would wait at a spot on the shore for the trawlers to arrive.[134]

With the spadework completed in Cox's Bazar, Baruah confidently headed to Bangkok for placing the order with the brokers, which was larger than the one made at Romania. The delivery, which was expected to yield an assortment of AK-47 assault rifles, pistols, grenades, rocket launchers, ammunition and explosives, would primarily be sourced from Chinese agents, and a small quantity from other agents who sold weapons manufactured in Europe. The ship would reach Cox's Bazar at a given date four weeks later, in the first week of December 1994. Apparently, ULFA's coffers were almost empty after footing the bill for the consignment in Bangkok.[135]

Baruah handpicked four experienced ULFA functionaries for receiving the weapons in Bangladesh. They included Lohit Deuri, who was summoned from the Bhutan camp. The squad landed at a hideout of the Rohingya leaders in Cox's Bazar near the coast, where they stayed for a day for the three trawlers to arrive. Late in the evening, they ventured deep into the sea to the pre-arranged location, but the ship was nowhere to be seen. They returned to the town early morning and set sail again the next evening to the same location on the sea. It was early morning at 2 a.m. that the ship was finally spotted.[136]

After drawing closer to the ship, Baruah climbed a rope ladder on to the deck of the ship, where two officers were waiting to receive him. They appeared more like navy officers than employees of a private ship ferrying merchandise.[137] Within a few minutes the crew began assembling medium-sized wooden boxes on the deck, which were then transferred to the trawlers with ropes. After an hour or so, the trawlers embarked on the return journey laden with weapons, but heading towards an estuary. The spot could be traced only after dawn. There a Rohingya squad had been waiting with two trucks since midnight. The wooden boxes began to be moved from the trawlers to the trucks.[138]

However, trouble was brewing again. No sooner had the loading of the trucks been completed than some forest department officials appeared out of nowhere. They watched the unusual activity from a distance and informed the police. The ULFA team was unnerved.

Would it mean confiscation again, and conviction? There was hardly any doubt that the police would dispatch a team for inspection of the site. There was no time to bury the consignment or to shift it to a remote spot. Finally, the Rohingya leaders' suggestion that the convoy should proceed towards Bandarban in the Chittagong Hill Tracts was accepted. They assured the ULFA squad that the police would be managed if there was any trouble. The Rohingya leaders had a rapport with most of the senior officials in the district. However, the police had already firmed up a plan to seize the consignment.[139]

The convoy came under a hail of gunfire only ten minutes after it began the journey across a stretch of semi-hilly terrain where policemen had positioned themselves for an ambush. The trucks screeched to a halt. One of the trucks suffered minor damage, with holes on its side. One of the Rohingya leaders leapt out from one of the trucks, raised his hands and spoke to the policemen. He went away with them to some unknown location and returned after a couple of hours. The convoy had been permitted to proceed, but only after a deal was struck.[140] A few police officials would have to be paid a handsome amount very soon. The ULFA group heaved a sigh of relief. A month later, Paresh paid the amount to the police and a commission to the Rohingya leaders, as committed to them earlier.[141]

At Bandarban, ULFA cadres had already arrived from the camps in Satcherri and Bhutan. Paresh had also devised a plan for the stocking and distribution of the weapons, which was known only to a few functionaries. Three quarters of the consignment would be immediately transferred to the camps at Satcherri and Srimangal, and the rest to other destinations in Bhutan and Assam in smaller quantities by different routes.[142] In all probability, the Indian security agencies would gather intelligence about the arrival of the consignment, with the result that surveillance would be mounted along the border. So it was necessary to hoodwink them into believing that the entire consignment would be transported through only one route.[143] Baruah had a plan to ferry a fraction through Myanmar's hilly terrain in Chin State to the camp of the People's Liberation Army (PLA), further north near Manipur. Thus was born the idea of 'Operation Ambrosia', or 'Amrit Mission', one of the most perilous operations ever to be undertaken by rebels from the Northeast in foreign territory.[144]

Within no time a debate ensued among the ULFA leaders as to whether the assignment could be successfully accomplished. The terrain was not only thinly populated but completely unfamiliar to ULFA. Would the Chin National Army (CNA), which had been active in the region and fighting against the Myanmar Junta for many years, allow passage of the weapons through its territory? Finally, the consensus evolved that the mission must be led by functionaries familiar with the route and terrain. This meant either hiring guides or joining hands with other rebel groups well-versed with the region.[145]

The only outfit from the Northeast whose cadres had journeyed between Myanmar's Chin State and Bangladesh was the NSCN(IM). Towards the end of 1993, 250 cadres of the outfit had trekked all the way from the borders of Manipur to reach the newly established camps in Bangladesh at Ali Kadam and near Cox's Bazar, which was very close to NDFB's camps. It was a gruelling march, spanning more than seven weeks, which had also claimed the lives of a few cadres.[146] NSCN(IM) functionaries based in Bangladesh were pessimistic about taking the route when some ULFA leaders contacted them for guidance. More than from the Myanmar army, there was the danger of the hostile terrain and scarcity of food as villages were scattered over very long distances. Nor was the Naga outfit able to furnish ULFA with any local contacts who could have acted as guides for the operation.[147] Did ULFA have any other option?

A glimmer of hope for ULFA appeared two weeks later, when a senior PLA functionary, Captain John Singh, informed them that he was familiar with Myanmar's Chin State since cadres from Manipur had trekked through the route earlier to reach Bangladesh. What he disclosed was the opposite of the NSCN(IM)'s gloomy estimation of the track, stunning the ULFA leaders. He disclosed that the mission could be successfully completed if the march proceeded close to the Mizoram border, which was dotted with villages at regular intervals. He also offered to provide more than a hundred cadres for the mission to ferry the weapons, which meant that some rifles and ammunition would also have to be shared with them. The total strength of the group could well cross 150; the All Tripura Tiger Force (ATTF) was also keen to participate with its own contribution of cadres.[148]

Paresh gave his nod for the mission after weeks of vacillation. By January, a deal was struck with PLA—all weapons to be carried by its cadres would belong to them. On its part, the group would steer the marching cadres through the jungle, arrange for food and shelter, and accommodate them in one of its camps along the Manipur-Myanmar border till was feasible for them to embark on the subsequent journey to Bhutan. The operation was scheduled tentatively for the first half of March, before the onset of the rains.[149]

Even as hectic preparations began for the assignment, Anup embarked on a mission to the UN-sponsored World Summit for Social Development at Copenhagen between 6 and 12 March 1995 as an environmental activist. He had already enrolled as a member of the Dhaka-based Institute for Environment and Development Studies, which was engaged in afforestation schemes. The real motive was to lay a network among NGOs and a presence with global organizations that espoused the rights of marginalized indigenous communities. Anup's goal was also to forge closer ties with a UK-based medical practitioner, Dr Mukul Hazarika, who had been requested by ULFA to attend the conclave. Hazarika, who hailed from Nagaon in Assam, had already championed ULFA's cause at different venues in Europe and had been keen to meet the leaders.[150]

In Copenhagen, Hazarika introduced Anup to a London-based NGO named Liberation, which was a consultant to the UN and known to assist organizations fighting oppressive governments in highlighting their grievances at global platforms. Next, ULFA secured membership of the Society for Threatened People, which operated out of Germany and was engaged in similar activities but mostly with communities facing threat of extinction around the globe. Acquaintance with these groups opened up avenues for ULFA with other forums, such as the Unrepresented Nations' Peoples Organisation (UNPO) and the annual congress of the UN Sub-Commission on the Promotion and Protection of Human Rights at Geneva, where representations were made between 1995 and 1997.[151] For honing their diplomatic skills, ULFA deputed chairman Rajkhowa and foreign secretary Shashadhar to avail of a course in Bangkok facilitated by Liberation.[152]

ULFA's activities at the international fora stirred other separatist groups from the Northeast into action. NSCN(K) chairman S.S. Khaplang, sent a missive to Paresh from Myanmar expressing his desire to present the case of the Nagas in Myanmar and India at Geneva. ULFA assured him that the task would be accomplished and all hurdles cleared for his journey to Geneva. Khaplang was equipped with a Bangladeshi passport under the surname of 'Lyngdoh'; this would mean he belonged to the Khasi community from Sylhet. But it was only two years later, in 1997, that the Naga chief was able to reach Geneva after crossing over to Bangladesh from Meghalaya in the Northeast.[153]

CHAPTER 5

MARCH OF DEATH

Operation Ambrosia

BY THE END of February 1995, the temporary camp at Bandarban was overflowing with cadres of ULFA and ATTF pouring in from different destinations. Another camp was erected further up in the hills, close to the border with Myanmar, where a wide array of weapons to be ferried were dumped, including the different versions of the Kalashnikov assault rifle, 9 mm and .32 pistols, Universal Machine Guns (UMGs), rocket launchers and ammunition.[1] Fifty-seven cadres were chosen by ULFA for the march, to be led by a Kachin-trained veteran, Dilip Rongpi, who would be assisted by senior functionaries, including foreign secretary Shashadhar. And they would be joined by twelve cadres from the ATTF and around 100 from the PLA in the long march to Manipur.[2]

Each functionary was tasked to carry up to around 30 kg, which was even more than the load they had to carry on their assignments in Kachin. There were very few in the group who had the experience of undertaking such an arduous task. The saving grace was the brief duration of the journey, estimated by the PLA to be completed within three weeks.[3] According to the plan, the march would commence on 16 March from the camp after sunset to a location above the tri-junction of Bangladesh, Myanmar and India. Darkness was preferred, as the Indian security forces deployed along the border in the Indian state of Mizoram above the tri-junction had a network of informers in the region. The plan was to trek through a sliver of territory in the state on the next day before setting foot in Myanmar. The PLA group under Captain John Singh would get attached to the group on the next day, ahead of reaching Mizoram, where its cadres had already pitched tent.[4]

Anup, Paresh and ATTF president Ranjit Debbarma arrived at the camp a couple of days before the start of the operation. They briefed the cadres about the journey, the dos and dont's, and the items to be carried by each cadre, including rice, medicines, clothes and a flask of water, besides the large quantity of weapons and ammunition. They shook hands with all the cadres as they began the march on an ascending hilly path leading to the border with Mizoram. The climb was relaxing and unhurried; the track was not very narrow and the cadres switched on the lights they carried since there was no fear of police. A medical unit at the rear, equipped with all the necessary medicines, including injections, was at ease as there had been no case to attend to so far.[5]

Around 2:30 a.m. an alarm broke out, halting the march. The cadres at the front tasked to act as guides had taken a wrong turn, which could lead the column to a location far from where the PLA had been waiting for them.[6] And of course it would mean inviting danger if they surfaced near any outpost of the India border guards. The entire group was instructed by Dilip Rongpi to retrace their path to a point and wait until further orders as some select cadres began to scout for the precise route. The search continued and a pathway spotted two hours later, but it was headed in the southern direction, which might have led to the Parva area at the tri-junction of the three countries.[7] It was not before the wee hours of the next day that the track was finally discovered. The march resumed, with a break around 9 a.m., when a brunch of rice and boiled vegetables was cooked. Thereafter, there was no confusion till the PLA camp came into view late in the evening.[8]

The next morning, the enlarged group stepped into Mizoram through a secured spot along the Bangladesh-India border decided earlier, which was devoid of the presence of the Indian border police. The group crossed over to Myanmar's Chin State three days later, with a change in direction to the north. So far, everything was proceeding according to plan, but food was getting scarcer towards the month end. The first village the rebels stumbled upon in Myanmar was small, with only about thirty households and without any surplus rice to spare. A bigger village came into view two days later, where rice was available but not vegetables. The marchers' stock was somewhat replenished. The rice was combined with boiled wild banana flower, which was their diet for the next week.[9]

On 25 March, the trek was again halted, but for a different reason altogether, and that was to have an adverse effect on the operation. A group of about a dozen, who identified themselves as belonging to a faction of the Chin National Army (CNA), requested the senior functionaries of the marching group to proceed to a village for a meeting with their leaders. In the village, however, the behaviour of Captain John astonished the cadres from the other two groups. He frantically requested the Chin leaders to show them the route that led to Manipur! So, did he pull a fast one when he claimed that he was well-versed with the terrain? He was often spotted trying to make sense of a hand-drawn map marked with mountains and rivers. To make matters worse, he did not carry a compass, and there was nobody else in the PLA who knew the direction. The Chin rebels were willing to assist them, but only if part of the consignment was given to them.[10]

There was no way to relay the message to Paresh in Bangladesh for an opinion as the batteries of their walkie-talkies had been exhausted long ago. A long negotiation ensued between John and the Chin leaders, but there was no decision in the end. The CNA was unwilling to accept the plea that it would be provided with weapons from Bangladesh after completion of the assignment. The PLA was determined not to part with anything, and it would not let either the ULFA or ATTF forward their opinion. Soon they left the village to resume the march, but they proceeded on an erroneous route leading further into the interiors of Myanmar.[11] This was also when the Myanmar army decided to checkmate the rebels, thinking that their motive was to launch attacks in its territory.[12]

In fact, the Myanmar government had been apprised of Operation Ambrosia three days after the march had begun from Bandarban. Accompanied by an associate, Paresh called on high-ranking officials at the Myanmar Embassy in Dhaka with a request for 'safe passage' for the group. The officials agreed and even suggested that the group ought to carry a white flag whenever there was the possibility of coming face to face with the army. However, it is doubtful if the message could be relayed to the army in the remote Chin hills immediately, as that area was one of the most underdeveloped regions in Myanmar.[13]

A couple of days after the meeting with the CNA, a helicopter hovered close to the column for several hours. Alarmed that there could be an assault, the leaders issued orders to the entire group to duck for cover in the jungles. The objective of the sortie, presumed to be from the Indian army, was probably to determine the precise location of the marching cadres. It was only in the evening that the trek was continued, after the helicopter had disappeared. Nobody knew where they were headed to, but fear of an encounter with the army was beginning to grip everybody. Nothing untoward happened for the next four days and a detour on the wrong path halted when a few elderly residents at a village revealed the correct direction to them.[14]

However, by the second week of April, a group of young cadres began to display signs of extreme fatigue and were unable to keep pace with the column. But there was no option except to keep marching till the destination was reached. So far, there had been no major obstacles in the journey except scarcity of food and water. The PLA leaders kept insisting that its camp in Manipur was only a short distance away, whereas it was actually far away, which become evident within a few days. Nonetheless, their claims helped to keep the morale of the entire group high for a few more days. [15]

The group reached a big village on 12 April, where it decided to halt for the night. Rice was purchased and distributed among the cadres. The plan was to relax and stay for another night, but Captain John ordered resumption of the march in the morning. Barely 2 km from the village, the rear section of the column came under heavy fire in what turned out to be the first major encounter with the Myanmar army. Since the attack was also launched from the front, the group surmised that it was a combined effort with the Indian army to halt its advance. All the cadres scurried for safety behind trees and boulders. Not a single shot was fired in retaliation, as it would entail wastage of ammunition.[16]

After the firing subsided, Captain John, Dilip Rongpi and Shashadhar discussed the situation and resolved to create a platoon for defence and to hit the trail back to the village. John devised a plan to mend fences with the Myanmar army. He instructed Choudhury to write a letter to the commander of the Myanmar army, which would be delivered by a messenger in the village. It was inferred that the army had an establishment or a camp at a location nearby which had launched the attack on the cadres. The letter explicitly mentioned, '... we are not your enemy, which explains why we have not fired a single bullet. And we hope you will not consider us as your enemy. So we nurture the hope that you would not launch any further attack on us.'[17]

An elder from the village agreed to deliver the letter as well as the response from the army to the group. But his absence till late afternoon made everybody jittery, until the captain issued an order for resumption of the march. In fact, the army never moved from its position, and it had been waiting for the group to return. Again, a torrent of gunfire greeted the cadres who were instructed by the captain to return fire and proceed with the trek. While the ULFA and ATTF factions were able to escape unscathed and move beyond the danger zone, the PLA squad was left far behind and was detached from the column. At night, the entire group halted at a village, where the PLA also caught up, but a few of its cadres were missing.[18]

After dinner, three young ULFA cadres who had been complaining of weakness almost collapsed and expressed their inability to proceed further on the journey. In all probability, they were infected with malaria or mokhlong and were administered injections. The PLA was faced with the same predicament after two cadres, one of whom had sustained bullet injuries during the attack, expressed reluctance to proceed further. Waiting for them to recover could put the entire group at risk since information would certainly reach the army about their presence in the village. Carrying them on stretchers was unfeasible, since everybody was already burdened with the extra load of weapons. So a decision was arrived at to leave all the five cadres behind after the senior functionaries spoke to the village chief. They were accommodated in two huts; medicines and some money were given to them in the hope that they would soon recover from their illnesses and be able to resume their journey. It was a heartbreaking moment for everybody in the morning at the time of departure when the sick ULFA cadres requested the group to deliver the message at their homes that they were no more.[19]

Everybody moved on with a heavy heart, only to experience another depressing episode in the afternoon. Another ULFA cadre who could no longer walk had to be abandoned, but in much harsher conditions. A shed was erected for him near a waterfall with a sheet of polythene covering the top, and he was provided small quantities of medicines and rice, a machete and some money. Two more cadres, who were in a particularly concerning state of health, were somehow dragged to the camp set up in the evening at the summit of a hill. They were administered injections, which helped them recover in time for the trek the next morning.[20] But the situation only turned worse during the day, resulting in more confusion and fragmentation of the marching column.

The army had anticipated the path of the rebels and had already taken positions for another ambush. In all likelihood, the letter sent to the commander had either not been delivered or was ignored. So, no sooner had the cadres begun descending the hill after breaking camp than gunfire and mortar shells rained on them, killing at least half a dozen from across outfits on the spot. The rest dived for cover in the jungle on the side of the narrow pathway and returned fire, which might have also caused casualties to the army. The encounter raged on for five hours, with both sides determined not to abandon their positions. Finally the army withdrew, but there were many functionaries among the ULFA and PLA, including Captain John, who also disappeared, along with many cadres. They were definitely not killed in action, as their dead bodies would have been found if that were the case. The column was scattered, with the cadres splintering in different directions—and some of them might have also preferred to abandon the assignment and chart a different path ahead.[21]

That the Myanmar army would continually launch offensives against them was least expected by the group when the assignment was conceived. Battered and tired, around seventy cadres from all the marching outfits clung together, but were unable to decide on the next course of action. PLA appointed a sergeant major, George, as the new commander of Operation Ambrosia, while Dilip Rongpi continued to lead ULFA. Somebody suggested that the dead bodies ought to be buried, but there was no time to dig graves for them. The danger zone would have to be crossed at the earliest.[22]

So the journey continued, with some cadres carrying the rifles and ammunition of their slain colleagues. A village was spotted after three hours. They decided to spend the night there, despite the danger of a raid by the army. It was 28 April, but the group had still no clue as to how long it would take them to reach Manipur. Rice was purchased in the village and the chief agreed to provide a dozen porters who would act as guides and carry the extra rifles up to a certain distance.[23] In the evening, the army pounced on the rebels again with a few minutes of continuous gunfire. The encounter lasted only for an hour or so, and saw the same sequence of events as earlier—cadres diving for cover, firing in retaliation and dispersal of the group. Finally, it was now only about fifty cadres from the original marching group that pitched camp near a waterfall in the hills.[24] A small squad that was detached during the encounter succeeded in reaching the camp late in the evening. The group swelled to sixty cadres when the march began again in the morning in the direction the porters had indicated.[25]

Operation Golden Bird

Information about the arrival of the weapons in Cox's Bazar had reached R&AW by mid-January after the rebel groups had already finalized the plan for Operation Ambrosia.[26] The army top brass was briefed about the development in New Delhi and entrusted with the mandate to thwart the rebels' mission. By the last week of March, a tentative plan of action emerged, following a series of meetings convened by the Dimapur-based 3 Corps in Nagaland. Finally, the 57 Mountain Division in Manipur was assigned the task, codenamed Operation Golden Bird.[27]

The army estimated that the rebels would be neutralized within a week.[28] The immediate challenge for the army was to assemble a large force of 300–400 soldiers, as availability of troops in Mizoram was scarce. Mizoram was among the peaceful states in the Northeast; militancy had drawn to a close after the accord between the government and Mizo National Front (MNF) in 1986. The 8 Mountain Division had been transferred to Jammu and Kashmir following an increase in terrorist activities in that state. So, troops had to be airlifted by helicopter from different units stationed in other states of the Northeast, with Assam Rifles and para-commandos also pitching in to augment the numbers.[29] They landed in a terrain wholly unfamiliar, where the army had ceased to operate years ago. All these years there had been no effort to intercept rebel groups such as the NSCN(IM) and PLA that had been frequenting the Indo-Myanmar border along the route from Bangladesh.

Nonetheless, the general officer commanding of 57 Mountain Division, major general M.S. Gill, landed at the Assam Rifles post at Twangklawng with the senior officers stationed at Aizawl for the conduct of the operation. With hardly any time to lose, the army plunged into tapping as many sources across the border as possible for actionable intelligence on the rebels' movement and routes. Feelers were sent to all the three groups active around the tri-junction at Parva—the National Unity Party of Arakan, Chin National Army and a Bangladeshi group called Shanti Bahini. The Chin outfit agreed to provide the army information as it was already peeved with the rebels for their refusal to spare them some weapons.[30]

Information soon began to trickle in on the movement of the rebels after they crossed Ltulphungtlang village in Myanmar in a northern direction, conveying the impression that they would soon cross the Kolodyne river. The army's plan was to set up interception lines at convenient locations along the border to stall their advance. Accordingly, troops were to be positioned at a vantage point along the river and at a second interception line near the villages of Zawngling, Khengkhong, Tuipang and Tuithminhar in Mizoram. It was presumed that the marchers would replenish their stocks of rice and water and possibly halt for the night at these hamlets. However, on the ground, the turnout of events was different from what was envisaged by the army at the headquarters of 57 Mountain Division in Manipur. The rebels inadvertently charted a meandering track touching the territories of both countries, which had the effect of throwing the army into tremendous confusion. The rebels succeeded in dodging the interception along the Kolodyne river by digressing further east into Myanmar. The army decided on hot pursuit for a couple of kilometers, but it was hardly of any use as the rebels trotted faster than them, reaching a safe zone.[31]

Additional forces were flown in by the army and readjustments made in the deployment, with interceptions at certain points further north and east that sometimes strayed into Myanmarese territory as well.[32] It was envisaged that the meandering trek of the rebels would touch upon these points within a few days. On 13 April, the army came close to confronting the rebels at Fartlang across the border, but the same story as earlier was repeated, with the rebels giving them the slip by venturing deep into the hills. However, this time around, another unsavoury experience was in store for the Indian army after a platoon came face-to-face with a company of the Myanmar army led by a non-commissioned officer. The officer had no qualms in ordering the Indian squad to return to its own territory. For the Myanmar army, there was no reason for the Indian army to execute an operation in their country.[33] In all possibility, they were never briefed by their headquarters about Operation Golden Bird, information about which remained confined to the Indian army as subsequent developments were to prove. It is also doubtful if efforts were made at all by the Indian army with its Myanmar counterpart for a combined operation!

When the episode was reported to 57 Mountain Division, an order was issued to move deeper into Myanmar to a new line of interception, with the rider that no casualties in the Indian army would be acceptable.[34] The commanders were puzzled, as the insurgents had moved to the interior, resulting in an encounter with the Myanmar army on 17 April at Hlamphie. Again, the Indian army bumped into a Myanmar column, leading to an outcome much more severe than its previous encounter. Efforts were made to convince the Myanmarese officer to join hands with the Indian army for the operations, but they were in vain and the officer even threatened to launch an offensive if the Indian army did not step back into its country![35] No reply was forthcoming from the General Officer Commanding (GOC) at 57 Mountain Division when he was informed about the incident.

The army column crossed over to Mizoram and was instructed a day later to proceed to a place east of Zongling in south Mizoram along the border. At night, another message was received that a large squad of Assam Rifles was also heading for the same destination, following receipt of inputs from multiple sources that the rebels would soon cross the area. However, instead of challenging the rebels, Assam Rifles ended up firing at the army column in the dark, resulting in the death of an army personnel, prompting the headquarters to summon an emergency meeting of all the commanders engaged in the operation.[36]

All the columns began heading towards the Assam Rifles battalion at Serchip in Mizoram, where a detailed evaluation of the operation was held. That the rebel column could not be halted came as a surprise to 57 Mountain Division, but there were abundant reasons for the army's dismal performance. To begin with, a limited number of maps of the areas of operation was issued to the commanding officers on their reaching Mizoram. The confusion was compounded by the army's unfamiliarity with the terrain and the limited availability of wireless equipment, which severely curtailed the army's operational reach and effectiveness. While the army had Self-Loading Rifles (SLRs), the rebels were carrying Kalashnikov assault rifles and universal machine guns. On certain occasions, the columns were left with limited or no rations, and there were cases of malaria resulting from lack of medicines. Moreover, staff officers from 57 Mountain Division or Assam Rifles were not available in adequate numbers for coordination.[37]

The briefing at Serchip was the first time that operational instructions were explicitly given and maps of the new area of deployment issued. All the troops were divided into two task forces under the commanding officers of Assam Rifles and 15 Kumaon.[38] A tactical headquarters was established for coordination in Khwabung, an existing post of Assam Rifles. The possible route of the rebels along the border was charted, and new positions for the army identified for deployment. It was evident that the insurgent group, despite pressure from the Myanmarese army, had actually moved deeper into Myanmarese territory rather than crossing over to the Indian side. Though not very advantageous, it was decided to set up interceptions in and around Farkawn Bulge in the north since the Indian squad could no longer move freely across the border.[39]

On 25 April 1995, after an intelligence void of a few days, information was received about the movement of the insurgent group and a column was hurriedly positioned to stall its advance along the border adjacent to Klangpi in Myanmar. For the first time, the results were encouraging for the army. In an encounter that lasted for about fifteen minutes, six insurgents were killed and five weapons, fifty-two rucksacks with approximately 500 rounds of ammunition and about five quintals of rice were recovered. Getting wind of the skirmish, about eighty Myanmarese troops arrived on the spot. They were requested again to carry out joint operations with the Indian forces, but the request was turned down. The same stance was maintained by the senior Myanmar army officers who had arrived in Imphal on 28 April for the Indo-Myanmar Liaison Conference. The Dimapur based 3 Corps of the army immediately issued orders to the commanding officers not to cross the international border.[40]

A flurry of minor episodes unfolded in quick succession towards the fag end of April. In a village near Vaiphei, close to the border, the army stumbled across bags of ammunition and rifles near a river. Further ahead was the dead body of an ATTF cadre who had probably contracted some disease and could not keep pace with the rest of the group. Two army personnel also passed away after contracting malaria. A couple of days later, the bullet-ridden bodies of a Mizo couple who were shot by the rebels were recovered. Another local resident, who had succeeded in avoiding contact with the rebels by hiding in the jungles, told the army that an official of the Intelligence Bureau and a translator who were with the couple were also shot dead before the rebels proceeded on their journey.[41]

Subsequently, three squads of the rebels comprising functionaries of ULFA and PLA, which had broken away from the main column following the ambushes by the Myanmar army, were apprehended in Mizoram. Among them were ULFA foreign secretary Shashadhar, who had managed to cross the border to Lunglei in south Mizoram with another injured functionary, Avinash Bordoloi. The duo had all but abandoned the plan to continue the trek to Manipur. Their plan was to reach Silchar in Assam from Mizoram and then cross the border to Bangladesh. They hopped on to a truck after threatening the driver, but the vehicle was intercepted by the army at a barricade.[42] ULFA functionary Diwakar Moran, who had been hit in the palm by a bullet, was with another group and was the first to be interrogated by the army. He had crossed the border into Mizoram with a group, but was left behind after he fell unconscious from loss of blood. Moran had a narrow escape after a hail of bullets descended all around him, one of them piercing his left palm. He woke up in the morning in a paddy field and then managed to reach a small hut where he requested the occupant for food. He was offered rice, which he ate, and but he again dozed off in a few minutes on the earthen floor of the hut. In the evening, he was woken by the kicks delivered by a dozen army personnel, who then dragged him to the nearest outpost of Assam Rifles.[43]

An interesting episode happened with Moran and his squad before they crossed the border into Mizoram. After straying from the main column, this group twice came under attack by the Myanmar army, resulting in the death of more than a dozen PLA and ULFA cadres. As they continued with the trek after the encounter, a resident of a village came with a message from a small group of Myanmar army personnel that they did not intend to clash with the rebels anymore. Not only that, they were also willing to show them the route leading to Manipur. The army personnel were temporarily putting up in the village the messenger hailed from, and the village was visible from a distance. Although the ULFA and ATTF cadres were willing to befriend the Myanmar army, the PLA squad was longing for retaliation after losing so many of their colleagues in ambushes by the army. A heated debate ensued among the rebels, but there was no way that PLA would relent. They instructed the messenger to inform the army personnel to come empty-handed, which they did after half an hour. The group consisted of six men in tattered uniforms, and none of them appeared to be an officer. The ATTF and ULFA cadres requested the PLA once again to rethink their decision, but to no avail. The six men were surrounded by the PLA functionaries and taken to a secluded spot some distance away from the village. They were then shot by two cadres after being forced to kneel down.[44]

The group comprising ULFA and ATTF cadres decided to split from the PLA and march on their own. After a couple of hours, they met some Myanmar army personnel who had no qualms about guiding them towards the route to be taken. The rebels were puzzled by the army's changed behaviour and surmised that this group was still ignorant about the fate of their colleagues who had been shot. But there would also be a reason why the army was no longer obstructing their passage. They also inferred that the combined operations with the Indian army to foil their mission must have drawn to a close, which also meant that it would be safer to walk on a track in Myanmar rather than along the border between the two countries. The border was not only indistinguishable, but none in the group had knowledge about the route. In all probability, they would have to drift into Mizoram occasionally, where the Indian army could be waiting to ambush them. And that is precisely what happened within the next couple of days, as the entire group was apprehended after they inadvertently ventured into Mizoram. There was no ambush as the army had taken up positions at vantage locations after receiving inputs from the Chin National Army about the rebels' movement. The rebels surrendered as they were too tired and demoralized to retaliate.[45]

End of Operations

Meanwhile, amid the uncertainties, the larger column of the rebels, comprising about fifty cadres from all the three outfits, continued on their journey in the northern direction. Neither the PLA nor the ATTF had equipped themselves with certain essential ingredients before embarking. ULFA's stock of medicines was fast depleting after distributing them to the functionaries of the other outfits who were suffering from malaria or other ailments. The trek's pace had slowed as four sick persons had to be carried on stretchers all the way, following a decision by the group leader that they would not be abandoned in villages or secluded spots in the jungle.[46]

Ambushes by the Myanmar army continued at regular intervals whenever the group stepped deep into the country. Even if there was a change in the army's policy towards the rebels, it had not yet been conveyed to all the battalions stationed in the country's Chin State. Sometimes the encounters lasted only for a few minutes, but on some occasions for several hours, resulting in casualties and injuries. On 2 May, there were two ambushes in a span of just one and a half hours in a quick manoeuvre by the army that caught the rebels by surprise. On the next day, two PLA cadres were blown to pieces after stepping on a landmine on a descending path from a hill. Then a gap of about a week ensued without any encounters, till the cadres reached a spot where the army had been waiting in large numbers for the final ambush, reminiscent of the first clash on 13 April. Many PLA and ULFA cadres were killed and commander George lay injured with four bullets in his body. Before dying, he issued orders to the group to resume the march and leave him behind in the jungle.[47]

It was not until 26 May that an unexpected episode impacted the remaining part of the rebels' journey. The group had begun its march a bit late in the morning after a hearty meal of rice and horse meat. A horse had been killed the previous evening.[48] Around noon, two farmers working in a field were approached for rice and direction to Manipur. They replied saying that the Myanmar army had kept a letter for them in the village, which they soon fetched. The letter, written in English, read:

> Dear Friend
>
> You should reach Manipur soon which is only 9 kms from Burma. Don't fire if you come face to face with the BA. If you do, then none would be able to escape from here. We had to engage in fighting with you without knowing anything. We have lost many soldiers and perhaps the same mishap has befallen you. This was a conspiracy of the Indian army. But we soon realised our mistake. Now our villagers will arrange food for you and will show you the route to Manipur. Please leave Burma at the earliest.[49]

The group jumped with excitement, not so much at the changed attitude of the army as much as at the information from the farmers that their destination had been almost reached. They were also informed that another rebel group that had arrived a week ago after an ambush was also proceeding in the same direction. A senior ULFA functionary, Biju Deka, wrote a letter in Assamese and told the villagers to hand it over to any squad that might reach the village over the next few days. It was a message that they should proceed to the PLA camp along the border with Manipur.[50]

What propelled the volte-face by the Myanmar army?

The letter left no room for doubt that it did not trust the Indian army and also explained its unwillingness to engage in a combined operation with it to thwart the mission undertaken by the rebels. It is possible that the decision to allow safe passage to the insurgents might have been arrived at by the Tatmadaw weeks ago, but there was delay in transmitting the message to the units in Chin State. The Indian army understood the reasons behind the Tatmadaw's gritty reluctance to engage in a combined operation to check the rebels. On 4 May, the Indian government had conferred pro-democracy leader Aung Sang Suu Kyi with the Jawaharlal Nehru Award for International Understanding. She had been put under house arrest at Yangon since 1990, but the damage was done. The development came on the heels of a long chain of events that had irked the Tatmadaw to no end. The pact between R&AW and KIA had been followed by the Indian government's support to the pro-democracy movement in Myanmar.

Rajiv Gandhi's visit to Myanmar in 1987 was the first by an Indian prime minister in nineteen years, but he did not depart from the policy of idealism. Refugee camps were opened in Manipur and Mizoram for activists of the pro-democracy movement fleeing the crackdown in Myanmar, and later a parliamentary panel was informed by the government that none would be forced to return. The All India Radio (AIR) had also broadcast anti-military propaganda for a few months in Burmese before it was stopped following complaints from Yangon. In 1992, India joined a United Nations' resolution sponsored by the US and western countries condemning the Junta for its violations of human rights.

The policy took an about-turn from the early nineties, culminating with the visit of Myanmar's deputy foreign minister U. Nyunt Swe to New Delhi in 1994, during which he held meetings to improve bilateral relations. A memorandum of understanding was inked to increase cooperation between the border authorities of the two neighbours and to prevent 'illegal and insurgent activities'. A second agreement stipulated regularization and promotion of border trade through Manipur and Mizoram. However, this was just the beginning of a new chapter in bilateral relations, which would see rough patches in the years to come. In reality, the two governments were yet to feel at home with each other, and ties between the two were yet to be fully normalized.

After the award to Aung Sang Suu Kyi was announced, there were intelligence inputs with the Indian security agencies about the free passage offered by the Tatmadaw to the insurgents.[51] Some Indian soldiers in Mizoram had also witnessed Myanmarese army personnel shaking hands with the rebels across the border before the operation against them was suspended.[52] The Indian army decided to set up new positions along the border at Champhai, further north and nearer to Manipur, for intercepting the rebels. The main purpose of the fresh deployment was to nab the individuals or small groups separated from the main column following encounters with either the Indian or Myanmar army. For the next two weeks there were a number of encounters, resulting in the elimination of some rebel cadres and confiscation of weapons and ammunition. At a later point, the Mizoram police was roped in by the army, leading to a small group of insurgents being nabbed, along with their weapons. Operation Golden Bird was officially called off on 21 May after information reached the army that the main column had reached the border in Manipur. The army did not have the mandate to extend the operations to that zone.[53]

There are differing estimates of the number of casualties that resulted from the operation and the distance trekked by the rebels from Bangladesh to Manipur. The main column of the rebels was engaged in as many as thirteen encounters with the Indian and Myanmar armies during the trek.[54] According to an assessment by a senior ULFA functionary who participated in the march, the majority of the rebel cadres killed in ambushes or by disease belonged to the PLA. There were nine dead from ULFA, while eight more were left behind in the villages or jungles during the arduous journey that extended over almost ten weeks.[55] Days after the operation ended, the army estimated that fifty-eight insurgents were killed, including thirty-one from the PLA, and fifty weapons, consisting of assault rifles and pistols, were seized. Three Indian army personnel were killed while another three succumbed to malaria a few days after the operation had drawn to a close.[56]

Then there were the forty-four rebel cadres who were apprehended in Mizoram and interned for many days in army custody before being handed over to the police.[57] Most of them went through the same ordeal of torture, which usually happens when an insurgent is apprehended by the army. The army did not know that in the group was ULFA foreign secretary Shashadhar, who was brutally thrashed with rifle butts, resulting in a severe injury to his lower spine.[58] For one of the groups, though, the agony lasted only a couple of days as a senior officer ordered lenient treatment of the rebels and even summoned a doctor to diagnose their diseases.[59] Some of the rebels suffered another round of battering by local convicts at the jail in Mizoram for killing a Mizo couple during their journey.[60] About a month later, the ULFA functionaries were transferred to jails in Guwahati and Dibrugarh, where they were lodged for two years. Subsequently, after serving their sentences, most of them crossed the border to the camps in Myanmar, Bhutan or Bangladesh.[61]

In hindsight, the nature and fallout of the operations were beyond the expectations of either the army or the insurgents. Neither the Indian troops nor the rebels were conversant with the terrain, but the latter had to take a greater pounding as they had become the target of both the Indian and Myanmar armies. And it seems likely that the Myanmar army confronted the insurgents not so much by design but as a natural reaction to rebels from a neighbouring country in its territory. And perhaps the aggressive action by the Indian troops left them with no choice but to put in efforts to stall the rebels' operations.

For the Indian army, Operation Golden Bird offered valuable lessons, beginning with the fact that the exercise exposed the loopholes in its strategy. The entire operation was marked by the absence of a definite operation plan, resulting in the ad-hoc mobilization of troops and inadequate logistical support. The two task forces were given little time to prepare for the operation after they were constituted and pressed into service. After the first briefing on the situation on 19 April 1995, the deficiencies of the first phase were somewhat curbed and the operations became more focused. But certain glitches, like lack of medicines and transport, continued until the end of the operation.[62]

Ideally, in such an operation, a briefing centre ought to have been set up, a helicopter provided and the police involved, which would have generated more actionable intelligence and might even have prevented some of the insurgents from escaping in small groups by private transport or on foot.[63] The 57 Mountain Division wanted to wrap up the operation at the earliest after orders were received from the army headquarters in New Delhi, which had swung into action after receiving information from R&AW on the rebels' plan. So, what becomes apparent in this episode is a case of passing the buck by one department to another and of fixing the responsibility for action on somebody else without doing the necessary follow-up. The army could not fathom that diplomatic efforts with Myanmar were imperative for the success of the operation. Perhaps the Ministry of External Affairs (MEA) was never informed about Operation Golden Bird, which explains the announcement of the award to Aung San Suu Kyi on 4 May.[64] It could have been done a few days later, after the operation had drawn to a close. In any case, Aung San was under house arrest and could not have arrived in India to receive the award.

These drawbacks notwithstanding, the army felt that the operation had been a great success as a large number of insurgents was either killed or apprehended. [65] The rebel group certainly suffered in terms of loss of equipment and was demoralized. But it must be borne in mind that the outfits had different objectives to fulfil from the operation. For PLA and ATTF, it meant gaining weapons and ammunition at a time when it was not easy to get access to them or to transport them to their camps. PLA lost more than thirty cadres, but it was still able to transport more than fifty assault rifles and a few universal machine guns, besides a large quantity of ammunition to its camp.[66] The gains were relatively less for ATTF, but its decision to allocate a dozen cadres for the operation strengthened its ties with ULFA. Its leadership had correctly envisaged that the camp in Bangladesh's Satcherri would be utilized by ULFA in the future for storage of weapons.

Some ULFA functionaries engaged in the assignment were convinced that Operation Ambrosia had mixed results.[67] The casualties could have been avoided with more planning and better information about the terrain, but they still succeeded in ferrying some weapons and ammunition to their ultimate destinations. They were ignorant of the plans that had already been firmed up by Paresh even before the consignment had arrived in Cox's Bazar. It was a closely guarded secret, known only to a few senior functionaries in the outfit.[68] Subsequent developments were to prove that the operation fulfilled the most vital goal of ULFA.

The key objective of Operation Ambrosia had been to keep the attention of the Indian security forces and agencies riveted on the India-Myanmar border and to convey the impression that the entire consignment was being ferried through this route. However, in reality, only about 10–15 per cent of the total consignment was taken by the rebels to the camp of the PLA.[69] Soon after the operation had started, Baruah busied himself with implementing the next plan of transporting as much as 50 per cent of the weapons in Bangladesh to the camps in Bhutan and other hideouts of ULFA in Assam.[70] In the course of time, rebel groups such as the UNLF and Kamtapur Liberation Organisation (KLO) were also given weapons from these camps at concessional rates.[71]

Multiple routes were identified along the international border of the Northeast for the subsequent operation. The weapons were to be distributed equally among all the routes as a precaution against seizures by the security forces. Five porous stretches that had scant presence of the Indian Border Security Force were selected, with entry points at Dhubri in Assam, Garo and Jaintia Hills in Meghalaya and two spots in Tripura not far from the Satcherri camp in Bangladesh.[72] A few functionaries from the camps in Bhutan and Bangladesh had already been instructed to station themselves at certain locations along the border to receive the weapons.[73] Their task was to arrange for the logistics and routes for transportation of the weapons to the camps in Bhutan. With the exception of Dhubri, which had a riverine border with Bangladesh, the rest of the entry points were far off from the camps in Bhutan, in Meghalaya and Tripura. The consignments would again have to travel a long distance and pass through multiple check points along the national highways, including the Nalbari-Barpeta zone in western Assam, which had a heavy deployment of the army.

Onward to Bhutan

By 22 June, all the rebels who survived Operation Ambrosia had reached their destination along the India-Myanmar border in Manipur, where they were received by a squad of the PLA.[74] After putting up at a small village for three days, another journey commenced to a camp of the outfit further north in Myanmar, which too was equipped with a training centre. A message sent by Paresh by radio instructed the thirty-odd ULFA cadres to deposit all the weapons at the camp's armoury and wait until further orders. So, for the next three months, it was the same curriculum of drills, games and the daily errands of a rebel camp, except that there was no danger of raids by the army.[75]

A month after their arrival, the group was asked to take part in raiding a police station in Manipur, which was blown up after an encounter lasting half an hour. Within a fortnight came another operation against a CRPF convoy, which was not as successful as the previous one. All the CRPF vehicles were able to scrape through to safety after a brief exchange of fire.[76] Even as preparations were on for the next encounter, a message from Paresh instructed the cadres to head for Bhutan in small groups. While most of them flew from Imphal to Guwahati, a few among them slipped out of Manipur in buses and taxis to Barama in western Assam, close to the border with Bhutan.[77] A year later, the weapons from the PLA camp were transferred to ULFA hideouts in eastern Assam bordering Arunachal Pradesh.[78]

Eventually, all the functionaries converged at the ULFA camp in Bhutan's Deothang, where the weapons from Bangladesh had begun to arrive in small quantities, ferried through multiple routes by different squads from the border. Among all the routes used for their transportation, the corridor through the border district of Dhubri in Assam was found to be the safest. There a senior functionary, Lohit Deuri, was deputed to supervise the operation. From Dhubri, the weapons were brought in trucks to Bongaigaon and then across the border to the nearest camp at Nganglam. Finally, the weapons that reached Bhutan consisted of around 300 Kalashnikov assault rifles, rocket launchers, grenades, pistols and ammunition.[79]

ULFA's presence in Bhutan had expanded since it had set foot in the kingdom four years ago. By mid-1995, around 400 cadres were stationed at the four camps, with the biggest at Deothang, which doubled as a training centre. It was bifurcated to create another camp near Sukuni Basti, which controlled the armed wing and was called the General Headquarters (GHQ). At the helm of all of ULFA's political activities was the Central Headquarters (CHQ) further east, near Kawoipani in Samdrup Jongkhar. The Barpeta Camp was at Nganglam, located some 100 km west of GHQ and which was soon to assume an important role in the outfit's subsequent operations.[80]

The expansion was propelled by ULFA's finances getting into shape, with funds pouring in at regular intervals. ULFA's kitty was primarily filled by means of money extorted in Assam and contributions made by the ISI from time to time.[81] Usually, after receiving funds, the district units were supposed to cover their expenses and transfer the remaining amount to Dhaka. In reality, the collected amount was never consistent and auditing was yet to be adopted as a regular practice in the organization. So, diversion of funds by cadres and commanders for personal gains, which had commenced at the formative phase of the organization, continued without any checks, causing occasional periods of scarcity at the camps.[82] The GHQ in Bhutan alone expended about Rs 2–2.5 lakh every month owing to its large size, while the expenses were even higher in the camps in Myanmar as food had to be transported over long distances over hilly terrain. Then there were expenses incurred by the senior functionaries at Dhaka and their foreign travels. The annual budget of ULFA was approximately Rs 3 crore, excluding expenses on weapons and ammunition.[83]

In Bhutan, ULFA had laid out an elaborate but cautious strategy of cultivating the support of the local populace, in a manner that it did not upset the Bhutanese ruling elite. The officialdom abhorred the Lhotsampha, the migrant Nepalese population inhabiting the southern districts of the kingdom. The residents not evicted during the backlash in the late 1980s continued to be deprived of all developmental schemes of the government.[84] The presence of the rebels came as a boon to a section of the Nepalese residents in Bhutan. The camps provided them the means to earn extra money. Instead of going to the distant markets to sell their surplus agricultural produce or depending on unscrupulous agents, many farmers could now sell it at higher prices to middlemen appointed by ULFA for supply to the camps. The camps were also medical centres of sorts for the locals suffering from serious ailments.[85]

Taking advantage of the intimate ties it had developed with these villages, ULFA organized a network of informers among them. Cadres with radio facilities were also stationed in some settlements, and they would report all untoward developments and keep a tab on suspicious people.[86] This was the outer layer of security, following the defence camps set up at vantage points and the continuous patrolling around the bigger camps. The fear was of the Indian army, which had been constantly making efforts to demolish the rebel establishments. The army was alerted barely two months after the first camp was established at Uttarkuchi, which led to a series of meetings at the GOC 4 Corps in Tezpur.[87] It decided to swing into action by raiding the camp at Uttarkuchi early in 1992, resulting in the capture of four cadres, including two women.[88] The relocated camp at Dimla, east of the previous camp at Uttarkuchi, was again attacked three months later.[89] The third assault was by a combined team of the police and CRPF across the border at Gerowa in Bhutan, where training was being imparted to a new batch of recruits. The raids were halted only after the camps were shifted to the interiors near Deothang, Sukuni Basti and Oraon Basti in Bhutan's Samdrup Jongkhar district towards the end of 1993.[90]

The army realized that continuous operations in Bhutan's territory without the permission of the Bhutan government could sour the friendly ties between the two neighbours. In the latter half of 1993, a meeting was convened in New Delhi among top officials of the home and defence ministries to discuss the rebels' presence in Bhutan. A decision was arrived at to initiate dialogue with Thimphu for permission to allow the army to conduct operations in its territory. The efforts bore fruit some months later when permission was granted by Bhutan to the Indian army to raid the two camps at Deothang and Nganglam.[91] Again, the operations met with limited success. At Deothang, the army succeeded in destroying only a small camp and in capturing two ULFA functionaries. The encounter at Nganglam continued for almost two hours without much damage to the rebels. Thereafter, the attacks were halted inside Bhutanese territory for a few years, enabling ULFA to conduct its activities with greater ease.[92] New Delhi continued to keep a tab on the outfit's expanding activities in Bhutan and reminded Thimphu occasionally about the dangers of allowing the rebels a free hand in its territory.[93] In particular, the Indian government was concerned about ULFA's growing network among a section of officials in the Bhutanese government and its plans to set up more camps at different locations.[94]

The reports received by the Indian intelligence agencies were accurate. Before the arrival of the weapons at the camps, Deuri had indeed been making the rounds of several government offices in Samdrup Jongkhar and Trashigang. He met senior government officials in both the districts for creating goodwill among them and to deliver the message that ULFA meant no harm to anybody in the kingdom. Among the officials who developed close ties with Deuri was an army officer, captain Ugyen Sonam, who later provided information against the outfit, about its operational plans. The congenial ambience in Bhutan prompted ULFA to invest funds in the coal mines at Samdrup Jongkhar, which ensured it a steady profit for a few years. Houses were taken on rent in Thimphu and Phuentsholing for the UFLA senior functionaries to stay in whenever they landed from Bangladesh or Assam.[95]

With everything so hunky-dory in Bhutan, Paresh finally gave the nod for the general council to be convened at Deothang. Senior functionaries stationed at different locations were instructed to reach the destination a month ahead of the event scheduled for December.[96] Secured routes would have to be charted as the counter-insurgency operation was on in full swing in Assam. The general council was unexpectedly long, commencing towards the end of November and extending well into January. Again, there was brainstorming on many issues, including the relevance of Marxism, the counter-insurgency operations in Assam and the offensive by a section of SULFA activists. After a week, the focus of the meeting shifted to restructuring of the organization and making it more effective militarily. Baruah assumed a vocal role, very different from his role at the session at Narayanganj, when he had chosen to be a silent spectator. His proposals for a new organizational structure, which were discussed earlier at Narayanganj, were approved for immediate implementation. They entailed a complete overhaul of the political and military wings.[97]

So, the earlier district committees comprising representatives from both the civil and military wings were abandoned with the bifurcation of the departments. The central headquarters would now execute organizational and political work under the east, west and central zones, with political commissars and functionaries under new designations. But, similar to the earlier district formations was the pyramidical structure, again with regional councils under a zonal council in each of the zones, and above them the central executive council. Finance, publicity and culture were to be separate departments with representation in the councils. The sessions at Deothang also decided to make military training mandatory for all ULFA functionaries, to set up a treasury at the central headquarters and to conduct annual audit of the funds gathered and expenses incurred by the different departments. The establishments in Assam, Myanmar and Bangladesh were named Kopili, Rongili and Rupahi.[98] It was specifically laid down that nobody below the age of fifteen was to be recruited; this was lower than the age limit prescribed by some other rebel outfits in the region.[99]

The armed wing, which was designated as the United Liberation Force of Asom, or Sanjukta Mukti Fauj, was to consist of two battalions—7 and 28—to be launched on 16 March 1996 and placed under the command of the general headquarters in Bhutan. There were plans to launch the 27, 109 and 709 battalions in the future, depending on the situation and availability of resources.[100] There was a rationale behind the numbers allotted to each battalion, signifying certain episodes in ULFA's history. Thus, Battalion 7, which was put in charge of the camps' security in Bhutan, was derived from 7 April, which ULFA considers as its foundation day, while 109 and 709 were drawn from 1979, regarded as the year in which the outfit was launched; 28 denoted ULFA's protest day of 28 November, which overlapped with the launch of Operation Bajrang five years ago; 27 July was the outfit's martyrs' day, coinciding with the incident in 1991 when five civilians were shot at Dipila by the Border Security Force after a bridge was blown up by ULFA.[101]

Associated with the changes in the armed wing were resolutions on the framing of new bylaws and redesignation of the ranks of the functionaries. The highest rank was 'colonel', for Paresh, who was the chief of staff heading the general headquarters. The lowest was a 'private', and three privates were entrusted to a lance corporal. Above lance corporal, in units of three, were the posts of sergeant, sergeant major, second lieutenant, lieutenant, captain, major and lieutenant colonel. There were to be four staff officers at the general headquarters, under divisions G1 and G2, with the latter also being in charge of all the military operations. While Bening Rabha and Robin Neog were to man the posts in G1, Raju Baruah and Lohit Deuri were appointed for G2 with clearly defined roles. Belying expectations, the post of 'deputy chief' was deliberately left vacant as Paresh was apprehensive of separate power centres within the wing. Eventually, Raju Baruah came to be known as the 'deputy commander' in charge of operations all over Assam on account of the wide responsibilities he was vested with.[102]

Paresh's rationale for the new structure stemmed primarily from two factors. He was concerned about factionalism, which was taking a heavy toll on the organization. There had been instances when cadres from one district were reluctant to cooperate with their counterparts from another. Occasionally, operations were even aborted due to enmity among district commanders. The zones and battalions implied that functionaries could be shifted to serve in regions far away from their home towns, which was perceived as an effective tool to put an end to cliques surfacing in the outfit. Paresh was of the firm opinion at the meeting that getting rid of the earlier structure would also enable optimum utilization of the large pool of functionaries that ULFA had enrolled, including the batches that had already been trained.[103]

The justification for the change was convincing to the majority of the participants at the general council, but months later Paresh also decided to constitute another group of six senior functionaries in Dhaka for executing operations independent of the battalions. He envisaged that there would be a number of tasks in the future—such as the fetching and transfer of weapons to different destinations, organizing meetings with representatives from other organizations and receipt of funds from locations along the India-Bangladesh border—that would have to be accomplished by trusted functionaries.[104]

The conclave at Deothang ended with a discussion on the impending assembly polls in Assam, to be held after five months. The debate centred on whether the strategy of non-interference followed during the 1991 elections ought to be repeated. The majority view in the council was to support the AGP in the polls so as to extract optimum mileage from the next government. It was resolved to set up pressure groups in all the districts to draw up agreements with AGP candidates, who were to be coerced to give a commitment to ULFA that the issue of self-determination would be raised in the assembly. Written assurances were extracted ahead of the elections from a few contesting candidates of the party in Nalbari, Nagaon and Dibrugarh.[105]

ULFA was extremely hopeful of a return to the heydays of the late 1980s when it was able to set up a parallel government. It was upbeat as it was equipped with greater fire power and more cadres to take on the government forces, besides having bases in all the neighbouring countries. Japanese radio sets for long-distance communication, which were to reach the camps after three months, considerably improved communication between the high command in Bangladesh and the establishments in Bhutan, Myanmar and Assam.[106] ULFA was on the cusp of another upswing that was to continue for three years until mid-1999, marking a sharp break from the downslide of the past four years when operations were at a low ebb due to scarcity of funds and weapons, and the crackdown by the government.[107]

Between 1993 and 1995, around twenty-five to thirty persons were shot dead by ULFA, which was less than the number of people gunned down by the National Democratic Front of Bodoland (NDFB). The surrenders that began in 1992 continued sporadically throughout the Congress regime, with more than 180 functionaries laying down weapons, although it is extremely doubtful if all the surrendered cadres were rebels who had enrolled with ULFA. More than thirty ULFA functionaries were killed in encounters during the same period, either with the police or army.[108] There were incidents that grabbed a great deal of attention—the abduction and release of two senior government employees after payment of ransom, an attempt on the life of state health minister Bhumidhar Barman and the assassination of Ujjal Barman, the son of former Congress minister Ramani Barman.

CHAPTER 6

BOLTS FROM THE BLUE

Ill-Fated Beginning

THE UNFOLDING EVENTS in Assam in the run-up to the assembly polls were anything but favourable to the ruling Congress. The party suffered a severe jolt in April 1996 when chief minister Hiteswar Saikia passed away two weeks ahead of the assembly polls from kidney failure. The vacuum created was not only difficult to plug, but it spawned intra-party squabbles for the top post. Added to this was the threat from ULFA, especially in eastern Assam and Nalbari, compelling many Congress candidates to restrict their campaigning to safer zones.[1] The party candidate from Margherita, Binu Chetia, who had a lead role in the formation of the Jatiyo Rakshi Bahini in the late 1970s, was shot dead by ULFA before the elections. This was followed by the assassination of cabinet minister Nagen Neog and his security personnel at Golaghat. The end result was absence of a poll strategy in the Congress to counter the anti-incumbency wave that had gripped the state.

The AGP, on the other hand, did not leave any stone unturned to trounce the Congress. The two factions led by Bhrigu Kumar Phukan and Chandra Mohan Patowary decided to bury the hatchet and merge with the parent organization. The AGP entered into a pre-poll alliance with the CPI and CPI(M) and assured the Bengal-origin Muslims that it had no intention of harassing them on the pretext of identifying illegal migrants. The issue of illegal immigrants that had rocked Assam during the historic six-year agitation of 1979–85, and on which the party had swept to power a decade ago, was conveniently buried.

Unsurprisingly, the coalition bagged a comfortable sixty-eight seats to form the government out of which fifty-nine were won by the AGP. The Congress was reduced to only twenty-eight from sixty-six. On 15 May 1996, the new government was sworn in, only to be rattled by incidents, one after another, for the next three days in an uncanny replay of what had marked the beginning of the Congress regime five years ago. On 16 May, the day after the swearing-in, the superintendent of police of Tinsukia, Ravi Kant Singh, was shot dead by ULFA along with his bodyguards in a meticulously planned operation by half a dozen functionaries. Around a dozen police personnel were also killed. The outfit decided to target Singh following receipt of information that he had orchestrated a series of operations at different places in Dibrugarh and the adjoining region some months earlier, resulting in atrocities against innocent residents.[2]

On 17 May came another assassination, which made for one of the most sensational episodes of the troubled times in Assam. Executive editor of *Asomiya Pratidin* Parag Kumar Das was shot dead by unidentified assailants in Guwahati when he was heading home after picking his son up from school. The son too sustained bullet injuries in his hand. Protests erupted in different parts of the state and the calls for a shutdown by MASS and ULFA received wide support.[3] A month later, the police identified surrendered ULFA functionary Prafulla Bora as the prime accused in the killing. Bora, who had joined the ranks of SULFA in 1992, sensed danger and had already gone underground after he was summoned for interrogation by the police.[4] The government was rattled again when, on the next day, at least thirty-five people were killed and around thirty villages set ablaze after clashes erupted between a section of the Bodos and Adivasis in Kokrajhar.

Among all these incidents, it was Das's assassination that attracted the maximum publicity and which was to have far-reaching implications for the AGP regime. Soon after the episode, three theories were being speculated on by different sections of people, with each trying to link Bora with the murder. The first, articulated by some former ULFA functionaries, suggested that Das fell a victim to politics within the outfit. They were of the opinion that he had grown extremely close to the ULFA leadership over the past year and was all set to join the outfit as vice chairman. This would have upset the power equations in ULFA, and the role of some leaders would have diminished. In particular, Paresh was suspected of having orchestrated the murder through SULFA functionaries.[5]

A month before he was shot dead, Das had graced ULFA's raising day celebrations at its general headquarters in Bhutan on 7 April, which was also attended by Paresh and other top leaders. Present at the event were senior activists of People's War Group, including Ganapaty, who was later appointed the chairman of CPI(Maoist).[6] Das delivered a long speech evaluating ULFA's role and drawbacks and the dire need for regular introspection.[7] It was decided at the camp that Das, along with Anup, would attend a conference on human rights to be organized by Forum Asia in Bangkok. In Bangkok, Das also took a detailed interview of Rajkhowa, which was published in *Asomiya Pratidin* after he returned to Guwahati. The dateline of the piece mentioned the location of the interview as 'somewhere along the India-Myanmar border'.[8]

In Guwahati, Das had broached the topic of joining ULFA with some close associates, including Ajit Bhuyan, but he was unable to arrive at a final decision.[9] So, it cannot be said with certainty that he would have joined the outfit if he were not assassinated. It is also extremely unlikely that the SULFA functionaries would have carried out the murder on the instructions of Paresh, since they were already on the warpath with ULFA. As a matter of fact, Paresh had called Bora to ask him why he had pulled the trigger on Das, to which the latter had replied that he had no role in the incident.[10]

According to the second theory, which gained acceptability among civil society groups and journalists in Guwahati, it was a state-sponsored act to eliminate an ULFA ideologue who had been swaying a large section of the people in support of the outfit. Das had already served jail sentences twice after being arrested under the National Security Act and Terrorist and Disruptive Activities Act. One of his books, *Swadhinatar Prastav,* had been banned for justifying sovereign status for Assam and ULFA's campaign. The theory went that the conspiracy to exterminate Das had been hatched months ago, but it was Singh's assassination in Tinsukia that had prompted an intelligence agency to get rid of Das at the earliest. The SULFA squad that was hired executed the task the next day by getting Bora to identify Das ahead of the operation. This theory identifies R&AW as the agency that masterminded the operation, in collusion with a police officer who was related to the slain superintendent of police, Ravi Kant Singh.[11]

The gunning down of a high-profile editor like Das could not have been planned in twenty-four hours unless the assassins had been preparing for the operation for several days before 16 May, when Singh was shot dead by ULFA. This would mean that the killers had detailed information about ULFA's plan to target Singh, which was most unlikely. Then, firming up the plan to assassinate Das would have taken at least a few days since the killers would have had to choose a convenient spot for the killing and ensure their exit route after the act. Finally, the AGP's win in the assembly polls would have certainly compelled the killers to exercise extra caution since the party was known to be sympathetic to ULFA. That ULFA had supported the AGP during the elections was also an open secret.

The third theory says that Das fell victim to a plot by a group of SULFA functionaries who had been annoyed with his writings for quite some time. The group decided to take the extreme step of killing him since he did not 'mend his ways' despite being warned several times. The plan had been on for a long time but had been expedited after ULFA shot Congress candidate Binu Chetia dead in Margherita in the last week of April. Chetia had assisted ULFA in the early eighties and had later developed a cozy relationship with the SULFA group. The SULFA group was convinced that ULFA was provoked by Das to order Chetia's killing, which was allegedly reflected in some editorials he had written in the Assamese daily. So it formed a squad that got in touch with its accomplices in Guwahati to identify Das and to select a suitable spot for the operation.[12] The possibility of the group being provoked by a senior police officer to execute the act at the earliest too cannot be ruled out.[13]

The government ordered a CBI probe following the police's inability to make headway in the case. Four years later, the investigating agency submitted charge sheets in the Kamrup District and Sessions Court against four SULFA activists, who were identified as Das's killers. Three out of the four accused were dead by the time the charge sheet was submitted.[14] One of them, Nayan Das, was lynched in Dibrugarh by a mob for what was considered continuously appalling conduct that had become intolerable. Two others, Tapan Dutta and Diganta Barua, were shot dead by ULFA in Guwahati in separate encounters. And in 2009, a district court in Guwahati acquitted the lone surviving accused, Samar Kakati, for lack of sufficient evidence.[15] Prafulla Bora, who was identified by the police as the prime accused soon after the incident, was not named in the charge sheet for lack of evidence.

While delivering the judgment, the Kamrup District and Sessions judge, Dilip Kumar Mahanta, reprimanded the CBI for its faulty probe, which had weakened the prosecution's case and allowed the accused to walk away scot-free. A SULFA activist who reportedly played a key role in the conspiracy and who was to join a political party years later was never interrogated.[16] Several witnesses who were interrogated by the agency later declined to appear before the court, fearing for their lives. Two other suspects in the murder case—Promode Gogoi and Prabin Sarma—who had been arrested by the police, could not be charge sheeted by the CBI for lack of evidence.[17] A day after the judgment, Samar Kakati, whose name was doing the rounds as one of the accused, told a TV news channel that the CBI had never interrogated him seriously although they had asked him some questions on a few occasions.[18]

Incidentally, the CBI submitted the charge sheet after a PIL in Gauhati High Court by a group of eminent intellectuals, led by professor Hiren Gohain, who made a fervent plea for early completion of the investigation. The widespread assumption among some sections of people was that the investigating agency was in no mood to bring the probe to a logical conclusion. The uproar that followed after the charge sheet was submitted prompted the family members of the slain editor to file a review petition seeking annulment of the judgment passed by District and Sessions judge of Kamrup and remand of the case for retrial. In 2012, the petition was dismissed by the court on the plea that there was no sufficient ground for a retrial.[19]

The episode left a deep scar on CBI's image as a competent and impartial investigating agency. The loopholes in the probe were interpreted by some people as further testimony to the government's role in Das's murder and its complicity in shielding the accused. Certainly, there were reasons for this view to gain currency, given the number of questions that remain unanswered. It is worthwhile to recall a few intriguing aspects of the probe listed in the revision petition filed by Pallab Kumar Das before the Gauhati High Court. It was widely expected that the CBI would challenge the session judge's order within ninety days, but the agency abstained from filing any petition in the high court to prosecute the accused. It is not known why the agency never bothered to trace the blue

Maruti car without a number plate, allegedly used by the assassins and left abandoned at the place of crime. Incidentally, the police had also refused to seize the car, which was later believed to have been sold in Siliguri. The petition further alleged that the agency had disregarded the materials gathered by the police during its investigation in the case and also did not bother to examine the possession of unauthorized firearms by one of the accused.[20]

So, was it simply another bungling of a case by the CBI or was it a cover-up involving a deeper conspiracy? Certainly, not all the lapses in the agency's probe could have been coincidental. The agency had taken more than three years to wind up the investigation and to submit the charge sheet in court. If it was deliberate, then was the government also involved in Das's murder, as alleged by a large section of the people, including a few senior ULFA functionaries?

The Nepal Connection

Before he was shot on 17 May, Das had been advised by some close associates to exercise caution in his movements. His colleague and editor of *Asomiya Pratidin,* Ajit Bhuyan, who had been equally active as a human rights crusader and had been arrested several times, had sensed the danger to Das's life, especially after receipt of information that the army had been awfully upset over an editorial published in the daily the previous month. Das, however, did not believe that a plot to murder him would be hatched for his overtly critical opinion about the role played by SULFA and the security forces in committing human rights abuses.[21] He was wrong. That something was cooking against Das was known to some people in Guwahati, including a section of government officials. A middle-rung police officer who was close to Das had advised him to approach the government for a personal security officer.[22]

The conspiracy to murder Das was hatched by a group of SULFA activists hailing from the districts of eastern Assam. The CBI charge sheet claimed that one of the accused had vowed to avenge the death of Binu Chetia in the presence of some witnesses at the residence of the deceased in Margherita.[23] Therefore, contrary to the popular notion among a section of people in Assam, the possibility of government agencies being involved in the plan to assassinate Das appears extremely remote. The group of assassins was apprehensive that further harm could be caused by Das if he was not exterminated.[24]

After the plan was firmed up, a three-member squad from Dibrugarh reached Guwahati in a Maruti Esteem vehicle about a week before the assassination. After arriving in the city, they sought the assistance of a group of select close associates for the operation. A recce of the spot in the Rajgarh area of the city was carried out, the exit route chosen and a blue Maruti 800 car arranged by the killers for the operation. The car's number plates were changed in the evening ahead of the murder. It was decided that two persons would be seated in another vehicle stationed some distance from the spot where Das would be gunned down.[25]

In the afternoon on the next day, two persons emerged from the rear of the Maruti vehicle upon spotting Das and shot him at point-blank range. The squad sped away in the same vehicle, which was later found abandoned at a spot about a kilometre from the scene of action. Fourteen empty bullets of different calibers were recovered from the place of crime, indicating that the assailants had used different firearms in the murder.[26] It is highly possible that the killers departed from the city within a few hours of the murder.[27]

The police registered an FIR on Das's murder, but the investigating officer, Rameswar Lalung, who was also the officer in charge of Chandmari police station in Guwahati, was unable to take the probe to its logical conclusion. Apparently, Lalung had been able to identify a few members of the assassination squad after he interrogated some SULFA activists picked up from different places in the city. He came under severe pressure from some of his seniors to submit a fabricated report without identifying the individual(s) who had pulled the trigger. On one occasion, he was threatened by an unidentified caller over the phone that his family would be wiped out if the report mentioned the names of the assailants. Soon he sought a transfer and the police headquarters was glad to shift him to the vigilance and anti-corruption department. It was becoming increasingly clear to the top brass of the police that the government did not want any progress in the investigation.[28]

Lalung was intimidated by two senior police officers who were instructed in categorical terms by a powerful minister in the AGP-led government who was not unhappy with the demise of Das, to shield the accused. The minister received support from some of his colleagues in the party, who were of the opinion that the AGP could not afford to toe a soft line towards ULFA as it had during the late 1980s. The police heaved a sigh of relief when the case was taken over for investigation by the CBI. Weeks later, a sub-inspector who was soon to get involved in the state-sponsored 'secret killings' in the late 1990s, facilitated transfer of the blue Maruti car used for the crime away from Guwahati, never to be found again. To eliminate all evidence, another businessman, Mitra Dev Mahanta, known for his links with ULFA and who knew all about the plot, was shot dead near his residence in Guwahati by the same conspirators who had hatched the plot to kill Das, after being instructed to do so by a powerful AGP minister.[29]

With the dust settling on the killing, all the assassins and their accomplices were certain that they would never be prosecuted. The SULFA activists who had fled to Nepal fearing arrest also returned to Assam. Surprisingly, one of them who was involved in Das's assassination vanished after three months from Guwahati, never to be seen again. Nor did the matter attract media attention, although an FIR was supposed to have been lodged at a police station by the deceased's wife. The episode was buried, but some SULFA activists were certain that it was linked to the sensational killing of former minister and member of Parliament in Nepal, Mirza Dilshad Beg, on 29 June 1998 in Kathmandu.[30]

Beg was gangster Dawood Ibrahim's point man in Nepal. Hailing from Uttar Pradesh, he began his career as a petty criminal but later relocated to Nepal, where he became a member of the Nepal Sadbhavna Party. However, he was soon expelled for anti-party activities. He became a minister twice in the Nepal government after joining the Rashtriya Prajatantrik Party. A member of Parliament from Krishna Nagar on the India–Nepal border, he began to facilitate safe passage of criminals from India, especially from the Dawood gang, and operatives of Pakistan's ISI into India. Beg had also assisted some of the accused in the Bombay serial blasts in fleeing from India via Kathmandu to Dubai.[31]

Beg's empire of crime covered a wide gamut of illicit activities in Nepal. Most of the auto-lifting in northern India was done by the syndicate he headed, which had begun to spread its tentacles to the Northeast as well. Incidentally, the SULFA activist involved with the gang that had shot Das had been associated with a few of Beg's crime syndicates in Nepal to earn a livelihood. This apart, reports compiled by the Uttar Pradesh police and Indian intelligence agencies claimed that Beg was involved in almost every sphere of ISI-sponsored activity in Nepal.[32]

By June 1998, the Indian government had decided to request Nepal for Beg's extradition. The CBI was tasked to prepare a dossier detailing his criminal activities in India.[33] But Beg was extremely influential in Nepal and it was uncertain whether he could be brought to India to face trial. Knowing the circumstances, a top official of a central intelligence agency had already begun to explore the possibility of assassinating Beg, using his underworld contacts.[34] The person chosen for the job was Dawood's arch rival and former Mumbai underworld don Chhota Rajan, who was based in Malaysia. Rajan planned to execute the task through his associates engaged with crime syndicates in Nepal who were adversaries of Beg. He was certain that Beg's assassination would trigger an uproar in Nepal, leading to a high-level probe to track the killers. He felt that the operation must be executed by non-Nepalese citizens who would exit the country immediately after the operation.[35]

After a couple of months, with Rajan unable to finalize a plan, the intelligence official decided to explore another option to assassinate Beg. He got in touch with a senior government official in Assam who was known to be pally with the SULFA activists. The official was briefed about the plan on Beg and told to examine the possibility of engaging the activists in the operation. They agreed to execute the task but with the precondition that they must be allowed to return to Guwahati with an assurance that they would not be charge-sheeted by the CBI for Das's murder.[36]

The preconditions were not easy to fulfil, as they would call for manipulation at a high level in a case that was extremely sensitive. Usually, it is a norm with security agencies to protect their assets, barring in exceptional circumstances when they are disowned. It was another two months before it was finally decided by the officials that the preconditions would be fulfilled as it was more important to get rid of Beg.[37] On their part, the SULFA activists agreed to keep the whole episode under wraps as leakage of the details would only embarrass the Indian government.[38]

As per the plan, Rajan would claim responsibility for the killing, which he did after Beg was shot dead in Kathmandu on 29 June 1998.[39] With the SULFA activists were more members in the squad who had agreed to take part in the operation.[40] Years later, the names of Farid Tanasha, Bharat Nepali and Sanjay Ghate, all of whom were members of Rajan's gang, cropped up as conspirators in the killing, but nowhere was the SULFA activists' name ever disclosed.[41] They returned to Guwahati after almost a month of the incident in Nepal.[42]

But the situation took a different turn when the activist who assassinated Beg threw a hint before a small gathering of other SULFA members about his involvement after getting drunk.[43] He had already taken to drinking heavily and there was a high risk of the secret being revealed to more people. Subsequently, within two weeks, he was shot at an apartment in the city and buried in its outskirts.[44]

This episode happened at a time when the gang involved in Das's murder began to be actively involved in 'secret killings' in Assam. The government, both at the state and Centre, deemed it necessary to offer incentives and protection to all the groups of secret killers made use of by the security forces. It was widely believed by some sections that the CBI was instructed at the highest level to wind up the probe on Das's murder at the earliest and name all the three people who were already dead as the killers. It was also presumed that the agency was told to let Kakati off the hook, which could explain why it never appealed against the judgment of the Kamrup District and Sessions Court.[45]

In retrospect, the government's involvement in Das's killing was discernible when efforts were successfully made to scuttle the investigation and eliminate all evidence that could have indicted the killers. Many factors coalesced at different levels to ensure that the conspiracy and the actual sequence of events leading to the assassination remained hidden. There were other incidents linked to the murder, which still remain a matter of speculation. A senior police officer who threatened investigating officer Rameswar Lalung went missing under mysterious circumstances till he surfaced in Assam two years later. There were widespread rumours that he was being shielded by powerful politicians who also pulled strings in the capital to ensure his return to Assam at a convenient time. This trigger-happy officer was apparently ducking for cover from a powerful and outspoken legislator who had warned him in the presence of many people! Apparently, the officer had killed a close associate of the legislator two years ago in a fake encounter. The legislator believed that the officer had devised a plan to kill him too, which did not work out.[46] Years later, there would be more allegations against the officer that he had framed innocent people as poachers and killed them in and around Kaziranga National Park.

A Narrow Escape

The tremors from Parag Das's assassination were accentuated by other incidents in Assam that happened at frequent intervals almost until the end of 1997. Among the immediate high-profile killings by ULFA were the murder of two officers of the rank of deputy commandant working with the Central Reserve Police Force and Assam Police, followed by the assassination of an inspector general in the heart of Guwahati. Attacks against the army were stepped up, with as many as thirteen personnel being killed on a single day in separate ambushes. More dreadful for the government was the armed campaign by the Bodoland Liberation Tigers (BLT) which had no compunction in unleashing terror against civilians. On 30 December, six bogies of the Delhi-bound Brahmaputra Mail were blown up near Kokrajhar, killing thirty-five people and injuring more than 100. Clearly, the late 1990s was one of the bloodiest epochs in Assam in the post-Independence period.

Furthermore, the Special Branch of the Assam Police had been receiving information about efforts being made by a section of radicals in the twin hill districts of Dima Hasao (North Cachar Hills) and Karbi Anglong and among the tea tribes and Bengal-origin Muslims to form insurgent outfits. During 1996–97, an outfit called Dima Halam Daogah (DHD) emerged in Dima Hasao; its goal was to carve out a separate state for the Dimasa tribe. The increasing attacks by the NDFB on the tea tribes prompted local leader Bir Singh Munda to float the Birsa Commando Force, while the NSCN(IM) was also exploring various options to organize some Karbi youths into a rebel outfit.[47]

In Bangladesh, the ISI was encouraged to strengthen its presence owing to the congenial ambience that prevailed during the BNP-led regime, which was distinctly pro-Pakistan. Although the BNP was defeated by the Awami League in the 1996 general elections, the ISI was able to continue with its efforts to assist more rebel groups in India's Northeast. Besides the ethnic outfits, the agency had firmed up a plan to support Muslim Fundamentalist Organizations (MFO) whose immediate goal would not be to confront the Indian security forces but to work covertly for furthering the goal of 'Brihot Bangladesh' (Greater Bangladesh). The MFOs could be utilized to facilitate demographic invasion and communalize the situation by engineering riots.[48] These efforts were further evidenced by the arrest of four ISI operatives in Guwahati in 1999 and MFO activists in the late 1990s from different parts of Assam in the subsequent years.[49]

Predictably, the consequence was a series of meetings in the capital's North Block among the home ministry, army headquarters and the state government, with the goal of putting together a mechanism for effective counter-insurgency operations. The result was a unified command structure, constituted on 20 January 1997, which was more elaborate than the previous versions formed in the wake of Operation Bajrang and Operation Rhino. A strategy group headed by the chief secretary of Assam was established; its other members were the General Officer Commanding (GOC) of the Tezpur-based 4 Corps, the inspector general of police in charge of operations, and representatives from the paramilitary organizations, intelligence agencies and the state home department. For operational purposes, a unified headquarters headed by the GOC-4 Corps was set up for better coordination among the police and army for operations and deployment. The third component was the coordination committee at the district level, which was a miniature replica of the unified headquarters.[50]

Although it was laid down that all operations must be conducted in the presence of police officers, this agreement was rarely followed by the army. While the AGP government and most police officers were willing to turn a blind eye to the high-handedness of the army, some were unwilling to watch this in silence for very long. Police chief P.V. Sumant was vocal against the army's excesses committed during the counter-insurgency operations.[51] Soon, complaints began to pour in from the army headquarters against Sumant, who was transferred from his post. Apparently, the home ministry was also of the opinion that efforts to weaken the rebel groups must not suffer because of squabbles between the army and the police.[52]

The differences between the army and police in tackling militancy in Assam were deep-rooted, stemming from a combination of many factors. The police in the mid-1990s was still struggling to come to grips with the challenges of combating insurgency in

Assam. A special squad called Black Panthers had been formed, but it still suffered from a weak and corrupt leadership, which was most apparent from the shocking flight of police chief Ranju Das, along with chief secretary Arunodoy Bhattacharjee and two senior officers from the state. They quit on medical grounds soon after the results of the assembly polls were declared, never to return to Assam for fear of retribution from the AGP and ULFA. Das was suspended for dereliction of duty four months later.[53]

These episodes only served to reinforce the army's assumption that the police could not be relied upon as an ally in the battle against militancy. The army's opinion in the early 1990s that the police had been infiltrated by ULFA remained unchanged. As such, the army conducted many operations without informing the police, in spite of the guidelines laid down when the Unified Command Structure was constituted.[54] And there was another fundamental reason behind the dissimilarities in their approach to the problem. Unlike the police, the army officers and their units were deployed for a brief tenure of three or four years at every location. There is intense pressure to produce results, but it was not always an easy task to create an efficient network for gathering intelligence in a brief span of time. No wonder many operations executed by the army were based on inaccurate information, resulting in human rights abuses.

Nonetheless, the revamp of the strategy to combat militancy was in sync with the new role assumed by chief minister Mahanta in national politics. The AGP, which had won five Lok Sabha seats out of the fourteen seats from Assam in the general elections of 1996, became a coalition partner in the United Front government at the Centre. It bagged two berths in the council of ministers, besides a position for Mahanta in the steering committee of the coalition government. In the changed scenario, it was imperative for him to shed his previous image of being pro-ULFA. The outfit would have to be reined in, vanquished if possible, but it was a task that the police could not be expected to fulfil. Besides ULFA, there were other rebel groups on the rampage in different regions of the state. There was no alternative but to allow the army the upper hand in the counter-insurgency operations.[55]

All these developments were an unambiguous message to ULFA that the AGP had no intention of honouring its pre-poll commitment of repealing the Armed Forces (Special Powers) Act, lifting the ban on the outfit or raising the issue of self-determination in the assembly. The ULFA leadership was convinced that the party's hostility towards the outfit pivoted on none other than the chief minister, who was also suspected of playing a dubious role during the late 1980s when he had snatched the political wing of the home department from home minister Bhrigu Kumar Phukan.[56] Efforts by a section of the AGP legislators led by Atul Bora to pressure the Centre for withdrawal of the army from Assam came to naught even as the All Assam Students' Union (AASU) warned of a state-wide agitation and reminded the party of its pre-poll promises.

The ULFA leadership resolved to take the extreme step of adopting the same policy towards the AGP as it had with the Congress. And first on the list would be the chief minister, to send a message to the entire party to mend its ways. It resolved to assassinate Mahanta at the earliest so that his coterie would be sidelined in the government and the ministers who were still sympathetic to ULFA would come to the centre stage. The staff officers at the ULFA general headquarters in Bhutan were instructed to fine-tune the plan, which had to begin with a report on the strategy to be adopted. A senior functionary who was deputed to Guwahati submitted a report within a month, making a case for a blast using TNT and gelatin. But the challenge was to find a convenient spot to minimize the collateral damage.[57]

In the first week of May 1997, a four-member squad consisting of Alok Goswami, Munna Mishra, Ton and Sanglot descended from Bhutan with explosives and made its way to a hideout on the outskirts of Guwahati. The team decided to trigger the blast on the day Mahanta would return from the capital to Guwahati.

They selected a spot on the road adjacent to the Nilachal Hills near Lalit Chandra Bharali College, which linked the airport to the city. There was a culvert on the road, which was found ideal for planting the bomb. It had thick shrubs on the side towards the college. The wire for triggering the blast could be taken to a safe place near the college, which too would not raise suspicion as it was covered with shrubs. The team plunged into action upon receiving the information that Mahanta would arrive at Guwahati on 8 June from New Delhi.[58]

The operation began in the wee hours a day ahead, when a bomb was strapped below the culvert and a suitable place identified about 100 metres away, where Sanglot would sit with his finger on the button the next day. It was to be pushed when Munna gave him the green signal. Goswami waited at the airport with his radio pager to inform the duo at the culvert about the chief minister's arrival. This was done and the button was pressed, but a tad too late as the convoy had already crossed the culvert. Apparently, the reason for the failure was Munna's delay in issuing the order to Sanglot. Still, the blast ripped the culvert and created craters on the road.[59]

Mahanta equipped himself with more security to thwart further attempts on his life. He was also more determined than ever to wage war against ULFA. The Unified Command furnished details to the government about new plans for a counter-insurgency grid across the state with a focus on the state's borders with Bhutan, Nagaland and Arunachal Pradesh.[60] This was envisaged to generate pressure on the outfits' functionaries to lay down arms and return to the mainstream. To give more punch to the strategy, the state cabinet resolved to offer greater incentives to surrendered rebels through a new package at the earliest.[61] The achievements and failures of the previous surrender policy were evaluated. Between 1 June 1992 and 31 March 1997, as many as 4,843 militants, including 3,439 from ULFA, were rehabilitated under the scheme at an expenditure of Rs 99.3 crore. After laying down their arms, some 813 rebels were given employment in different government departments. The flip side of the policy was that it could not provide employment to all the surrendered cadres; neither were the loans repaid to them.[62]

In the new policy unveiled in mid-1998, the surrendered rebels would not be given soft bank loans to launch business ventures. This policy was applicable to cadres surrendering after 1 April 1998 with at least one weapon, but surrendering militants who did not have weapons could also be considered for rehabilitation in exceptional and deserving cases. Monetary incentives would be provided for the surrendered weapons. Those who surrendered them would be provided vocational training with a monthly stipend not exceeding Rs 2,000 per month for a period of twelve months. Return to the mainstream would not grant amnesty to the cadres for their crimes, which would be subject to the due process of law. And, finally, unlike the previous scheme in which the state government contributed to the expenditure, the Centre would bear the entire cost of the new rehabilitation programme.[63]

At the diplomatic level, New Delhi made a forceful plea before Bhutan for a proactive policy against the rebels' camps and training facilities.[64] Thimphu understood New Delhi's concerns but it categorically rejected any request for intervention by the Indian army to dismantle the camps. Thimphu was in favour of a policy of dialogue to persuade the rebels to vacate the kingdom. The Indian government was informed that Thimphu needed time to evaluate the situation, gauge public opinion and forge a consensus through parliamentary deliberations. Even if the military option were to be exercised by Bhutan, its armed forces would require time for amassing resources and additional troops.[65]

With Bangladesh, the focus of India's dialogue was entirely on clinching an agreement on the sharing of river waters and the return of the Chakma refugees from Tripura to their homes in the Chittagong Hill Tracts. The twin objectives were achieved, and there was an understanding as well not to allow insurgents to operate from each other's territories. But there was hardly any action against the rebels from the Northeast in Bangladesh owing to political instability in New Delhi and its failure to follow up on the matter with the Bangladesh government.[66] Still, many senior functionaries of rebel outfits decided to vacate Dhaka for a few months and head to different locations within the country and in Southeast Asia. One of the destinations was the Philippines, where a senior ULFA functionary interacted with leaders of a rebel outfit and officials of intelligence agencies from different countries, but without any fruitful outcome.[67]

The top brass of ULFA was extremely upset with the botched operation against Mahanta. ULFA resolved to continue to target high-profile personalities in Assam. Orders issued to check the activities of development worker and activist Sanjoy Ghose in Majuli were carried out on 4 July, when he was detained by some ULFA functionaries and whisked to a remote location on the river island.[68] Ghose's disappearance sparked a major crisis, attracting wide media coverage and demands for his release from different organizations. ULFA never expected this episode to escalate into a massive uproar, which was soon to produce irrevocable consequences.

Dream Gone Sour

Sanjoy Ghose hailed from a reputed Bengali family in Mumbai. He had decided to chart an offbeat track after graduating from Elphinstone College. He chucked away an opportunity to study at the prestigious Indian Institute of Management, preferring to join the Institute of Rural Management (IRMA) in Gujarat. Subsequently, he was associated in development activities with the Tribhuvandas Foundation at Anand and then went on to set up the Uttar Rajasthan Milk Union Limited (URMUL) in Bikaner, where he worked for close to a decade.[69] His next halt was New Delhi, where he was appointed as general secretary of the Association of Voluntary Agencies for Rural Development (AVARD), started by Jayprakash Narayan decades ago.[70]

Around the same time, Sanjoy launched a communication network called Charkha, which was also a platform for development workers to write on related issues and influence the mainstream media.[71] Charkha facilitated Sanjoy's visit to different parts of the country, including the Northeast, which began to capture his imagination as a land offering immense scope for voluntary action. Majuli, one of the biggest river islands in the world, fascinated him in particular in his quest for a more 'challenging' assignment. Sometime in April 1996, Sanjoy and his wife Sumita decided to pack up from New Delhi and head to the island. There they began work under the banner of 'AVARD-NE' after cobbling together a small team of seven dedicated persons, some of whom had already been associated with them in Rajasthan.[72]

Indeed, there was a need for effective intervention in Majuli to arrest the decaying state of affairs. Located about 320 km east of Guwahati, the island is home to twenty-two *Vaishnavite Satras,* or monasteries, and is the seat of the Assamese Vashnavite culture. But Majuli was and still is a fast-disappearing island. The geographical area of the island was 733.79 sq. km in 1914, as depicted by the Survey of India map. The twin problems of floods and erosion had brought it down to 502.21 sq. km by 2004.[73] In the 1960s, the government had constructed embankments to protect the island from floods, but they offered very little protection. They were often breached during floods, inundating vast areas of the island. Erosion continued unabated, with the river gobbling up large chunks of land, resulting in shrinkage of the island.

AVARD-NE decided to set up offices at Kamalabari on the island and in Jorhat for coordinating operations. It plunged into action by joining hands with two student organizations—AASU and AJYCP—and a local outfit named Seuj Bandhu, to bore tube wells to provide drinking water to the families that had abandoned their homes and were living on the embankments because of the floods. Medicines were distributed to them by means of a boat that sailed around the island for several days at a time.[74]

There was more scope for work once the flood waters receded. Within weeks, two rehabilitation projects were launched—a nursery with the assistance of Seuj Bandhu and loans for the poorest women in eight villages for the winter crop. An Assamese newsletter, *Dweep Alok,* aimed primarily at young people, was started. It featured columns on self-employment, news about government programmes and how to make use of them. A bit of investigative journalism unearthed a scam on Indira Awaas Yojana at Bongaon where the local panchayat president, Parul Bora, was found to have awarded a contract for building houses to her son. Photographs of the incomplete scheme were prominently displayed in the newsletter.[75]

The subsequent works of AVARD-NE in the island focused on anti-erosion, resulting in the creation of more than 30,000 man-days of labour and the beginning of an experimental scheme to protect 1.7 km of its coastline from erosion. Then, in a brief span of time, schemes were unveiled to make changes in the design and production of bamboo craft items and handloom weaving; to train sixteen health workers; and to set in motion a process to create libraries in twenty villages.[76] The organization had just begun to generate support among the people when danger came knocking on the door. ULFA was extremely upset about AVARD-NE's activities and wanted the group to pack up and leave Majuli![77]

The clash with ULFA had been building up since the time AVARD-NE set foot in Majuli. At the first meeting, which was held within a month of its arrival on the island, ULFA suggested that AVARD set up its office at Bongaon. This suggestion was declined as Kamalabari was well connected with the mainland. No sooner had the NGO begun providing relief to the flood victims than came the arrival of the army in search of militants, fuelling speculation about the NGO's links with the intelligence agencies. ULFA's suspicions were amplified when the police nabbed one of its senior functionaries, Mahendra Khound, from the island.[78]

By the end of 1996, a section of the ULFA leadership was convinced that AVARD-NE was working as a cover for R&AW. It had to be driven out soon before further damage was done.

The rebels firmed up a three-pronged strategy to achieve this goal. A protest rally was organized on the island, where people carried placards saying 'Sanjoy Ghose Go Back'. A memorandum was submitted to the sub-divisional officer by a few residents, highlighting the receipt of funds from the Tata group by the NGO, allegedly at ULFA's behest, and requesting him to deport Sanjoy from the island. The NGO's links with the Tatas was considered suspicious since the group always focused on tea gardens in the state and was never interested in having a presence in the island. Posters came up at many localities in the island on many occasions, hurling abuses against AVARD-NE and accusing its functionaries of being spies.[79]

Incidentally, ULFA's campaign found support among a section of the people in Majuli whose feathers had been ruffled by AVARD-NE. Many of their misdeeds on the island that included the faulty execution of projects by contractors were exposed in the newsletter *Dweep Alok*. Clearly, for AVARD-NE, the writing was on the wall. The situation worsened from April when people associated with AVARD-NE were quizzed by ULFA. They were coerced to give false statements against the NGO. In the same month, a local worker named Bhagirath Das, a key functionary of the NGO and a vehement critic of ULFA, was shifted to Jorhat after the rebels threatened to kill him if he did not resign from the organization. Then came the turn of other workers, like Mailika and Jamini, who were at the forefront of the organization and instructed to dissociate from AVARD-NE. All of them were told that they were pawns in the game and that they were being exploited to further certain objectives of Indian organizations.[80]

The turning point came at a public meeting convened by AVARD-NE on the issue of the continuous threats it was receiving from ULFA, in which a resolution was adopted supporting the work done by the NGO on the island. This was almost like throwing ULFA a challenge, and the latter could not take it lying down. The meeting was also interpreted by ULFA to mean a serious effort to trigger a movement for the rebels' expulsion from the island.

Senior members of ULFA's east zone resolved to interrogate Sanjoy and serve him and his group a deadline to exit from Majuli at the earliest.[81] On 4 July 1997, Sanjoy and his associate Chandan Doley were detained by the rebels at Mekheli village, which the two had visited to meet local residents and discuss the possibility of starting a goat farm.[82]

Finding Sanjoy and Chandan missing at Kamalabari, Sumita and a few associates came to Mekheli the next day. They were informed that Sanjoy and Chandan were spotted in the village in the afternoon, cycling away with two ULFA functionaries, Shiraz and Phatik. There was no information about the destination they might have headed to from Mekheli. A company of police and the paramilitary landed at Mekheli, only to draw a blank.[83] Some details of the episode tumbled out only after Chandan landed at Kamalabari the next day.[84]

Chandan revealed that he and Sanjoy were stopped by two ULFA functionaries, Shiraz and Phatik, when they had just started cycling back towards Kamalabari. They were requested to travel with the functionaries to a nearby village for a discussion. There they were threatened for the 'undesirable' activities of the NGO on the island. They were shifted to another village, where there were joined by six other functionaries who were armed, and then to still another village, all in a short span of time. There, dinner was served and Chandan was taken to a different destination by two men. On 5 July, Chandan and these two functionaries cycled from one village to another, seemingly without any objective, and he spotted the four men who had at some point detained Sanjoy. But Sanjoy was not with them. The squad told Chandan that he was being interrogated by 'Sir'. At night, Chandan was able to escape from where he was held. He jumped into the Brahmaputra and swam till he reached a safe spot on the island, on the southern bank facing Jorhat.[85]

Chandan's version was hardly convincing to anybody. First, the distance he said he swam was a whopping 18 km. Swimming in the swollen river and in its fast-moving currents would be no mean feat. Also, if he was escaping from his abductors, why did he not choose the easier option of swimming down the river along the same bank instead of going across? Chandan's story of escape will remain a riddle. The mystery over Sanjoy's whereabouts was laid to rest when, on 9 July, Paresh called up some dailies in Guwahati to inform them that Sanjoy had been arrested for being an agent of R&AW. The charge against him was that he was passing information to the army and inciting the people against ULFA. And he would soon be tried in a people's court and then punished accordingly.[86]

Over the next two weeks, the AVARD-NE team sat on a dharna at Bongaon demanding Sanjoy's release and information about his whereabouts. A peace committee of prominent citizens was formed to make contact with the abductors and negotiate for his release, but without any success. Nobody had any clue where Sanjoy had been taken. There were the occasional rumours that he had been spotted at different locations on the island. A police operation at Gereki in Majuli, after receipt of information that Sanjoy was being detained there, also yielded nothing. A ray of hope came on 19 July with a press release by an elderly well-known resident, Dulal Barua, stating that he had been contacted by some ULFA leaders to convey the news that Sanjoy would be released as soon as the 'misunderstanding' had been resolved.[87]

Three days later, hope gave way to despair when the local dailies began to receive conflicting press releases from ULFA. On 22 July came a faxed message from ULFA stating that Sanjoy, along with two other abductors, had drowned when their canoe overturned on the Brahmaputra. After a few hours, the newspapers in Guwahati received a second message from ULFA, contradicting the first, saying that Sanjoy was alive and safe in their custody. The statement in Assamese went on to say that the first message was false, meant to discredit the ULFA and sent by people who had no respect for life.[88]

To add to the confusion, the police came up with its own explanation that Sanjoy had been killed on the day he was abducted. The basis of this theory was a confession extracted from an ULFA functionary, 'Tulen Baruah', in police custody, who named Siraj Bora and Phatik Hatimota as the functionaries who had abducted Sanjoy.[89] Interestingly, there was no ULFA functionary by that name either in Majuli or anywhere else in the vicinity of the island.[90] This version continued to be peddled, and also came to be accepted by a large section of people as they were ignorant of the actual sequence of events leading to Sanjoy's disappearance. The truth was that that the police and the intelligence were at the receiving end for not being able to derive accurate information on the episode.[91] So, it became imperative for them to disseminate their own version of the abduction to ward off criticism. No intelligence agency could boast of any network on the island until this incident—and the situation was similar in many regions in the state where ULFA rebels operated with ease.[92]

Transmission of messages from Majuli was a slow process for ULFA. There was no cell phone, radio or wireless transmitters with the ULFA functionaries. A proposal had been approved by ULFA's east zone for a radio set in the island, but it had not yet been implemented. The nearest transmitter was at Lakhimpur, further upstream, on the north bank of the Brahmaputra. The river had to be crossed by ferry for delivery of messages, or the messages had to be relayed from the public call offices on the island, which were shut after Sanjoy's abduction. No wonder the ULFA high command itself was in the dark for a long time about the actual incidents happening in Majuli.[93]

In the midst of all this came another press statement, this time from Paresh of the ULFA high command, saying that Sanjoy would be released if three conditions were fulfilled—AVARD-NE would have to wind up its activities in Assam; it should make a public apology to the people of Assam for injuring their sentiments, and all operations by the security forces would have to be suspended. Sanjoy would be released and handed over to a foreign organization if these three conditions were fulfilled. Further, ULFA would not be responsible if Sanjoy died in an encounter. Complying with this

ULFA diktat, AVARD-NE left Assam towards the end of July after issuing an apology to the people of the state. Before this, Paresh had repeated the demands over the phone to Sumita.[94]

Following a request from Sanjoy's family members, the government directed the security forces not to undertake any operation that could jeopardize his life. It was also agreed that some representatives of the International Commission for Red Cross based in New Delhi could get in touch with the abductors for securing his release, as desired by his family.[95] Sanjoy was finally all set for release from ULFA captivity. The optimism was short-lived. On 7 August, ULFA claimed that Sanjoy had died after falling off a cliff in Arunachal Pradesh![96] That was the last statement from ULFA on Sanjoy's abduction for a very long time.

Speculation about Sanjoy's fate continued for some more time, fuelled by conflicting media reports. In April 1998, a story carried on the front page of many local dailies and some other publications said a skeleton had been found north of Majuli near Lakhimpur by some labourers who were digging the land. The police confirmed that it was Sanjoy's, only to deny it two days later.[97] The police continued to stick to its earlier theory that Sanjoy had been killed in Majuli soon after he was abducted. This also found mention in the statement tabled by home minister Indrajit Gupta in Parliament on 14 August, seemingly as a matter of duty, which summed up the entire episode, beginning from the abduction on 4 July and ULFA's last press release declaring Sanjoy dead.[98] The statement simply dished out the police version of the episode which was not totally correct.

What Happened to Sanjoy?

Almost a month after ULFA's first meeting with AVARD-NE in mid-1996, at which the latter had turned down ULFA's suggestion to shift its office to Bongaon, a report was submitted to the ULFA central headquarters in Bhutan by a political commissar of the outfit, Bhaskar Dutta, deployed in the east zone. It delved into the background and details of the NGO's activities and provided a list of all the people engaged in the schemes that were being implemented in Majuli. The report claimed that Sanjoy was closely linked with many different agencies of the government; that his dad had been former prime minister P.V. Narasimha Rao's close acquaintance and that the NGO had received Rs 700 crore from the government for anti-erosion work in Majuli. Further, the report said Sanjoy had held a series of meetings with R&AW in New Delhi before deciding to pitch tent in Majuli. His mandate was to demolish ULFA's base on the island.[99]

The report stopped short of recommending the steps to be taken by ULFA in the matter. This, it was expected, would be decided by the high command. However, the report lay on the desk of organizing secretary Asanta Bagh Phukan in ULFA's central headquarters for some time. He never apprised the high command of its contents. The leaders in Dhaka were upset over Sanjay's activities in Majuli, but there was no instruction from them either to mete out punishment to him or to abduct him.[100] Their silence prompted other senior functionaries of ULFA to put in efforts to draw the attention of the leaders to Sanjoy's activities. A meeting hurriedly summoned by ULFA's 28 Battalion in Dibrugarh resolved to depute Mrinal Hazarika to Bhutan for a decision on AVARD-NE. However, the stalemate could not be broken as the top leaders in Dhaka were reluctant to issue instructions on what to do about the NGO.[101] Most of them were preparing to depart for Geneva to attend a series of conferences.[102]

Eventually, the situation in Majuli was hurtling towards more conflict after ULFA embarked upon interrogating and threatening members of the NGO.[103] The events that unfolded in the subsequent months seemed to confirm the rebels' suspicion that there were links between AVARD-NE and the government. They were in no doubt that the army's deployment on the island and a police operation were based on inputs forwarded by Sanjoy. A warning issued to a worker at the NGO, Bhagirath Das, had no effect on the NGO's activities. Das continued to be actively involved in its schemes after his relocation to Jorhat. AVARD-NE was certainly in a defiant frame of mind, which was further evidenced by its summoning a meeting to generate 'public opinion' against ULFA. The meeting was convened around two months ahead of Sanjoy's disappearance. These were clear indications that the NGO would have to be compelled to leave the island.[104]

Towards the end of June 1997, a meeting convened at Dhakuakhana on the north bank of the Brahmaputra by ULFA functionaries belonging to the east zone resolved to serve a deadline to AVARD-NE to leave the island. A ten-member squad formed for the task quizzed Sanjoy on 4 July when he visited Mekheli village with Chandan. He was also told in categorical terms to exit the island within a week.[105] But Sanjoy was determined not to give in to the threats so easily. He allegedly assumed a defiant posture, replying that he would continue his development schemes in Majuli. The ULFA team was flabbergasted by the response. It decided to detain Sanjoy and Chandan till the arrival of a senior member from Dhakuakhana where he had gone for a meeting.[106]

Sanjoy and Chandan were interned at Sikari Chapori, a semi-flooded sandbar detached from the island, for two consecutive nights. On 6 July, there was an operation by the police and army on all the households in Bongaon known to have provided shelter to ULFA functionaries, in the hope of getting information about Sanjoy's abductors. The four cadres—Amrit Dutta, Bhaskar Barua, Arup Barua and Siraj Bora—tasked with keeping Sanjoy in captivity, grew uneasy at the thought that the police would soon set forth to rescue Sanjoy and head to where they were hiding. A decision was quickly taken to relocate to another place by boat late in the evening.[107]

Accounts of what happened afterwards take a hazy turn at this juncture, and a diversity of views on these developments have been shared by different people. Dr Sunil Kaul, a member of AVARD-NE who was working in Majuli, was informed by some locals at Mekheli that Sanjoy had been hacked to death on the evening of 6 July, which could mean that the incident happened after the operation to trace him was launched by the police and army.[108] This version is believed by a section of ULFA functionaries who were stationed at different locations far away from the island.[109]

However, a majority of the rebel functionaries, including some of the top leaders, believe that the group met with an accident when it was travelling to another spot on the island by boat after the search operation at Bongaon.[110] They were of the view that the swirling waters of the river perilously tilted the boat at some point, and Chandan escaped by jumping into the waters. In all likelihood, in the ensuing commotion Sanjoy also got flung into the river and sank within seconds, never to be seen again. Incidentally, the river is infamous for its fierce underwater currents at many places and has been known to have devoured even good swimmers earlier. All that the ULFA squad could do in the dark was to make continuous rounds on the boat at the location for endless hours. Many branches and logs that had floated down the river and got stuck on the banks were checked, but there was no trace of Sanjoy.[111]

News of this incident had not yet reached the ULFA high command, which was still under the impression that Sanjoy was safe in the custody of the abductors. It was only sometime in the third week of July that the message about the accident could be relayed to Paresh in Dhaka, after a letter written by a senior member from Dhakuakhana reached Bhutan.[112] On 22 July, ULFA faxed a press release to the media declaring that Sanjoy and two of his abductors had drowned in the Brahmaputra. However, no input was relayed from Majuli to the high command saying that two ULFA functionaries had also drowned along with Sanjoy.[113]

The ULFA high command was eager to ascertain the truth about the episode. It appointed operations commander Raju Baruah and organizing secretary Asanta Bagh Phukan as members of a committee to probe the episode. It was also apprehensive that the drowning incident could fuel more negative publicity for the outfit. So the leaders also resolved that it would be declared as false—which was done in a subsequent press release. In Bhutan, the committee deputed a functionary, Pulak Saikia from Darrang, to visit Majuli for a report. He returned to confirm that Sanjoy had died from drowning.[114] Fearing a greater damage to it image, ULFA decided not issue a release again saying that Sanjoy had actually died of drowning. Instead, it resolved to feed a false story to the media that he had met his end after falling off a cliff in Arunachal Pradesh. Incidentally, the idea about the mishap on the cliff struck the leaders after a functionary of outfit named Paresh Goswami was killed in an encounter with the army in Lakhimpur, bordering Arunachal Pradesh.[115]

Still, among the senior functionaries of ULFA there was confusion over the actual sequence of events leading to Sanjoy's disappearance, owing to the different theories that were doing the rounds among the residents of Majuli. Another version that was gaining ground was that Sanjoy had been deliberately pushed into the river by the abductors after Chandan escaped. So, Pulak was again deputed from Darrang to visit Majuli for the second time on a fact-finding mission. He began the task of gathering information after reaching the island. But he vanished before he could submit a report from his investigations. It was surmised by ULFA that he was shot dead after being apprehended by the security forces.[116]

By September 1997, the police had arrested sixteen persons suspected of involvement in the abduction and murder of Sanjoy.[117] The case was transferred to the CBI, which named eleven persons in its charge sheet submitted in 1999. The agency had interrogated nearly 250 people and surmised that Ghose was shot on the very night of the abduction.[118] Of the eleven accused, five were killed in separate encounters with security forces over a period of time. Phatik Hatimota, a local functionary, was arrested in 2011 while three others, including ULFA's armed wing chief Paresh, continued to evade arrest by the police.[119]

The award of life sentences to two ULFA functionaries—Kania Hazarikia and Moni Neog—had raised eyebrows among the local groups and residents in Majuli who were acquainted with the details leading to Sanjoy's disappearance. It appears that these two were not involved in the plan to summon or detain Sanjoy. They were simply instructed to lend a helping hand to the squad after it had detained Sanjoy and Chandan at Mekheli village.[120] The statement given by Chandan on the involvement of Hazarikia and Neog in Sanjoy's abduction was evidence enough for the court to pass the sentence against them. The judgment by the District and Sessions Court of Kamrup in 2003 was upheld three years later by the Gauhati High Court which said there was 'absolutely no reason' to interfere with the verdict.[121] Hazarikia and Neog were released in 2018 after serving eighteen years in jail.

Almost six months after the Sanjoy's abduction, the ULFA functionary who had played the most crucial role in ordering Sanjoy's detention was called to Bangladesh by the leaders to explain the episode. His explanation appeared genuine to the high command. He justified the decision to summon Sanjoy for interrogation since he believed Sanjoy was an undercover agent of R&AW. The functionary is also believed to have supplied Paresh some other details that confirmed the linkages between the NGO and the intelligence agency. The situation spun out of control because of the floods and the raids conducted by the security forces in the vicinity where Sanjoy and Chandan were detained. Chandan's daring escape by diving into the river and the resulting commotion in the boat were unexpected. The account corroborated the information received by Paresh from different sources about AVARD-NE's agenda on the island.[122]

ULFA's opinion of AVARD-NE was starkly different from that of a large section of Majuli's populace, which was convinced about its noble intention of ushering in positive changes in the island. So, was AVARD-NE actually working at the behest of R&AW or the government? It is necessary to point out that ULFA had been obsessed with R&AW since it became active in the early 1980s. Certain incidents over the past decade or so seemed to have strengthened suspicion among the outfit's leaders about the agency's designs in Assam. In 1990, just three weeks ahead of Operation Bajrang, the agency had air-lifted employees of some tea gardens, along with their families, from Doom Dooma to Guwahati as an act of rescue from ULFA. Then there were widespread allegations that R&AW had been involved in imparting training to a section of Bodo youths near Tezpur in the late 1980s to destabilize the AGP government. Further, it was R&AW's pact with the KIA that had compelled ULFA to leave Kachin.

R&AW's operation in Doom Dooma or the training imparted to the Bodo youth were exceptions to its activities in Assam rather than the rule. The agency's mandate lies beyond the country's borders and not within, although it maintains offices called Special Bureaus in many border states. Intelligence operations within the country, including counter-intelligence activities, are executed mostly by the Intelligence Bureau (IB), which is under the administrative control of the home ministry. So, the prospect of AVARD-NE being a front of R&AW or any other government department appears quite slim. Sanjoy had high-level contacts in the government, which might have helped the NGO procure funds for its schemes in Majuli. At the same time, Sanjoy and his group had been accused of being 'anti-national' in Rajasthan as well, when they began questioning certain projects like the family planning programme and the 'famous' Rajasthan canal implemented by the government.[123]

There's no gainsaying that AVARD-NE was serious about its work in Majuli. That the NGO's schemes had become popular on the island was best reflected in the resolution adopted at the open meeting convened by residents of the island, approving continuation of its activities. But there was a coterie of contractors and government officials whose interests were jeopardized by AVARD-NE's schemes. They stood the risk of being exposed and penalized by the government. The possibility of this group provoking ULFA to chase the NGO away from the island cannot be ruled out.[124]

ULFA's unease was primarily due to the NGO's growing recognition among the Mishing, who were not active supporters of the outfit. It was concerned about the likelihood of a situation on the island similar to the movement that had emerged in Lakhimpur-Dhemaji in the late 1980s, when a large chunk of the community had turned against the outfit at the instigation of URMCA. The rebel functionaries felt that the NGO's continuous defiance of its orders would not only contribute to the erosion of its authority in Majuli but was also an indication of the shape of things to come in the future. The final straw came on 4 July, when Sanjoy supposedly told the ULFA functionaries that he would not leave the island under any circumstances. This was something ULFA could not take lying down. In all likelihood, even if Sanjoy had not drowned, he would have been detained in remote locations till such time as he agreed to wind up operations on the island.[125]

AVARD-NE would have surely done better to gain experience of working in conflict zones before landing in Majuli. The NGO went too far too soon without the necessary safeguards. A book on Sanjoy's diaries that was subsequently published, with an afterword by his wife Sumita, opining that the abduction was linked to the fundamental issue of the 'right to voice one's opinion on the prevailing state of affairs and the right to work in any part of the country without fear of intimidation'.[126] That is certainly the right observation, but there are stages that a society and a country pass through everywhere over a long period of time before the rule of law is firmly established; conflicts either fizzle out or diminish in the process of nation-building. The 1990s were a turbulent phase in the Northeast with armed rebellions in most of the states, which was a stark reflection of the challenges of national integration in the frontier region. Unlike the metropolises, the situation in conflict zones is vastly different, and freedom of expression and work can be curtailed not only by rebel groups but also by the government. There can be many unexpected happenings in these regions that would be awfully astonishing to people living in undisturbed regions.

Geneva—the Turning Point

In Dhaka, ULFA's three-member squad of Rajkhowa, Anup and Shashadhar were in high spirits as they prepared to leave for Geneva to participate in two UN-sponsored conferences—for the

International Day celebrations of the World's Indigenous Peoples, held every year on 9 August, and the Sub-Commission on the Promotion and Protection of Human Rights.[127] Rajkhowa had prepared the speeches to be delivered, while Anup and Shashadhar equipped themselves with documents to be submitted explaining the condition of the indigenous communities in Assam and the rationale of the demand for sovereign status for Assam. Although ULFA had been frequenting these venues since 1995, it was for the first time that it would present its case before a large gathering of diplomats and delegates from organizations across the world.[128]

Even as the spadework for Geneva was on, news about Sanjoy's disappearance in Majuli trickled in. The ULFA delegates grew worried about the possibility of adverse repercussions of the episode on the organization at the conclaves. And they were not wrong in their assessment. The shape of things to come was evident at Bangkok, where they landed for a few hours to catch a connecting flight to Geneva. They were asked a volley of questions on Sanjoy by functionaries of the Unrepresented Nations Peoples' Organization (UNPO), who were also headed to the UN conference. In particular, they wanted to know if ULFA had abducted him, to which Anup replied saying that he would be released if he was still alive.[129]

At Geneva, while Rajkhowa and Shashadhar busied themselves with locating low-priced accommodation, Anup left for Madrid to attend a conference on the Zapatista movement in Mexico, which was an uprising of the indigenous communities that had erupted at Chiapas in 1994. He joined the others two days later, only to find that the pitch had already been queered for ULFA following a vigorous campaign by Indian diplomats on the outfit's terror activities in Assam. ULFA had figured in the list of participants at both the UN-sponsored conferences, but its entry was deleted ahead of the commencement of the programmes.[130] Leading the tirade against the outfit was India's ambassador at Geneva, Arundhati Ghose, who was supported by members of Amnesty International.[131] Ghose, who was Sanjoy's aunt, began the campaign by approaching the diplomats of the countries from where NGOs had offered their banner and sponsorship to ULFA. In particular, two NGOs caught her attention—Society for Threatened People, a Germany-based organization that works in close collaboration with the German government, and the UK-based Liberation.[132]

Ghose's task was rendered easier by the red-corner notices issued by Interpol against Rajkhowa, Anup and Paresh on charges of murder and extortion after ULFA confirmed Sanjoy's death in Arunachal Pradesh.[133] Instructions had also been received by the Indian embassy in Bern to make a case before the Swiss Interpol for the arrest and repatriation of the ULFA leaders. But there was no action against them, and Ghose observed that Chetia had free access at the UN building and at the sub-commission meetings. She took up the matter at different levels, but Interpol did not have the powers of arrest. The agency approached Geneva police, and Ghose made a representation before the director of the UN office in Geneva. The staff at the UN security cell swung into action and questioned Anup, but there was no way they could arrest him. He had a valid Bangladeshi passport under the name John David Salomar and a Swiss visa to enter Switzerland.[134]

Sensing danger, Anup slipped out of the conference room into another chamber which housed cyclostyle machines before going down to the basement by a lift. He headed to a café on the same premises, where a lawyer and two human rights activists from Jammu and Kashmir advised him to exit the place immediately. Anup was never seen again at the conclave.[135] Rajkhowa and Shashadhar had already left the venue, along with the representatives of other rebel outfits in the Northeast, that included PLA's general secretary Sanasam Gunen, vice chairman Manohar Mayum Pravin Kumar and president of the All-Tripura Tiger Force, Ranjit Debbarma. All of them had begun preparations to return to Bangladesh.[136]

Anup evaded arrest, owing to the legal wrangle involving the Swiss authorities and the UN legal cell. The relations between the host country and the UN are governed by an agreement. After the representation from Ghose, the UN legal adviser in Geneva referred the matter to the UN headquarters in New York, but the latter's reply was somewhat ambiguous. It drew on the host country agreement with the UN and the US, in which it was mentioned that the host country cannot stop any representative of an NGO from attending a UN meeting. A caveat was added, however, that this did not convey immunity against any crime which may have been committed by the individual concerned. The Swiss Permanent Mission chose to interpret this letter as giving all NGO representatives immunity from arrest and refused to take any action against Anup.[137]

Anup reached the apartment where he was putting up at Geneva, hurriedly packed his bags and landed in London, where he headed to the apartment of Dr Mukul Hazarika, who had already begun to be associated with ULFA. Anup was certain that he would be arrested if he returned with the same passport to Bangladesh since Interpol had been alerted and the Awami League-led government was friendly to India.[138] So he got on with the task of arranging another passport, although he knew it was not an easy task in the UK. The first few attempts were futile, as all the contacts offered by Hazarika expressed their inability to help him with the task. After many more attempts at different places, he was able to come in contact with a national from South Africa, Azizur Rahman, who had fled that country and had requested the UK government for asylum. Rahman agreed to sell his passport to Anup for $2,500. Rahman's photograph on the passport was replaced with Anup's, and a business visa to Bangladesh secured from the country's High Commission in London.[139]

Anup was all the more worried when he heard that Rajkhowa and Gunen had been detained at the airport in Dhaka for several hours. Rajkhowa was quizzed by sleuths of the National Security Intelligence (NSI), but he was able to convince them that he was actually William Momin Sangma, as mentioned in the passport he was carrying, and not a senior functionary of ULFA they were looking for.[140] The agency could possibly have unravelled the truth with a bit of investigation, but it decided to let him off in the evening. It was easier for Gunen to convince the agency that he was a citizen of Bangladesh since there was a sizeable Meitei population in Sylhet. The rest of the rebel functionaries who had returned from Geneva were able to scrape past the prying eyes of the security agencies at the airport without any hassle.[141]

Anup decided to return to Bangladesh four months after the conclaves at Geneva, assuming that the security agencies were longer on ULFA's trail. True to his assessment, he was not quizzed by any official at the airport.[142] But unknown to him, his residence at Mohammadpur had been put under surveillance by a security agency.[143] So, on 21 December, detectives of the Special Branch took him into custody along with two junior functionaries of the outfit, Babul Sarma and Lakhi Goswami, who were present at his residence when the squad arrived.[144]

In custody, Anup and his associates were under the impression that they would be set free within a few days. Inspector Mujibul Haque of the Special Branch who was entrusted with the case was almost certain that they would not be produced before court. On his suggestion, Anup penned a letter for prime minister Sheikh Hasina Wajed, attaching to it photographs showing his presence at the conclaves held in Geneva to establish that they were freedom fighters and not terrorists. However, the letter was never forwarded by the inspector general who headed the Special Branch. A week later, it was confirmed that the three would be produced in court.[145]

The department was unable to decide on the charges to be levelled against Anup and his associates. Anup told the department that they did not want to be extradited to India. He was concerned that in Bangladesh he would be charged with only a single offence of illegal entry into the country, which would mean a lighter jail term and subsequent extradition. He requested the detectives to prepare a charge sheet that also mentioned illegal possession of a satellite phone and foreign currency so he would be awarded a longer sentence in jail. The Special Branch agreed to Anup's suggestions, resulting in these charges also being made against the two other accused who were apprehended with Anup. In court, the judge's attendant asked Anup how long he would like to be incarcerated, to which Anup replied 'two years'. The attendant told him it would be difficult for the judge to pass a verdict sentencing him to only two years in prison.[146]

Anup agreed to a longer sentence. So, finally, the jail terms were four years for foreign currency possession, two years for illegal entry and seven years for illegal possession of a satellite phone, on which the judgment came later. However, the jail terms for all the cases were concurrent. And there was a law that good conduct in jail would lead to a deduction of three months of every year in jail. All this added to a total of only five years and three months. The verdicts seemed to fit perfectly with Anup's plan to avoid being handed over to India. He hoped that BNP would sweep to power in the next general elections in Bangladesh scheduled for 2001. His release from jail, along with Sarma and Goswami, would coincide with the coming to power of the BNP regime, which would certainly be unwilling to accept India's demand for his extradition.[147]

Anup's conviction sent shock waves among the rebel outfits from the Northeast based in Bangladesh. They knew that more leaders could be nabbed if the government decided to crack the whip against them. ULFA, ATTF and NDFB, with their training centres in Bangladesh, had a more conspicuous existence in the country than the other outfits such as the PLA, UNLF, NLFT and NSCN(IM), whose establishments were more in the nature of hideouts. The political instability in New Delhi was a breather for the groups as the Indian government was unable to keep the pressure on Dhaka to go after more rebel leaders. Neither these camps nor the hideouts were disturbed by the Bangladesh government.[148]

Nonetheless, Sanjoy's abduction, his disappearance and Anup's conviction were a turning point in ULFA's history.[149] Fourteen years later, Rajkhowa would publicly apologize for the Sanjoy episode at a public meeting in Majuli's Bongaon.[150] The outfit's chapter with the UN agencies and its ties with NGOs such as Liberation and Society for Threatened People drew to a close, never to be revived again. ULFA continued to maintain links in Europe for some more time, but they were intermittent and with some individuals rather than with organizations.[151]

Maggie Bowden, the general secretary of Liberation, subsequently sent an 'equivocal apology' regarding the incident to Michele Fedoroff at the NGO Section in the UN, in which she said:

> Liberation accepts that Anup Chetia deceived us and we genuinely regret this. We obviously were not in a position to check passports or to detect forgeries, neither do we have the practical or financial facilities to vet every single individual with an application where the application is made for and on behalf of an organisation. In this case the application applied for was on behalf of Assam Watch, which is a Human Rights organisation, and has been affiliated to Liberation for the past four years.[152]

At the same time, it is difficult to envisage a drastically altered situation in Assam should ULFA have been able to surge ahead with its plans at Geneva. It is unlikely that resolutions by UN-sponsored organizations at foreign venues would have caused a decisive impact on the separatist campaign in Assam. More important was the change in the power equations within the outfit after these incidents. The clique led by Anup and Shashadhar, which had advocated ULFA's presence at the UN forums and links with global organizations, suffered a serious setback. Paresh had never been favourably disposed towards these ideas as his focus had always been to forge stronger ties with the ISI and security agencies in the neighbouring countries. For him, all that mattered was the military wing and the creation of circumstances in India that would force it to cede the Northeast. There was no place for politics and diplomacy in a separatist movement. His position became more dominant, with the inevitable corollary of the political wing being eventually relegated to a more marginalized role in the organization.[153]

CHAPTER 7

TURNCOATS AND SECRET KILLERS

Tea, Tata and Tapes

EVEN BEFORE SANJOY'S abduction had snowballed into a storm, the seeds were sown for an equally shocking episode when three ULFA functionaries met in Guwahati in the latter part of June 1997. ULFA functionary Phanindra Medhi had just arrived for a brief sojourn in the city from New Delhi without any specific task. He interacted with a junior functionary and an agricultural engineer, Munna Mishra, who had enrolled in the outfit two years ago and had risen up the ranks owing to his acumen in executing operations successfully. But Mishra had already been converted into a mole by a police officer a few months ago. Before boarding the flight to Delhi, Phanindra had innocently disclosed all the details of his mission in the capital to Mishra, who passed on the information to his police handler.[1] Top police officials went into a huddle with chief H. Hrishikeshan for a plan of action, which was firmed up without delay.[2]

Phanindra's visit to Guwahati came after a meeting at Thimphu early in May where two senior leaders of ULFA had come together to work out the route by which the outfit's cultural secretary Pranati

Deka could be sent for treatment to Mumbai. Pranati was at an advanced stage of pregnancy but she had developed complications, for which she would have to be treated in a hospital. Present at the meeting in Thimphu was her husband Chitraban Hazarika, who was the finance secretary of the outfit, and another leader. It was decided that Phanindra and a woman functionary, Mridula Changmai, would remain attached to Pranati till they returned to Bhutan after the delivery.[3] The three flew to New Delhi, where they stayed for a week at a hotel before shifting to a rented accommodation. In the capital, they were briefed by Dr Brojen Gogoi, a senior functionary of Tata Tea Limited, who informed them that all arrangements had been made for Pranati's treatment at Mumbai's Jaslok Hospital.[4]

In Mumbai, where Dr Gogoi was also present, the hospital advised Pranati to return after two months for the diagnosis. Since staying in the city in a hotel was expensive, the three decided to go to New Delhi, where they shifted to the same Uttam Nagar accommodation they had rented earlier. Phanindra also returned from Guwahati for the subsequent trip to Mumbai, with Pranati and Mridula, in the first week of August. Pranati delivered a baby boy in mid-August without any complications. With the trip successful, the team booked tickets for New Delhi on 23 August 1997. But they were picked up within a few minutes of their arrival at Santa Cruz airport by a squad of the Mumbai police, which had been tracking their activities over the past several weeks.[5] On 7 September, Assam police chief H. Hrishikeshan dropped the bombshell before the media in Guwahati—Tata Tea Limited had sponsored the medical treatment of a senior ULFA leader in Mumbai. The episode, which featured on the front page of most national dailies, took the corporate sector by storm.

Tata Tea Limited knew it could land in deep trouble for doing what it had, but it assumed that underplaying the issue would be an appropriate tactic to douse the controversy. It affirmed that its Specialised Medical Assistance Scheme had a 'non-discriminatory' screening system. It reiterated that the company was not aware if

Pranati had availed of the benefits of this scheme.[6] The company's claims that it was ignorant of the expenses incurred on Pranati's treatment is contrary to the evidence on the incident, which tumbled out very soon. Many top officials of Tata Tea Limited had been aware of Pranati's actual identity, although she was admitted in the hospital as Bonti Barua.[7]

The bonhomie between ULFA and Tata Tea Limited was the outcome of a string of incidents dating back to 1990, when the outfit compelled tea companies in Assam to shell out money. Tata Tea Limited, which owned twenty-one gardens and employed about 20,000 workers in Assam, received demands for funds too, but it was able to convince ULFA that it could not deviate from its long-standing policy of not contributing funds to any rebel group.[8] Instead, it offered to construct a referral hospital at Chabua, which ULFA accepted. Three years later, the abduction of the Tata Tea Limited regional manager, Bolin Bordoloi, by the NDFB provoked ULFA to step up its demand for cash. If the company could pay Rs 1 crore as ransom for Bordoloi's release, then it could also bend the rules to pay cash to ULFA.[9]

Sometime in November 1995, Paresh placed a demand for 100 walkie-talkie sets in a letter written to Tata Tea Limited managing director R.K. Krishna Kumar.[10] On 4 January 1996, the company's executive director, S.M. Kidwai, replied to Paresh expressing the company's inability to fulfil the demand, but said it would be willing to invest in more schemes for the benefit of the workers and the people living near the tea estates.[11] The company was concerned about the possibility of an AGP win in the impending assembly polls and a relapse of the situation to what it was in the late 1980s.[12] So the company decided to keep the door open with ULFA for future negotiations. And to ensure that it did not ruffle the feathers of the Assam government, the state home secretary, B.V.P. Rao, was apprised about the exchange of letters with ULFA. Chief minister Hiteswar Saikia, however, instructed Rao to inform Tata Tea Limited that it should discontinue its interaction with ULFA.[13] The matter subsided for a while until after the elections when Paresh told the company to send a delegation for talks to Bangkok.[14]

AGP had formed the government and there were widespread rumours that the party would step up the demand for lifting the ban on ULFA.[15] Hence, at Tata Tea Limited, a four-member team comprising general manager S.S. Dogra, Dr Brajen Gogoi and two more employees was constituted without delay ahead of the Bangkok meeting. Again, to ensure that the company was not on the wrong side of the government, the additional director of the Intelligence Bureau, Ratan Sehgal, was kept in the loop. He insisted that the Assam government should not be informed of the matter.[16]

The details of the covert meeting in Bangkok, held on 25–26 May 1997, found their way into a report in *The Indian Express*. More details, including the minutes of the meeting, also became available to the media in Guwahati, possibly being released by Assam police.[17] At the meeting, the Tata Tea Limited representatives furnished a list of ten development schemes implemented in Assam as evidence of the company's commitment to the welfare of its workers and the people living near the estates. Not impressed with the claims, Paresh alleged that Tata Tea Limited had never been concerned about the aspirations of the local youth, which was apparent in their low representation in the management ranks. He made a case that the company should invest its entire profits of Rs 50–60 crore (per annum) in the state instead of the meagre amount that it had been spending.[18]

Finally, Paresh placed eight demands before the delegates, out of which supply of walkie-talkie sets, relocation of the company's office from Kolkata to Assam and payment of an annual tax to ULFA were discarded, on the rationale that they militated against the company's policies. The representatives replied in the affirmative to the other demands, such as upgradation of the hospital at Chabua, more funds for investment in development schemes and greater opportunities for the local youth. The company had already invested a sizeable amount in the packaging industry in the state.

On the Assam Tea Plantation Security Force, which Paresh wanted withdrawn, the representatives said Tata Tea Limited was opposed to the creation of the force, which was why the estates owned by the company were the last to get security from it.[19]

After the meeting, the company replied to Paresh offering scholarships to children of the outfit's functionaries who had been killed, assistance to widows for self-employment, supply of medicines and medical facilities to patients recommended by ULFA at Apollo Hospital and Tata Memorial Hospital in Mumbai.[20] The plan was to execute all these schemes over a period of time, but immediate on the agenda were medical facilities, which were implemented towards the end of the year, when an ULFA nominee was offered treatment at Apollo Hospital in New Delhi.[21]

As such, the ULFA–Tata Tea Limited links had already been established before Pranati's case was unearthed by the police. The company had been able to resist ULFA's demands for a long time till the mid-1990s, when it too succumbed to the pressure. Further, the police probe eventually led to seizure of the letters written by senior Tata Tea Limited officials to Shalimar Hotel and Jaslok Hospital in Mumbai recommending accommodation and treatment for Bonti Barua, who was none other than Pranati.[22] All these revelations punched glaring holes in the company's claims that it was unaware of Pranati's antecedents, including the long statement issued by the company on 12 September 1997.[23]

Thereafter, events unfolded a frenetic pace—events involving government officials and ministers at the highest level and some of the most well-known names in the country's corporate sector. Assam police chief H. Hrishikeshan received a call from union home secretary K. Padmanabahiah, indicating that the probe against Tata Tea Limited ought to 'slow down'.[24] This incident coincided with the interrogation of three senior officials of the company—S.S. Dogra, S.M. Kidwai and R.K. Krishna Kumar—by the Assam police in Guwahati. They were confronted with a host of facts gathered by the Special Operations Unit (SOU) of the police, which exposed as hollow the company's repeated claims that it was ignorant about Pranati's identity. The most clinching evidence for the police was the company's letter to Jaslok Hospital requesting upgrade of Pranati's room from class-B to class-A.[25]

Tata Sons chairman Ratan Tata called on chief minister Mahanta at the capital with a reiteration of the same message doled out in the press releases—there was no question of militancy funding by Tata Tea Limited and Pranati's case was a glitch, at the local level, in the implementation of the company's Medical Assistance Scheme. However, the conversation took a serious turn when the chairman informed Mahanta about the role of Ratan Sehgal—the additional director of the Intelligence Bureau—who had advised the company to go ahead with the meeting with Paresh in Bangkok. The chief minister got in touch with the Prime Minister's Office (PMO) and the home ministry to unearth Sehgal's actual role. Then he briefed the core committee of the ruling United Front government about the incident. However, there was no response either from the PMO or the home ministry. He also thundered at a press conference in Guwahati that the Intelligence Bureau had 'no right' to authorize Tata Tea Limited to talk to militants in Bangkok.[26]

More trouble was brewing for Tata Tea Limited when police gathered evidence of its links with the NDFB. Early in 1997, a four-member team, including S.S. Dogra and Dr Brojen Gogoi, had met a delegation of the NDFB at New Delhi's Taj Palace hotel and the company had paid for the return flight of the rebel functionaries. So, Tata Tea Limited officials were summoned again for interrogation by police. Dogra was arrested while an Interpol alert was issued for Dr Brojen Gogoi, who was believed to be in the US at the time. The company was instructed to secure his return within two weeks.[27]

Dr Brojen Gogoi was already staying at a company guest house in Kolkata after his return from a study trip to the US on 6 September. Five days later, he checked into Hotel Rutt Deen in his own name and then got himself admitted at Woodland Nursing Home, from where he contacted the Tata Tea Limited office. On

16 September, the company secured anticipatory bail for Dr Brojen Gogoi, R.K. Krishna Kumar and another senior executive, K. Sridhar, from the Mumbai High Court.[28] Therefore, the company's claims that it was unaware about Dr Brojen Gogoi's whereabouts, which Ratan Tata too reiterated before chief minister Mahanta in New Delhi, were simply not true.[29]

The company realized it had committed another blunder by feigning ignorance about Dr Brojen Gogoi's whereabouts. Sensing more trouble if the deadline of two weeks from the Assam government was not met, Dr Brojen Gogoi presented himself before the police in Guwahati on 24 September. He was arrested for waging war against the state in collusion with ULFA, and not for the Pranati episode since anticipatory bail had already been obtained in that case.[30] The arrest came as a jolt to the company as it did not anticipate such a move from the Assam police. The top brass was panic-stricken that the axe might fall on some more executives. In sheer desperation, it pulled strings and made all efforts, roping in contacts at high-level offices, to wriggle out of the muddle it had got into in Assam, only to trigger another distressing controversy.[31]

Early in October, *The Indian Express* published recorded telephone conversations among some top corporate honchos engaged in the rescue mission for Tata Tea Limited. The incident, which became famous as the 'Tata tape controversy', proved that the company knew of Dr Brojen Gogoi's location in Kolkata although it preferred to give a false statement before the Assam police. The discussions, which were held over a few days between Bombay Dyeing chairman Nusli Wadia, Mahindra and Mahindra chairman Keshub Mahindra, industrialist and Rajya Sabha member Jayant Malhoutra and Tata Sons chairman Ratan Tata, focused on the ways and means to be adopted to put an end to the controversy. Ratan Tata had held consultations with home minister Indrajit Gupta and home secretary K. Padmanabhaiah on the matter. Some of the others who were approached to bail out the company included former prime ministers Chandra Shekhar and H.D. Deve Gowda, special secretary Vijay Mathur and field marshal Sam Manekshaw for his access to Assam's retired governor lieutenant general S.K. Sinha.[32]

But on whose orders were the conversations recorded? And who leaked the tapes? For a section of bureaucrats in the capital, the needle of suspicion pointed to a highly placed official in the Intelligence Bureau. The government was quick to deny that it had ordered the tapping of phones and pushed for a probe into the incident.[33] The uproar continued for several days, prompting efforts by different sections of people to broker a truce between the Assam government and Tata Tea Limited. West Bengal chief minister Jyoti Basu landed in Guwahati for a series of meetings and issued a statement appreciating the role of the tea companies in Assam. A large delegation of tea companies also called on Assam chief minister Mahanta in Guwahati to assure him of their support in the battle against militancy. Tata Tea Limited reiterated as much in a press release, saying it supported the government's efforts to curb militancy in Assam.

Chief minister Mahanta received the message—he ought to bury the hatchet since he had won the battle against Tata Tea Limited. He agreed. After all, the tea sector was too crucial for Assam's economy to be distressed for very long. Security was beefed up at the estates, but most of the tea companies in Assam continued to shell out money to the rebel groups.[34] There was no charge sheet against Dr Brojen Gogoi, who was released after three months in jail.[35]

The controversy fizzled out, but speculation as to the reasons that had prompted Mahanta to train the guns so assiduously against Tata Tea Limited continued for some time. Many were convinced that he was extremely upset with the tea companies when he had visited Kolkata to raise funds for the party ahead of the assembly polls. Most of these companies had either donated a meagre amount or had refused to donate, as in the case of Tata Tea Limited. So, he had an axe to grind against them. Pranati's case was too good an opportunity to be missed for settling the score.[36] Even as the drama unfolded, Tata Tea Limited's plan to establish a cancer hospital at

Chabua with an allocated corpus of Rs 350 crore was cancelled, and the funds were redirected to West Bengal.[37]

Blunder in the Snow

When the ULFA delegates were preparing to leave for Geneva, Paresh was focused on fixing an arms deal in China. He was prompted to scout for more weapons following a decision by the state-owned China North Industries Group Corporation (NORINCO) to embark on modernization and dispose of its obsolete weapons.[38] Brokers in Southeast Asia were looking for buyers for these weapons, to be sold at concessional rates in China. A consignment had already been procured jointly by the NDFB and NSCN(IM) and successfully ferried to different camps in the Chittagong Hill Tracts after being offloaded at Cox's Bazar from a ship.[39]

Paresh flew to China's Yunnan, where a deal was firmed up with brokers for a consignment of assault rifles, pistols, grenades and ammunition. However, the brokers proposed an alternative route for transshipment of the weapons, which was considered less expensive than delivering them directly via the sea at Bangladesh's Cox's Bazar. Their suggestion was for the consignment to be dropped at a convenient spot, either along the Sino-Bhutan or India-China border in Arunachal Pradesh, devoid of army presence. Paresh found the idea exciting. He felt the option of a route bypassing Bangladesh was worth exploring. He told the brokers that a recce would be carried out for convenient spots along the border and a route finalized for the weapons to be ferried.[40] Within a week of his return to Dhaka, he instructed two senior functionaries from Dibrugarh to survey the border region at the Dibang valley in Arunachal Pradesh.[41] The general headquarters in Bhutan was tasked with the same job, but focusing on the border districts of Bumthang and Haa in the kingdom, as suggested by Paresh.[42]

Chosen for the task in Bhutan was an experienced functionary, Lohit Deuri, who was instructed to cross over to China at Bumthang and establish contact with the nearest outpost of the Chinese PLA from the border. If his efforts were successful, and the terrain favourable, then the consignment would be dropped at the outpost, from where it must be ferried to the camps. Deuri was about to step across the border with some locals he had befriended in Bumthang when he was accosted by the police, quizzed and even threatened with arrest. The charges could be extremely serious as Deuri was not a Bhutanese national. Fortunately, the police handed him over to the deputy commissioner of Bumthang. Deuri's explanation that he was an Indian trader exploring the possibility of trade at the border did not convince the district head, who had almost made up his mind to prosecute him. It was only when Deuri called a highly placed official in Thimphu over the telephone that he was permitted to leave Bumthang. Subsequently, he was assigned by Paresh to survey another spot on the border at Haa, about 300 km west of Bumthang.[43]

Meanwhile, the general headquarters in Bhutan decided to explore the possibility of a route through Paro too, where a squad comprising two experienced functionaries, Biju Deka and Ram Gogoi, succeeded in establishing contact with a local smuggler who assisted them in crossing over to China. They walked for eight days at a snail's pace over snow-clad mountains to reach a market where they stayed for two days, but not before Deka had a miraculous escape that saved him from slipping into a deep crevice. The layers of snow concealed the craggy surface and sharp edges of the terrain, where one wrong step could lead to lethal consequences. A Chinese army establishment could be spotted at a significant distance from the market, but reaching the place would mean a walk of two days. Ferrying weapons from this spot would be an impossible task. Paresh instructed the two to return to Thimphu after he was provided with all the details of their journey over radio.[44]

The ULFA team that went to Arunachal Pradesh met with the same fate and was unable to proceed beyond a certain point in the Dibang valley abutting China. Unlike the circumstances in Bhutan, the weather was crippling for the functionaries, and the hilly terrain at certain points too steep to negotiate. Even the locals with whom the ULFA squad interacted were reluctant to venture too deep into the wilderness, which meant that carrying weapons down that route was probably unfeasible.[45] Incidentally, among all the spots along the India-China border in Arunachal Pradesh, the Dibang Wildlife Sanctuary, through which a route was sought to be established, had the least presence of the Indian army because of the tough terrain.

At Haa in Bhutan, the task was easier for Deuri as the terrain had less snow and no presence of either the police or the army. He crossed the border with the assistance of some locals to reach the Chinese army outpost, where a PLA officer told him that the consignment would arrive at a nearby spot within a couple of weeks of his intimating another person at a far-off location. However, the weapons must be ferried from the spot within forty-eight hours. Deuri returned to Haa and paid a local merchant to arrange for 200 yaks to be taken across the border. The plan was to use these yaks for transporting the weapons. He returned to Thimphu, where Paresh and a few other senior functionaries had already arrived to supervise the operation.[46] Even as preparations were on for the operation, a Bhutanese senior intelligence official hurriedly summoned Paresh to his office the next day. The officer sounded extremely worried.[47] What had gone wrong?

The official told ULFA in categorical terms that it would have to abandon the plan of transporting weapons from China. The Indian government had gathered extensive details of Deuri's preparations to fetch the consignment from across the border. Thimphu had been alerted and was requested to take immediate measures to foil the import. It was revealed that Deuri had made a mistake by overtly inquiring about the availability of yaks. He was neither a Bhutanese citizen nor an Indian trader who frequented the valley.

Eyebrows were thus raised when he claimed that he wished to ferry some commodities from across the border. Incidentally, Haa has the biggest presence of the Indian army among all the districts of Bhutan; it is where the headquarters of the Indian Military Training Team (IMTRAT) is located. It had received information about Deuri's suspicious activities from multiple sources.[48]

Paresh was concerned as he had already footed the bill for the consignment. Left with no alternative, he fell back on the other option of accepting delivery of the weapons on sea and then bringing them to the camps in Bangladesh. Almost four trucks of weapons were delivered by ship, comprising assault rifles, anti-aircraft guns, sniper rifles, heavy machine guns and a colossal quantity of ammunition. While half of the consignment was kept at Satcherri, the rest were dispatched to different locations in Assam, again through different routes, including through locations along Bangladesh's border with West Bengal, in vehicles registered in Bhutan as they are not checked in India.[49] The Indian intelligence agencies had received information about the possibility of more weapons being procured by ULFA. The Border Security Force (BSF) was alerted along some vulnerable stretches of the India-Bangladesh border in Assam and Meghalaya, but this did not yield any results.[50]

ULFA was clearly on the ascendant, with the threat from the Indian security forces being minimal for the time being. The enhanced ambience of safety prompted the outfit to offer training to the Kamtapur Liberation Organisation (KLO) and a group of youths from Arunachal Pradesh, under the banner of Arunachal Dragon Force, with the twin goals of checking the expansion of NSCN(IM) and exploring the possibility of a route from China for ferrying weapons to Assam.[51] The training module was standardized; specialized sessions in bomb-making and wireless communication began and a refresher course was introduced for the senior cadres. All these were eventually implemented at the camps in Myanmar and Bangladesh.[52]

It was during this period in the late 1990s that the number of trained combatants in ULFA reached the highest figure of around 2,000, which was in addition to the non-combatant members, comprising 1,000 more, with the maximum numbers stationed in Bhutan.[53] This was almost equal to its cadre strength in the late 1980s, although there were few combatants at that time. In the late 1990s, the most essential precondition of funds for sustaining a larger establishment was fulfilled. An efficient system for regular flow of cash to the different camps in the three neighbouring countries had been set up; it was primarily dependent on extortion.[54]

So, more schemes were conceived and implemented at the camps in Bhutan, aimed at enhancing the efficiency of the combat units and the optimum utilization of the women cadres. A specialized squad called Volcano was constituted for targeting industrial and strategic installations. Three targets were assigned to the group, although only the oil pipeline in Nalbari's Pagladiya could be blasted. Attack on the other targets was kept in abeyance, following multiple proposals from some senior functionaries who were in favour of a drastic expansion of the Volcano unit.[55]

Amid these recommendations were covert ventures for the creation of an intelligence wing, known only to a handful of senior functionaries. The wing assumed different shapes over a period of time, with the first squad of three functionaries being trained by deputy commander Barua at the general headquarters. They were to be posted at the three zones covering the entire valley, with the mandate to submit monthly reports on the political activities of the councils.[56] Even as this unit was activated came a suggestion within a month from Paresh for constitution of another squad with the broader objective of covering the ULFA battalions and identifying the moles in the camps. Some leaders were concerned after two spies of an Indian intelligence agency were identified in the camp; they were awarded capital punishment.[57] So the military intelligence unit (MIU) was given shape. It consisted of forty experienced cadres from both the political and armed branches of ULFA, with

Paresh as the head and Raju Baruah as his deputy.[58] It was assigned multiple goals.

Regular reports were received from MIU functionaries stationed in Guwahati, Nalbari, Dibrugarh and Tezpur on the activities and performance of the battalions and councils. They mixed with the new recruits to identify the spies; they gathered information on the movements of the army and on the cadres who were released from jail to find out if they had disclosed vital information about the organization to the security agencies. Another mole planted by police was put before the firing squad in Bhutan after being identified by MIU.[59] Again, on the recommendation of the wing, all the cadres were encouraged to maintain diaries and contribute to the wall magazines at the camps in Bhutan.[60] The assumption was that the personality of the cadres, as well as their motives and degree of commitment to the organization, could be gauged from their writings. The results were encouraging, but plans for expanding the unit were hamstrung by the dearth of eligible functionaries. By early 1998, MIU was merged with another specialized group called Enigma, with enhanced functions and more women as its members.[61]

More than an Enigma

By late 1997, circumstances were ripe for ULFA to launch a bigger specialized squad. This was Enigma, which was entrusted with the twin mandates of gathering information and executing specific operations in the Brahmaputra valley. Two developments hastened the formation of the squad in Bhutan. ULFA was in receipt of information from its sources in the government that a massive offensive was being planned against the outfit through a variety of strategies drawn up after the failed attempt to assassinate chief minister Mahanta.[62] The outfit's leaders perceived that scaling up attacks on security forces and government installations could be an apt approach against the government plan.[63]

Secondly, some ULFA leaders had been mulling the possibility of a battalion consisting exclusively of women, to be tasked with a range of objectives and with a focus on information gathering. Their idea was to completely segregate the wings of intelligence and operation in the organization for greater efficiency and to prevent leakage of information. Based on previous experiences, it was realized that the execution of operations was easier in the rural areas. In the urban areas, information about the target had to be accurate for an operation to be successful. Usually during an operation, there is an officer in charge of the squad, a second-in-command and another in charge of security. They are provided all the necessary details by the group that gathers intelligence. The timing, place and other aspects would then be chalked out among the three functionaries ahead of the operation. It was presumed that if women were engaged for the information gathering group, there would be less chances of leakage and security would be better maintained.[64]

These issues were topics of intense intermittent discussion for several weeks over radio among Paresh and the staff officers of the general headquarters in Bhutan. Finally, they resolved that the objective could be better fulfilled by a group that combined both operations and information-gathering instead of two separate wings. So, the idea of an exclusive battalion for women was discarded in favour of a smaller unit, which would be attached to the MIU. It would comprise experienced functionaries selected from all the camps. Thus was born the idea of Enigma, which was fine-tuned by deputy commander Baruah with suggestions from Munna Mishra, who was entrusted with a vital role in the project. Enigma was envisaged as a secret group within ULFA whose activities would be independent of the battalions.[65]

Information about the members of Enigma, such as their place of origin and other details, were to be known only to the senior functionaries since secrecy was an essential precondition for the success of any operation. In reality, the engagement of many experienced functionaries for the squad was widely known from the beginning, and especially the functionaries who were chosen from the general headquarters. Preference was given to cadres presumed to possess the skills to arrange safe houses, funds, cover-ups and strategies for execution of an operation. All the cadres were to undergo a specialized training module of three months, to be supervised by Barua at a camp established near Deothang between the general and central headquarters. Among the trainers was Munna Mishra, who was given the authority to access all the details of the members of Enigma.[66]

Around 200 cadres, including thirty women, were selected and divided into two sections, Enigma A and Enigma B. The former group, which was bigger, consisted of cadres drawn mainly from the general headquarters who were to focus only on operations in the rural areas. Women were to be attached with the latter, tasked with operations in the towns and cities and with information-gathering. Their faces had to be covered with a black cloth whenever they stepped out of the camp to visit other camps. After completion of training early in 1998, the first batch of thirty cadres was instructed to settle down and acclimatize in the bigger cities, such as Guwahati, Dibrugarh and Tezpur, under fake identities. They were briefed about the targets to be identified and told to submit reports to the headquarters in Bhutan for further action.[67]

As many as five batches rolled out from Enigma over regular intervals of time, and the cadres were either stationed at the camps in Bhutan or sent to different locations in Assam. By mid-2000, before the squad's activities were trimmed, more than thirty small and big operations were executed, including a few sensational killings and ambushes.[68] The most well-known was an incident involving a brigadier in Guwahati who was assassinated after being trailed for almost two weeks by a two-member squad. A lieutenant colonel suffered the same fate near the 4 Corps headquarters in Tezpur within weeks of another senior officer from the Special Services Bureau (SSB) falling prey to another team of Enigma at the same place. Among the prominent ambushes was one carried out deep inside Manas Wildlife Sanctuary, in which some personnel of a patrolling army column died, and one near Uttarkuchi along the border with Bhutan, where a major was reportedly killed.[69]

Women played a key role in many of these operations, and especially in the assassination of high-profile officers. From the group of thirty, six women were selected for continuous deployment in operations for over two years. Their reports were invariably found to be precise, enabling the Enigma command centre to station shooters at the right time and spot for the killings. One of the operations executed entirely by women was the blasting with RDX of an oil storage depot at Thekeraguri, located about 80 km east of Guwahati, causing huge losses to Indian Oil Corporation. On many occasions, the hideouts the women arranged in Guwahati and Tezpur rendered the execution of commands much easier.[70]

The Enigma group demonstrated how women have advantages over men in certain situations, owing to their ability to perform multiple tasks. And yet, contrary to the plans of the ULFA leadership, their role in operations had to be curtailed within one and a half years of Enigma being launched. A functionary of the squad was expected to arrange the necessary logistics on his own after being assigned the location for an operation. Women were found lagging behind when it came to arranging the logistics for an operation. In a few instances, extra support was necessary from Bhutan for settling some women in the towns. Eventually, most of the women were engaged for office work and radio communication at the camp in Bhutan. The disappearance of three women from different hideouts over a period of time was another setback that contributed to the curbing of their role in operations.[71]

Nonetheless, the enhanced and focused role of women as combatants in Enigma was an almost unparalleled chapter in the annals of insurgency in India's Northeast. Almost all the major rebel groups in the Northeast had enrolled women, with some among them, like the PLA, UNLF and NSCN(IM), even forming separate wings for women. However, instances of their engagement in combat roles or assignments to faraway missions were indeed very rare. An exceptional example comes from the Naga National Council, which in the late 1960s chose twenty women in its second batch for a long and arduous trek to China as part of its training.[72] PLA and UNLF engaged women in a few operations, but it is doubtful if this was sustained on a long-term basis.[73]

In Enigma, women reported diverse experiences of the tasks assigned to them. While some were satisfied to have taken part in operations like their male counterparts, another section was frustrated to have been confined to the camp. And there was another group of women that was critical of the role played by the leadership in managing the affairs of the secret squad.[74] Their varied opinions notwithstanding, Enigma marked the peak of women's participation in ULFA. The extinction of Mahila Kalyan Parishad and the chaos that followed the post-Operation Bajrang phase caused a gap of a few years in women's involvement in the movement. It picked up only in the mid-1990s, when they began to be recruited in small numbers for the armed wing and other branches and stationed at the camps in Bhutan and Myanmar.[75]

Similar to the previous phase, the triggers that drove men to join ULFA were the same for the women—a deep angst and many grievances about the existing socio-political conditions in Assam, a desire to effect radical change in society, or sometimes simply peer pressure. There were also a motley group of high-school dropouts, widows, siblings and wives of men who had joined ULFA earlier.[76] By the late 1990s, women constituted around 10 per cent of all ULFA functionaries, numbering between 200 and 250 cadres—many more than in the late eighties before the launch of the army's operation.[77] Apart from these categories, there were women engaged with ULFA mostly in an unofficial capacity. They were the wives of functionaries at the camps, some of whom had also completed their training in Bhutan and were assigned non-military tasks from time to time. A few women embarked on perilous errands to gather food for the camps at a later stage, when the supply routes were choked by the Royal Bhutan Army; this was similar to the occasional errands women cadres had to run in Myanmar too.[78] Then, there were also those stationed in the Brahmaputra valley with the primary task of relaying messages, running propaganda and even arranging logistics for other members.[79]

ULFA's top echelon seemed to have been convinced about the merits and demerits of women cadres and the functions that could be performed by them.[80] Women were found to be more disciplined and dedicated than men, which was evidenced by the fact that fewer women become turncoats or surrender before the government. Besides, many women withdrew from ULFA silently without availing of the benefits offered by the government for surrendered cadres. On the flip side, women were found unable to follow other women as leaders but performed better if they were attached with squads led by principled male commanders. Then, their roles naturally became restricted after they married and gave birth to children, as no commander wished to send women in such positions on faraway assignments. The role of many competent women cadres was thus restricted and confined to the camps after they got married.[81]

Nonetheless, there was immense scope for ULFA to link its campaign to women's issues and develop a broader agenda. But it is doubtful whether such topics were ever deliberated on by the leadership in the sporadically organized meetings where policy decisions and amendments to the outfit's constitution were discussed. And there were other developments that certainly pointed to a bias against women among the ULFA leadership. In the military wing, only three women—Moni Hazarika, Meghali Khargoria and Santi Rajkumari—were able to rise to the rank of second lieutenant with their outstanding performances.[82] In the non-military departments, Pranati Deka attained the highest position of secretary in the culture department, but that was one of the least active branches of the organization.

By the beginning of 2002, the ULFA leadership was compelled to merge Enigma with the battalions and its cadres shifted to two different locations.[83] This decision was preceded by a furious debate among the leadership over whether Enigma had actually been able to fulfil the purpose for which it had been created. Paresh was in no doubt that it had caused more harm than good to the organization and that its operations could also have been executed by the battalions. Deputy commander Baruah's views were somewhat different. He felt that Enigma's story was one of mixed successes and failures. His opinion was echoed by some other functionaries, who felt that the experiment offered vital lessons for the organization.[84]

Paresh was extremely upset with Baruah for his inability to identify in good time the moles planted by the Assam police in the squad. He knew something was amiss and had sounded a note of caution when many functionaries stationed in different towns and cities stopped reporting to the high command a while after the completion of their training.[85] They were never traced again. A few senior functionaries sent on specific tasks were also shot dead by the police under mysterious circumstances.[86] Alarmed by these developments, the leaders made serious efforts to check further damage, and they began by compiling a list of suspects and scrutinizing their past activities. The needle of suspicion pointed at Munna. Soon the leaders arrived at the conclusion that he was the one who had informed the police about Pranati Deka's treatment in Mumbai after Phanindra disclosed the details to him in Guwahati. And that it was possibly Munna again who deliberately pressed the button on the bomb a few seconds late to prevent the assassination of chief minister Mahanta in Guwahati. A decision was taken to put him on trial in Bhutan at the earliest, which would possibly lead to capital punishment before the firing squad. It was a challenging task, as Munna had already sensed danger and had begun to take safety measures.[87]

Former SSB senior instructor Biraja Nanda Chowdhury, who held classes on guerrilla warfare at his residence in Margherita.

(Credit: Rita Choudhury)

Founder chairman of ULFA Budheswar Gogoi *(left)* at his residence in Moran.

(Credit: Special Arrangement)

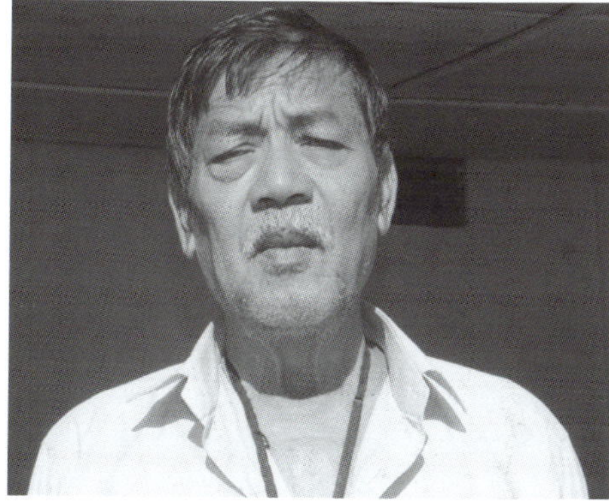

Former finance secretary and founder-member of ULFA Bhupen Borgohain.

(Credit: Rajeev Bhattacharyya)

Former vice chairman and founding member of ULFA Suren Dihingia.

(Credit: Rajeev Bhattacharyya)

Former defence secretary and founding member of ULFA Someswar Gogoi.

(Credit: Special Arrangement)

Former commander-in-chief of ULFA Budheswar Gogoi.

(Credit: Rajeev Bhattacharyya)

ULFA chairman Arabinda Rajkhowa *(centre)*.

(Credit: UB Photos)

ULFA general secretary Anup Chetia *(left)*.

(Credit: UB Photos)

Chief of staff and supremo of ULFA's anti-talks faction Paresh Baruah *(left)* with NSCN(K) chairman S.S. Khaplang *(centre)* and NDFB(S) interim president I.K. Songbijit at a camp in Taga in Myanmar's Sagaing Region.

(Credit: Rajeev Bhattacharyya)

ULFA vice chairman Pradip Gogoi at Sivasagar after his release from jail in 2010.

(Credit: Special Arrangement)

NSCN general headquarters Kaisan Chanlam (Challam Basti) in Myanmar's Sagaing Region, where ULFA functionaries were trained.

(Credit: Hseng Noung Lintner)

A group of ULFA functionaries of the first batch in Kachin (1987).

(Credit: Lohit Deuri)

Officers of the Kachin Independence Army (KIA) who trained ULFA.

(Credit: Lohit Deuri)

Army operation at Lakhipathar during Operation Bajrang in 1990–91.

(Credit: Pradip Gogoi)

A squad of ULFA functionaries ferrying weapons through Myanmar in Bangladesh's Bandarban ahead of Operation Ambrosia.

(Credit: Special Arrangement)

ULFA general headquarters at Samdrup Jongkhar in Bhutan.

(Credit: Lohit Deuri)

ULFA functionaries with locals at Samdrup Jongkhar in Bhutan.

(Credit: Retired brigadier Ranjit Barthakur)

ULFA cultural secretary Pranati Deka (*middle*) with functionaries of the outfit at a camp in Bhutan.

(Credit: Special Arrangement)

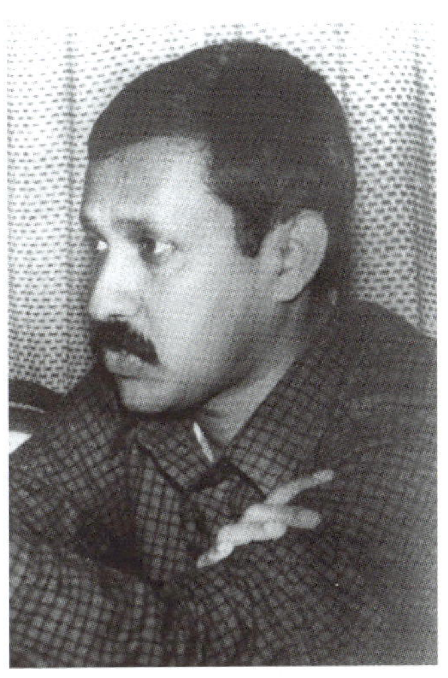

Parag Kumar Das, executive editor of *Asomiya Pratidin*, who was assassinated in 1996.

(Credit: Special Arrangement)

Sanjoy Ghose (*seated, second from right*) with the AVARD-NE team in Dimapur.

(Credit: Dr Sunil Kaul)

Commander of ULFA's 28 Battalion Mrinal Hazarika (*middle*) briefing the media at Sadiya on 26 June 2008 after ceasefire with the government.

(Credit: Rajeev Bhattacharyya)

Delegates of People's Consultative Group (PCG) at North Block in New Delhi after a meeting with home minister Shivraj Patil (*third from right*) in 2006.

(Credit: Hiranya Saikia)

Morning drill of ULFA functionaries at a camp in Taga in Myanmar's Sagaing Region.

(Credit: Rajeev Bhattacharyya)

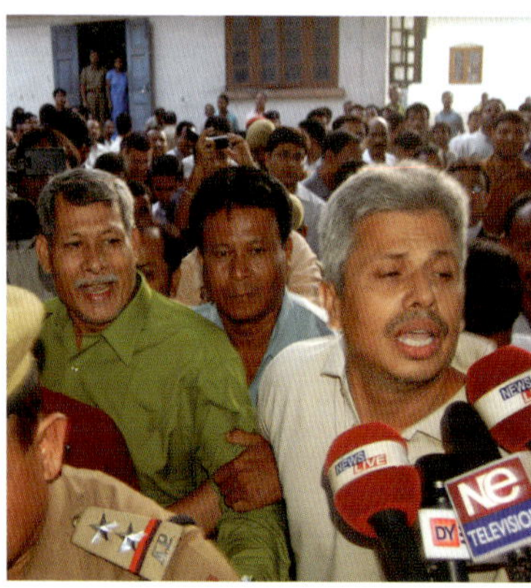

ULFA finance secretary Chitraban Hazarika *(left)* and foreign secretary Shashadhar Choudhury in Guwahati after they were handed over to India by Bangladesh.

(Credit: Special Arrangement)

Former ULFA chairman of anti-talks faction Dr Mukul Hazarika delivering a lecture at the outfit's camp in Taga in Myanmar's Sagaing Region.

(Credit: Special arrangement)

The Killer Moles

Surinder Kumar Mishra, alias Munna Mishra, was born in Duliajan in Dibrugarh district to a lower-middle-class family that had migrated from Uttar Pradesh in the early 1960s. He graduated from the Biswanath College of Agriculture after passing out from Central School in his home town, where he was known for being a good sportsman and passionate debater.[88] He first came in contact with ULFA functionaries at Biswanath when he was still a student, but it seems that the meeting had a lasting impression on him. A couple of meetings with members of the outfit convinced him that his destiny lay in being a rebel fighting age-old injustices than as an agricultural scientist. By the end of 1995, he had already joined ULFA and completed his training at a camp in Bhutan.[89]

Munna's enrolment did cause a flutter among a few senior functionaries for a while, as they were unable to fathom what motivated him to take the plunge into ULFA. There were other people from the Hindi-speaking and Bengali communities who had assisted the outfit in a variety of ways, especially in gathering funds, during the late 1980s. A small section from these communities had been associated with the schemes launched by the ULFA-backed Jatiya Unnayan Parishad in the late 1980s. In Sadiya, Suresh Modi, who belonged to a Hindi-speaking community, was allegedly beaten to death by the security forces on suspicion of being an ULFA functionary.[90] But instances of recruitment of non-Assamese functionaries like Munna were very few.

Munna's conduct made him stand out from the crowd from the time he landed at the camp in Bhutan. He was of medium height and build and sported a thin beard. He occasionally broached philosophical topics and spoke about well-known writers like Khalil Gibran, whom his colleagues had never heard of.[91] The leaders were clearly impressed. Munna began to be trusted all the more after his brother was gunned down in Duliajan by government-sponsored secret killers who were unaware of his role as a spy in ULFA. It wasn't long before he was selected for advanced training in Pakistan after completing the course in Bhutan.[92] Subsequently, he was tasked with getting settled in Guwahati for specific operations against high-profile targets.[93]

In Guwahati, Munna operated as a businessman from a rented accommodation in a locality inhabited mostly by Hindi-speaking residents. His performance was considered outstanding as some of his work had resulted in abductions that yielded the outfit hefty sums of money or in extortions from wealthy businessmen who had not been spotted earlier.[94] Then, sometime in the second half of 1996, he disappeared for almost four months while on a journey to Nagaon to contact a few ULFA functionaries for an operation assigned to him by the general headquarters. The leaders assumed that he might have been apprehended and shot dead by the security forces. But he surfaced in Bhutan with a convincing explanation—he had indeed been apprehended at Nagaon but had somehow managed to escape from police custody.[95] It was during this time that his suggestion for a specialized squad contributed towards fine-tuning of the concept of Enigma. His work was part of a plan to infiltrate the organization further and reach the top leaders.[96]

Almost two years later, after Munna's role had been unravelled, a section of the leadership believed that he was converted into a mole after being blackmailed by a police officer in Nagaon. It is true that he was apprehended and brought to Guwahati in 1996 and handed over to another senior officer who was to assume a lead role in the infamous secret killings two years later in Assam.[97] Munna was brainwashed continuously for over two months and threatened with incarceration in jail for the rest of his life if he did not fall in line. He finally agreed to execute the lethal plan suggested to him and struck a deal with the officer.[98]

Munna would embark upon the mission with the precondition that he would withdraw if the situation warranted and after that would be given a job in a government department in New Delhi.

The officer agreed and briefed him about the objectives he would have to fulfil—gathering as much information about the camps in Bhutan as possible, the outfit's hideouts in the towns and cities, the networks that ensured the flow of funds and efforts to reach Bangladesh for assassination attempts on the leaders. No time frame was fixed for the execution of these tasks.[99]

Meanwhile, at the camp in Bhutan, Munna was tasked to train the first two batches of Enigma, which he successfully completed within six months. He instructed many among them to get settled in different towns, mostly as petty traders and daily wagers.[100] Subsequently, he was stationed in Guwahati for a few months by the leadership for better coordination among the Enigma functionaries who were scattered in different parts of the valley. And this was what Munna had been waiting for to fulfil part of his mission. It is estimated that during this period he killed at least fifteen functionaries, including three women and two senior functionaries, in collusion with the police. Another woman succeeded in escaping from his clutches, but not before being raped by Munna for many days.[101]

The ULFA leaders began to feel suspicious about Munna when a senior functionary in Bhutan who had a high-level source in the police headquarters was tipped off about his motives.[102] There were more episodes in the next four months providing further evidence of Munna's plans. A senior functionary of ULFA, Dhristi Rajkhowa, had got in touch with Munna in Guwahati as he wanted to halt for a night in the city. Rajkhowa was taken to a rented house on the outskirts of the city, but he decided to shift to another location after Munna had left. At night, the house was raided by the police. It was a pattern that repeated weeks later in the case of another functionary, Ashim Dutta, who too had a narrow escape.[103] The leaders knew that Munna would never turn up at the general headquarters if ordered to do so. At the same time, he might put in efforts to prove that he was not a mole by undertaking risky missions. So it was decided to station him in Shillong for a few months and task him with ferrying weapons from the Bangladesh border.[104]

According to the plan, Munna would receive a consignment of six AK-47 rifles from an ULFA functionary along the India-Bangladesh border in Karimganj and then hand them over to the central zone functionaries at Nagaon. Another senior functionary was tasked to collaborate with him for execution of the assignment. The weapons were fetched and the vehicle was on its way to Nagaon when Munna disembarked after Shillong was crossed, never to be seen again. Munna offered his version of the incident to the leaders over the phone, but they had already made up their minds to punish him and bring an end to his association with the organization. He was told to proceed to Dhaka, supposedly because Paresh wanted to engage him in an operation for fetching weapons and explosives from another country.[105]

ULFA also wanted to detain him in Dhaka and then put him on trial at the camp in Satcherri.[106] Munna's plan was to try and pull off the most important component of his mission—to assassinate Paresh or any top leader of the outfit. He discussed the plot with the senior police officer who activated a few contacts in Dhaka after getting in touch with R&AW. Munna was tasked to contact these people after gathering details of Paresh's residence and movements.[107] After a date was fixed for his arrival at the border in Meghalaya's Garo Hills, two ULFA functionaries were sent from Dhaka to receive him, but he was nowhere to be traced. It is likely that Munna might have gauged the outfit's plan and decided to chart an alternative path to reach Dhaka.[108] Paresh received information from Bangladesh Rifles (BDR) that he did cross the border surreptitiously and was headed for Dhaka. But Munna never reached Dhaka. Instead, there was a rumour among the ULFA leadership that he was putting in serious efforts to send a pistol to a R&AW agent in the city linked to the underworld for assassinating Paresh.[109] The subsequent developments also sent ULFA into a tizzy.

A week later, Paresh was informed by a government official in Bangladesh that Munna had been apprehended in Bangladesh but the authorities were compelled to release him after a senior official from the Indian High Commission intervened.[110] And, almost a month later, he surfaced at Assam House in Shillong, where he was found making attempts with a group of SULFA cadres to nab ULFA functionaries and coerce them to work for Assam police's Special Branch. Even as Munna continued with the operations in Shillong, an Assam police team nabbed him and five other SULFA activists from the city, only for them to be released a few hours later. The officer who had issued the order was ignorant about Munna's actual role.[111] ULFA failed to put him on trial as he soon shifted to New Delhi to work for an intelligence agency.[112]

Nothing was heard of Munna again until 2011, when he got in touch with a SULFA activist, Prabin Das, in Guwahati. Das had narrowly escaped from a squad of SULFA activists who were operating at the behest of some police officers (who came to called `secret killers') many years earlier. He was in dire financial straits and making efforts to make both ends meet. So he was excited when Munna offered him a job at Siliguri with a high salary, which meant working for an intelligence agency. But it was not the Special Branch this time around but a central agency, and the tasks also did not entail engaging in anti-ULFA operations. Das shifted to Siliguri, where Munna had also settled for the new assignment. Trouble came knocking once again after a year, when Munna was picked up by the police for interrogation in a case of abduction and disappearance of a well-known Indian businessman in Nepal who was also the brother-in-law of a Bollywood superstar![113] Munna confessed to blackmailing and murdering the businessman. He was convicted with life-term imprisonment and incarcerated at the Siliguri jail. Das was also arrested and convicted for being an accomplice in the crime.[114]

Munna's chapter drew to a close, but there was a spin-off incident that unfolded a year ahead of his departure from Assam in 2000. He came into contact with an ULFA functionary named Dalim who was stationed at Tezpur after completing training for Enigma in Bhutan. Dalim was introduced to the senior police officer who brainwashed him with the same tactics as had been used with Munna to become a mole in ULFA.[115] Dalim was trained as a medic for a month and was equipped with a huge quantity of medicines and instructed to return to the general headquarters under the plea that his life was under threat in Tezpur. He did as told, and his explanation for his return was convincing to the ULFA commanders in Bhutan. But Dalim knew that an attempt to assassinate the senior functionaries at the camp would be suicidal as there would be no chance to escape. It would have to be executed at a safer location, outside the camp. The opportunity came a couple of months later when he was included in a sixty-member squad for Operation Saraighat to blow up a CRPF camp in Barpeta. The assignment, to be led by deputy commander Raju Baruah, necessitated a trek through the hills about 100 km west of the general headquarters.[116]

Dalim's conduct had aroused the suspicion of Baruah on the first evening of the trek, when he tried to convince the other members in the team to take anti-malarial injections. In the evening on the fourth day, the squad reached a village near the CRPF camp at Bhuyanpara, where it halted. The squad decided to lay an ambush on the next day instead of storming the camp. The ambush was cancelled after CRPF personnel were tipped off by their informers about the presence of ULFA functionaries in the village. The village was surrounded, resulting in a gun fight that went on for almost three hours without any casualties. The ULFA squad retreated deep into the jungle to a safe zone for the night.[117]

At the hideout, Dalim sprang a surprise with a complaint that he was unwell and requested permission to return to the general headquarters. He was allowed to hit the return trail in a group of nine functionaries, as Baruah was convinced that his presence in the group could be harmful. The first halt of the group was at a village near Nganglam, where Dalim succeeded in pouring sedatives into the food meant for the functionaries. At night, he shot six of them who were sleeping in the same hut and decamped with their rifles with another functionary, Champak, whom he had succeeded in brainwashing. Baruah dashed to the village the next day after receiving the message on radio from the functionaries sleeping in the adjacent hut who were able to escape from being targeted by Dalim. However, Dalim did not live long to reap the success of his operation. Even as he crossed the border, he was shot dead by CRPF personnel who mistook him for a rebel armed with weapons. Champak was saved from the hail of bullets after he ducked for cover. He surrendered before the police at Barpeta within a couple of days.[118]

Dalim was dead, but he had succeeded in achieving for the security forces the larger objective of spawning an ambience of suspicion at the ULFA camps in Bhutan.[119] The distrust at the camps seems to have been reinforced also by the activities of a group of SULFA activists who had joined hands with a section of the police and army to carry out what came to be called secret killings. The degree of interaction among the functionaries was reduced and any slight aberration in the conduct of anybody in the camp was enough for him to be suspected as a mole. Munna and Dalim were cogs in a killing machine deviously engineered as a policy to counter ULFA. It was a tactic that had borne results in Punjab against the terrorist movement. The conditions in Assam were perceived to be the same, where a similar experiment could be repeated with success.

An Eye for an Eye

Sometime in mid-1999, ULFA functionary Prabin Das was handcuffed and shoved into the rear of a Maruti van after being picked up from the outskirts of Guwahati by a squad led by a police officer nicknamed 'Kanphuli'.[120] Das was to be taken to an apartment in the heart of the city where a group of SULFA activists lived. Das knew that his end was near, for he had heard harrowing tales about how victims were sometimes hacked and then shot dead by the gang before being buried in the jungles. Fortunately for him, he managed to escape from the parking lot of the apartment when the police personnel had gone upstairs to inform the SULFA activists about the arrival of a new victim. For some reason, there were no guards at the gate when the vehicle was parked in the premises. Das was able to break his handcuffs at a friend's residence in a neighbouring locality where he put up for the night. He left Guwahati the next day to a safer destination across the Brahmaputra, returning almost a year later when the killings were halted. He was among the very few who had been able to escape from the clutches of the secret killers.[121] Most of the people on their hit list were exterminated in meticulous operations.[122]

The term 'secret killings' gained currency in Assam in the late 1990s. They went on for almost two years till about mid-2000; they consisted of unidentified assailants murdering relatives and associates of prominent ULFA functionaries, linkmen of the outfit and surrendered functionaries perceived to have been engaged with the outfit. The phenomenon had its origins during the previous regime of the Congress when a section of SULFA was co-opted by the security forces in counter-insurgency operations to combat ULFA. They were mostly utilized as informers to identify the rebel cadres, their hideouts and networks and to entice them to surrender. Information received by the security forces from them were occasionally made use of to exterminate linkmen, but the operations were erratic and less organized.[123] Very rarely were family members of ULFA functionaries targeted, not even when a bloody feud was on between the under- and over-ground factions after the first ULFA split in 1992. Among the unusual incidents was the murder of Paresh's brother, Dinesh Baruah, two days after he was reported missing from his home at Dibrugarh's Jeraigaon.[124]

The second phase of secret killings that began in the late 1990s were preceded by some important developments that seemed to have convinced the government to make them part of the policy for countering insurgency in the state. ULFA's campaign against the AGP was a reason for the party's dismal performance in the mid-term Lok Sabha polls in 1998. The party failed to secure even a single seat, even as the Congress won ten of the total of fourteen in the state. The AGP leadership, and especially Chief Minister Mahanta, were desperate for effective strategies that could check ULFA from causing further harm to the party. The creation of a Unified Command notwithstanding, 1997 had been one of the worst years for Assam in terms of insurgency-related incidents. As many as 213 civilians were killed by militants in a total of 400 incidents that included extortions and abductions, in which ULFA was involved in 231 cases.[125]

To cope with the situation, some police officers began toying with the idea of systematically involving a larger section of the SULFA in counter-insurgency operations. The name of former Punjab super-cop K.P.S Gill, who was earlier posted in Assam, had cropped up in several media reports and publications as the person who had brainwashed these officers into carrying out extra-judicial killings in the same manner as had been done in Punjab. Gill had been accused of active involvement in the preparation of a blueprint to raise a squad of secret killers to eliminate the kith and kin of ULFA activists and sympathizers.[126] These speculations surfaced after Gill's visit to Assam in mid-1997 as president of the Indian Hockey Federation to promote the sport, when he also had meetings with a few police officers in Guwahati.[127] However, he had not only denied his role in framing the killer doctrine in Assam but also refuted allegations that he had employed similar tactics to eliminate terrorists in Punjab.[128]

Whatever might have been Gill's role in the secret killings, the governments both at the state and Centre were certainly not averse to implement the policy in Assam.[129] Intelligence reports continued to portray a grim picture of ULFA's resolve to continue with its campaign and extortions.[130] The government's plan was to achieve multiple objectives with the secret killings—deliver a message to

ULFA that there would be fierce retaliation to its actions, strike terror in the hearts of sympathizers and compel them to stay aloof from the outfit. The operation was also aimed at eliminating the linkmen who assisted the outfit with information and identification of sources of funds and recruits.[131] The green signal from the top prompted an inspector general who had been fervently making a case for such tactics to form a core team of six trigger-happy officers, including sub-inspectors, inspectors and an additional superintendent of police.[132] Even as efforts were on to put in place a system for implementation of the lethal plan came an incident that made the task hugely easier for the group.

On 10 August 1998, Dibrugarh-based SULFA activist Tapan Dutta was shot dead along with his associate Madhurjya Mahanta in Guwahati by ULFA. Dutta and his group were being watched by ULFA for quite some time for their alleged role in activities perceived to have harmed ULFA. However, the order to gun him down came as a surprise to many senior functionaries in ULFA, who were unable to fathom why the decision had been arrived at by a section of its leaders.[133] Incidentally, there were several meetings among the senior functionaries of ULFA after Gill's visit to Guwahati. In Sivasagar, a list was compiled as well of all all the policemen and persons among the police and SULFA activists who could be engaged in the secret killings and their consequences for the organization evaluated. While some were in favour of adopting the same 'secret killing' tactics against those on the list, the majority view was against that since ULFA was a revolutionary outfit and not a bunch of killers.[134] The consensus was to desist from any activity that could trigger a replay of the conflict with SULFA in the early 1990s. Moreover, the SULFA numbers were soaring with surrenders every year, some of them genuine and some occasionally faked by the government.[135]

Dutta's killing had the instant effect of galvanizing a group of the SULFA into action against ULFA. They were scared, convinced that sooner or later they would be targeted for walking out of the outfit. It made perfect sense to them to join hands with the police and army for a counter-attack as that could entail several benefits for them.[136] But first, a retaliatory strike was immediately called for to deliver a stern message to ULFA that its actions would provoke a severe reaction in future. So, on the same night, a squad of SULFA members, their faces wrapped in black cloth, descended on the house of ULFA publicity secretary Mithinga Daimary at Barama, 80 km west of Guwahati, and shot dead his mother, sister, brother and sister-in-law. Hours later, in the morning, ULFA chairman Rajkhowa's elder brother, Dimba Rajkonwar, who was an employee of Assam State Transport Corporation, was gunned down in Dibrugarh. The police in these districts were informed in advance so as to prevent any action that could throw a spanner in the operations.[137] The entire strategy could suffer a setback if any SULFA activist were to be apprehended for involvement in these acts. In due course, the words 'lima tango' (a message that there would be an operation by the gang of secret killers and to avoid any action by the district police on the squad) were sent on wireless to police officers to denote an impending operation.[138]

The success of these operations prompted the police team and SULFA to expedite the creation of a larger apparatus to cover the affected districts. Three groups of different people were soon identified to continue the operations until the end of the AGP regime. Around twenty SULFA activists who were mostly close associates of the core group were chosen from Guwahati, Nalbari, Dibrugarh and Sivasagar for taking part in all the operations. Another group of surrendered cadres from a rural background, who had been recruited earlier into the police, was attached as escort to the SULFA activists. And, finally, a wide network was created to garner information on the activities of ULFA functionaries and their sympathizers. Eventually, a few among them were also engaged in killings, as were some police officials beyond the core group whose names remained shielded from the public domain. As part of the deal, it was agreed that the SULFA squad would be allocated government contracts in some departments, permitted to run syndicates and impose illegal taxes on trucks carrying goods from other states into Assam.[139]

Concurrent with these preparations were the overtures from some army officers to the police and these groups to get attached with the killer squad. Their rationale for unleashing terror in Assam using extrajudicial methods was in sync with that of the police officers and the SULFA group. A brigadier hailing from a north Indian state was keen not to miss the opportunity to exterminate people who were sympathetic to the ULFA cause. He assumed the lead role in collaborating with the SULFA team in the killings. And, similar to the police squad, the brigadier also gathered a small group of army officers who were loyal to him and would execute his orders.[140]

Sometimes the interactions between the police and the army were facilitated by a middleman who was neither a SULFA activist nor a government employee. A local daily had flashed his name as being one of the masterminds of the secret killings, which was not true. He was no more than a crank based in Guwahati who nurtured ambitions of becoming a secret agent and chief of R&AW after being heavily influenced by James Bond movies.[141]

What happened during the next two years were killings at regular intervals, some of which were immediate reactions against operations of the ULFA. On 7–8 March 1999, as many as seven people were gunned down after ULFA hurled a grenade at an apartment in Guwahati where some members of the core SULFA group lived. Babul Ingti, who tossed the grenade, was shot dead within a week, but the secret killers showed no mercy to his aged parents and sister either. In the same episode, the grandparents of another ULFA functionary, Nirmal Boro, were shot dead in the outskirts of Guwahati, as well as the parents of Dhristi Rajkhowa at Goalpara. In later incidents, brother of ULFA foreign secretary Shashadhar Choudhury and brother-in-law of deputy commander Raju Baruah fell victims at their residences in Nalbari. Some incidents sparked brief agitations, as happened in Nalbari after the killing of Jyotish Sarma, who was the brother-in-law of ULFA functionary Subhash Sarma. Sarma was targeted after ULFA gunned down a SULFA activist, Avinash Bordoloi, for being part of the secret killers' gang.

As the killings continued, differences cropped up among the different factions of the secret killers. A clash was averted by the intervention of the police officers who were part of the covert project. The SULFA group from western Assam expressed discontent over what it alleged as 'preferential treatment' to the gang from the eastern districts by the government. By mid-1999, the former group shifted from their common residence at an apartment on R.G. Baruah Road in Guwahati to another location at Beltola, from where they continued to operate. Earlier, the group's attempt to occupy some flats at an apartment in the city's upmarket Uzan Bazar failed after local residents vehemently opposed their presence in the locality.[142]

Secret Killers Run Amok

The murders were one aspect of the secret killers' wide gamut of illicit activities. They were also granted the licence to make as much money as possible by every means possible. Besides the illegal taxes imposed on the trucks and goods coming into the state, many government departments were compelled to dole out a percentage of their budgetary allocations to the SULFA. The racket received a boost with the patronage of some politicians, ministers and government officials who received a cut from the extortions.[143] For the police and army officers involved in the killings, it meant grabbing land, accumulating ill-gotten wealth and gratifying all their desires. One case that had hogged the media limelight for several days was a sensational triple murder of SULFA activists, allegedly by Major Jamir Ahmed Khan in Dibrugarh. Khan had seized a few crore of rupees from an ULFA hideout with their assistance but he did not want to share the booty with them.[144] Years later, an army court of inquiry found his 'possible involvement' in the crime and he faced trial in a civilian court in a case registered at a police station in Dibrugarh.[145]

Most of the men in uniform engaged in the killings were smarter and luckier than Khan. Topping the list was the additional superintendent of police in the killer squad who amassed the maximum wealth, mostly in terms of the prime land he acquired in Guwahati and other districts through a variety of tactics. There were places in the city, such as the 10 and 4 Assam Police Battalions at Kahilipara, where the victims were sometimes interned before being killed.[146] Occasionally, the officer would get drunk before posing the last question to the victims: 'What is your last wish?' Invariably, the victims would frantically plead for mercy, which was of no consequence. The decision to shoot them dead had already been taken. There were a few instances when some of the victims were set free with a warning to keep their mouths shut due to interventions by politicians or senior officers.[147]

The lower-ranking officers in the killer group were encouraged to follow in the footsteps of the additional superintendent. Very soon, they also acquired plots of land and hefty sums of cash extorted from businessmen and victims who were identified as being close to ULFA and threatened with death. One member among them, known to be a sexual pervert, went a step further by undertaking two contract killings, one for a businessman who wanted a SULFA activist exterminated and the other for a politician who wished to get rid of a man who had been stalking his wife for many months.[148]

However, as the operations continued, the ULFA leadership decided to retaliate by targeting some AGP ministers and their relatives to deliver the message that the 'secret killings' policy must be buried at the earliest. So, after days of planning, an IED was blasted in Nalbari, which killed minister of public works department and forests, Nagen Sarma, along with four others.

Agriculture Minister Chandra Mohan Patowary's brother was gunned down and an attempt was made on the life of a relative of the health minister, Kamala Kalita. The party was jolted when a faction within the party made an ardent case for an immediate end to the policy. But there was also a group, including some ministers, which believed that its continuation would deliver a body blow to ULFA, from which it would never be able to recover.[149] With the government showing no signs of relenting, ULFA issued a press release claiming that an agreement had been reached with the AGP ahead of the assembly polls—that the issue of Assam's self-determination would be raised in the state assembly—following a series of meetings between the senior leaders of the two groups. It followed this up with an ultimatum to the government that the killings must come to an end.[150]

The gang of secret killers only changed their modus operandi at some places by focusing more on abductions than on barging into their victims' residences in the dead of night. Among the many people who disappeared were some who were neither functionaries nor linkmen of ULFA. The information received by the squad from their informers was considered gospel truth and was never verified.[151] A much-discussed case was one from the Fatasil-Ambari area of Guwahati, where a priest vanished without a trace after being abducted on the same suspicion. He was believed to have been chopped into pieces at Chandrapur near the city and buried in the jungles.[152] One of the most inhumane operations happened in Moran in the eastern district of Dibrugarh, when the killers exterminated farmer Uma Kanta Gogoi's entire family, including his wife and three children, with bombs, accusing them of being ULFA sympathizers. The dreaded SULFA activist who led the operation was even offered bodyguards by the government. He was able to duck for cover until 2011, when he fell a victim to ULFA's bullets.[153]

Predictably, public opinion was swinging drastically against the government, as increasing evidence of its involvement in the secret killings came to light. As it appeared, the ministers who had advocated the murders were fast losing control of the killer group, which operated with impunity and without any fear of being prosecuted. Some junior officers who were against the killings boldly defied the orders of the inspector general who headed the killer squad. Once, a superintendent of police warned the inspector general that his entire gang would be gunned down if it were to get involved in any killings in the district under his control. But the majority of the officers preferred to turn a blind eye to the operations and agreed to fall in line with the policy.[154]

All the First Information Reports (FIR) registered at the police stations against the secret killings were put in cold storage, never to be probed.[155] Public anger was aggravated by the miraculous tales of escape of some victims, which found wide publicity in the vernacular media. Among the bigwigs who had a narrow brush with the gang was former editor of *Asomiya Pratidin*, Ajit Kumar Bhuyan, who had been arrested earlier and was later to be elected to the Rajya Sabha as an independent candidate.[156] The case of an AJYCP activist, Ananta Kalita, was the most damaging for the government. His chilling account of his escape from the clutches of the killer squad also featured in the international media and in reports compiled by some global organizations.[157] Kalita's case established beyond doubt that a large segment of the police apparatus was engaged in the clandestine scheme.

Kalita was picked up from his residence at Hajo on the night of 16 September 1999 by unidentified armed men. He was kept for two days at the barracks of the 10 Assam Police Battalion in Guwahati, where he was tortured and quizzed about the activities of ULFA. Two days later he was taken to Jorabat on the outskirts of the city, where he was shot in the head and pushed down the slope of a hill. The bullet reportedly passed through his cheeks. He regained consciousness at around 4 a.m. and climbed up the hill to the highway, from where he was taken in a truck to the AJYCP office in Maligaon. Strong protests erupted, compelling the government to order a judicial probe, which never made any headway. The Assam Human Rights Commission asked for a report from the police, but it denied any involvement in the incident.[158]

Kalita's escape came on the heels of a sensational report in *The Telegraph* detailing the discovery of a severed head and leg at Hudompur Dokhola on the banks of the Brahmaputra near Guwahati. This was vigorously followed up by all the dailies. Later, it emerged that the victim was senior ULFA functionary Parameswar Das who was picked up by the secret killers and hacked to death.[159] The pattern was found repeated in the case of many people who had gone missing over the past few months in Kamrup and Nalbari.[160] Thereafter, from around mid-1999, more events unfolded, convincing the AGP leadership that measures to undo the damage caused by the killings were called for. Governor S.K. Sinha spoke to Chief Minister Mahanta making a case for an immediate end to the policy after more dead bodies were recovered from different regions of the state.[161]

The killings somewhat came down after the commandos attached to the SULFA group as escorts were replaced with police personnel. Some SULFA activists were arrested, but the kingpins remained untouched.[162] Cases of missing persons continued to be reported sporadically until the constitution of a commission of enquiry under Justice Safiqul Haque just a few months ahead of the assembly polls. The commission's failure to bring the probe to a logical conclusion was no surprise. But its constitution was an indication that the government had changed its mind on the policy of secret killings. It was time for the leaders of the SULFA squad to escape from Guwahati. The illegal syndicates they had created in Guwahati were taken over by another gang of SULFA which was not involved in the killings. But many of their businesses in the eastern region remained intact as there was none to challenge them.[163]

Whatever was left to uproot the policy of secret killings in Assam was done by the Congress government after being elected to power in the assembly polls in mid-2001. The killings became a major issue in the elections, which the Congress was successfully able to make use of to trounce the AGP. The pre-poll pact between the AGP and the BJP made it easier for the Congress to convince the electorate that the secret killings had the blessings of both parties. That SULFA would have to be kept under check was reinforced by another sensational episode that happened within a month of the new government assuming power, when an internecine clash among two SULFA factions at Moran Polo Club in Dibrugarh left fourteen dead and several injured.[164] Within no time the inspector general and the other police officers in the killer squad were transferred to insipid posts with a warning to refrain from such activities in the future.

However, as it turned out, the Congress government's abhorrence for the secret killings never went beyond transfer of the tainted officers. Two commissions appointed by the government to probe the episode failed to reach any logical conclusion—the Justice (Retd) Meera Sarma Commission never received funds and staff to execute its mandate, while the report compiled by the Justice (Retd) Jogendranath Sarma Commission was not accepted by the government.[165] Chief minister Tarun Gogoi was well aware that ULFA was still a force to reckon with since all its bases in the neighbouring countries were intact. The battle would have to continue with the police at the vanguard, and nothing was to be done that would demoralize the force. He was not in favour of the AGP's policy of entrusting the army with the upper hand in counter-insurgency operations in the state.[166]

The government was certainly glad when the Justice (Retd) K.N. Saikia Commission submitted a report on the secret killings in 2007 without identifying the killers, which was despite the fact that all the suspected SULFA activists, police personnel and former chief minister, Mahanta, were quizzed. As per its recommendations, the government decided to launch its own investigation into eleven cases, besides awarding a compensation of Rs 3 lakh to each of the victim's families. And years later, in 2018, the Gauhati High Court rejected the Saikia Commission's report on the ground that it was not 'valid'. The court also absolved Mahanta of any involvement in the secret killings.

Nonetheless, the conclusions arrived at by the last commission, which probed thirty-five cases, confirmed the earlier suspicions about the involvement of the police and army with the SULFA in the killings. However, some of its findings have also raised doubts among some sections as to whether the commission was actually competent to carry out the probe. For instance, it said the army was 'involved everywhere', whereas it was the police that was involved in the majority of the cases.[167] Then, it concluded that the modus operandi of the killers was to persuade the relatives of ULFA functionaries to convince them to surrender and they were gunned down only when they failed to do so.[168] Incidentally, an overwhelming majority of the victims never had any inkling that they would be targeted by the secret killers. So, the commission's conclusion that the killers persuaded some of the victims' relatives is extremely doubtful.[169]

In the end, it emerged that around 150 people were murdered by the secret killers in Assam.[170] The numbers were small compared with the figures in Punjab, but the impact was huge, though not immediately discernible.[171] The AGP leadership's assumption that the strategy would fulfil the twin objectives of delivering a decisive blow to ULFA and securing its own future proved to be only partially correct. The secret killings dealt as much of a lethal punch to the AGP as it did to ULFA, with long-term consequences. The party leadership failed to realize that a replication of counter-insurgency tactics that had borne results in a far-off state under different social and economic conditions could have very different implications in Assam. AGP's support base among a large chunk in the Assamese heartland was lost forever, never to be revived. The centrifugal tendencies in the party which had been dormant for a long time, were again entrenched, triggering irreversible consequences. Chief minister Mahanta's expulsion from the party after a couple of years was followed by a split that further weakened the party. For ULFA, however, the devastating impact of the killings was in addition to another crisis that had been silently brewing in the organization for quite some time.

'Shaken, Not Stirred'

Concurrent with the secret killings in Assam were other episodes that unfolded in a sequence to produce multiple debilitating effects on ULFA. Some of them were the consequence of deliberate efforts being made by the government to win the battle against the rebels. And there were incidents that occurred thousands of kilometres away on issues far removed from militancy, but they certainly impacted the situation in Assam in a manner that was only favourable to the government. Added to this were ULFA's systemic flaws, spawning obstacles in the implementation of pragmatic polices by the outfit for coming to grips with the crisis.

Besides the secret killers, there was another category of rebels, belonging to the Bodoland Liberation Tigers (BLT), who were engaged by the security forces intermittently in operations against ULFA and NDFB. Towards the fag end of the 1990s, BLT had sent feelers for a negotiated settlement, which was accepted by the government. As it usually happens in a peace process, an informal ceasefire was firmed up between the two sides without delay, enabling the security forces to make use of a section of the rebels in operations against the active rebel groups, ULFA and NDFB. This continued almost till the accord with BLT was clinched in 2003.[172]

Besides these operations that remained shielded from the public glare was the revamp that Assam police had undergone since the mid-1990s for combating militancy. A three-pronged strategy was adopted by inspector general N. Ramachandran who headed the Special Branch: creation of an intelligence battalion and widening of the network of informers, digitization of records and devising of training modules with the engagement of the central intelligence agencies.[173] Small teams were formed, including the Special Operations Unit, for specific tasks with deadlines. Similarly, a commando battalion, trained in Punjab, was established, and squads were attached with the regular battalions across the valley. Assault and self-loading rifles in large numbers were made available to the police after the approval of the home ministry, which gradually replaced the vintage .303 rifle.[174]

Around the same time, surveillance was rendered easier with the new interceptor device acquired by the police and army after being put on trial for a month at Hashimara in north Bengal. Unlike the previous version, the new equipment was able to track the location of anyone placing a phone call and it worked with cellular phones too.[175] Most of the rebel outfits were delighted when cellular phone services began in Assam in 1998. Faster transmission of information enabled rapid collection of funds and precise execution of operations for a few months.[176] The advantage was short-lived. The task of identifying their locations and associates became much easier for the security agencies with the advent of the cellular phone. Realizing the danger, ULFA issued instructions to functionaries in the valley to use the device minimally and to evolve codes while delivering messages. But enough damage had already been done.[177]

Amid these developments was the unexpected Kargil War in mid-1999, triggering a nationalist fervour across the state at the same time that public opinion was against the government for the secret killings. Three soldiers from Assam, captain Jintu Gogoi, Uddhab Das and Nandchand Sinha became martyrs in the war. Their heroic deeds in the operations against the Pakistani infiltrators at Kargil were the stuff of stories on the front page of all dailies in the state for many consecutive days. But in an act that betrayed total disregard for the popular sentiment, ULFA issued an appeal exhorting all Assamese personnel employed in the Indian army to refrain from taking part in the war, saying that Kashmir had been illegally occupied by India.

ULFA's appeal had the reverse effect of what was intended. There were reports of rebel functionaries returning to the mainstream and some of them being lynched at some places in the state when the war was on. For ULFA, the war was an opportunity to demonstrate its loyalty towards Pakistan's ISI, on whom it had become dependent for assistance, including funds. There were ample indications that Paresh called up many people for information on the army's positions in the Northeast during the war. The outfit also triggered three blasts in north Bengal, halting the movement of trains for a day.[178]

Consequently, by the latter half of 1999, a large part of ULFA's network had been ruptured in the valley. More than 5,000 cadres surrendered between 1997 and 2001, and the security forces, as part of counter-insurgency operations, gunned down 984 rebels, some of whom were functionaries from other outfits too.[179] Besides the linkmen and associates who were killed, there was also a section that agreed to dissociate itself from ULFA and NDFB and work as informers for the police.[180] These were the people who had actively assisted the outfit with providing hideouts, supplying information on potential sources of funds and recruits, and also sometimes gathering funds for a commission. Then, the murder of relatives of rebel functionaries was a huge discouragement for the potential recruits. The fallout was an inhospitable situation for ULFA beyond its camps and hideouts in the neighbouring countries and states. The leadership was compelled to instruct all functionaries to hit the trail to the camps for safety.[181]

Funds for the camps almost came to a stop, with the result that a severe financial crisis gripped the organization. More affected were the camps in Bhutan, as there were more cadres and families there than either in Myanmar or Bangladesh.[182] On a couple of occasions, arrangements were made by Paresh to transfer cash to the camps, but it was hardly enough to stave off the funds crisis for very long. The expenses in Bhutan were covered by the funds gathered in Guwahati and western Assam where the secret killers had been most active. As the operations against ULFA intensified, a large sum that had been gathered by some linkmen was siphoned away, never to be deposited. There were a few cases of middle-rung functionaries who preferred to surrender after extorting money from traders instead of heading back to Bhutan.[183]

This crisis was in addition to the escalating confusion in ULFA following the creation of zones and battalions that replaced the earlier district committees. The change entailed the transfer of functionaries to regions far away from their home terrain; also, their postings in distant locations triggered conflicts between them and the locals of those areas who were indirectly associated with the outfit.[184] The ULFA functionaries were ignorant of the ground realities in the localities where they were posted. More grave was the gulf that emerged between the armed wing and the other departments in the organization. The army took orders only from the general headquarters and not from the central executive council, as envisaged earlier during the general council in Bhutan.[185] This was in sharp contrast to the previous norm, under which the army would implement decisions arrived at by the district committees headed by presidents.

A large chunk of the armed cadres was young and non-committed and had been recruited without any background checks. The training of three months was inadequate to teach them the techniques of retaining local support while remaining shielded from the enemy. The situation was acute in the east zone, which covered five districts, including Dibrugarh, where more than fifty cadres were killed by the security forces in the late 1990s.[186] So, most of the functionaries were instructed to shift to safer regions in neighbouring Arunachal Pradesh and to the 28 Battalion camp in Myanmar. The resulting vacuum in the eastern zone continued until almost early 2001, when ULFA's recruitment started and its operations were intensified.[187]

Internal squabbles in ULFA were not confined to the districts. Factionalism reared its ugly head at the general headquarters in Bhutan following serious differences between deputy commander

Raju Baruah and staff officer Lohit Deuri. Many functionaries were upset with Deuri for the failed mission to transport weapons from China through Haa Valley. They felt the operation was scuttled because of his imprudent conduct while surveying the border region, which had alerted the Indian government. At a later stage, Deuri rented a house near the town of Samdrup Jongkhar, where he would often stay for long durations, raising the suspicion of the senior inmates in the camp. Paresh sought to bridge the gulf between them, but it was too late. Deuri had already decided to surrender, which he did by getting in touch with the Special Branch after reaching Siliguri. Later, he would reveal that he was also upset with the high command for not appointing him the deputy commander-in-chief, a post that had been given to Paresh for a long time.[188]

Paresh, in particular, was crestfallen with Deuri's exit.[189] After the 1992 split, his surrender was the first among the top functionaries. Paresh was also concerned that Deuri's absence could mean a more dominating role for Baruah in the general headquarters—which he did not like.[190] Moreover, the leadership was already extremely jittery about the continuing crisis as there was no possibility of an immediate turnaround of the situation in Assam. In all likelihood, the BJP-led coalition government which had swept to power in the general elections after the Kargil War would support the hardline approach of the AGP government for defeating militancy in the state. ULFA had called for a boycott of the general elections, but it went largely unheeded with the turnout being a high 70 per cent.[191]

Nonetheless, the ULFA high command firmed up vital decisions to be executed over the next year and a half. The battalions were to be rejuvenated for an all-out campaign against the AGP ahead of the assembly polls scheduled for mid-2001.[192] A network of associates would have to be created anew for funds, and for operations to be successful. Some senior functionaries who had completed the refresher and mandatory military courses in Bhutan were instructed to return to their respective areas for the task.[193] Second, covert support would be extended to the Congress, but with the condition that the policies unleashed by the AGP would be abandoned if it were to win the elections.[194] Some sort of an agreement was arrived at between Paresh and some Congress leaders about three months ahead of the elections. Senior Congress leaders in Assam assured the outfit that the secret killings would be brought to an end, the killers compelled to shift to other locations and efforts made to resolve the conflict between Assam and India.[195]

And, finally, ULFA resolved to target the Hindi-speaking communities in the state, which was a trend that was to be repeated intermittently till 2008. ULFA knew that the ramifications of attacks on the Hindi-speaking communities would be felt across the country. The BJP, especially, would be rattled, since its support base was primarily in the Hindi-speaking states of the country. Many local dailies and analysts opined that the killings of Hindi speakers were carried out by ULFA at the behest of Bangladesh's DGFI to foment internal strife in India.[196] The role of the ISI or a section of the DGFI in coercing Paresh to embark upon a path of indiscriminate killing cannot be ruled out, given his proximity with and dependence on these agencies. Leaflets of 'Assam Tiger Force' were found strewn at a killing site, which indicates that ULFA was apprehensive of a ferocious public reaction and wanted to put the blame on a fictitious outfit.[197]

The situation in Assam underwent a change from the second half of 2000, making the task easier for ULFA to implement its resolutions. The government's decision to put the brakes on the secret killings meant that a large section of informers of the police and SULFA killer squads across the state became inactive. They grew apprehensive of retaliation from ULFA, especially after three informers were shot dead in Nalbari for collaborating with the police. All these factors facilitated the ULFA rebels' reentry and recruitment of cadres, which was most perceptible in the eastern districts of the valley.[198]

By September 2000, the groups vested with the responsibility of the operation against the Hindi-speaking communities had selected the target localities and were ready to strike.[199] The massacres that began on 23 October continued almost at regular intervals till 7 December in the districts of Tinsukia, Dibrugarh, Sivasagar and Nalbari, leaving 120 dead. The worst was the operation at Sadiya, where twenty-eight people were gunned down by a dozen rebels within a span of ten minutes.[200] A majority among the dead belonged to low-income groups who earned their living as daily wagers or as petty traders. In the bloodbath on 30 November that occurred at three locations killing twenty-two people, many victims were from third-generation Hindi-speaking families.[201] Joining the ranks of these chilling episodes were the killings orchestrated by the NDFB and the Karbi Anglong-based United Democratic Peoples' Solidarity (UPDS) on these communities, albeit on a scale lesser than ULFA's.

Operations were again intensified by the security forces to hunt down the killers, but they had already crossed over to Arunachal Pradesh and Bhutan, beyond the reach of the security forces.[202] For ULFA, the strategy was to lie low for some time and embark on operations against the AGP ahead of the assembly polls.[203] It was certain that the AGP would lose, but the party's pre-poll alliance with the BJP created doubts among ULFA leaders for a brief span of time. Plans were redrawn to include BJP workers in the list of targets. The campaign that commenced almost a month prior to the elections in May led to the killing of as many as 34 people and the injuring of 129, compelling the security officials to compile a list of 'highly vulnerable candidates' contesting the polls, which included 138 from the AGP and the BJP combined. Additional companies of the paramilitary were deployed, but they were unable to check the offensive launched by ULFA. Among the dead were BJP candidate for Dibrugarh, Jayanta Dutta, and his two campaign managers. And three days after the polls, ULFA issued a press release warning the Congress not to repeat the earlier mistakes of the Hiteswar Saikia regime.[204]

Chief minister Tarun Gogoi was a veteran politician who grasped the situation better than anybody else. He knew that ULFA had been traumatized but that it could embark upon a path of revival again. A minister who agreed with Gogoi and was also close to him euphemistically remarked in a cabinet meeting that ULFA was 'shaken, not stirred', and it was only a matter of time before it trained its guns on the Congress. Gogoi agreed with the minister. He lost no time in unveiling his two-pronged strategy after the new government assumed power. Counter-insurgency operations would be continued with the same vigour, while efforts were also to be made for a peace process with the outfit.[205]

Gogoi was not very optimistic about ULFA smoking the peace pipe, given Paresh's dominating role and the existing conditions that were in its favour.[206] Besides, there was no indication that its bases in the neighbouring countries would be dismantled soon. In Myanmar, an informal agreement for cessation of hostilities had been firmed up between NSCN(K) and the Junta.[207] There was every possibility of the anti-India Bangladesh Nationalist Party (BNP) and its allies sweeping to power in the country's general elections scheduled towards the end of 2001, which would mean continuation of the facilities enjoyed by the rebel groups in Bangladesh.[208] Bhutan was still undecided on the camps in its southern districts, prompting New Delhi to make renewed efforts at convincing Thimphu to make a decision.[209]

CHAPTER 8

THE DRAGON'S THUNDER

The Gathering Storm

BHUTAN ASSURED THE Indian government again that it was confident about persuading the rebels, through peaceful means, to vacate the kingdom.[1] Its resolve to shun the military option stemmed from multiple factors. The Royal Bhutan Army was not only ill-equipped, with a strength of only 6,000, but highly inexperienced for an operation against the rebels.[2] The kingdom had last gone to war 138 years ago, when it fought the British in the Anglo-Bhutanese war of 1865. The British won and they came to exercise much influence in Bhutan's affairs. The victory also gave the British unrestricted trans-Himalayan access for trade with Tibet. The Royal Bhutan Army (RBA) developed principally as a force for protection of the royal family. It was due to these reasons that the Indian army has been allowed to permanently station some units in the country and manage its border with China.[3]

The Bhutanese government was also apprehensive of a backlash by the rebels if the military option were to be exercised. It was of the opinion that coercive policies would affect the lives of as many as 66,464 people in 304 villages across its southern districts.[4] Trade routes to at least twelve of the twenty districts of Bhutan have to pass through Assam.[5] Bhutanese traders are heavily dependent on Indian merchants in the two states of Assam and West Bengal for merchandise. Disturbances could hamper the local economy and make access to goods for the landlocked kingdom difficult.

Following its commitment to New Delhi, Thimphu prepared a roadmap for dialogues with ULFA, NDFB and KLO. By mid-1997, invitations had been sent to the camps of the outfits with specific dates for talks at Thimphu.[6] Predictably, the focus was on ULFA, given its larger presence in the kingdom and the Indian government's concerns over its mounting activities. The importance accorded to the talks can be gauged from the high-profile delegation, comprising senior parliamentarians and ministers, chosen to represent the government. Its objective was also to acquaint parliament with the ground reality so that a resolution could be adopted in support of the policy concerning the rebels.[7]

ULFA was the first to respond to the offer of talks by holding a meeting at the central headquarters after receiving the green signal from the high command in Dhaka. Finance secretary Chitraban Hazarika and deputy commander Raju Baruah were chosen to represent the outfit in the talks held at Thimphu. The Bhutanese delegation, led by a senior minister and seven parliamentarians, explained the pressure being exerted on the country by New Delhi for dismantling the camps. The two ULFA representatives were told in categorical terms that the presence of the militants in the kingdom could strain the ties between the two neighbours. Therefore, there was no option for the outfits but to shift to some other location. The ULFA delegates replied saying the issue would be discussed with the senior functionaries and efforts would be made to resolve the matter through peaceful means.[8]

The ULFA high command was not alarmed over the development, although Paresh was quick to reach Bhutan for participation in the next round of talks with Hazarika. He wanted to evaluate the government's motives and gauge the situation for himself. Convened early in 1998, the meeting was a repetition of the first, with the same demand and explanation by the government delegates. The meeting continued into the next day, when Paresh proposed that Bhutan ought to assume the role of an intermediary to resolve the conflict between Assam and India. The delegates wanted to know the details of the separatist movement in Assam, which were explained to them. The proposal was not discarded, even as the earlier demand for the camps' dismantling was stressed upon by the government representatives.[9] An interesting twist at the end of the talks was the offer of financial assistance by the Bhutanese delegation to ULFA for relocation of the camps to some other site outside the kingdom. ULFA remained non-committal but assured the government of continuing the dialogue for a peaceful resolution of the issue.[10] Paresh left for Dhaka with the firm belief that the government's demand was not serious enough to merit greater attention.[11]

The government understood that the rebels did not attach the required importance to the matter, which was evidenced in the two rounds of discussions with ULFA. The NDFB and KLO were yet to respond to the offer of talks, despite being invited several times. To exert greater pressure on them, the Bhutanese parliament adopted a three-point resolution in 1999 after extensive discussions in the national assembly, which supported measures to stop rations and supplies from reaching the camps, prosecution of Bhutanese or Indian nationals found assisting the militants in the kingdom, and further dialogue with the outfits for a peaceful solution.[12]

King Jigme Sinye Wangchuck also decided to visit the camps with senior army officers, with the twin objectives of delivering a stern message to the outfits and gathering first-hand information on the camps. ULFA's central headquarters was the first camp he turned up at with his senior army officers, carrying boxes of oranges for the inmates, chocolates for the children and medicines for Mama, who was the senior-most functionary. The king greeted the cadres warmly, shaking hands with all the inmates, interacting for a while with Mama and then huddling with the senior functionaries for over two hours for talks. The discussions centred on the camp, supply of food and medicines and the common problems that were being faced. The king graciously reminded the representatives what was told to the ULFA delegates earlier—about dismantling of the camps, their relocation, and assistance for the exercise. Before departing, an invitation was offered for another round of talks at Thimphu.[13] The same sequence of activities was repeated at the ULFA general headquarters, where he landed four months later, and at an NDFB camp in the following year. [14]

The third round of talks was convened in mid-2000 after another invitation. The government delegation led by home minister Lyonpo Thinley Gyamtsho was determined to achieve a breakthrough with ULFA, represented by Hazarika and Mama.[15] The discussions began with the Bhutanese team reiterating its appeal for dismantling of the camps and relocation of the ULFA functionaries from the kingdom. But the request came with a warning to ULFA this time around—the Indian army would raid the camps if they were not dismantled soon. The Bhutanese team was unwilling to accept ULFA's vacillation on the appeal. The ULFA representatives said that four camps would be immediately dismantled, as per a decision already arrived at by the leadership.[16]

The home minister ordered a large map to be placed on the table; it had markings of red and blue where the rebel camps were located. He asked the delegates to mark the camps that were to be dismantled, which included the two zonal (mandal) camps at Bongaigaon and Darrang, a training centre near the general headquarters and the Enigma camp near Deothang. Gyamtsho demanded that the central and general headquarters be included in the list, to which Hazarika replied by requesting for more time. After the meeting, the home minister spoke to Paresh, to confirm if he was agreeable to the decision. Paresh answered in the affirmative and gave his consent to a proposed agreement to be signed by Hazarika and the parliamentary secretary. The agreement laid down the deadline for the dismantling of the camps: 31 December 2000.[17]

The official delegation that inspected the sites in the last week of December was thrilled with ULFA's fulfilment of its commitment. The officials did not know that the Enigma camps had been shifted to remote locations—Enigma A to Uttarkuchi and Enigma B further up in the hills, north of a place called Twenty-Eight. Enigma's operations had been drastically reduced, but the high command had not yet taken the decision to disband the squad. It was envisaged that its expertise in operations could be utilized ahead of the assembly polls in Assam, which were scheduled to be held four months later.

The government followed up its success with ULFA with efforts to conclude similar agreements with the KLO and NDFB. Another invitation delivered to KLO elicited no response. NDFB chairman Ranjan Daimary, who was present in Bhutan, dashed to Thimphu, for the first time, with publicity secretary B. Erakdao, after receiving a warning from the government. The king himself briefed the two leaders about the situation, with the appeal that they would have to leave the kingdom within a specified time frame. The home minister offered to bear the expenses of the transfer of their camps to any location they chose. In the end, what the NDFB committed was more than what the government had been hoping to wrest from the outfit. Daimary assured the king that all the camps would be dismantled within six months, which was mentioned in the agreement inked between the two sides.[18]

There was unanimous support in the NDFB camp for implementation of the agreement. Daimary was deeply touched by the appeal made by the king himself. So, before leaving Bhutan, he held a meeting with senior functionaries to plan the transfer of their 700-odd cadres from Bhutan to Bangladesh, Myanmar, Arunachal Pradesh and to the hill district of Dima Hasao in Assam. They were scattered in eight camps across Sarpang and Samdrup Jongkhar districts in Bhutan, which included the camps of their First and Second Battalions.[19] The plan was to persuade NSCN(K) and ULFA for assistance to relocate some of the cadres to Myanmar and Dima Halam Daogah (DHD) in Dima Hasao. A week later, Daimary departed for Bangladesh by boarding a flight from Paro.[20]

This breakthrough was ample reason for the Bhutan government to rejoice as the military option could be avoided. Its plan was to invite ULFA for another round of talks in mid-2001 to create a roadmap for the dismantling of the rest of its camps.[21] The top functionaries at the central headquarters went into a huddle a day after the invitation was delivered at the camp. They were certain that the government would insist on another agreement for their relocation with a final deadline. So, it made perfect sense for either Rajkhowa or Paresh to be present at the next meeting. The message from the central headquarters prompted a quick decision at Dhaka, and Rajkhowa was deputed for the talks. His twin mandate was to prevent a military offensive and to explore the possibility of talks with the Indian government. From Thimphu, he would head to the central headquarters for a long stay to address all the concerns of the functionaries and make efforts at streamlining the organization.[22]

Rajkhowa and his secretary and former publicity secretary Ruby Bhuyan landed at Thimphu in the first week of December with a three-month visa on their Bangladesh passports.[23] The king's reiteration at the meeting of the earlier appeal to them to vacate the kingdom was no surprise. He went a step further, with an offer to facilitate talks between ULFA and the Indian government. The delegates were thrilled, and they assured the king they would get back to him soon after discussing the matter with Paresh and the other leaders at the central headquarters. However, what astonished the two delegates was the impolite behaviour of home minister Gyamtsho, who almost threatened them of dire consequences if they did not make their way out as soon as possible. These were confusing gestures, compelling the two to ponder over the motive of the government for a long time. Did the king really mean what he said? Had the decision for an offensive already been taken?[24]

Most of the senior functionaries at the central headquarters supported talks with the Indian government. They resolved to appoint Nibaran Bora as the interlocutor for the peace process.[25] Bora was a well-known and respected leader who had been among the vanguard of almost every nationalist cause in Assam. He was an author, columnist and the founder-chairman of the regional party Purbanchaliya Lok Parishad (PLP). His son Javed Bora, was a prominent functionary in the outfit and had been based in Dhaka for some time. He was shot dead in Dibrugarh by unidentified assailants. The king would be requested for assistance to kickstart the peace process with New Delhi after receiving consent for the role of interlocutor from Bora.[26]

A letter written by Rajkhowa offering to assume the role of the interlocutor was to be delivered to Bora in Guwahati. Ruby Bhuyan was to make the delivery, but an unexpected incident unfolded as she prepared to embark upon the journey. A message from Paresh to the central headquarters barred him from proceeding on the errand! Paresh was vehemently against starting the peace process with the Indian government.[27] Rajkhowa was extremely dejected. Other functionaries at the central headquarters were startled at Paresh's about-turn on the peace process. He had agreed to the plan ahead of Rajkhowa's departure from Dhaka.[28]

Paresh had his own reasons to scuttle the efforts for the peace process. He was of the view that Anup, who was expected to be released from jail within a couple of months, must be engaged in the decision. A decision as important as talks with the Indian government must have the approval of the general secretary of the organization.[29] There was speculation among some functionaries that Paresh was compelled to halt the effort owing to Pakistan's opposition to the plan.[30] And there was another group that believed that talks with the Indian government at that juncture would have fuelled demoralization and dissension within the ranks of the organization. It was extremely doubtful if New Delhi would have accepted the offer of talks from ULFA when earlier offers had been spurned by the organization. All these factors might have been taken into consideration by Paresh when he opposed the endeavour.[31]

Rajkhowa was at a loss as far as charting the future course of action was concerned.[32] The king would have to be informed that the proposal for talks with the Indian government had not been approved by the organization. The only option would be to dismantle the camps and transfer all the functionaries out of Bhutan, which the government would certainly insist on, along with a deadline, in the next round of talks. ULFA was still undecided, unlike the NDFB which was quick to firm up a roadmap for the relocation of its camps. But, unknown to ULFA, Thimphu's growing concerns over other developments in southern Bhutan were soon to have an effect on its stance towards the rebel outfits.[33]

Crossing the Rubicon

The tranquil phase in southern Bhutan after the eviction of the Nepalese immigrants in the late 1980s and early 1990s did not last long. The displaced Nepalese lodged at the refugee camps in Nepal's Zhapa joined hands with dissident Bhutanese nationals to float the United Front for Democracy (UFD) in 1997, demanding political reform and greater respect for human rights in Bhutan. Poster campaigns and grassroots activities were observed in several districts, provoking a crackdown by the government. At least 150 people were arrested, of whom the majority were Bhutanese nationals and monks belonging to the Sarchop community. They were charged with collaborating with the 'ngolops', or anti-nationals. The government viewed their demands as seditious and capable of fuelling political turmoil.[34]

The crackdown somewhat checked the movement from spreading its wings for a few years.[35] But new ideas of revolt began to germinate at the refugee camps. And this time the stimulus came from the burgeoning Maoist movement in Nepal, whose primary goal was to overthrow the monarchy. The Nepalese Maoist leaders found similarities among themselves and the disaffected sections of the populace in Bhutan, which was enough reason for them to explore the scope of a movement with them. The result was the formation of a core committee among the refugees, enrolment of members and visits by the key functionaries to the Nepalese-inhabited areas in southern Bhutan.[36] From mid-2000, posters and cassettes explaining the Maoist doctrine were distributed, and speeches heard over loudspeakers exhorting the locals to join the movement. A few activists also contacted ULFA for weapons, but were sternly refused.[37]

All this was enough to trigger panic among the Bhutanese ruling elite, who grew apprehensive of renewed turmoil in the southern districts. Since the rebel outfits were annoyed with the government's appeal to them to vacate the kingdom, they felt they might as well join hands with the Maoists and the Sarchop Bhutanese nationals for an armed campaign. Thimphu's concerns were aggravated after a briefing from the Indian government that underscored the Maoists' efforts to procure weapons from ULFA and the birth of an outfit, Bhutan Gorkha Liberation Front, among the refugees in Nepal.[38]

ULFA's silence on talks with the Indian government was no less disturbing for the Bhutanese government. Nobody from Thimphu had heard from Rajkhowa, who was supposed to have discussed the matter with the senior functionaries for finalizing the roadmap for the talks. The three-month visas granted to him and his secretary had also expired.[39] Nor was there any indication that the NDFB would fulfil its commitment of dismantling its camps. KLO sent a team of middle-ranking functionaries for talks, which was extremely annoying to the Bhutanese delegates.[40] Although the KLO's presence was of no consequence, the government was concerned about the possibility of its links with the Maoist movement.[41] The king decided to visit the camps again for the last time.

He first turned up at the NDFB camp at Kalikhola near the border of Assam and West Bengal, where the issues discussed five months ago with the outfit's leadership at Thimphu were reiterated.

The chairman was in Dhaka and a decision to not implement the earlier plan of relocating to outside the country had already been arrived at. A majority of the functionaries were of the view that it would be next to impossible to carry on with the campaign in Assam from far-off locations such as Myanmar or Dima Hasao. At the same time, there was a section among them that firmly believed, an offensive would be launched by the government to dismantle the camps sooner rather than later. All that the senior functionaries, including general secretary Gobinda Basumatary, could do was to listen to the king without conveying their opinion.[42]

Months later, in mid-2002, Rajkhowa decided not to reveal the real picture before the king when he arrived at ULFA's central headquarters. Instead, his reply to him focused on buying more time from the government, on the ground that an executive council meeting had been planned in Bangladesh.[43] Paresh had already firmed up a plan for the meeting, where a host of decisions were to be arrived at, including a decision on the camps in Bhutan. No timeline for the final decision could be given to the king, which possibly indicated to him that there was no possibility of the camps being dismantled so soon. Nonetheless, the king renewed the earlier appeal with the offer of financial assistance to cover the expenses of relocation. He also suggested that only one camp ought to be maintained till the executive council meeting was convened and the rest dismantled.[44] The king's displeasure with ULFA was amply evident when he landed at the general headquarters after a couple of days. There was no prior intimation of his visit, unlike on the previous occasion. His attitude had also undergone a marked change. He refused to accept the traditional Assamese gift of the gamusa (a towel) or even to interact in the casual manner that he had earlier.[45]

In Thimphu, a series of meetings chaired by the home minister with leading parliamentarians and highly placed government officials gauged the implications of the rebel outfits' disinclination to exit from the kingdom. The pros and cons of an offensive to flush them out came up for discussion again, with the majority expressing the view that the armed forces were ill-equipped for such an exercise. At the same time, the outfits' disregard for the government's appeal could not be ignored for long, lest it should convey the impression that the regime was scared to crack the whip on them. It was a dilemma for the government, and there appeared to be no resolution. Pressure from New Delhi was mounting; it made an offer to provide men and materials to Bhutan for the operation. The Bhutanese government was apprehensive that this might lead to many more casualties at the camps, including women and children, if the Indian army was given a free hand to conduct a flush-out exercise.[46]

The uncertainty, however, lasted only till the end of 2002, when more information flowed in from the Indian intelligence agencies about the future plans of the Maoists in Bhutan. More meetings had reportedly been convened by the Maoists at the refugee camps in Nepal to expedite the organization's activities in southern Bhutan. They were convened after favourable reports were submitted by a couple of activists who had toured the Nepali-inhabited zones in the kingdom. The conditions were ripe for the outfit to expand its activities among the disgruntled populace, which included a section of Bhutanese nationals. A name proposed for the outfit, the Communist Party of Bhutan, Marxists-Leninists-Maoists (CPB-MLM), found acceptance among the participants at the meetings. It was decided that the formal launch of the outfit would take place in the following year, but the date would be decided at a later stage based on the convenience of all parties involved. Present at the meeting were senior functionaries of the Communist Party of Nepal (Maoist), who pledged support and assistance to the new outfit.[47] Details of all these activities were compiled into a report and delivered at Thimphu by an official delegation from New Delhi, which was followed by the visit of the Indian Army Chief General N.C. Vij and National Security Adviser Brajesh Mishra.[48] Their message to the Bhutan government was simple—evict the rebel groups before they join hands with the Maoists! India again assured the kingdom of all kinds of assistance that it would require for the offensive, including an offer of joint operations.[49] The Bhutan government finally decided to go ahead with preparing for the offensive.

An elaborate strategy was firmed up after a series of brainstorming sessions chaired by the king. The option of a peaceful resolution to the impasse would not be abandoned while the groundwork was being laid for the military option. An appeal to the rebels would be made for the last time through a parliament resolution after a few months. In the meantime, the supply routes to the camps would be choked, traders and middlemen who supplied rations and essential commodities to them would be prosecuted, markets near the camps shut down and the Nepalese-inhabited villages that provided shelter to the rebel functionaries identified and their population configuration altered by settling people of other ethnicities there and relocating the locals elsewhere. The idea was to compel the rebels to leave so that an offensive could be avoided. And if they still refused to leave, the government would be left with no choice but to flush them out.[50]

For the operation, though, a more prudent approach was adopted by the Bhutanese government, keeping in view the limitations of the Royal Bhutan Army. A long list of issues was drawn up for discussion with the Indian government for framing the blueprint for the operation. Of utmost importance was the need to equip the Bhutan army with the capability to take on the rebels through advanced training, superior fire power and augmentation of its numbers. The Indian army was to be involved, but only selectively, and greater engagement on their part could be called for elsewhere, only if the rebels put up a resistance and retaliated against the army. Additional Indian forces could be on standby near the zones where the operation would be launched.[51]

The Indian government went all out to fulfil Thimphu's demands. It was a hard-won success for New Delhi, coming as it did after almost seven years of diplomatic efforts to convince the Bhutan government to take stern action against the rebels. An extensive plan was rolled out early in 2003, following extensive sessions in the capitals of the two countries among senior government officials. The Royal Bhutan Army was to be expanded by recruiting more soldiers, who were to be trained by the Indian army. A select group of officers would undertake a course at the Counter Insurgency and Jungle Warfare (CIJW) school in Mizoram's Vairengte. Weaponry, including artillery guns for the shelling of camps, was to be supplied by India.[52] Many officials engaged in the formulation of the operation were of the opinion that resistance by the rebels was to be expected.[53]

The operation in its first phase would focus on the Deothang-Kawoipani region in Samdrup Jongkhar, where the biggest of the ULFA camps were located.[54] Reports indicated that there were over forty rebel establishments in the southern districts, including around ten big camps. ULFA had the maximum, with more than thirty camps; NDFB had eight, while KLO had the smallest presence, with one camp in Bhutan near Kokrajhar and a training centre in north West Bengal.[55] More spots, including some NDFB camps which were scattered in the districts of Zhemgang, Pema Gatshel and Sarpang in Bhutan would be targeted and shelled from a distance. A grid created by the Indian army at certain spots along the Assam-Bhutan border was expected to help apprehend the fleeing rebels. Finally, it was decided that the operation would be launched after the rainy season, when all the preparations were complete.[56]

All these sweeping developments were not unknown to the senior ULFA functionaries in Bhutan. The sources they had developed over the years in the Bhutan government were prompt in briefing them about the plans for the operation. Some of these informers were supposedly identified by the government, shunted to insipid posts or penalized.[57] Two names that were doing the rounds among the India security agencies was military adviser to the king, Brigadier V. Namgel, and a highly placed official in the foreign ministry,

Wangchuk Dorji, who had developed a rapport with ULFA.[58] There were rumours that a Bhutanese army captain who used to pass on sensitive information to ULFA was jailed.[59]

What ULFA's sources disclosed was confirmed within a couple of months when the markets near the camps were shut down and a crackdown began in a few villages inhabited by the Nepalese. Over a hundred people, mostly traders in the local markets and farmers suspected to have assisted the rebel groups, were jailed, and some families compelled to relocate to far-off locations. Bhutanese families were settled in the villages, and they became the eyes and ears of the government.[60] With the supply chain dismantled, a crisis began to brew again in the rebel camps, triggering attempts to establish alternative routes for fetching food and essential commodities. The camps were not prepared to face a crisis or an emergency.[61]

Soon it became unsafe for ULFA functionaries to descend from the hills to the plains. Increasing cases of attacks by the Indian army were being reported. They began with the raid on the Enigma A camp at Uttarkuchi. There were no casualties among the inmates but the camp was burnt down.[62] Another instance was an encounter near Simla Bazar, which raged on for many hours, in which three ULFA functionaries were killed.[63] Sometimes the operations were allegedly carried out in the interiors of Bhutan without the knowledge of the Bhutan government. An attempt was made to nab ULFA publicity secretary Mithinga Daimary who was operating from a rented accommodation at Bumthang in north Bhutan. He moved to a secret location at Six Kilo near Deothang, from where he continued to operate till the launch of the military operation.[64]

Clearly, the pace of preparations for the operation ahead was picking up. The districts of Samdrup Jongkhar and Trashigang began to swarm with more army personnel, including large numbers of the Indian army. The rebels were in no doubt that at least two new battalions of the Royal Bhutan Army were being raised and trained in these locations.[65] They watched the developments, discussed them and speculated on the next move that would be taken by the high command. A decision would be possible only at the executive council meeting in Bangladesh, for which the dates had not yet been decided.

Amid these developments came an unexpected missive from Paresh that heightened the anxiety at the central and general headquarters—an air raid on the camps was imminent and would happen within a week. He ordered evacuation of the camps, which was done on the very next day. Temporary shelters were erected in the jungles for the functionaries, at safe distances from the camp. There was no air raid, but helicopters hovered above the camps at regular intervals for many days. It was almost a month before the rebels considered it safe to return to the camps. Defensive measures at the camps were strengthened and night patrolling intensified to ensure greater security.[66]

Rajkhowa decided to slip out of Bhutan before the situation turned more hazardous. His visa had expired long ago and there was no way that he would be able to catch a flight from Paro to Dhaka.[67] Moreover, it could be unsafe for him to go to the airport as the Indian security agencies were aware of his presence at the central headquarters and that he would soon leave for Bangaldesh.[68] So he decided to walk a long distance through the hills, along routes considered safe and devoid of Indian army presence. A twelve-member squad, including his secretary Ruby Bhuyan, would accompany him on the journey to western Bhutan, from where they would sneak into Bangladesh through Cooch Behar. The rest of the senior functionaries from Bhutan would follow suit for the executive council meeting in Bangladesh after the dates were finalized.[69]

Political Wing Abolished

Rajkhowa's meandering journey through the hills to western Bhutan was interspersed with regular halts at unsuspecting villages to avoid detection. The Indian army and intelligence agencies had carved out an extensive network of informers along the border, enabling frequent flow of information on the movements of the rebels. Still, there were many safe places for shelter as there were people sympathetic to the rebel groups. The camps had been a source of livelihood for many impoverished families in the region, which was almost devoid of development activities by the government.[70] Rajkhowa's trek came to a halt at ULFA's Bongaigaon camp in Bhutan, where he stayed for a week to interact with the cadres. The same queries that came up at the central headquarters were made to him again, about the future plans of the outfit and the camps in Bhutan. All he could do was to explain the king's proposals and the impending meeting in Bangladesh, where a slew of decisions was expected to be arrived at.[71]

From the Bongaigaon camp, Rajkhowa and his team reached Pheuntsoling, which is the penultimate halt in Bhutan before the descent to north West Bengal. The plan was to put up for a couple of nights in the town with ULFA functionary Rustav Choudhury, who had been stationed there with the task of facilitating the entry and exit of leaders and consignments of weapons from Bangladesh. On the next day, a hawker arrived at Rustav's residence to sell vegetables, but his gestures alarmed Rajkhowa. He spoke Hindi and, with his typical north Indian features, resembled a soldier of the Indian army. The chairman knew that he had been tracked down, and it made perfect sense to hit the trail again at the earliest. The other members of the squad, who were living in a hotel, were instructed to pack up and join Rajkhowa. In the evening, they left for another destination west of the town and then to Bangladesh through Cooch Behar a day later. At night, Rustav was gunned down by unidentified assailants when he stepped out of his residence for a stroll![72]

The dangers in Bhutan were in sharp contrast to the prevailing situation in Bangladesh. ULFA and the rebel groups from the Northeast had never felt more secure in any country. There was no fear of surveillance or crackdown any longer. The pro-Pakistan Bangladesh Nationalist Party (BNP)-led alliance had swept to power in the elections with an absolute majority. The congenial ambience there encouraged Paresh to tie up with the ISI for more weapons and RDX directly from Pakistan. One consignment, offloaded at Chittagong in mid-2002, was concealed in rice bags and then transported in trucks to the camp at Satcherri.[73]

ULFA's growing arsenal was a matter of envy for the other outfits, whose leaders did not have as many contacts as Paresh did in the grey market for weapons in China and Southeast Asia or his capability to fix deals. Within no time, other outfits such as the PLA and UNLF approached him for weapons, which were provided at concessional rates from the dump at Satcherri. And soon there came a message from the People's War Group (PWG) in Andhra Pradesh with a similar request. A senior PWG functionary, Kishenji, who later became a politburo member of CPI(Maoist) and the chief military strategist of the group, arrived in Dhaka after crossing the border in north West Bengal to purchase weapons from ULFA.[74] Two consignments consisting of RDX, pistols and assault rifles were delivered to the group at convenient locations along the India-Bangladesh border in West Bengal.[75] The third met with a mishap when the truck carrying the weapons was confiscated at Bogra in Bangladesh. This incident made headlines in the local media, which also mentioned the possible involvement of the All Tripura Tiger Force (ATTF) in the episode.[76]

The increasing availability of weapons coincided with ISI's resolve to offer greater support to rebel groups in India.[77] The training modules in Pakistan had already been restarted, with a greater fervour to include as many outfits as possible from the Northeast and Islamist groups from Bangladesh.[78] Apparently, the batch of eight functionaries from ULFA and ATTF that boarded the flight from Dhaka to Karachi in mid-1996 was the first after a gap of four years, when the Awami League-led alliance was in power.[79] By 2004, close to 40 ULFA functionaries, out of 100 functionaries from all the rebel groups in the Northeast, including the NDFB, NLFT and PLA, had undergone training in Pakistan in five separate groups.[80] All the trainees were provided Bangladeshi passports by a group of intelligence officers in Bangladesh who were on ISI's payroll.[81]

The training modules imparted to the groups were of unequal durations, ranging from seventeen days to three months, with the number of trainees varying with each batch. One group, which was also stationed at Tora Bora in Afghanistan, had the longest session of over three months.[82] Besides the usual exercises and firing weapons of all kinds, there was greater emphasis on indoctrination and bomb-making for all the groups.[83] There were lessons on remotely triggered bombs and in a technology that used light for detonation. The most complex gadget was the Programmable Timer Device (PTD) involving multiple circuits and more ingredients than the ordinary bomb. The Pakistani trainers spent hours feeding the trainees propaganda, the underlying message of which was to cause harm to the Indian government and population. Among them was an officer named 'Khan Baba', who would often remind the rebels of the importance of rape as a weapon and the necessity to increase the Assamese community's population. He was extremely well-informed on India's Northeast and especially of the stretch between Nagaland's Dimapur and Guwahati. The functionaries returned motivated to renew their campaign in Assam.[84]

The Pakistani army officers were no less thrilled to engage with the new batches. The flattering feedback from the trainers prompted lieutenant general Asfaq Pervez Kayani, who was soon to be appointed chief of ISI and later chief of army staff, to arrive at the camp for a brief interaction with the trainees.[85] It was during one of these sessions in mid-2003 that Paresh visited Islamabad for a discussion with his ISI handlers on the situation in Bhutan. However, his stay in Pakistan was curtailed following developments in Bhutan that further indicated the government's hardening stance towards the rebel outfits. The meeting of the executive council could no longer be delayed. He rushed back to Dhaka for the meeting, instructing the senior functionaries in Bhutan to reach Bangladesh by mid-August.[86]

In Bhutan, things were indeed unfolding at a fast pace. The government had set 30 June 2003 as the deadline for the rebels to leave the country and threatened the use of military force to expel them if they did not pull out on their own.[87] The deadline was timed to coincide with the eighty-first national assembly, to be convened between 28 June and 18 August. As anticipated by the government, there was no response from the outfits, and the process for a parliament resolution was set in motion. Home minister Lyonpo Thinley Gyamtsho informed the assembly that ULFA had an estimated 1,560 functionaries in thirteen camps; NDFB had 740 in twelve camps while KLO had 430 militants in five camps.[88] While the figures for ULFA and NDFB were almost accurate, KLO's strength was nowhere beyond 100, with many of its functionaries putting up at ULFA's central and general headquarters.[89] The assembly mandated the use of force against the outfits, but only after making one last attempt at persuading the rebels to leave the country.[90]

However, the ministers and government officials knew that they were was drifting towards an operation. The Deothang-Kawaoipani zone in southern Bhutan was gradually getting into war mode—there were occasional flag marches, briefings in the towns and villages by the army on the measures to be adopted for safety during war and digging of trenches at some locations.[91] There were unmistakable signs of an offensive, which was continuously being brought to the notice of the ULFA high command by the senior functionaries in Bhutan.

NDFB inferred as much from the developments, especially after the king's visit to the camp at Kalikhola and the briefing it received from its sources in the Royal Bhutan Army. Chairman Daimary's reminder to Paresh about the Bhutan government's plan fell on deaf ears.[92] Paresh still would not believe that Bhutan was serious about evicting the rebels by force from the country. Most of the senior ULFA functionaries were bewildered at his rigid stance.[93] Did Paresh not order vacation of the camps some time ago after receiving information about the possibility of an air raid? Many among them hoped to derive definitive answers from the executive council meeting scheduled for the second week of September in Bangladesh's Sherpur.[94]

At the meeting, Paresh continued to harbour doubts about Bhutan's capabilities to physically drive out the rebels, but he was all for implementing the king's appeal, which was made during his last visit to the central headquarters, to reduce the number of camps. So, it was resolved unanimously to dismantle all the camps except one, which was to be called the Central Command Headquarter (CCHQ), after the merger of the central and general headquarters. Mobile camps would be in existence in Bhutan for fulfilling a variety of tasks, including operations. The bulk of the functionaries were to descend from the hills, for three battalions (109, 27 and 709) to be created for western and central Assam. These would new additions to the existing two formed earlier. All the battalions were to be controlled by the CCHQ, which was to be placed under the charge of organizing secretary Asanta Bagh Phukan.[95] The post of operations commander was left vacant after Raju Baruah raised an objection over the proposal to appoint Phukan to that position. Baruah was extremely aggrieved when he was stripped of the post of military spokesperson and deputy commander and shifted to Bangladesh.[96]

Most importantly, the political wing was to be abolished, along with the zones, and all functionaries were to be incorporated into the army and assigned ranks. So, ULFA was transformed into a military outfit, although the roles and functions of the chairman and other leaders in the political departments remained unchanged.[97] Underlying this momentous decision was the undivided opinion among most senior functionaries that drastic measures were called for to address the hitches that had crept into the organization and to counteract the damages inflicted by the Bhutan government.[98] It was assumed that merging the political wing into the armed wing would engender cohesion, besides creating greater political awareness among the functionaries, which was deemed necessary.[99] All these changes were made permanent with a constitutional amendment before the conclave drew to a close.[100]

Most of the functionaries were elated with the revamp, except the women at the camps, who felt betrayed by the new resolutions. A clause was added in the constitution that women would be allowed to retire after they attained the rank of second lieutenant, fuelling confusion and multiple interpretations. The three second lieutenants among the women were of the opinion that they would not be allowed to move above that rank even if they chose to remain in the organization. They registered their protest, but there was no reply from the seniors.[101] Others inferred that no ranks would be given to the wives of functionaries who did not avail of training, but that norms would be formulated for promotion of the women functionaries who had already completed their training.[102] Whatever the truth, the fact was that enrolment of women had decreased in the post-2000 period owing to the turmoil in the organization.[103] Commanders always preferred not to have too many women cadres at the camps in Bangladesh and Myanmar, for security reasons.[104]

This confusion notwithstanding, most of the participants at the meeting were convinced that a reduction in the number of camps in Bhutan would stall a flush-out campaign by the Royal Bhutan Army.[105] Cadres had already started shifting out of the camps in Bhutan to man the new battalions, while another group was transferred to Myanmar almost a month after the executive meeting was convened.[106] Only around 600–650 inmates remained in Bhutan, including women and children, who were to be shifted to the newly constructed CCHQ.[107] It was time to send a delegation again to Thimphu to apprise the government about the resolutions at the meeting, which was assumed by the ULFA leadership as total acceptance of the king's previous year's appeal at the central headquarters. The request for a meeting elicited an immediate response from the king's office, and it was scheduled for the last week of October. ULFA foreign secretary Shashadar flew out from Dhaka to join two senior functionaries, Asanta Bagh Phukan and Mama, who had travelled from the central headquarters to Thimphu. The meeting sprung surprises for the ULFA leaders.[108]

The Bhutanese delegates, led by prime minister Jigmi Y. Thinley, were in no mood to allow the rebel outfits to stay any longer in the country. They offered to facilitate the transfer of all the functionaries to another country, which would be chosen by ULFA, with a financial package of Rs 200 crore![109] All the women and children would be taken care of by the government and subsequently handed over to India. For the ULFA delegates, there was no option but to accept the offer. Sensing that an operation was imminent, they assured the delegation that Paresh and Rajkhowa would land in Bhutan within a week to implement the terms laid down by the government. ULFA's commitment was converted into an agreement, which was signed by three of its participants at the meeting.[110]

Thimphu never expected any response from ULFA. The government's motive was to retain evidence of the efforts it had made to resolve the issue peacefully, ahead of the operation. It knew that relocation of the rebel functionaries to another country was an unfeasible proposition. No country, not even Myanmar or Pakistan, would openly give asylum to so many rebel cadres. At the most, the Bhutan government might have entertained the possibility of compelling the rebels to surrender so that a flush-out could be avoided.[111] Moreover, in Dhaka, Paresh stuck to his earlier view that Bhutan did not have the nerve to exercise the military option against the rebels if the agreement was not implemented.[112] Within a month, the Bhutan government also convened a meeting with three senior NDFB delegates, making the same offer as the one that had been extended to ULFA by the prime minister. But no agreement could be concluded following the vague response from the NDFB. The outfit was already prepared to disperse from the camps if an operation were to be launched.[113]

By early November, the two governments firmed up the final part of the operation plan, with 15 December being finalized as the date for the launch.[114] Codenamed 'Operation All Clear', it was to be executed with the help of 7,000–8,000 troops of the Royal Bhutan Army and active support from the Special Frontier Force (SFF), which operated under India's Research & Analysis Wing (R&AW).[115] A team of Indian army officers led by major general S.S. Dhillon was stationed at Thimphu for supervision of the operation with the chief operations officer of the Royal Bhutan Army, lieutenant general G.G. Lam Dorji, who reported directly to the king.[116] Forty-eight hours ahead of the offensive, a notice was served by the government to ULFA, NDFB and KLO through *Kuensel*, the country's national newspaper, that it was left with no option other than to entrust the Royal Bhutan Army 'with the sacred duty of removing the militants' from the country.[117]

ULFA's central and general headquarters were oblivious about the notice in the *Kuensel*, as its circulation was limited to a few towns in the country.[118] On the contrary, functionaries were upbeat when a major in the Bhutanese army informed them that the king would visit the central headquarters on 15 December. Speculation arose in the camps about an immediate offensive after a warning from another army officer some days ago was dismissed. And, as was the case on earlier occasions when the king was to visit, the camp was decked up and preparations were begun to receive the king. The women at the camp became busy baking pithas to be served to the guests.[119] An appointment was also scheduled between the prime minister and a delegation of the NDFB at the border town of Nganglam.[120] The gameplan was sinister, and it caught the rebels by surprise.

Operation All-Clear

The fifteenth of December 2003 was a typical winter day in the hills of Bhutan. The unpleasant cold was aggravated from time to time by an infrequent breeze, and the sky was cloudy. But it was also unlike other days at the ULFA central headquarters, as the king's visit had always been an occasion of excitement. And now that he was expected to announce the final deadline for dismantling of the camps, there was already a buzz among the functionaries that the issue had almost been resolved in the last round of the talks at Thimphu. Brunch was served early at the camp to ensure the attendance of all the inmates when he arrived. The women had also finished assembling all the ingredients in the kitchen for serving refreshments to the guests.[121]

A gunshot at around 8.30 a.m. seemed to signal the king's arrival. Some functionaries, including Mama, who were supervising the reception, assumed the firing by the cadres stationed below at the defence camp of the central headquarters was meant to welcome the king. Then, a couple of more shots were heard again, within a few seconds of the first—louder than the first. There was no cause for alarm, they seemed to think, until a shell exploded after a minute at the hut where Mama lived. He instantly knew what was happening—the offensive had begun! Mama yelled at the top of his voice asking everybody to vacate the camp and rush to the jungles. Then it was a torrent of blasts, at intervals of a few seconds to a minute, all over the camp.[122]

The mortars were fired from a distance of 2–3 kms from at least three locations in the adjacent hills. Hira Sarania, a senior functionary, suffered a minor injury after being hit by a splinter in his left leg. But his comrade Champak was not so lucky; he died on the spot.[123] The accuracy of the shelling left nobody in doubt as to the involvement of the Indian army in the operation.[124] Orders were issued for vacation of the camp. A group of functionaries rushed to the barracks where the two dozen women and children lived. They were herded together, with whatever belongings and foodstuff could be grabbed, and taken on a descending route along the northern flank of the camp to a spot beyond the range of the mortars. They were joined by Mama and other senior functionaries, all of whom were in a state of total confusion over the next step to be taken. Other functionaries from the camp scattered in different directions amid the shelling that continued until afternoon.[125]

The scene was worse at ULFA's general headquarters, which housed around ninety inmates, including twenty women and children.[126] It came under attack a few minutes after the central headquarters did, and the defence camp near Sukuni Basti below the hills was pounded with mortar shells. The reaction here and the ensuing chaos made for a replication of the scenes as at the central headquarters—a hurried evacuation to a safe spot beyond the range of the shells. The bombardment was even more precise at the general headquarters, so much so that all the big camps were hit and three senior functionaries, including Rahul Dutta, along with his child, lay dead after being hit by splinters. Two more cadres sent to fetch food from the kitchen in the afternoon were killed; another had his leg ripped apart in a blast.[127]

In these dire circumstances, all that the senior functionaries at both locations could do was to continually try to establish radio contact with Dhaka, which yielded results only three hours later. Paresh delivered a stern message to the rebels not to retaliate against the Royal Bhutan Army; the trigger was to be pulled only if the Indian army arrived at the camps. He might have been under the impression that the offensive would not last long.[128] Nonetheless, the decision against a counter-attack made sense, what with the women and children in an extremely precarious situation in the jungles. Paresh assured the inmates that efforts to speak to the king and end the offensive were on.[129]

So, late in the afternoon after the shelling had ended, some functionaries silently watched from a distance when a company of the Royal Bhutan Army reached the central headquarters. The ULFA flag was lowered and Bhutan's was hoisted. They inspected the entire premises; 'important' was inscribed on some barracks that were not damaged from the shelling. Their departure within an hour prompted an ULFA squad to crawl out, at snail's pace, from an adjacent hill and get into the camp in search of food. The army kept its eyes constantly on the camp from a distance. Just when the group was retreating with an abundant stock of food, the mortars boomed again from a monastery, killing one cadre on the spot.[130] The army had entrenched itself in several locations around the camp and it could be only a matter of time before the rebels' hideout was identified and raided. Time was running out for the rebels, and there was no escape route to safety.[131]

A different scenario emerged at the other camps located west of the ULFA headquarters, which were almost simultaneously attacked although the shelling was for a shorter duration.[132] The camps were small, with fewer functionaries, and devoid of women and children. The commanders were hardly in doubt that their base in Bhutan had drawn to a close. There was no reason to wait for further instructions from Paresh, except to abide by his earlier command not to engage in a counter-attack against the Royal Bhutan Army. They dispersed speedily. Grabbing as much food and weapons as possible, the commanders and functionaries scraped through the numerous gaps in the hills without any encounters. The NDFB and KLO cadres were also not cornered in the offensive as they too evacuated their camps with the same swiftness.[133]

Both ULFA headquarters continued to be pounded on the next day too, compelling all inmates to remain in the jungles. Paresh was unable to speak to the king; neither was he able to give further instructions to his functionaries in Bhutan on the next course of action. The situation was turning worse, with at least six functionaries succumbing to their injuries at the hideout near the general headquarters.[134] The status quo was broken on the third day with a flurry of developments that began with the army burning down the central headquarters around noon.[135] After Dhaka was informed of this, Paresh ordered that the women and children be separated from the functionaries for surrender.[136] He was no longer in doubt that the army was determined to bring the rebels' presence in Bhutan to an end. The next day, the women and children were transferred from the general to the central headquarters' hideout via a secret route after radio contact was established between the two locations.[137]

Two decisions were promptly arrived at among the functionaries in the hideouts—they decided to inform the Bhutanese authorities of the surrender of the women and children, with whom Mama and a few senior functionaries were to be attached, and to disperse the rest to safer zones in small groups.[138] Three heavily-armed squads, including a dozen functionaries led by Hira Sarania, exited from the hideout to head westward, where the presence of the army was presumed to be less.[139] The forty-nine-member group near the general headquarters, which included many senior functionaries, such as Asanta Bagh Phukan and Bening Rabha, decided to move out together in the opposite direction before beginning their descent from the hills.[140]

But how was the surrender of the women and children to be managed? Evacuating all the women and children from the hideout involved too great a danger for anybody to recommend it. The impasse was broken on the next day, when Mrinmoy Hazarika and another functionary volunteered to turn up at the nearest camp of the Royal Bhutan Army with a letter declaring ULFA's commitment not to engage in counter-attack and with a request for immediate assistance for the injured, women and children, and an appointment with the king. The next day, the duo descended from the hideout, as planned, with a gamocha held high, signaling that they came in peace.[141]

The first village below the hills was found to be deserted. The residents had been shifted to a safer zone days ahead of 15 December in anticipation of an offensive by ULFA. At the next, which was about a kilometer away, the two functionaries were in for a surprise—they were surrounded by the residents and tied up with ropes. They were informed that there were instructions from the army to apprehend the fleeing rebels from the camps.

Interestingly, this was one of the Nepalese settlements that had been an important link in the supply chain to the central headquarters. For some reason, they were not evicted during the crackdown ahead of the operation. Perhaps they had been warned by the Bhutanese authorities to desist from maintaining links with the rebels, which explained the drastic change in their attitude towards ULFA. The saving grace for the detainees was the few familiar faces in the crowd, who patiently heard their reasons for landing up at the village. Two elderly persons agreed to accompany them to the nearest camp after intimating the army in advance through a messenger.[142]

The reception at the camp was along expected lines. Hazarika and his associate were tied up with ropes and shoved into a barrack within minutes of delivering the letter. Their ordeal ended the next morning, when they were untied, served food and briefed about the instructions received. A commander ordered the junior officers to reach the ULFA hideout, confiscate all the weapons and assemble the inmates at the nearest monastery. They reluctantly agreed to do this only after being repeatedly assured by the two ULFA functionaries that no harm would befall them, as the women and children were desperately waiting to be rescued. In the evening, after arriving at the hideout, the officers escorted the group of fifty-odd people, Mama and a few senior functionaries, to a monastery on an adjacent hill after taking possession of six AK-47 rifles and three pistols that the functionaries had surrendered.[143]

Meanwhile, one of the three teams of rebels that had exited the central headquarters managed to chart a circuitous route through the hills till they reached a spot where they were compelled to halt. About 50 metres away were six personnel of the Royal Bhutan Army, waiting to ambush any rebel cadres descending from the hill. There was simply no way to cross the zone without alerting them. The functionary leading the group, who was armed with a universal machine gun, pulled the trigger on the army team, killing all of them on the spot. They were apprehensive about more army personnel in the area, but there were none. The rebels quietly surged ahead on their journey after grabbing whatever food they found on the personnel's dead bodies.[144]

The squad led by Hira had a narrow escape from being spotted by the army at Kawoipani as they lay hidden in the shrubs. There was no way to reach the eastern flank of the town, which might have offered them another track for the onward journey. Two NDFB functionaries who were also on the run joined the group as it was retreating to a safer location near a river bank for the night. But their presence did not go unnoticed. Soon there came a volley of fire and mortar shells, killing four members of the party, including the two NDFB functionaries. The rest of the members somehow managed to vanish into the jungle. They trekked the whole night until they arrived at a village before daybreak. They were offered food by a resident and a hut to sleep in for the whole day.[145]

In the evening, as the group resumed its march further west, a radio news bulletin revealed that Mama had died along with the women and children![146] The group was stunned and speechless for some time. They thanked their stars for their prudent decision to leave their hideout in time. But they were unaware about the spate of fake news in the media surrounding Operation All Clear owing to the absence of information from the governments and the deliberate peddling of misinformation. The media was further convinced about the death of Mama following a statement from ULFA that he had been shot in custody after being captured while he was leading a group of women, children and injured rebels holding a white flag.[147] However, all of them were safe in the monastery, awaiting transfer to another location.[148]

It was only on 18 December that tidbits of information on the operation were released by both the governments. All the press releases said was that the rebels had been 'dislodged' from all the camps in the kingdom and that the Royal Bhutan Army was pursuing them in the dense jungles to flush them out.[149] Earlier, on the day of the operation, a statement from the Bhutan government explained that the rebels' presence had 'seriously affected' economic development, education, cultivation and commercial activities in several districts of the country. The government argued that the presence of the terrorists had endangered the safety of travellers in those areas and had caused disruption in the transportation of the goods through the traditional and convenient routes to and from India.[150]

There was ample justification for Thimphu to exercise the military option against the outfits when the other tactics had failed. Perhaps no other head of state would have turned up at the rebel camps so many times with an appeal to the rebels to move out of the country. That the rebels had disregarded the traditional authority was not in doubt. But the allegation by Thimphu that the militants had caused disruption in trade between the two countries was simply not true. The survival of the rebel camps depended on the cooperation of the neighbouring settlements, which was also true of their establishments in the other neighbouring countries. If found engaging in misconduct, ULFA functionaries were never spared by locals anywhere.[151]

Nonetheless, within three days it was apparent that Operation All Clear had fulfilled its immediate objectives. All the camps, except the remote Bongaigaon camp of ULFA in the dense jungles north of the Manas National Park, had been burned or dismantled, and even the Bongaigaon camp was demolished two weeks later.[152] An overwhelming majority of the rebels had already vacated the kingdom and dispersed in different directions after crossing over to Assam and West Bengal.[153] That there was no counter-attack by the groups, except for a couple of sporadic instances, was a huge relief for Thimphu.[154] Its focus was riveted on the group in the monastery, and it was devising the means by which they could be handed over to the Indian authorities at the earliest.[155]

Missing in Action

The turnout of events was more rapid a week after the launch of Operation All Clear. Not surprisingly, Paresh's evaluation of Thimphu's motives had been wrong, compelling him to issue an appeal to the king for halting the operation in view of 'the traditional bond' between the people of Bhutan and Assam. ULFA was not critical of Bhutan during the first week of the operation, although it lamented that the crackdown was being used as a ruse by the Indian army to suppress the outfit's movement for self-determination and was launched without a 'clear ultimatum'. However, with the appeal having no effect, ULFA's stance hardened and chairman Rajkhowa declared Bhutan the enemy.[156]

Nonetheless, the Bhutan government was making serious efforts to hand over the captured functionaries to India. The sojourn of the ULFA squad at the monastery ended five days later, after the Bhutan government decided to shift them to the nearest army camp located around 8 km away, in Samdrup Jhonkar. At the army camp, all items in their possession were seized, and new clothes were provided. They were served food and allocated rooms. On 25 December, after two days at the camp, the group was again relocated to a larger camp, which had been a polytechnic institute earlier. The male functionaries, who numbered around twenty, were separated; they were blindfolded, their hands tied with ropes, and then they were shoved into jeeps.[157] Senior leaders like Mama and Robin Handique were spared, along with the women and children who stayed behind and watched in horror the spectacle unfolding before them.

The ULFA group's ordeal began a couple of hours after it was handed over to the Indian army. Non-stop thrashing for fifteen minutes was followed by half an hour's helicopter ride to another destination, which some functionaries assumed was an army establishment in Assam. The battering started again, and it was more brutal this time, with more men pouncing on the detainees and delivering kicks and blows all over their bodies. The army wanted to gather the names of politicians, lawyers and doctors in Assam who had assisted ULFA, and the names of the traders who facilitated supply of food to the camps in Bhutan. The names of a couple of lawyers who had secured bail for some of them years ago were revealed by the detainees. The interrogation, which continued the next day, covered all aspects of ULFA's activities in Bhutan. Subsequently, the detainees were handed over at a police station in Assam's Rangia.[158]

Meanwhile, the squad with most of the senior functionaries that had exited from the hideout near the general headquarters had been roaming in the hills in search of a safe track that could lead them away from the army's presence. On 23 December, they decided to take a chance at night, taking a route along a river bank near Deothang. But no sooner had they reached the river than came a volley of screams in Hindi from the jungle warning the group not to proceed further. Within seconds they were surrounded by the Royal Bhutan Army from all sides, including from the opposite bank of the river. The functionaries dropped all their weapons since escape was next to impossible. Their hands were tied and they were marched for a long time and lodged at the former polytechnic institute. They were handed over to the Indian army within a couple of days. The army passed their custody on to the police in the same manner as it had the previous batch.[159] However, about a dozen senior functionaries, including Asanta Bagh Phukan, Robin Neog and Bening Rabha, who had been apprehended with these two groups and lodged in separate rooms at the institute, never reached Assam. They were reported missing after a few days! Where did they vanish?

Interestingly, even as the ULFA squads were apprehended and lodged at the former polytechnic institute, media reports quoting Indian intelligence agencies said that several leaders of the outfit including, Mithinga Daimary, Bening Rabha, Robin Neog and NDFB publicity chief B. Erakdao, had fallen into the net of the

Royal Bhutan Army.[160] Among these four functionaries, only Daimary was handed over to Assam police by the Indian army about a week after the launch of the operation. Daimary thought he would be shot when he was blindfolded and thrashed by the army at its Tamulpur brigade near the border with Bhutan. With him were two middle-ranking NDFB functionaries who were also handed over to the police.[161] Incidentally, Erakdao had reached Nganglam a day ahead of the operation along with two NDFB functionaries for the appointment with the prime minister, but they never returned to the camp.[162]

According to ULFA, as many as twenty-six functionaries were missing in action after the operation, including a newly recruited woman from Barpeta.[163] NDFB's tally of missing men from the camps was presumed to be less, but the count was at thirty-six some years later as many functionaries remained untraceable after the operation.[164] The Indian government remained mum about this, despite efforts made occasionally to elicit information on the missing persons. Five months after the flush-out in Bhutan, ULFA abducted Assam minister G.C. Langthasa's son with a demand for information on the missing functionaries in exchange for his release.[165] He was set free but the government was unable to disclose their whereabouts.

In 2007, the Gauhati High Court directed the Assam government and the ministry of defence to furnish information on the missing cadres within a week in response to a petition by Shyamalee Gogoi, whose husband was untraceable in Bhutan. The ministry filed an affidavit stating that the list of ULFA cadres handed over by the Royal Bhutan Government to the Indian authorities could not be made public as it was an unpublished official document.[166] The statement prompted the wives of some of the missing functionaries to go on a hunger strike in Guwahati for some days demanding information from the government, but nothing was disclosed.[167]

There are different theories explaining the leaders' disappearance during the operation. The widely articulated version comes from a section of government officials and overground rebels—that they were dead within a week of their being apprehended by the Royal Bhutan Army. They ruled out the possibility of the functionaries being incarcerated in some secret jail of the Indian army or at some remote detention centre in Bhutan.[168] And, how did they die? Many officials and rebels believe they were shot dead, but there is no unanimity on the sequence of events that led to it.[169] They were last spotted at the former polytechnic institute in Samdrup Jongkhar by another section of captured ULFA functionaries who were subsequently jailed in Assam.

The controversy over the missing functionaries notwithstanding, Operation All Clear was perceived to have been a success by the two governments. By 27 December 2003, the Royal Bhutan Army declared that all the rebel camps had been burnt and more than 500 AK 47/56 assault rifles, an anti-aircraft gun, 328 other assorted weapons including rocket launchers, mortars and 100,000 rounds of ammunition confiscated.[170] The two governments doled out contrasting data on the number of rebels who were killed and captured. Indian army chief N.C. Vij's statement that 650 militants had either been killed or apprehended did not tally with the numbers released by the Bhutan government, which came up with the figure of 485 rebels dead or captured, in addition to the 11 personnel of the Royal Bhutan Army killed during the operation.[171] Estimates by ULFA functionaries were even lower—234 apprehended in Bhutan, including 168 functionaries, 27 children and 39 women;[172] a total of 15 were killed, including 13 functionaries, 2 women and a child, and 5 apprehended in Assam after escaping from Bhutan.[173] NDFB suffered 10 casualties in the operation and as many as 150 of its functionaries were captured in Assam after crossing the border from the camps.[174] And only one functionary from KLO was killed, while many were captured.[175]

Operation All Clear triggered a protest in Guwahati and a flurry of letters by ULFA and human rights organizations to the UNO calling for its intervention in bringing an end to the flush-out campaign. Senior and prominent citizens of Assam made the same request via appeals to the king of Bhutan and the president of India. ULFA chairman Rajkhowa wrote to the president of China with a request for providing asylum to the functionaries who had escaped to the mountains in north Bhutan.[176] Certainly, there were no functionaries in that far-off region in the kingdom. However, ahead of their relocation to the monastery, functionaries at the hideout near the central headquarters did contemplate sneaking into China through Tawang in Arunachal Pradesh, but did not do so.[177] It was a difficult proposition since crossing over to Tawang would have entailed trekking a long distance through Bhutan's Trashigang, one of the most militarized districts in India. In all probability, Rajkhowa must have been aware of this; he simply wanted to gauge China's response to the situation and whether there was any scope of pitching tent in that country. There was no response from Beijing. Nor was Paresh's offer of talks a couple of days later to the Indian government accepted, since it came with the riders that they must focus on Assam's sovereignty and involve a third-party mediator.[178]

The confusion among the leadership compounded the demoralization of the functionaries who had survived the operations after fleeing from the camps. They were fortunate to have crossed the border, but there was no place where they could take refuge. The government had envisaged their predicament and was prepared for psychological operations.[179] A surrender of eighty-six functionaries belonging to ULFA and NDFB, which had been finalized weeks earlier, was staged two days after the launch of the operation with wide media publicity.On 23 December, chief minister Tarun Gogoi declared a general amnesty to all militants who would surrender before 31 January 2004.[180] Many rebels considered acceptance of the offer a sensible option for returning to the mainstream.[181] By the end of January, there were an estimated 178 and 58 cadres from ULFA and NDFB, respectively, who surrendered before the government, in a trend that continued intermittently throughout the year.[182]

ULFA's network was severely ruptured in the region stretching from central Assam to the western districts. Work on constituting new battalions was delayed as the active functionaries who had not surrendered were ducking for cover, seeking safe places.[183] And there were other far-reaching consequences of the operation. The elimination of the rebel base in Bhutan had the instant effect of putting the final nail in the coffin of the KLO, which could never revive again. Its chairman, Jeevan Singha, continued to stay in Dhaka in close proximity to the ULFA leaders.[184] More important was the split set in motion in the NDFB after the offensive, when a faction led by Gobinda Basumatary inked a ceasefire agreement with the government in 2005. The limited resources of the outfit ruled out the possibility of more cadres from Assam being accommodated at the camps in Bangladesh. There was no alternative for Basumatary and the NDFB functionaries in the valley except to buy peace from the government through a ceasefire.[185]

Paresh appeared to be deeply embarrassed about his faulty assessment of the situation in Bhutan. Still, despite the setback, he gathered his nerves to firm up plans to recreate the organization in the central and western regions of Assam. He got in touch with all the high-ranking cadres hiding at different locations, instructing them to begin work for constituting the three new battalions.[186] More important in his scheme of things was the Myanmar-based 28 Battalion, which was placed under the command of Mrinal Hazarika. It was envisioned to play a vibrant role in the outfit's future campaign in Assam. The battalion had been able to sustain its operations in the eastern zone of the state despite all-out efforts by the security forces to keep them in check. Just a month ahead of Operation All Clear, the battalion had struck terror again among the Hindi-speaking communities by killing eleven daily-wagers in Tinsukia. This was followed by one of the most daring and successful attacks against the army, when the Daisa camp was blown up in the same district. The raiding party lost two cadres when the army ambushed it before it crossed the border into Myanmar. These operations were followed by an attack on the CRPF outpost at Maibela, which was destroyed completely, on the day news of Mama's death in Bhutan had arrived.[187]

The favourable conditions in Myanmar and Bangladesh hugely contributed to ULFA's revival in a brief span of time after the reverses suffered in Bhutan. Contrary to the expectations of a section of Indian government officials, Operation All Clear had neither any effect on the policies of the two countries towards the rebel outfits nor on ULFA's capabilities to recover, which was similar to the situation after Operation Bajrang.[188] This was despite the fact that the SAARC summit in Islamabad convened immediately after the flush-out campaign in Bhutan signed the Additional Protocol on the Suppression of Terrorism, which sought to check the financing of terrorist networks by making it a criminal offence. Soon, Pakistan amended the Anti-Terrorism Act of 1997 to sync it with the Additional Protocol. It was certainly a smokescreen to ward off global pressure after the 9/11 attacks in the US, which had reaffirmed the Pakistan government's links with terror groups. Even as the SAARC summit was being held, ISI was making sincere efforts under ULFA's name for offloading the largest-ever consignment of weapons in Bangladesh.[189]

CHAPTER 9

TRAIL OF CALAMITIES

Disaster at Chittagong

THE LANDSLIDE VICTORY of the BNP and its allies in the Bangladesh general elections in 2001 spurred Pakistan to chalk out ambitious plans aimed at fulfilling the twin objectives of consolidating its presence in the country and triggering further disturbances in India. Its defeat in the Kargil war continued to rile Islamabad, prompting a search for strategies for retaliation against India. ISI plunged into action by convening a series of meetings at its headquarters in Rawalpindi for a roadmap to ensure the continuity of the regime headed by the BNP and to strengthen the militant outfits in India. Subsequently, officers tasked to execute the project held meetings with select members of the pro-Pakistan lobby in the ruling political parties and intelligence agencies in Bangladesh.[1]

For the first objective of fortifying the BNP-led regime in Bangladesh, a group of pro-Pakistan political functionaries had already been discussing a plan to weaken the Awami League and its allies. Some BNP leaders proposed choking the flow of funds to the parties and prosecuting as many leaders as possible on either real or fabricated cases. Others supported the plan of a few Jamaat-e-Islami (JeI) functionaries for radical measures that would forever weaken the Opposition parties in Bangladesh—letting loose killer squads to exterminate all the top leaders of the Opposition parties. But such a plan could be suicidal and take the country to the brink of large-scale disturbance.[2]

Finally, the blueprint hammered out by the political functionaries entailed the selection of a small group of assassins by a section of the Bangladesh intelligence agencies opposed to the Awami League. Their gaze fell on the Harkat-ul-Jihad-al-Islami Bangladesh (Huji), which had sent many of its functionaries to participate in the war in Afghanistan. Within a month, two veteran functionaries of the organization who agreed to execute the operation were selected. They put together a group of half-a-dozen members, who were further briefed by the intelligence sleuths in Dhaka. According to the plan, blasts would be triggered at a location, to be decided in advance, so that the plan could then be fine-tuned to perfection.[3] The Huji functionaries were assured a hefty sum of money to execute the operation and the members were even assured passage to a safe destination if the situation were to turn hazardous for them.[4]

Even as the operation against the Awami League was being finalized, ISI decided to broach the plan of arming rebel outfits in India using Paresh and a few loyalists—BNP minister of state for home Lutfuzamman Babar and director of NSI, retired brigadier general Abdur Rahim. They were to ensure the arrival of weapons at Chittagong and their transshipment to secured destinations in the country. The weapons were to be stored until plans for their distribution in India were decided.[5] ISI's plan was to procure as large a consignment as possible through a disguised network. ULFA would be shown as the buyer from a firm based either in the Middle East or Southeast Asia, which would receive the weapons from the state-owned NORINCO in China.[6]

Paresh was vested with the responsibility of receiving the weapons from the ship with the help of trawlers and then ferrying them to the camps of the outfit after consulting the other members of the group. He would also have to make efforts to convey the impression that it was a transaction wholly managed by ULFA. And there would be no better way to create the smokescreen required than to gather advance payment for the weapons from some rebel groups in the Northeast. Paresh succeeded in the endeavour with the help of some outfits from the Northeast, which included the NSCN(IM), UNLF and NDFB.[7]

For the ISI, the immediate objectives now were to arrange funds and to pull strings in Beijing to get the weapons released at concessional rates from the state-owned NORINCO. It knew that ULFA did not have the financial prowess to cough up a huge amount for the weapons in a brief span of time. Paresh was convinced that ISI's plea for weapons at concessional rates would not be turned down by Beijing.[8]

Moreover, disturbances in India would certainly not be detested by China. He was proved correct when the ISI informed him in early 2003 that the deal had almost been clinched. A month later, Paresh told his trusted aides in ULFA to be prepared for the operation at short notice. The consignment was to be kept in underground chambers constructed at the camps in Sherpur and Satcherri.[9]

On 28 March, a five-member squad of senior ULFA functionaries assembled at the Chittagong port for the operation. They were joined by a well-known smuggler from Chittagong, Hafizur Rahman, and two officials of the NSI who helped them hire ten trucks for ferrying the weapons. The plan was to cover the weapons with bags of salt after they were loaded on to the trucks. The four trawlers set sail towards Sittwe in Myanmar with a five-member team, including three ULFA functionaries. The ship, which was believed by some functionaries to be owned by Chittagong member of parliament Salauddin Quader Chowdhury, was spotted almost eighteen hours later, at a location much farther than the spot they had decided on. The unloading of weapons from the ship, which began in the wee hours of 30 March, continued almost till noon, when the crane broke, bringing the operation to a grinding halt![10]

Only two trawlers, 'Amanat' and 'FB Khazardan', were loaded, but the ship's captain was not willing to wait any longer. He decided to depart from the spot as he was apprehensive about being accosted by the Myanmar navy. The trawlers hit the return trail and moored near Teknaf at Cox's Bazar. In the morning, Paresh instructed the ULFA squad, by satellite phone, to hit the seas again at night with the two empty trawlers in search of the ship. This was done, but without any success. On 2 April, they returned to Teknaf and headed with the other two trawlers to the jetty at Chittagong owned by Chittagong Urea Fertiliser Limited (CUFL) on the Karnaphuli river. Hafizur Rahman and the ULFA functionary were ready with cranes to receive the consignment.[11]

The situation at Chittagong took an unexpected turn. The NSI pair that had helped ULFA hire the trucks was nowhere to be seen on the day the trawlers arrived with the weapons. A few police personnel visited the jetty a few hours ahead of the trawlers' arrival, as if they had prior information about the consignment. They left after a few minutes but returned when the trawlers entered the jetty late in the evening. Hafizur Rahman and the ULFA functionary, who identified himself as Abul Hussain, claimed that it was their consignment that was being transported with the government's approval. The weapons began to be transferred from the trawlers to the trucks.[12]

The two were concerned about the presence of the police personnel, but Paresh instructed them to continue with the loading as he was confident that there would be no trouble. Six trucks were loaded within three hours, when trouble began with the arrival of senior police officers, led by Abdullah Baki. They issued orders for the operation to be halted. Rahman sternly said the police was not authorized to seize the weapons since the consignment had been approved by the government. Baki issued orders for the confiscation of the trucks and apprehended all the people engaged in the operation. Within an hour came a posse of correspondents from TV news channels and dailies, who began to take photographs of the weapons. It was no longer possible to keep the matter under wraps.[13]

The five ULFA functionaries and about a dozen daily-wagers engaged in the operation were taken to the police station near the port. Hussain's efforts to persuade the police commissioner, who too arrived at the station, to release the consignment were in vain. The commissioner politely told him that the weapons could be released only with the approval of the home ministry. A phone call did come from the ministry early in the morning, but only with the instruction to free the ULFA functionaries without registering cases against them! Within minutes, the group was dropped by the police at the outskirts of Chittagong with strict instructions to depart from the city at the earliest. They dispersed and settled at different locations for a couple of months before returning to Dhaka. For some time, Paresh was confident that the weapons would be handed over to ULFA by the government, but that did not happen.[14]

The seizure of its consignment at Chittagong was not the first time ULFA had lost some of its weapons. Two years ago, a ship carrying a consignment had vanished near the Andaman and Nicobar islands after being caught in a cyclone.[15] Then, in 2001, UNLF chief Sana Yaima was reportedly apprehended in Myanmar with a large group of functionaries but set free after payment of a hefty sum of money to the army. However, the weapons that were confiscated were not released. Many ULFA functionaries claimed that their organization had footed a part of the bill and almost half of the consignment belonged to them.[16]

Nor was the episode at Chittagong the first instance of weapons being confiscated in Bangladesh, but it was certainly the biggest ever in the country's history.[17] The 1,500 boxes the police seized were new Chinese munitions worth an estimated US$ 4.5–7 million. They consisted of a wide array of weapons, including T-56-1 7.62 mm assault rifles, Uzi and T-85 submachine guns with integral silencers, T-69 40 mm rocket-propelled grenade launchers, optical sights T-69 RPG launchers, T-82-2 hand grenades, RPG warheads, ammunition and walkie-talkie communication sets. That a small quantity of non-Chinese weapons was also included was evident from the presence of the Uzi submachine guns, which had originated in Israel years ago. Although their place of manufacture is unclear, it is highly probable that the ship received the submachine guns and other non-Chinese items in Singapore after sailing from Hong Kong.[18]

The government was in a fix as the episode snowballed into a major controversy, grabbing media attention across several countries. There was an uproar in India when it became known that the weapons were meant for ULFA and other rebel groups in the country. The issue gained added significance when Chittagong City Mayor and Awami League leader A.B.M. Mohiuddin Chowdhury claimed that the weapons were sent by the US and Pakistan to arm Indian rebels stationed in the Chittagong Hill Tracts. Opposition leader Sheikh Hasina demanded an international probe while pointing fingers at a section of BNP leaders for their involvement in the incident.[19]

Deeply embarrassed by the episode, the Bangladesh government appointed a five-member high-powered inquiry committee headed by home secretary Omar Faruk. However, no deadline had been fixed for the committee to file its report. The home secretary confirmed the involvement of three persons in the smuggling, pinned the blame on the police for failing to arrest them, but found 'no political links' to the incident.[20] Within a month, the CID was also allowed to probe the incident after investigating officer Ahadur Rahman was relieved of the task for his controversial role in the episode. A report on 11 June 2004 named forty-three people in the case filed under the Arms Act. Around three months later, a supplementary charge sheet was submitted by another investigating officer, where one more name was added to the existing list. He also probed the arms smuggling case and submitted the charge sheet in November, accusing forty-five people.[21]

So, what went wrong with the operation?

Certainly, the police would not have dared to seize the consignment if there was no instruction from the home ministry. And yet, several bigwigs were involved in the operation from the outset, including at least two ministers from the government and highly placed officers from the intelligence agencies. Several theories were doing the rounds among the ULFA functionaries in Dhaka after the confiscation and constitution of the probe. According to the first, the Central Intelligence Agency (CIA) of the US was tipped off about the arrival of the consignment by its loyalists in the DGFI who were not part of the operation. The CIA grew apprehensive that a major portion of the weapons would be grabbed by the burgeoning fundamentalist outfits in Bangladesh, which would only make the situation in the country similar to that of Afghanistan. Subsequently, the American government pulled strings in the BNP-led government to foil the operation.[22]

The second theory suggests that an Indian intelligence agency had received information about the weapons deal, probably from its sources among the overground rebel groups in the Northeast. The agency began to make efforts at a higher level to prevent the weapons from falling into the hands of ULFA. Two key functionaries of the BNP—state minister of home Lutfozzaman Babar and prime minister Khaleda Zia's son Tarique Rahman—were persuaded to get the weapons seized after they arrived at a consensus following promises of business deals. They swung into action by issuing instructions to the police in Chittagong a couple of days before the trawlers arrived at the jetty.[23]

Anup did not believe it was a case of 'back-stabbing' given his interaction with two police personnel in Dhaka jail, where he was incarcerated when the seizure was made. The two personnel had been convicted after being caught stealing a few weapons from the seized consignment. They arrived at the jetty in Chittagong when the weapons were being transferred from the trawlers but they did not know that it belonged to ULFA. They assumed it was a case of smuggling, which could offer them scope to earn a quick buck. They only realized their plan was not feasible when Hafizur Rahman told them sternly that the consignment had the approval of the government. Subsequently, they informed their seniors, who reached the spot within a few minutes.[24]

These theories notwithstanding, it is difficult to ignore the fact that it was an extremely ham-fisted operation at Chittagong. If the weapons had not been confiscated, at least three more trucks would have been necessary for transporting the consignment from the two trawlers. Arranging for more vehicles would have certainly caused more delay in completion of the operation. And if the crane had not broken, all the four trawlers would have been packed with weapons. And this would have necessitated at least twenty-six trucks at the jetty, which was not anticipated by ULFA.[25] In all probability, the operation would not have remained shielded from the media.

For ULFA, though, there was no immediate impact from the calamity, as its arsenal was still big enough to sustain its campaign in Assam. It had shelled out around Rs 1 crore as payment for the two trawlers that had fetched the weapons from the sea.[26] Paresh was left embarrassed before the rebel outfits from whom he had taken advance payment for the weapons. His reputation as the reliable gun merchant took a serious hit.[27] It was a quirk of fate for ULFA that two of the biggest seizures of weapons were made not during the regime of the Awami League but that of the BNP, which distinctly favoured the rebel groups from the Northeast. It was not until 2014, after the Awami League-led coalition returned to power, that the probe reached its logical conclusion. Charge sheets were compiled and the court awarded the death sentence to fourteen persons. The long list included Paresh, former industries minister and Jamaat-e-Islami chief Motiur Rahman Nizami and former minister of state for home affairs and senior functionary of BNP, Luftozzaman Babar, and two former chiefs of Bangladesh's intelligence agencies.[28] Paresh would be at a safe destination, away from the country, when the verdict was delivered.

Double Blast Whammy

ULFA's 28 Battalion had begun to give shape to a plan for the customary blast on 15 August, India's Independence Day. In 2004, there were more reasons for the outfit to trigger a bigger explosion on that day. The message that neither Operation All Clear nor the Chittagong arms haul could dent the outfit's ability to continue its campaign in Assam had to be delivered. But it would have to be at an unexpected location as there was a heavy deployment of security forces in the districts on the south bank of the Brahmaputra in eastern Assam. In these districts, as many as eleven blasts had been triggered by the battalion between January and July that year, targeting oil pipelines, trains and other government establishments.[29]

In June, the battalion had dispatched a two-member squad to survey the districts of Lakhimpur and Dhemaji on the north bank of the Brahmaputra, with the objectives of identifying convenient spots for a blast and of framing a strategy to enlarge the outfit's support base in the region.[30] After a recce that lasted over a month, they decided to zero in on Dhemaji, for the simple reason that the Independence Day celebrations there were always held at the large playground of Dhemaji College. There was ample space for the bomb to be planted, far away from the spot where the national flag would be hoisted. After receiving approval from the senior functionaries, the two dug a spot for planting a Programmable Timer Device (PTD) about two weeks ahead of the event.[31]

The routine call by ULFA and other separatist outfits for boycott of Independence and Republic Day was certainly diminishing in its effect, with more people participating in the celebrations every year. The Dhemaji district administration unwittingly decided to hoist the flag at a new spot, close to the place where the bomb was buried, to facilitate a larger congregation in the playground.

Bomb squads were activated in advance to search for concealed explosives. For some reason, the squad at Dhemaji could not detect the PTD, probably because the spot was not scanned effectively.[32] On 15 August, the PTD, programmed to blast at 9 a.m., went off without a hitch just as the programme commenced. All the children participating in the event were lined up in a row near the PTD. Not surprisingly, ten of the thirteen who were killed on the spot were children, and another twenty-five were seriously injured.

The death of ten children became news almost all over the world. Instances of so many children being killed as a result of a strike by an insurgent outfit was almost unheard of in the country. ULFA's immediate reaction was to deny its involvement in the heinous crime, but nobody believed the statement issued by Paresh.[33] Reports in the vernacular media accused Assam Water Resources minister Bharat Narah of being involved in the blast, which he denied as a baseless allegation.[34] Operations were intensified in the districts to nab the criminals, but they had already taken refuge far away. The two functionaries were not punished by the outfit as their version tallied with the report of the inquiry committee constituted by the battalion to probe the episode. The damage was not intended and had resulted from the district administration's plan to hoist the flag at a different spot in the playground from earlier. The report, however, pointed a finger of suspicion at the government for allowing the explosion to take place despite having received prior information about the PTD.[35]

The impact of the Dhemaji blast had been as adverse for ULFA as the disappearance of Sanjoy Ghose from Majuli seven years ago. Any hope of expanding the outfit's base into the north bank of the Brahmaputra was almost ruined forever. There was a general revulsion towards ULFA in these two districts and in a large part of the valley, which continued at least for a couple of years. Whatever little support was left among the middle class also came to an end, never to be revived. The media assumed a more critical stance towards ULFA, which was certainly tilting more towards a terror campaign.[36] Years later, both Paresh and Rajkhowa apologized for what they considered the most tainted chapter in ULFA's history, but that hardly helped improve the outfit's image.[37]

In Myanmar, panic gripped the functionaries again when rumours that a flush-out campaign similar to Operation All Clear would be launched by the Myanmar army began to make rounds. The apprehension was over the safety of the fifty-odd women and children in the region around the First and Second Battalions (of NSCN-K), where schools had also been started. Within a week, a plan to relocate them to safer locations in Assam and Arunachal Pradesh began to be implemented, and as part of it, a few were stationed as far as in Siliguri and Nepal. But there was no raid by the army as it did not want to renege on the informal agreement arrived at with the NSCN(K) three years ago on cessation of hostilities. The ULFA battalion was able to sustain its activities with the same momentum as earlier on the southern bank.[38]

The ULFA functionaries who had planted the PTD at Dhemaji were shot by the security forces after about three years near Dibrugarh, from where they hailed.[39] Fifteen years later, in 2019, the Dhemaji District and Sessions Court convicted six of the fifteen accused. Four among them were sentenced to life imprisonment, and two others were sent to jail for four years, in addition to being imposed with a fine of Rs 5,000 each. Most of them were locals who had provided shelter to the two functionaries and had assisted them in planting the PTD in the college ground. Rosid Bharali, who was identified as one of the masterminds of the blast, was absconding when the verdict was delivered.[40] In 2023, the Gauhati High Court acquitted five of the accused due to lack of evidence in a judgment that severely indicted the police for its shoddy investigation.

Even as the effect of the Dhemaji blast was still lingering, news about another blast in less than a week trickled in—this time in Bangladesh—causing just as much damage to ULFA once again. The conspirators from the BNP, JeI and the intelligence agencies had finally decided to let loose the Huji killers on the Awami League leaders, including its president Sheikh Hasina, at a rally in Dhaka's Bangabandhu Avenue on 21 August. A grenade on a truck exploded two yards from the makeshift stage on which Hasina was standing. More grenades exploded in the next minute and a half, with as many as thirteen of them ripping through the rally premises.[41]

However, the plot failed. Many party leaders and security personnel created a shield around Hasina as she ducked behind the truck while the grenades missed their target and landed on either side. She was instantly huddled into her bulletproof vehicle and her security personnel fired blank shots to clear the way as they wheeled her away through the gunfire and thick smoke. The assailants fired at Hasina's vehicle, puncturing the rear wheel and leaving a large hole on the rear right side of its windshield. At least three bullets hit the right side of the front windshield, just opposite the front seat where the former prime minister was seated. She had a narrow escape, but many others around the place were not as lucky. Twenty-three were killed, including Awami League women affairs secretary Ivy Rahman and Dhaka Metropolitan unit advisor Rafiqul Islam, and over 400 were injured in the incident.[42]

The Awami League blamed the BNP-led government for the attack and demanded its immediate resignation. Twenty people were arrested after the incident, but seventeen of them were released as no proof of their involvement could be established. The three that remained gave statements admitting their role in the attack. The one-member inquiry commission of justice Joynul Abedin blamed a foreign enemy's role in the episode. The commission also claimed to have identified the perpetrators, but their identities were not disclosed. This secrecy fuelled speculation among a section of the media in India and Bangladesh that ULFA and the rebel outfits from India's Northeast may have played a role in the attack.[43]

Quoting the preliminary investigation, some dailies published news items claiming that the grenades lobbed by the assailants were supplied by the rebel outfits from the Northeast to whom the ruling parties in Bangladesh had outsourced the job of assassinating its political rivals. The allegations cited a couple of previous instances where too the involvement of these groups was suspected. Besides the arms haul at Chittagong, which was still fresh in public memory, the seizure at Bogra almost a year ago, when a truck loaded with a huge quantity of arms and ammunition was confiscated, was widely cited in the press. Three persons who were arrested in connection with the seizure were found to be residents of Tiprapalli village in Habiganj district, Bangladesh, and functionaries of the ATTF, which functioned in close cooperation with ULFA.[44]

Neither the media reports nor widespread public criticism could compel the government to take the probe to its logical conclusion. It would have meant indicting its own ministers and senior officials of the intelligence agencies. The image of the rebel outfits took a nosedive again, although ULFA was quick to deny any role in the episode. The suspicion over ULFA's involvement in the blasts seemed to lend credence to the rumours that it had enrolled as a member of the Pakistan-based Muttahida (United) Jihad Council. Most of these reports were false, but they had the effect of alienating the secular parties from the rebel groups in Bangladesh.[45] Nowhere was ULFA mentioned in the judgment delivered in 2018 that sentenced nineteen people to death, including a former minister and deputy minister, both of whom were from the BNP. The verdict notwithstanding, a section of journalists and government officials in Bangladesh continued to believe that the grenades were sourced from ULFA's ammunition dump and that this fact was meticulously concealed from the investigators.[46]

The ULFA link to the grenade attack had almost faded away from the public memory in Bangladesh, when it surfaced again in 2007, when the chief of the Special Branch of the Assam police, Khagen Sarmah, dropped a bombshell by claiming that a jailed ULFA functionary in the state had confessed to his involvement in the attack against the Awami League. The functionary, Pallav Saikia, who was arrested in Shillong, supposedly admitted that a squad of ULFA cadres had tossed the grenades and fired from assault rifles at the rally in Dhaka following instructions from Paresh.[47] The Bangladesh High Commission in New Delhi was instructed by Dhaka to probe the veracity of the news report.[48] However, no vital leads could be gathered to confirm ULFA's involvement in the attack. There were certainly other objectives that prompted Sarmah and his cohorts to peddle the news in the media.[49]

Nonetheless, ULFA continued to be secure in Bangladesh during the regime of the BNP-led government. Paresh's links with all the agencies were intact, and he soon began to prepare to receive another consignment of weapons from China, to be ferried through a route in Myanmar. If the plan worked, this route could be utilized for more consignments in the future. So, a team of eight persons led by two senior functionaries travelled all the way from Changlang in Arunachal Pradesh through Kachin to reach China's Yunnan. It was a perilous journey that took close to three months. The presence of either the KIA or the Tatmadaw was extremely thin in the region through which the route passed.[50] But there were other dangers on the route that unnerved the ULFA team.

The group realized that ferrying a large consignment across the snow-covered mountains and through the slender pathways dotting the entire landscape was next to impossible. The route remained closed for more than three months in the year because of snow. Upon reaching Yunnan, the functionaries met with the agents, some of whom were retired personnel of the People's Liberation Army (PLA) closely associated with the state-owned NORINCO. Paresh had already footed the bill for the weapons, but it was not possible to transport the much larger consignment that he had expected. The ULFA squad was compelled to settle for less than 100 AK-56 rifles and a sizeable quantity of ammunition. There was no fear of ambushes, but the challenge was to negotiate the lethal hilly tracks while transporting the heavy load. Porters from the local Ruwang community were arranged with the assistance of the agents in Yunnan. After three months, the consignment reached the border of

Arunachal Pradesh, from where the weapons were taken to different destinations by groups of ULFA functionaries.[51]

Although there was no dearth of weapons for the 28 Battalion, a larger quantity was always welcome, given the frequent encounters with security forces. When the consignment from Yunnan arrived at the border, the army had already launched one of the biggest operations against ULFA at the Dibru-Saikhowa National Park in Tinsukia, which was larger in scale than the operations in the early 1990s. Extra troops were mobilized from different units across the region to cover as much of the area of the sprawling park as possible and choke the escape routes of the rebels.[52] And far away, in New Delhi, another process was beginning to unfold involving talks with ULFA—the second attempt to bring the outfit to the negotiating table.

The Second Peace Initiative

The Dibru Saikhowa National Park had been an ideal hideout for ULFA's 28 Battalion for many years. Spread over an area of 756 sq. km., the park is located on the eastern border of Assam, straddling the twin districts of Dibrugarh and Tinsukia. The park is bound by the Brahmaputra and Lohit rivers on one side, Arunachal Pradesh in the north and by the Dibru and Dibang rivers in the south. It was easy for the rebels to engage in operations, vanish into the thick forests and sometimes cross over to Arunachal Pradesh through the park. The army decided to launch an operation after it became known that ULFA had established a couple of camps in the park. It was assumed that the loss of this base would curtail its operations in the region.[53]

Early in 2005, two incidents hastened the implementation of the army's exercise, codenamed Operation Balwan.[54] Oil India Limited (OIL) planned to begin exploration in the park, but it had to be cancelled following a warning from Paresh, who knew that such activities could jeopardize the camps. Then, the army received information about the battalion's plan to hold a meeting in the park with the participation of some senior leaders from Myanmar.[55] By July, around 5,000 troops were deployed in a wide arc that reached as far as Pasighat in Arunachal Pradesh on the north bank of the Brahmaputra.[56] Efforts were made by the army to choke the supply lines to the hideouts deep inside the forest through intensive patrolling of the rivers by boat. Sensing danger, the rebels had already firmed up alternative supply routes that were still beyond the army's reach.[57] The army announced commencement of Operation Balwan on 30 August 2005.

There were around forty ULFA functionaries scattered across the park when the operation began to intensify from August.[58] The meeting was cancelled as all the functionaries were now focused on finding exit routes from the park.[59] The army assumed that all the functionaries in the park could be flushed out with sustained operations.[60] For the first week or so the focus was on extensive shelling of the zones where the rebels were believed to have taken shelter. Helicopter gunships would appear occasionally during the day to spray bullets from the air, but there was still ample scope for the rebel squads to relocate to safe zones amid the operation.[61] They began to suffer casualties only after the ground offensive was begun by the army in the following month. The fiercest encounter came when a squad of seven functionaries led by Montu Sonowal was engaged in a gun fight for at least five hours with the army. All the functionaries were able to escape except a woman cadre, Jahnobi Gogoi, who was allegedly shot dead after being apprehended by the army.[62]

Intermittent encounters over the next month led to the death of six more ULFA functionaries in the jungles.[63] Many among them were also able to exit the park as the army kept advancing into the interior. The army's progress was slow because of the floods that were affecting a large region of the park. However, around twenty functionaries, including senior members such as Mrinal Hazarika, remained holed up in vulnerable positions without any possibility of escape. In all likelihood, they would be killed if they were to be captured alive by the army. When Paresh was informed over the satellite phone about the dire situation, he instructed the functionaries to duck for cover, move to safer zones to the extent possible and stall the army's advance for a few days.[64] This was not only a turning point of the operation but also the beginning of another momentous chapter for ULFA.

Paresh lost no time in expediting the peace process with the government, which had already gathered steam. This initiative was supported by almost all the senior functionaries in Bangladesh and members of 28 Battalion.[65] The battalion perceived that a ceasefire would enable regrouping, deemed imperative to restore the network, without which the security forces would continue to have an edge over it.[66] The newly formed 709 and 109 Battalions in western Assam were also facing hardship in implementing plans that had been chalked out earlier.[67]

Months ago, the spadework for the peace talks had been done by noted Delhi-based Assamese litterateur, professor Indira Goswami, who urged prime minister Dr Manmohan Singh to take steps for a peace process with the rebel group. The Prime Minister's Office (PMO) had replied expressing its willingness for a dialogue with ULFA.[68] The outfit's chairman, Arabinda Rajkhowa, responded on a positive note, saying that he would participate in the talks if he received a formal invitation from the government. He also made a case for holding a plebiscite on Assam's sovereignty, which was rejected by the state government. The initiative for peace talks received support from a Jatiya Mahasabha (national conclave) in Guwahati under the aegis of the People's Committee for Peace Initiatives (PCPI), which urged the Centre to kickstart the process.[69]

ULFA dropped the first two preconditions for talks announced earlier—that they must be held in a third country and under the United Nations' supervision—but continued to insist on sovereignty for Assam as the core demand. Goswami met the prime minister twice for starting the talks, and the latter announced in Guwahati that ULFA would be invited for talks if it shunned violence. He said nothing about sovereignty, which was interpreted by ULFA to mean that that demand had been rejected. Paresh reacted sharply, proclaiming that the prime minister's statement was not different from that of his predecessors, which also indicated that the 'colonial policy' would continue in Assam.[70]

The deadlock was broken in mid-2005 when National Security Adviser M.K. Narayanan wrote to Rajkhowa indicating the Centre's willingness to discuss all 'core issues'. ULFA was also asked to forward its charter of demands.[71] The organization had finally managed to put Assam's sovereignty on the negotiating table with the government—a development unprecedented in post-colonial India. The government had never discussed sovereignty with any rebel group with whom accords had been inked. It was apprehensive that if it was granted to one group, then others would follow suit with the same demand in the future.[72]

ULFA's triumph generated euphoria among the people of Assam and hope that the talks would commence with the arrival of its delegation from Bangladesh. But ULFA was aiming to extract more concessions from the government. It was not in a hurry to take the plunge in the peace initiative. Welcoming New Delhi's decision to hold direct talks, ULFA came up with the demand that five of its top leaders—vice chairman Pradip Gogoi, advisor Bhimkanta Buragohain, central publicity secretary Mithinga Daimary, cultural secretary Pranati Deka and central committee member Ramu Mech—must be released from jail for the quorum at the central committee which must approve the talks with the government. It also sought information on the senior functionaries missing in Bhutan as a condition for proceeding further. The government grew uncomfortable and was unwilling to accept any further preconditions from the outfit. ULFA's insistence that 'sovereignty' must be unambiguously mentioned in the invitation for talks was also turned down by the government.[73] The stalemate again lasted for a few weeks.

It was at this point that the SOS from 28 Battalion, holed up in the park, prompted ULFA to constitute a nine-member People's Consultative Group (PCG) and two coordinators, including Goswami, to act as the facilitator for the talks.[74] In the group were four members who were sympathizers of ULFA and had served jail sentences years ago. Most of the other members had either been in close touch with the outfit's leaders or were trusted by them. Arup Borbora was one of the members who sought a clarification from ULFA on whether he represented the outfit or civil society in the exercise. He was informed that he would be representing civil society.[75] Therefore, PCG consisted of representatives from the civil society and also members nominated by ULFA.

Irrespective of their affiliations, the PCG members worked in earnest to fulfil the mandate assigned to them. In its very first meeting on 11 September 2005, PCG adopted a resolution inviting suggestions from the people on ways and means of facilitating dialogue between the government and ULFA. The response articulated by citizens from different age groups and communities was overwhelmingly in favour of the peace process.[76] PCG's plea before the government to withdraw the armed forces from Dibru Saikhowa National Park was accepted and the operation terminated within a couple of days after a memorandum by the PCG was submitted to Assam chief minister Tarun Gogoi. Close on the heels of these developments was the invitation from the government for the first round of talks, scheduled on 26 October, which was also to be attended by prime minister Dr Manmohan Singh.

At the meeting, the PCG briefed the government delegation, led by national security adviser M.K. Narayanan, on the significance of the exercise and the dire need for 'restraint' by the government and ULFA for the success of the talks.[77] The session with the prime minister and chief minister Gogoi began with a written proposal from the PCG saying that sovereignty was the 'core issue' that must be discussed for resolution of the conflict with ULFA. After giving the PCG a patient hearing, the prime minister replied saying that dialogue could resolve the conflict. He also asserted that he was first a representative of the people of Assam, having been elected to the Rajya Sabha from the state, and then a prime minister. Further, he reminded the members that the government was not 'scared' to discuss any issue with ULFA.[78]

This positive gesture from Dr Singh prompted the PCG to forward a few suggestions to expedite the process. It proposed that the five senior ULFA functionaries ought to be released from jail to facilitate a resolution by ULFA's central committee in favour of the talks. The PCG, however, clarified that it was not a precondition for the talks, in the same way that the plea before the prime minister for information on the missing leaders during Operation All Clear in Bhutan was. The prime minister preferred not to respond on these two issues, although he was quick to recommend another round of discussions at the level of the PMO for consolidating the exercise.[79]

It was exactly what the PCG had been hoping for. The interest the prime minister had shown was certainly a reason enough for the group to be extremely optimistic about the outcome of the peace efforts. However, even as the members anxiously waited for the next round of talks, a few disconcerting incidents began to unfold. These incidents did not augur well for trust building between ULFA and the government. In a span of two months, in December 2005–January 2006, ULFA triggered a series of blasts while the security forces killed a few rebel functionaries in encounters.[80] To make matters worse, retired governor lieutenant general of Assam Ajai Singh remarked that ULFA was a law-and-order problem, which sought to counter the ongoing initiative for a political solution to the conflict.[81]

The PCG began to harbour doubts as to whether the government was actually serious about the peace initiative.[82] The confusion was somewhat dispelled at the next meeting, on 7 February, when the government delegation led by National Security Advisor (NSA)

Narayanan reaffirmed its commitment for dialogue with the outfit. In addition, Narayanan stressed on the need for immediate confidence-building measures, an examination of the cases of human rights violations by the security forces and a discussion with the state government for the release of the jailed ULFA leaders. It was resolved that another round of talks would be held with the PCG to pave the way for a dialogue with ULFA.[83]

The PCG returned to Assam with high hopes again. Unknown to them, silent preparations were on for a massive demonstration by citizens at Kakopathar in eastern Assam to protest the killing of an innocent man, Ajit Mahanta, by the army. The situation turned worse when personnel of the Central Reserve Police Force (CRPF) took to firing at the protestors indiscriminately on 10 February, killing nine on the spot.[84] A continuous curfew was imposed for many days till the situation limped back to normalcy. Mahanta's innocence was proved when top army officers offered a cheque of Rs 1 lakh at his residence and a decision was taken to court-martial the personnel responsible for Mahanta's death.[85]

The PCG was disheartened with the hollow assurances of confidence-building measures by Narayanan at the meeting. It warned of the possibility of a withdrawal from the process if the aggressive conduct of security forces was not restrained; such a stance, it cautioned, would only jeopardize prospects for direct talks between the government and ULFA.[86] Still, the members had reason to hope for a positive outcome from the exercise. The assembly polls held in May were devoid of any violent action by ULFA. The Congress won with a thumping majority, prompting chief minister Tarun Gogoi to declare the government's intention to release the five jailed ULFA leaders after approval from the Centre.[87] And, within a week of the new government assuming office in Guwahati came the Centre's communiqué to the PCG about the third round of talks scheduled for 22 June 2006, which was also to be attended by home minister Shivraj Patil.

Façade of Talks

The third round of talks in the capital was almost a replay of the previous session, with the PCG reiterating its earlier proposals, which had not yet been accepted by the government. The death of nine persons at Kakopathar was underscored by the group to drive home the futility of the confidence-building measures that the government had committed to at the previous meeting. Nonetheless, to hasten the process of direct talks, the PCG proposed a unilateral declaration of ceasefire by the government and a halt to military operations in Assam. It assured the government that ULFA would reciprocate with a similar gesture within forty-eight hours. Further, it suggested that the period of restraint by both parties should extend to three months, during which time the date, venue and ground rules for the direct talks with ULFA would be finalized.[88]

Predictably, home minister Shivraj Patil assured the delegation that the release of the five detenus would be considered, in consultation with the state government. He requested the PCG to impress upon ULFA the need to exercise restraint so that the proposed direct talks could be held at the earliest. A joint statement was issued after the meeting, incorporating all the resolutions. The PCG returned home with lofty expectations yet again, reflected in the appeal it promptly issued to both the ULFA and the government to observe restraint.[89] However, its optimism was short-lived.

Within a fortnight of the joint statement, two ULFA cadres were shot dead in Assam's Baksa district, which was followed by another incident in Meghalaya, where four functionaries were killed. The PCG felt that both episodes were reminiscent of the cold-blooded killings by the security forces and could have been avoided since the cadres were unarmed.[90] Restraint was thrown to the winds when ULFA retaliated by orchestrating blasts that killed a few civilians. Also, there was no effort by the government to release the detained ULFA leaders, in spite of its repeated verbal commitments related to the matter.[91]

Amid the uncertainty were developments in New Delhi's corridors of power, triggered supposedly by an initiative from the PMO. The mandarins were compelled to shake off their procrastination and issue a declaration on 13 August enabling the temporary suspension of army operations against ULFA.[92] It was also a clever ploy to assess ULFA's intentions, which customarily indulged in violence on certain days of year, including the Indian Independence Day on 15 August. ULFA responded immediately with a statement honouring the government's decision and reciprocated with a declaration of a ceasefire. For the first time in a decade and a half, the Indian Independence Day passed off peacefully in Assam in 2006.[93]

The PCG hoped that the next step would be release of the jailed leaders to facilitate a resolution by ULFA in favour of talks with the government.[94] However, this did not happen, owing to many factors. Prompted by a variety of reasons, a section of government officials had gone on an overdrive to prepare the ground for the revocation of the ceasefire on 24 September. They successfully convinced their political masters that suspension of operations against ULFA should not continue as it was bound to be counter productive.[95] In fact, a memorandum to the prime minister by the PCG for the continuation of dialogue between them elicited an astonishing response. He remarked that ULFA was not interested in engaging in the peace process![96]

The PCG knew that the process that had begun with immense enthusiasm almost two years ago had crashed.[97] It had dragged on this far owing to the initiative of the prime minister, who was genuinely concerned about ending the conflict in Assam. And it was certainly at his insistence that NSA Narayanan had dispatched a letter to the ULFA chairman indicating the government's willingness to discuss the core issues.[98] However, the odds were heavily stacked against Singh, both in the government and his party, resulting in termination of the ceasefire.[99]

The security establishment was convinced that Paresh would never participate in or allow chairman Rajkhowa to get engaged in the talks for which the PCG had been putting in sincere efforts.[100] They were certain that Paresh was firmly in ISI's grip and that an end to the conflict in Assam was not in the agency's interest. No wonder the government delegates had repeatedly been inquiring at all the sessions whether the top leaders of ULFA would be present at the talks. Eventually, they began to insist on another letter from the outfit's leadership expressing its desire for direct talks with the government.[101] The home ministry also demanded that ULFA must declare the names of the representatives who would sit for talks before the five detenus were released from jail.[102] The PCG assumed they were unnecessary preconditions and tactics to derail the peace process.[103]

The ministry's concerns stemmed largely from the rising graph of ULFA's offensive in the first half of 2006, which was more intense than in the corresponding period a year ago. According to an estimate, ULFA triggered fifty-two explosions and carried out fifteen attacks on the armed forces between September 2005 and June 2006, resulting in the death of forty-one civilians and six security force personnel, and injuries to 170. During the same period, the security forces were engaged in twenty encounters with ULFA, in which twenty-one cadres were killed and forty-eight apprehended.[104] Clearly, there was a colossal deficit of trust between the two sides, which the three rounds of talks between the government and the PCG were unable to bridge. The ministry's opinion remained unchanged, despite the fact that ULFA abstained from indulging in violence during the entire period of the ceasefire.

The ministry's doubts over Paresh's intentions may not have been entirely misplaced. His objective seemed to have been to extract political mileage from the exercise and to gauge the extent to which the Indian government was willing to discuss Assam's sovereignty. He was certain that talks would not grant independence to Assam, which was possible only through military means.[105] In all likelihood, he would not have sat for negotiations with the government delegates even if it were to be held at a foreign venue, which the ministry seemed to have understood.[106] It is also difficult to accept ULFA's argument that the presence of the five jailed leaders was necessary for the quorum in the central committee and a resolution in favour of talks with the government. Most of these leaders were not present in Bangladesh when the constitution was amended in 2003 to abolish the political wing.[107] Moreover, their views on the peace process could have been solicited while they were in jail too. The government would not have blocked such an initiative by ULFA.

Conversely, if the government had continued with the ceasefire and released the leaders from jail, there is a big possibility that the outfit would have come under public pressure to explore the option of a negotiated settlement with the government. In such a scenario, ULFA might have suffered a split, with the pro-talks faction led by chairman Rajkhowa walking out in support of the peace process. He would have certainly received support from the majority of the leaders in Bangladesh and a large number of functionaries in Assam, including 28 Battalion, which was facing the brunt of counter-insurgency operations.[108]

The intelligence agencies surmised that ULFA's days were numbered in Bangladesh. It was secure in Bangladesh only as long as the BNP-led government remained in power. The regime's tenure was scheduled to end in October, after which the general elections would be held under a caretaker government. Intelligence reports predicted a thumping win for the Awami League and its allies in the backdrop of the anti-incumbency wave that had swept the country. The Awami League was expected to crack the whip against all rebel and fundamentalist groups considered close to the BNP and Jamaat-e-Islami.[109]

The home ministry's hesitant approach towards the peace process found support among a section of the army, police and Congress politicians who were determined to maintain the status quo in Assam. The situation might have taken a different turn if chief minister Tarun Gogoi had consistently supported the exercise, but his attitude underwent a change after the Congress was re-elected in the assembly polls.[110] In all probability, he was apprehensive that the presence of a popular overground ULFA faction in the state could upset his political calculations. Gogoi knew that collapse of the peace process would not cause a dent in the support base of the Congress, which was registering an upward swing.[111] The BJP's tardy expansion in Assam did not yet pose a threat to the party in the state.

The opposition by the army and a section of the police to the peace talks was rooted in the benefits they routinely derived from counter-insurgency operations. There was no dearth of incompatible statements from police officers, who were actually not authorized to speak, on the peace process.[112] States reeling under disturbed conditions offered immense scope for promotions and siphoning of funds allocated for surrenders and intelligence gathering. Between 1991 and 2012, Assam received Rs 1,357 crore from the Union home ministry for combating insurgency, which included funds for modernizing the police.[113] The security forces' expectations were heightened when a new surrender policy for militants was unveiled in 2005, when the peace process was gathering steam. It was considered an improvement over the earlier policy, involving a monthly stipend of Rs 2,000 for a period of three years for the surrendered rebel functionaries, training in a vocational skill of choice, and a fixed deposit of Rs 1,50,000 for each surrendered militant, to be made available at the end of the three-year period.[114] This was too lucrative for the officers in uniform to give up, and especially when it was not difficult to strike deals with the militants for a share of the booty.

The voice with highest decibel was that of Assam's retired governor lieutenant general Ajai Singh, who minced no words in questioning the relevance of the PCG when the Centre had already decided to explore the possibility of talks with ULFA. Singh knew the terrain well from his long association with Assam. It was under his leadership as the commander of Tezpur-based 4 Corps that Operation Bajrang had been launched to flush out ULFA. As such, his opposition to PCG's efforts and to resolution of the conflict through peaceful means was quite understandable. He epitomized the mindset of a large section of the army—that all rebel outfits in the country must be crushed before they are allowed to negotiate with the government. Revolt against the government is a crime that must never be tolerated, even if the movement is rooted in genuine grievances. The governor's conduct even prompted several legislators in the Assam assembly to make a case for his removal. They disclosed that he had incited the delegates of a political party to oppose the PCG.[115]

The failure of the peace initiative was a huge loss for ULFA and a missed opportunity in Assam as a whole, which the hardliners could not gauge. The government would never again offer to discuss the core issues raised by ULFA. In 1992, ULFA could afford to turn down the government's offer of talks as the situation in the state of Assam and neighbouring countries had been favourable for the sustenance of its separatist campaign. But it had undergone a vast transformation a decade and a half later—a fact that the government understood very well.[116] The BNP-led government in Bangladesh stepped down a month after revocation of the ceasefire with ULFA, paving the way for the general elections. The protective shield over ULFA in Bangladesh was gone, fuelling anxiety among the leaders, although the caretaker government did not seem to perceive any immediate danger. In Assam, knowing full well that the ceasefire would be short-lived, the government drew up a roadmap for the deployment of more troops in the zones where the outfit was active.[117] Paresh instructed the battalions to mount attacks on the security forces, on Hindi-speaking communities and in the commercial hubs of Guwahati and Tinsukia.[118]

Rebellion in the Ranks

Fast-paced events marked the post-ceasefire period in Assam, producing occasionally inadvertent results. Three broad trends were discernible during the period until early 2009—gradual domination of the security forces, increased retaliation by ULFA on soft targets and shrinkage of its operational space. The army was already prepared to resume operations in eastern Assam, which had been halted almost a year ago.[119] 28 Battalion no longer sought refuge in Dibru Saikhowa National Park but moved further north to remote pockets along the Assam-Arunachal Pradesh border, which became the focus of the army's exercise.[120] This apart, around 14,000 paramilitary personnel also landed in the state to give support to the police in conducting operations described by chief minister Gogoi as imperative to 'clear separatist bases in the jungles' and to instill 'confidence among the people'.[121]

The ULFA battalions were faced with a situation which was as difficult as in the late 1990s when the secret killings were in vogue.[122] They were compelled to continue the tactic of avoiding direct gun battles with the security forces and instead focus on setting off blasts in vulnerable zones. There were still enough gaps for the rebels to sneak in through and execute operations. Triggering explosions at the commercial hubs in Guwahati turned out to be the most challenging, given the layers of security that had to be breached.[123] And at times ULFA joined hands with smaller rebel groups like the Karbi Longri National Liberation Front (KLNLF) to execute operations in Karbi Anglong and the neighbouring areas of the hill district, which did not have a huge presence of security forces.[124]

The results were unexpected for the government. The fifteen months from revocation of the ceasefire to the end of 2007 turned out to be one of the bloodiest phases in Assam. Between 1 January and 10 June 2007, ULFA succeeded in carrying out sixty-eight attacks in eastern Assam and over sixty firings and grenade blasts inside Manabhum Reserve Forest in Arunachal Pradesh.[125] In January alone, as many as eighty-seven people had died as a result of these strikes, which included a large chunk of residents belonging to the Hindi-speaking communities.[126] The government scrambled to effect changes in the Unified Command structure by replacing the chief secretary with the chief minister as the head, but that hardly helped stem the ULFA rampage. Incidentally, Assam remained on the top of the list of casualties in insurgency-related violence in 2007 among all states in the country. According to data compiled by the ministry of home affairs, more than 290 civilians were killed by the militant groups in Assam and over 750 were wounded.[127]

More disconcerting for the government was ULFA's call for boycott of the thirty-third National Games, which was scheduled to be hosted at Guwahati in February 2007. Hundreds of crores had been spent on creating the infrastructure for the Games, which would be the biggest sporting event ever held in the country's Northeast.[128] All of this made holding the games a matter of prestige for the Tarun Gogoi government. The Games could not be cancelled because of the ULFA threat. So, after receiving the state government's green signal, the minister of Sports and Youth Affairs, Mani Shankar Aiyar, announced in New Delhi that the Games would be held in Assam despite the disturbed conditions.[129] It was also decided that Congress president Sonia Gandhi would inaugurate the sporting extravaganza in Guwahati.[130]

At the same time, the government continued to be anxious following ULFA's refusal to lift the boycott, despite appeals from leading sports personalities in the state. A week ahead of the inauguration, the chief minister renewed the appeal to ULFA to lift the call for boycott while also declaring that the outfit was planning to disrupt the Games.[131] Explosions in the midst of the Games would not only tarnish the government's reputation but could put an end to the possibility of hosting such events in the state forever. These anxieties, on the part of the government, sparked a hilarious chapter. Efforts were made by a section of government functionaries to reach out to the ULFA leadership for a truce. Finally, ULFA relented and called off the boycott four days ahead of the event, fuelling speculation among a section of the media on the reasons that might have led the outfit to change its stance. A news report on a local TV channel, NETV, that claimed the government had paid ULFA to get the organization to refrain from violence during the event evoked sharp reactions. The chief minister threatened to sue NETV, while ULFA asked the channel to shut down if it could not substantiate its claim with evidence within a month.[132] The controversy, which had attracted wide media publicity, ultimately fizzled out without any response from the news channel.

Nonetheless, despite the setbacks, it was established that ULFA's writ continued to matter in Assam, which the government could not ignore. After the Games, the outfit resumed its violent activities with a series of explosions, occasionally targeting even the areas inhabited by Hindi-speaking communities. But this win for ULFA came at a heavy price in terms of casualties and the increasing war-weariness among the rebel functionaries. According to one estimate, at least 80 cadres were killed by the security forces in the post-ceasefire period before the end of 2007, and this was in addition to those who decided to lay down arms for availing the surrender package.[133] Many functionaries were compelled to take refuge in extremely remote locations.[134]

For 709 Battalion, it meant venturing into Bhutan once again to examine the feasibility of reestablishing camps there.[135] A camp near Kawoipani was set up, which was followed by another in the northern region of Manas National Park. (The latter, however, had to be dismantled within six months.) It did not take long for the Assam police to receive information about ULFA's presence in the kingdom.[136] The flurry of statements on the outfit's renewed efforts in the neighbouring country prompted the Bhutan government to issue a clarification that there were no rebel camps in the country.[137] Finally, secured hideouts were established at Bongaigaon and Udalguri along Assam's border with Bhutan, which remained undetected by the security forces for several months. It was at these locations where 709 Battalion toyed with the idea of floating a rebel outfit named United Liberation Front of Bhutan among the disgruntled Nepalese citizens of the kingdom without the knowledge of the leadership. A group of about two dozen was even trained, but the fervour required to become a rebel was missing among the Nepalese.[138]

Still, the Nepalese squad managed to manufacture a few bombs and trigger serial blasts at Thimphu early in 2008, just a couple of months ahead of the historic elections in Bhutan. They were low-intensity blasts in which one woman was injured.[139] The Bhutan government had no doubt about the involvement of Nepalese militants in the incident, given their past efforts to form rebel groups in the southern districts of the country. It was of the opinion that the blasts were nothing more than a protest by a section of discontented Nepalese against Bhutan's decision not to allow the refugees from eastern Nepal to return to the kingdom.[140] The ULFA leadership in Dhaka arrived at a different version after it began to gather details of the episode and came to know about the training module organized by the ULFA battalion. It surmised that the plan was to trigger more blasts, which could not be implemented. The involvement of an Indian intelligence agency, whose plan might have been to link ULFA with the blasts, was also suspected.[141]

In greater peril was the 28 Battalion in eastern Assam, whose hideouts at Manabhum forest in Arunachal Pradesh came under attack by the army in a series of intensive operations codenamed Operation Blazing Khukri and Blooming Orchid, lasting for over a month.[142] Small squads of army paratroopers were air-dropped at different zones inside the forest. They were backed by a fleet of helicopters that did reconnaissance missions. Jamming devices were used to block ULFA communications even as the cadres were faced with food shortage after the supply routes were choked.[143] By mid-2007, the resistance weakened and most of the rebel cadres were compelled to relocate either to safer locations in the hill state or cross over to the camps in Myanmar. Consequently, the frequency of blasts and strikes against Hindi-speaking communities marked a drastic reduction in eastern Assam in the subsequent year.[144]

The eviction from Manabhum was the beginning of more hurdles for the battalion. Its commander, Mrinal Hazarika, was apprehended at Siliguri as he was returning to Assam after meeting his wife and children in Nepal.[145] His successor, Prabal Neog, met with the same fate at Tezpur within a few months, leaving the group without an effective leadership. Certainly, there must have been moles in the camp who had alerted the police about the movement of the commanders. The camps in Myanmar were demoralized, making many inmates increasingly turn in favour of reviving the peace process with the government, which had been stalled a year ago.[146] When a message was delivered by 28 Battalion to Hazarika and Neog at Guwahati jail about the prevailing ambience in Myanmar, they decided to take it up with the government with a formal proposal of ceasefire.[147]

Behind the decision by the two imprisoned leaders to push for a ceasefire was the rationale and conviction that there was no point in carrying on with the campaign for sovereignty when the Assamese community's survival was at stake.[148] So they engaged in a flurry of meetings with intelligence officials, although the government only gave the green signal for the ceasefire in March. Expediting the exercise was the army's consent following a meeting in Tezu in Arunachal Pradesh between some senior officers and a squad of the ULFA battalion led by Jiten Dutta.[149] While the Alpha and Charlie companies of the battalion agreed to a ceasefire, the Bravo's senior functionaries were doubtful as to whether the entire camp would be willing to agree to it. Still, the government decided to ink the ceasefire agreement with the two companies, comprising around 200 cadres, even without the Bravo company, which decided to stay behind in Myanmar.[150]

By early June, the process of relocation of the cadres from Myanmar to remote locations in Sadiya, Assam began. It was an unprecedented development, the biggest mutiny in the outfit ever since it became active two and a half decades ago.[151] And it was staged by a group that had been the pivot of ULFA's campaign for several years. Such an episode had a few parallels in the annals of insurgency in India's Northeast. It was somewhat similar to the split in NNC in Nagaland after the Shillong Accord was inked in 1975. Years later, the entire exercise by the two companies of 28 Battalion was to fuel a huge controversy when a senior functionary, Jiten Dutta, who had played a key role in bring about the ceasefire, was accused of murdering some hardliners opposed to the initiative. However, the allegations against Dutta, who responded with an elaborate reply on Facebook, could not be proved.[152]

On 24 June 2008, the two companies of the ULFA 28 Battalion led by Jiten Datta declared a unilateral ceasefire with the government from Sadiya after Hazarika and Neog were released from jail. The declaration was followed by an extensive briefing to the media two days later by the leaders in Sadiya, where they clarified that the ceasefire did not mean a split in ULFA. They were forced to revolt owing to the leadership's refusal to pay heed to the issues they had been raising for the past several years and its silence on the threat to the Assamese communities from illegal Bangladeshi migrants. They voiced their willingness to engage in talks with the government for a negotiated settlement and urged the leaders in Dhaka to follow suit.[153]

Another Editor Assassinated

In Dhaka, ULFA reacted with predictable fury to news of the ceasefire by expelling former commander of 28 Battalion, Prabal Neog, from primary membership of the organization. Paresh asserted that no leader of the organization at the battalion level had the authority to declare a ceasefire or sit for talks with the government, except for the central executive committee. He alleged that the ceasefire move was part of a conspiracy hatched to fuel doubts among the ULFA leadership about its lower-level leaders.[154] His opposition notwithstanding, the government inked the ceasefire agreement as there were immense benefits to be reaped from doing so. Its assessment was proved correct as the level of violence drastically reduced in eastern Assam in the subsequent years. The Bravo company of 28 Battalion found it difficult to fill the void as its area of operation was the region west of Sivasagar.[155] Security forces gathered vital inputs about its hideouts and routes from the ceasefire group, which helped in fine-tuning its counter-insurgency tactics, offering better results.[156]

The ceasefire group was lodged at designated camps in Kakopathar, Moran and Moiradanga. The cadres received a monthly stipend of Rs 3,000 each from the home ministry. They were allowed to retain most of their weapons since there was fear of retaliation by the ULFA functionaries in Myanmar.[157] And it was not to be designated as a group of surrendered cadres but as the 'ceasefire group', in a new category that was to be expanded within a few years. A memorandum listing demands, such as Constitutional safeguards for the indigenous communities, inner-line permits for entry into the state and grant of greater control to the local communities over the natural resources of the state was submitted by the group to the government with high expectations of talks. However, the government was unwilling to negotiate with the group without the engagement of a few central leaders.[158] The group refrained from contacting the leaders in Dhaka and chose to wait for their return in the future for resumption of talks with the government.[159]

Until then, there was no option for the group but to settle down in the designated camps and abide by the ceasefire ground rules. Some of the senior functionaries were permitted by the government to shift to their residences and engage in business. It was a period of stalemate, but the cadres never expressed regret regarding their decision to relinquish the campaign for Assam's independence. They were convinced that the ceasefire had saved the lives of their fellow cadres, who would have been surely killed sooner or later by the security forces that had unleashed a shoot-to-kill policy after the collapse of the peace initiative two years ago.[160] Apprehending rebels and submitting them to the judicial process was considered cumbersome and counter productive at times by the security forces. Many rebel functionaries, including some leaders, were found to rejoin the outfit after being released from jail. Among them were also a few who did not return to the jungles, but they continued to remain engaged with ULFA as overground workers.[161]

An apt illustration of the government's extermination policy, which hogged media headlines for many days, was the manner in which an executive director of the Food Corporation of India (FCI), P.C. Ram, was killed in the crossfire between the police and ULFA on 11 July 2007, three months after he was abducted from Guwahati. He had been handed over to ULFA functionaries by a squad of overground NDFB rebels almost two months after they abducted him from the city in collusion with his driver. The ULFA group took custody of Ram without the knowledge of the high command in Dhaka.[162] Subsequently, he was kept in captivity for a month in Baksa before a decision was taken to release him in Guwahati following appeals from his family. The ULFA leaders in Dhaka had also issued instructions to the senior ULFA functionaries in western Assam to ensure his release at the earliest.[163]

Ram was destined not to reach home. He was shot along with two functionaries of the outfit at a village near Guwahati by a police team led by a deputy inspector general. That the team fired indiscriminately at the hut without giving the abductors any opportunity to surrender was apparent when a group of journalists and human rights activists visited the spot the following day.[164] Ram's son Praveen charged the Assam police with killing his father and filed a petition in the Gauhati High Court for review of the probe that was being carried out by the CBI.[165] Two years later, CBI charge-sheeted seventeen persons in the case, but its plea to close the case was rejected by a local court in Guwahati, which ruled that the probe must be conducted by a 'responsible officer'.[166] This was yet another example of how the premier investigating agency had conducted a shoddy probe into a case that was not very complicated.

The extermination policy included fake encounters, sham surrenders and arrests on fabricated charges to eradicate militancy in Assam. Between 1998 and 2018, the National Human Rights Commission registered 521 complaints of encounter deaths in Assam, second only to Uttar Pradesh. There was an escalation in the number of cases in the state during 2007–08 from the previous years.[167] This also coincided with the period following the unveiling of the new surrender policy, which also meant greater allocation of funds for counter-insurgency operations. The terror of fake encounters undeniably compelled more people to agree to surrender as rebels, although they may not have been associated with any outfit at all. At times, the same rebel was coerced to surrender more than once after a tacit understanding with the officers concerned.[168] In all probability, the financial benefits from doing this were shared, with the lion's share being garnered by the officers. This bizarre situation prompted the Intelligence Bureau to compile a detailed report on the army's conduct in Assam, which was intimated to the defence ministry.[169]

The misdeeds of the army in Assam were unravelled from time to time but not that of the police officers, whose knowledge of the local terrain enabled them to remain shielded. Head and shoulders above everybody else in the racket was a suave police officer whose long list of misdemeanours began in the late 1990s, when he availed of the services of a section of the SULFA to dabble in some business in Mumbai's dockyard. Success in the venture emboldened him to form a group of loyal SULFA activists for the grabbing of government contracts and occasionally land, and the booty was equally shared. Eventually, as he reached a higher position, he expanded his operations, sometimes joining hands with the additional superintendent of police who was in the core group that had carried out secret killings in the late 1990s.[170]

In the post-2006 period, the officer retained an upper hand in the police department, dealing with cases of middle- and top-ranking ULFA functionaries who wished to surrender. The process was not very smooth for the cadres who chose to return to the mainstream. They had to separate themselves from ULFA and yet continue to extort as much funds as possible for some time. Half of what they gathered had to be shared with the officer at regular intervals. The arrangement worked well, with the officer even offering some senior functionaries in central and western Assam protection. Eventually, his focus shifted to grabbing land at prime locations in the state and extorting funds from the crime syndicates in the state. Years later, he was to land in a soup for making serious efforts to occupy a plot of land in Guwahati that had been lying vacant for several decades.[171]

Among the several highlights of the officer's crime graph was his role in the assassination of the editor of a vernacular daily in Guwahati, Anil Majumdar, by a SULFA activist whose name figured in the CBI charge sheet submitted in 2015. Interestingly, he was shot days after security officials warned journalists in the city that rebel groups could target some of them ahead of the general elections.[172] This was planted news, ensuring that the needle of suspicion pointed to ULFA. The Gauhati High Court ordered the CBI to take over the case three years after the incident following a petition by Majumdar's widow, Mallika, expressing her dissatisfaction over the probe by the CID. Three persons had been arrested in connection with the case, but the department was clearly not interested in taking the investigation to its logical conclusion.[173] The judgment described the conduct of the CID as 'strange' since it did not probe vital leads provided by Majumdar's brother, who also mentioned his suspicion of the involvement of a senior police officer.[174] And, four years later, the CBI also filed a closure report naming only a deceased ULFA militant, Bijoy Phukan, as the editor's assassin.[175]

The officer knew that he could land in trouble if Bijoy was interrogated. So, within a week, he entrusted another SULFA activist from Nagaon and a sub-inspector from his department with the task of killing Bijoy. Bijoy's bullet-riddled body was found near

Nalbari two weeks after Majumdar was shot.[176] While the officer had succeeded in derailing the CID probe, it is not clear if he was able to prevail upon the CBI to follow suit.[177] That the CBI could not gather evidence to indict the officer was astonishing, since his involvement in the episode was an open secret among senior police officers in Guwahati.[178] But what prompted the officer to murder Majumdar?

Hailing from Nalbari, Mazumdar began his career as a local correspondent of the highest-circulated Assamese daily, *Asomiya Pratidin,* and later joined another daily, *Aji* as a staff reporter in Guwahati. He had also launched and edited two weeklies, *Nishan* and *Janmat,* and later launched a daily newspaper, *Natun Din.* Eyebrows were raised when he acquired *Aji* and became its executive editor. It was rumoured that he was close to a few top functionaries of ULFA active in western Assam, who had invested funds with him in business, land and an Assamese daily.[179] Within a year of his purchase of the daily, there were widespread complaints against him for allegedly publishing unsubstantiated news stories with vested interests. In due course, he obtained lurid details about the personal life of a leading businessman in Guwahati whose efforts to strike a compromise deal with Majumdar were not fruitful. Subsequently, the businessman offered the police officer a 'supari' (contract) to get rid of Majumdar in exchange for a hefty sum of money. This was accomplished within a month.[180]

The officer's emphasis on amassing a personal fortune by all means led him to neglect the affairs of his department. This he had ingeniously covered up for many years. He had developed the right equations with some top Congress politicians and bureaucrats in the state Home Department. But his failures were too glaring to be ignored for too long. On most occasions the police had been unsuccessful in thwarting the bombings by ULFA, due to dearth of actionable intelligence. The most devastating were the serial blasts in Assam on 30 October 2008 triggered by the NDFB, which happened to be one of the biggest terror strikes in the country. Nine blasts across Kamrup (Metro), Bongaigaon, Barpeta and Kokrajhar killed 88 and injured 540, while causing large-scale damage to movable and immovable properties.[181]

The police could not prevent the lethal plan from being executed by the rebel outfit despite receiving information from a central intelligence agency and the Sashastra Seema Bol (SSB) about the possibility of a terror strike in the first week of the month.[182] Again, to cover up its inefficiency, the officer coerced a surrendered rebel to send a text message to a media house while posing as a functionary of an unknown Islamist terror outfit, Islamic Security Force—the Indian Mujahideen—and claiming responsibility for the blasts.[183] However, as subsequent investigations revealed, there was no involvement of any Islamist group in the serial blasts.

It seems that a major reason for the blasts was a pact between the NDFB and the ISI.[184] There are different theories explaining other reasons that sealed the deal between the two parties. Some Indian government officials believe that several operations were planned in India by a 'rogue coterie' in the ISI opposed to the appointment of Ahmad Shuja Pasha as the chief of the agency. In addition, this clique was unhappy with the policies of Bangladesh's army-backed regime that were aimed to crack the whip on the Islamist outfits in the country and cultivate close ties with the Indian military. So, a series of terror strikes targeting India were planned and executed in less than two months. The serial blasts executed by the ATTF at Agartala in Tripura on 1 October 2008 injured seventy-six, followed by the explosions in Assam on 30 October and the Mumbai terror attack on 26 November that year.[185] Years later, the ISI chief was quoted as saying that some retired members of the agency had trained the terrorists who conducted the operation in Mumbai.[186] Some Indian officials also feel that NDFB chief Ranjan Daimary may have been 'compelled' to agree to the plan in some way and was threatened with arrest by the ISI if he refused.[187]

A section of rebels based in Bangladesh is of the view that a combination of many factors prompted Daimary to take the plunge in the ghastly operation. According to them, Daimary always preferred to establish direct links with the ISI and not be dependent on Paresh or any middleman for transactions. His faction was in distress after the split in the NDFB, and he was exploring various options to revive the group. He might have assumed that cultivating closer ties with the ISI would also mean funds and weapons from the agency after the operation. In addition, Daimary was supposedly dejected after the overground NDFB faction in Assam rejected his suggestions concerning the framing of a charter of demands to be placed before the government. He wanted to deliver the message through the blasts that there could be no peace process between the NDFB and the government without his involvement.[188]

A series of meetings was held at Dhaka, and later at Chittagong, after a small group was assembled for the task by NDFB chairman Ranjan Daimary.[189] Police officers who probed the episodes in Assam and Tripura also point fingers at other rebel outfits and agencies that might have had a role in fine-tuning the plan for the operation in the two Northeastern states. It is possible that the pro-Pakistan lobby in DGFI might have assisted the ISI with arranging for the explosives and other ingredients for manufacturing the bombs. It appears that the ISI pinned more hopes on the NDFB than on the ATTF to produce better results, since the chances of people being killed were greater in Assam than in Tripura.[190] ATTF's areas of influence were limited and fast shrinking in Tripura following the unveiling of an aggressive strategy by the state government.[191]

Nonetheless, the serial blasts, combined with other incidents, convinced the home ministry to inform the political bosses in Assam of the need to 'cripple' the officer by transferring him to an insignificant department.[192] The Intelligence Bureau was extremely upset over the officer's repeated fake alerts on the possibility of terror strikes by Islamist outfits.[193] The government accepted the suggestion, but the officer still succeeded in grabbing the top position in the Assam police force owing to his persuasion skills. After retirement from service, he left no stone unturned in his attempts to grab the post of security adviser to the government in Assam. However, he was unsuccessful in the endeavour. Some ministers and bureaucrats knew that appointing him to the post would open the floodgates to his despicable activities again. They thus ensured that his hectic lobbying met with a dead end.[194] The reign of the monster in uniform had finally drawn to a close.

The Great Escape

Serial blasts rocked Assam on 30 October 2008, the eve of a major political change in Bangladesh. Two months later, after almost two years of army-backed emergency rule, democracy returned to the country as the pro-India Awami League-led alliance won more than two-thirds of the 300 parliamentary seats in the general elections held at the end of December 2008. The results were widely interpreted as having liberated the country from a further descent into the reign of terror unleashed by Islamist terror groups. Sensing the danger, the military-backed regime had already launched a severe crackdown against the outfits. Six prominent terror barons, including the infamous Bangla Bhai, were hanged and scores of activists prosecuted.[195] That the new government would continue the efforts to eliminate the extremist groups was a fact that the Awami League had hinted at after winning the polls. Party supremo Sheikh Hasina also proposed the setting up of a joint task force by south Asian countries for combined action against terrorism.[196]

New Delhi was thrilled with the developments in Bangladesh. In all likelihood, rebel groups from the Northeast would face the hammer from the new government as some of them like ULFA had been closely identified with BNP-Jamaat and their affiliates. The blasts gave ample fodder to the Indian security agencies to compile an exhaustive report on the activities of the rebel groups in Bangladesh, their camps, hideouts and linkages with terror networks, which was submitted to Dhaka within a month of the new government assuming charge.[197] Topping the list of the outfits was ULFA, since it had the most extensive network in the country. And among the leaders that New Delhi wanted apprehended at the earliest were Paresh and NDFB chairman Ranjan Daimary for his role in masterminding the serial blasts in Assam.[198]

The Bangladesh government proceeded with utmost caution in the operation. It had to be executed stealthily by a trusted squad not associated with the ISI or its loyalists in the intelligence agencies. There was danger of the leaders escaping from the country if information about the operation was leaked to them. A team for the crackdown, drawn mostly from the elite force, the Rapid Action Battalion, began to firm up a plan after meetings with Indian security agencies in Dhaka.[199] Since there was no extradition treaty between the two neighbours, the plan was to hand over all the apprehended rebels to India's Border Security Force (BSF) at the border. Arrest in Bangladesh was to be avoided as it could give rise to legal complications and delay the transfer of the arrested to India. Anup was still languishing in jail for more than ten years after he was arrested in Dhaka. The team decided that the first operation to nab Paresh would be launched at an opportune time in April.[200]

However, despite the best of efforts by the team to maintain secrecy, Paresh had already been informed about the developments by his allies in the intelligence agencies. He knew that his stay in Bangladesh was fast drawing to a close. For Paresh, more than the possibility of being apprehended was the danger of assassination, given the many attempts that had been made on his life in the past.[201] Perhaps no other rebel leader in India had faced as many assassination bids as Paresh; he was lucky to have escaped unscathed every time.

Paresh's close brushes with death began with an accidental episode in Bhutan a week after the general council meeting drew to a close early in 1996 at Samdrup Jongkhar. Paresh decided to travel up to some distance in the contiguous Trashigang district in the country in a vehicle with senior functionary Tapan Barua, who later headed 28 Battalion. Two hours into the journey, a speeding truck belonging to the Border Roads Organisation of the Indian defence ministry hit the vehicle from behind on the hilly road. The driver somehow managed to prevent the vehicle from hurtling hundreds of metres below into a gorge. The truck was overtaken after some time, stopped and the driver beaten up till he was almost unconscious.[202]

One of the planned attempts on Paresh's life, which almost killed him, happened at the Satcherri camp in Bangladesh, ahead of Operation All Clear. It was a meticulous exercise planned at least three years in advance by the Special Branch of the Assam police. A man in his mid-twenties, named John, was indoctrinated to perform the task in return for recruitment in the police and a hefty sum of money. It was decided that the attempt would have to be made at a convenient location in Bangladesh, either at Dhaka or at the Satcherri camp. John was trained not to make any query about Paresh or even about the organization after he joined ULFA to avoid being suspected of being a spy. He would have to simply wait for opportunity to strike, after which he would have to make a dash towards the border. If he was apprehended by the Border Security Force (BSF), he was to identify as being engaged with Assam's Special Branch.[203]

By a stroke of fortune, John succeeded in getting stationed at the Satcherri camp a year after enrolling in the outfit. It was six months later that he heard murmurs about the possibility of Paresh visiting the camp. The leader arrived a week after this, for a brief stay of only two days, during which he held meetings and interacted with all the functionaries at the camp. John's task was rendered easier when he was chosen to stand guard as part of a two-member squad outside Paresh's hut at night.[204] He was equipped with an AK-81 assault rifle, which he had never operated earlier. On the second day, his queries about the rifle surprised a few of his colleagues although they did not attach any importance to it. He was also noticed spending more time in his barrack with his bags, as if he were searching for something. On the next day he vanished from the camp, never to be seen again. Later, Paresh and the other functionaries surmised that he had not been able to gather the nerve to pull the trigger. Perhaps he realized that escaping from the camp to the nearest point on the Indian border in Tripura after executing the task was fraught with risks. So he quietly slipped out of the camp, crossed the border without being intercepted and reached Guwahati.[205] Years later, John admitted before the media that he had escaped from the camp with the assistance of a senior functionary of the ATTF but denied having undertaken any assignment to assassinate Paresh.[206]

Another attempt to kill Paresh made for a hilarious tale. A senior officer of Assam police, in a bid to siphon off a large corpus of funds, came up with the idea of assassinating Paresh through a crime syndicate in Bangladesh. Apparently, the syndicate demanded a huge sum of money for the operation, which could not have been paid by the Assam police alone. So, the officer firmed up a deal with the intelligence agency for a joint operation, following which he received the funds but probably paid only half the amount as advance payment to the syndicate. The syndicate gave him the impression that it had begun to prepare for the task in earnest after receiving the advance payment. Weeks later, the officer was also apprised about the time frame and spot in Dhaka where Paresh was to be gunned down by a team of assassins.[207]

The officer was confident that the operation could not fail since the syndicate had sharpshooters on its payroll. So it was unsurprising when, true to his expectation, the syndicate informed that Paresh had been shot at a restaurant while dining with a financial counsellor, Rumi Khan. Extremely thrilled with the development, the officer fed the media the story, which was featured on the front page of most dailies the following day. So, the intelligence agency was confused when its agent in Dhaka, who had been tasked to confirm the episode, cast doubts on the syndicate's claim. Adding to the uncertainty was Paresh's vanishing act, which lasted almost a month. He stopped interacting with senior ULFA functionaries in Dhaka and was nowhere to be seen. Neither did he call any senior journalist or acquaintance in Assam. The officer in charge was convinced that he had been killed. Still, the agency's reluctance to accept his claims compelled him to embark upon another operation to verify the claim.[208]

It was resolved to spread the news that Paresh had been killed at his native village of Jeraigaon. The ruse worked, as one of Paresh's relatives decided to go to Dhaka to confirm the news. Trailing him was a sub-inspector of police, who was somehow able to confirm that Paresh was still alive. The relative returned home, and Paresh surfaced with a bang to inform the media about the failed attempt to assassinate him. The officer knew he had been duped by the syndicate, which seemed to have understood the dangers involved in executing such a scheme, given Paresh's contacts in the government and security agencies in Bangladesh. There was also no way to retrieve the funds given in advance to the syndicate for the operation. Later, the officer circulated a story among some of his associates that the syndicate had carried out the attack at the restaurant and that Rumi Khan was killed. Paresh was supposed to have escaped by jumping off the first floor of the restaurant seconds after the gunman pulled the trigger.[209]

Within about four months of the failure of this operation came yet another assassination attempt in Dhaka. Paresh believed that this one was another endeavour by an Indian security agency. As the ULFA leader was on his way to meet an acquaintance in the city, a person hurled a big boulder at the vehicle in which he was travelling, smashing the windscreen. Paresh was seated in the front with the driver, but escaped unhurt again as the boulder missed its target. The details about this episode are fuzzy as Paresh could not gather any details about the plan or the persons involved. Why was a gun not used if the person was tasked to kill him? Probably, as Paresh surmised later, since the incident occurred at a crowded corner in Dhaka, escape from the spot would have been difficult for the assassin after pulling the trigger.[210]

All the attempts to kill Paresh had failed, but there was reason for him to be more concerned now with the changed circumstances in Bangladesh after the general elections. He was convinced that the Indian intelligence agencies had planted their moles in ULFA, which meant that more information on his movements and activities would be leaked. It could be easier to nab or mount assassination attempts on him since the earlier shield of protection from the pro-Pakistan lobbies in the Bangladesh government was gone. There was no alternative but to shift to a safe destination in another country at an opportune time.[211]

With this in mind, Paresh decided to board a flight to Karachi at short notice within a month of the new government assuming power. This was not very difficult for him to arrange. He made the necessary preparations for the sustenance of his family, consisting of his wife, two sons and the nephew of former publicity secretary Mithinga Damiary, who was brought from Assam after his parents were shot dead by the secret killers in 1998.[212] Paresh never had to wind up ULFA's business in Bangladesh worth billions of rupees, as had frequently been reported in the Indian national and regional media. ULFA never invested in any business in Bangladesh, although Paresh had individually invested in some sectors, such as crude oil, but his investments were never close to the amount reported in the media.[213] That the outfit had been under severe financial duress on several occasions in Bangladesh over the past two decades was little known. Some ridiculous news stories even narrated tales about how the ULFA's colossal deposits in Bangladesh's Sonali Bank were seized by the new government and how it had sponsored political parties in the country during elections.[214] Another fake story that had hogged the media limelight was of a meeting between ULFA general secretary Anup Chetia, when he was still in jail, with

Pakistan president Pervez Musharraf when the latter had visited Bangladesh in 2002.[215] Clearly, the Indian intelligence agencies had stolen a march over ULFA in the psychological war.

The climax was reached sometime in the second week of April 2009, when Paresh was playing football at a stadium in Dhaka. He spotted two sleuths from an intelligence agency trailing him as he exited the stadium. He knew that the operation to nab him had begun.[216] He gathered his suitcases from his residence at Dhanmandi after dodging the sleuths and headed straight to the airport. On the following day, he had already reached Pakistan. This became known to the squad tasked with apprehending the rebel leader only a day later.[217] Paresh soon flew to China's south-western province of Yunnan, where he settled down at an accommodation near Ruili, facilitated by an intelligence agency of the Chinese government.[218]

The rest of ULFA's senior functionaries in Dhaka knew that their days in the country were numbered. It was a matter of time before they were apprehended and handed over to India. Escape to Myanmar was an option, but it was not worth the risk. The journey from the neighbouring Rakhine State in Myanmar to the ULFA camps in Sagaing Division was too long and hazardous. The routes were unknown, funds were extremely scarce and there were no contacts that could have facilitated their journey.[219] In greater anxiety were a couple of functionaries who had weapons brought from the Satcherri dump stacked at their residences in Dhaka. They would either be jailed for many years or face capital punishment if caught with the consignments. Paresh instructed them over phone a couple of days later to deposit the weapons at a safe destination in the city, which they accomplished with utmost stealth and without any delay.[220]

CHAPTER 10

TWILIGHT ON THE HORIZON

Trouble in Paradise

THERE WERE CLOSE to fifty ULFA functionaries, including the outfit's leaders and some of their families left in the camps and hideouts at Dhaka, Satcherri and Sherpur after Paresh departed from Bangladesh.[1] Barring a few episodes, the rebel outfits from the Northeast had never faced any trouble from the government in Bangladesh, irrespective of the party in power. Once an ULFA functionary was apprehended at Satcherri, only to be released a week later. A middle-ranking cadre, Deep Jyoti Mahanta, was jailed after being picked up from a hideout at Sherpur and a small quantity of weapons was confiscated from him. This was followed by another incident two years ago, when the same hideout was surrounded by security forces for a few hours.[2] These were isolated incidents and not part of any government policy to eliminate the presence of the rebel outfits from the country.

To most of the ULFA functionaries, Paresh's exit from the country did not come as a shock, but they were certainly left groping in the dark over their own future course of action. That he chose to inform only chairman Rajkhowa about his plan before boarding the flight out of the country was interpreted by many top functionaries as an indication that he had parted ways with them. The friction between Paresh and the other leaders, fuelled by the interplay of many situations over the past decade, had been apparent for quite some time. The clash of opinions among the leaders was primarily over the future roadmap of the organization. Paresh was not agreeable to the suggestion of the other functionaries for talks with the Indian government without Assam's sovereignty on the agenda for discussions.[3] The other leaders were also unhappy with Pakistan's overbearing influence over ULFA. Most of them, unflinchingly, were of the view that Pakistan's shadow had changed the outfit's character from revolutionary to terrorist, and all that Pakistan wanted was to make use of ULFA for the perpetration of terror in Assam. So, an end to the conflict in Assam was not in Pakistan's interest.[4]

The third point of friction between them was Paresh's domineering role in the organization, which severely curtailed the functioning of the other leaders.[5] Eventually, from the mid-nineties, Paresh had become indispensable for the management of the finances, acquisition of weapons and ensuring the security of the base in Bangladesh. And it was Paresh who maintained the closest links with the allies in Myanmar.[6] Anup's absence only made matters worse, for he could have played the balancing act to prevent the gulf between the leaders from widening. The void left by Anup was difficult to fill, which made Paresh's task of exercising authority in the organization even easier.

Such a state of affairs could not drag on indefinitely. This prompted Rajkhowa to plan a meeting with Paresh and the other leaders sometime in the second week of April 2009. The meeting, however, never happened as there was no response from Paresh. Moreover, months earlier, he had told Rajkhowa that his presence could not be expected at any meeting that would be attended by former military spokesperson Raju Baruah and foreign secretary Shashadhar.[7] The conflict that had been brewing among them for a long time took a turn for the worse after Operation All Clear in Bhutan; it was an open secret among the functionaries of the outfit at other locations too.[8]

There was precious little that Rajkhowa and the other leaders could do in the precarious situation that they had landed in in Bangladesh. However, their premonition of an immediate crackdown was wrong, owing to the Bangladesh government's focus on putting an end the country's Islamist terror modules at the earliest.[9] The rebel groups from the Northeast were not a threat to the government as the Islamist terror organizations linked to the Opposition parties and ISI were. Still, the Indian government continued to exert unrelenting pressure on Dhaka for a crackdown on the rebel groups. New Delhi's concerns were accentuated by reports that serious efforts were on by some of the rebel leaders to escape from Bangladesh.[10] Although there were no such plans on the part of the ULFA functionaries, some top leaders of the NDFB and UNLF had seriously examined the possibility of crossing over to Myanmar and then reaching the camps further north in the country's Naga-inhabited region.[11] A small camp of the NDFB with about forty cadres had been established a year ago at Taga in Myanmar's Sagaing Division following permission from NSCN(K) chairman S.S. Khaplang. The plan was also to relocate the three dozen cadres in Bangladesh to safe locations in Assam, Arunachal Pradesh and north West Bengal over a period of a few months.[12]

The covert manoeuvres and the battle by the Bangladesh regime against the Islamist terror outfits was assiduously observed by several governments. The US embassy in Dhaka decided to go a step further by holding a few rounds of informal talks with a senior ULFA functionary to take stock of the outfit's future plans. It was a renewed interest by the US in ULFA after almost eight years, when a proposed meeting with the outfit's senior leaders had to be cancelled following the 9/11 terror attack. The US wanted the faction led by chairman Rajkhowa to resume talks with the Indian government for a negotiated settlement. It sounded quite confident that New Delhi would not be able to turn down an offer of talks if it were to be proposed by ULFA.[13] In all probability, the US had grasped the strategic significance of India's Northeast, the dire need for an end to the insurgent movements there and its own possible role in the region in the future.

ULFA did not have to wait for too long for the action to begin. The knock came two months after Paresh's exit, on the door of KLO chief Jibon Singh near Mirpur—a development that was least expected by the rebel leaders. Singh was wanted by the police in India too, for his alleged involvement in the theft of Rabindranath Tagore's Nobel Prize medal in 2004 from Visva Bharati university at Santiniketan. The police believed that the stolen item was in Bangladesh, thanks to some leads it had received about Singh's association with a person named Shiplu, who had already been arrested in Dhaka.[14] Singh escaped in time, but not an ULFA functionary, Derhagra Sarania, who was nabbed from his residence even as he was preparing to jump from the first floor of the apartment.[15] A very similar incident also occurred with ATTF chief Ranjit Debbarma, who fled from the city to Chittagong when he saw a team of sleuths approaching his residence.[16]

Sensing danger, the ULFA leaders decided to take the only option before them which might prevent their arrest in Bangladesh. They decided to revive the peace process with the Indian government, which had been stalled three years ago. They decided to convene an emergency meeting of the central executive council, where a resolution favouring talks with New Delhi would be passed. The date for this was tentatively fixed in the second week of November, but tragedy struck before the leaders could assemble for the meeting.[17]

On 1 November, Chitraban and Shashadhar were apprehended at their residences, triggering a rumour among a section of the functionaries that they had given themselves up to the authorities—which was not true. They were handed over to India four days later, in an unmistakable indication that the Indian government wanted all the rebel leaders in its custody.[18] Rajkhowa had not received anything in response to the letter he had written to Indian prime minister Dr Manmohan Singh, spelling out the outfit's desire for talks. Nor did Bangladesh prime minister Sheikh Hasina Wajed reply to his emotional plea for the remaining leaders to not be handed over to India. He began to explore other channels to reach out to the Indian government and revive the peace process.[19]

A slew of sweeping resolutions were adopted at the emergency meeting among ULFA leaders on 10 November. It was accepted that the ULFA movement was now alienated from the masses in Assam, which justified the restarting of talks with the Indian government and its demands for the release of its jailed leaders in India. Two persons earlier associated with the People's Consultative Group—senior executive of Tata Tea Limited Dr Brojen Gogoi and Rebati Phukan—were named as interlocutors in the peace process. In addition, four senior ULFA functionaries who were in jail—Anup, Shashadhar, Chitraban and vice chairman Pradip Gogoi—were named by the committee as responsible for preparing the ground for the exercise, which was a ploy to get them released. The resolutions were dispatched to the battalions with the instruction to cease the armed campaign against the Indian government.[20]

In all likelihood, Paresh had not expected this development. He was jolted into dispatching a long email to Rajkhowa, saying the meeting was unconstitutional since the executive council ought to have been dissolved in advance. He would not accept Rajkhowa's rationale that ULFA's constitution permitted the chairman to convene a meeting when the majority of the members of the executive council were either absent or had been apprehended by the government. This led to the two venting their grievances against each other, touching on a host of issues that had accumulated over a long period of time. Rajkhowa's replies echoed the sentiments of the other senior functionaries on the ills that plagued the organization. They also delivered the unambiguous message to Paresh that the die had been cast to revive the peace process with the Indian government.[21]

However, there was little scope for Rajkhowa to decide on talks with the Indian government. He was soon apprehended, along with military spokesperson Raju Baruah and both their families at Cox's Bazar, where they had assembled with other senior functionaries to discuss the future course of action. They were picked up from a hotel by a team of Bangladesh's Rapid Action Battalion (RAB), which seemed to have been on their trail from the time they boarded the bus at Dhaka.[22] They were handed over to India within a week, in early December 2009, amid speculation among a section of the media and government officials that they had surrendered before the authorities following a plan firmed up several weeks in advance with the RAB.[23] Rajkhowa has dismissed the allegation as a figment of fertile imagination.[24] This episode, which was followed within a month by the arrest of three middle-ranking functionaries, almost brought the ULFA chapter to an end in Bangladesh.[25]

The Awami League-led government seemed to be relieved that an unrelenting demand from New Delhi had been fulfilled and turned its focus to battling Islamist terror groups instead of continuing the hunt for more rebels from India's Northeast.[26] In all probability, the government wanted the rest of the rebel functionaries to move out of the country on their own without being apprehended. To deliver a stern message, two ULFA cadres were picked up early in 2010 by RAB from a hideout in Sherpur and interned for a few days. Only one among them was released while the other went missing, never to be traced, for unknown reasons.[27] In another operation five months later, NDFB chief Ranjan Daimary was nabbed in Dhaka after accurate intelligence about his movements was provided by an Indian intelligence agency. His efforts to pose as a genuine Bangladeshi citizen, which had worked a decade ago when he had been apprehended at the airport and set free after being interned at a police lock-up for three days, totally failed to convince the RAB this time around.[28]

The two-dozen ULFA functionaries and their family members left in the country were in a deep quandary, unable to decide whether to inform the government of their presence or cross the border into India.[29] Finally, the latter option was chosen following a consensus at a meeting. This was intimated to senior functionaries lodged in Assam's jails, who decided to take the Assam government into confidence with all the details of the plan. It was decided that they would cross over to India through Meghalaya's Garo Hills as it was considered safer than other locations on the border.[30] Only two senior functionaries were excluded from the group as they were determined to continue living in Bangladesh. It was decided that all their weapons would be left behind at the hideouts in Sherpur.[31]

The plan was to begin the journey from Sherpur in the dead of night on a track where patrolling by the border forces of India and Bangladesh was absent. The danger was mainly from wild elephants, whose movements were unpredictable in the region. A recce conducted by a two-member squad a day ahead of the journey zeroed in on one spot where a wide hole was punched in the barbed wire fence to enable the group to scrape through comfortably to the other side. On 22 July 2010, the group of thirty-two, including about a dozen women and children, successfully accomplished the journey without any mishap, although a bit of confusion ensued at a location in the jungle they landed in after they had crossed over from Bangladesh. The destination was a Garo village, which was reached early next morning, before sunrise, after a trek of almost six hours from Sherpur. Former ULFA publicity secretary Mithinga Daimary, who had been released from jail, arrived with some vehicles to take the entire group to his residence at Barama after a brief stopover at the Special Branch headquarters in Guwahati.[32]

So, by mid-2010, all that remained of ULFA in Bangladesh were the five jailed functionaries, including Anup, Paresh's family and less than a dozen cadres whose primary task was to keep a tab on the weapons and ammunition dumps in the jungles of Satcherri and Sherpur. They remained under wraps for some time until the Bangladesh army and RAB discovered the underground chambers.[33] Other rebel groups from the Northeast continued to have their presence in the country even as these operations continued. NSCN(IM)'s foreign affairs department Alee Command remained intact, with an office in Chittagong and small camps in the Chittagong Hill Tracts.[34] Its ally NLFT had a camp in the same region, although it was struggling to survive owing to an acute shortage of funds. The hideouts of groups from Manipur, such as the PLA and UNLF, remained undisturbed in some cities and localities inhabited by the Meitei community. They suffered less from the crackdown as they were more dependent on their base in Myanmar and their hideouts in the Southeast Asian countries.[35] UNLF chairman Sana Yaima frequented Bangladesh occasionally, and the Indian security agencies knew this. He was apprehended in October in Dhaka after he landed from a capital in Southeast Asia and was subsequently handed over to India.[36] ATTF chief Ranjit Debbarma, who was closely aligned with ULFA, managed to remain untraceable for some more time till he suffered the same fate as Yaima almost three years later.[37]

The Fourth Peace Initiative[38]

There was no doubt that the process of conflict resolution with ULFA would gather steam in Assam after the arrival of the rebel leaders from Bangladesh. The overwhelming opinion across the state was already in favour of reviving the peace process that had been stalled three years ago. The jailed leaders considered exploring the possibility of a negotiated settlement with the government—an option they believed to be more sensible than rotting behind bars ineffectively. They resolved to mobilize the opinion of civil society organizations in the state on the issue, with the twin objectives of securing greater support for the exercise and of prompting the government to release them early from jail.[39] Two former members of the PCG were tasked by the leaders with the responsibility of assembling representatives of civil society groups and prominent citizens at a national convention in Guwahati, called Sanmilita Jatiya Abhibartan, on 24 April 2010.[40]

Professor Hiren Gohain, who headed the presidium at the convention, clarified at the outset that the conclave's goal was to prepare the framework for the resumption of the peace process between the government and ULFA, without taking sides. The draft resolution adopted at the end of the session summed up the opinion of the 126-odd participating organizations, including the influential AASU and Asom Sahitya Sabha.[41] It said that the negotiations between the government and ULFA must be resumed. Before the talks began, the government was also required to provide free passage to the ULFA leaders and release its senior functionaries from jail to allow for a resolution at a general council meeting supporting the peace process. Further, it impressed upon the government the need to halt legal proceedings against ULFA leaders till a final settlement was clinched. A nine-member steering committee headed by professor Gohain was formed, with the mandate to incorporate all the suggestions from the civil society organizations into a 'charter of demands', to be placed before the government by ULFA.

So, the convention's brief went beyond the role of the former PCG, whose only mandate was to act as a facilitator of the peace process. In addition, the issue of Assam's sovereignty, which was ULFA's precondition for talks in the previous round, was dropped by the convention, although it insisted that all core issues raised by the outfit ought to be discussed.[42] Still, nothing could move forward without the consent of the ruling party in the state, the Congress, which had been reluctant to offer its support for PCG's efforts in the later phase. But, with just a year left for the assembly polls, the party's attitude had undergone a change. It realized that anti-incumbency could be a factor that could work against a win for a third consecutive term in the upcoming election. Reviving the peace process could help the party score brownie points in the

Assamese heartland, where the AGP still had pockets of support. The state cabinet seized the opportunity by approving the peace process, even without Paresh's participation.[43] Adding impetus to the exercise was the appointment by the government of the former director of the Intelligence Bureau, P.C. Haldar, as the interlocutor in the peace process.

Predictably, the government permitted ULFA to organize a meeting at the Guwahati jail to discuss the peace process. The rebel leaders resolved to convene the executive and general council meetings for endorsement of talks with the government, which would only be possible if they were released from jail. Paresh's absence was advantageous, since he had been against a negotiated settlement with the government on all earlier occasions. It was expected that he would oppose the move, but that could hardly halt the process if the green signal for talks with the government were given at the proposed meetings. Among the fifteen-member executive council, six leaders were in judicial custody while vice chairman Pradip Gogoi and former publicity secretary Mithinga Daimary had already been released on bail. The rest were either abroad or missing after Operation All Clear in Bhutan. All the eight leaders in Assam were unanimous in their opinion that ULFA must engage in unconditional talks with the government.[44]

A slew of resolutions was adopted at the executive council meeting at Nalbari chaired by Rajkhowa after a long gap of almost eight years.[45] It resolved to hold the general council by February to expedite dialogue with the government, and without Assam's sovereignty among the issues to be discussed as a precondition. A formal letter was to be dispatched to Paresh for his participation in the general council and an appeal made to the Centre for the early handover of Anup to India by Bangladesh.[46]

That Paresh would spurn the invitation was a foregone conclusion.[47] He responded with a long press release with videos from a camp in Myanmar to prove that he was not alone in keeping the flame of the separatist movement alive in Assam.[48] He had already issued instructions to the senior functionaries in Dibrugarh and Tinsukia to enrol new cadres and send them to the camps in Myanmar for training.[49] So, for the government, it meant executing the dual strategy of the peace process, with the overground faction led by Rajkhowa, and continuing the battle against Paresh's group, which labelled itself as ULFA (Independent).

Rajkhowa and his squad of delegates gathered the impression that the government was keen to ink an accord with them at the earliest after a meeting with home minister P. Chidambaram in the capital early in 2011.[50] The Congress regime in Assam continued to support the peace process after it won the assembly polls for the third consecutive term after a few months. Chief minister Tarun Gogoi even remarked that the law could be changed for final settlement of the outfit's charter of demands submitted to the Centre, which was an indication of special provisions for Assam similar to the hill states in the Northeast.[51]

The thirty-nine-page charter hammered out after almost a year of extensive discussions and debate by the nine-member committee of experts, with some additions by the pro-talks ULFA, covered all issues plaguing Assam since colonial times.[52] The charter said that 'A version of dual citizenship be put in place so as to dispel the anxiety and indignation of the people of Assam at the apaty and ineffectuality of the GOI (Government of India) in protecting the identity and interests of the indigenous people of the state and preventing the growing threat of foreigners as well as other people without a stake in the long term survival of the indigenous people acquiring political power to control their destinies.'

The charter made a case for a stringent regime for identification of foreign nationals in the state and preventing their influx, scheduled tribe status to six indigenous groups (Tai-Ahom, Koch-Rajbonshi, Moran, Motok, Chutia and the tea tribes), reservation of 88 per cent of seats in elected bodies, greater control over local resources for the indigenous communities, measures for a permanent solution to floods and erosion, and creation of employment avenues. In a nutshell, it envisaged a system prevalent in the other

Northeastern states where two categories of citizenship are in vogue.[53] Citizens from the indigenous communities are entitled to greater rights than those that have migrated from other states.

Interestingly, the charter stressed the need for discussing the 'issue of sovereignty' for an honourable accord, burying all speculation that the pro-talks faction was unwilling to broach the topic before the government.[54] It stated:

> The United Liberation Front of Assam reiterates that the ongoing issues between Assam and India can be honourably and meaningfully resolved peacefully only by a fresh look at the issues of sovereignty, so as to ensure that the people of Assam can assert their inalienable rights to control their land and their resources therein, which they inherit and occupy from their forefathers, for securing their honourable existence and for developing the economy and the society of their State, according to their needs and aspirations, and also to protect their own identity and develop themselves according to their genius ...[55]

The talks commenced on 10 February 2011 with the pep that had also been discernible in the peace processes between the government and other rebel groups. A 'suspension of operations' agreement was signed among ULFA and the state and central governments. The outfit would not surrender any weapons until the final agreement had been clinched.[56] The 700-odd lower- and middle-ranking functionaries who would abide by the stipulated ground rules were to be accommodated in five designated camps. Monthly stipends of Rs 80,000 were allocated to each of the eight leaders and Rs 3,000 for the lower functionaries lodged in the camps.[57] Certain demands, like Inner Line Permit for entry into Assam, were rejected as it was considered unfeasible in Assam due to the state's central location in the Northeast and its diverse population pattern. By 2013, both sides were in agreement on a majority of the issues except on the grant of scheduled tribe status to the six groups, which would entail a long procedure requiring approvals from the ministries of home and tribal affairs and a bill in parliament for a Constitutional amendment.[58]

The peace process was continued after the BJP-led NDA government swept to power in the general elections of 2014. The ministry of tribal affairs had habitually been disinclined to grant scheduled tribe status to more communities. It knew that acceptance of such a demand from Assam could intensify demands from other groups in the country. Sensing the grimness of the situation, the home ministry made a representation to the tribal affairs ministry explaining the exceptional circumstances in Assam and how the demand for inclusion of the six groups in the scheduled tribe category was also a safeguard against foreign nationals in the state. The home ministry produced the census figures of 2011 to illustrate the abnormal growth of the Muslim population in Assam, from 30.9 to 34.2 per cent of the total population, which was higher than the country's average. The tribal affairs ministry seemed to have discarded its reluctance when the issue was broached by none other than home minister Rajnath Singh with his counterpart Jual Oram in the Ministry of Tribal Affairs a couple of months later.[59] The logjam over the accord appeared to have been finally broken.

The ULFA delegation was thrilled with the briefing it received in Delhi in mid-2015 after a gap of one and a half years. It was told about the plan for a cabinet note for approval by the council of ministers, which would be the starting point of the procedure to amend the Constitution.[60] The Centre's urgency to take the peace process to its logical conclusion was also understandable, given that the assembly polls in Assam were scheduled for early next year. The BJP had emerged as a serious contender in the state, and it was strengthened by the defection to the party of senior leaders from the AGP and Congress. Prime minister Narendra Modi's thundering speeches on many occasions against illegal immigrants seemed to be a further indication of the Centre's commitment to firmly tackle the menace.[61]

However, in a bizarre turn of events, no cabinet note was prepared, and neither was ULFA apprised about the reasons that led to abandonment of the plan. The home ministry seemed to have developed cold feet following the growing opposition in Assam against inclusion of new groups in the scheduled tribe category.[62] At the vanguard of the movement was the Coordination Committee of Tribal Organizations Assam (CCTOA), whose campaign vigorously argued that the six groups not only did not fulfil the criteria for being granted scheduled tribe status but that including them in the category would eliminate the political rights and preferential treatment accorded to the genuine tribals of Assam.[63] The home ministry considered it a safer option to brush the issue under the carpet, what with the assembly polls knocking on the door in Assam. The BJP had already indicated its plans to firm up pre-poll alliances with tribal political parties in the state, who could be unhappy if the six communities named by ULFA were granted scheduled tribe status.

The ULFA leaders were extremely frustrated with the government's approach, so much so that some among them even thought of refusing to attend further meetings in the capital.[64] The stalemate in the talks was caused in no small measure by the uncertain position of interlocutor P.C. Haldar after the BJP-led NDA swept to power in the 2014 general elections. He was identified as being close to the Congress, which was reason enough for the government to decide on replacing him with another interlocutor.[65] Ideally, Haldar's successor Dineshwar Sharma, who was also a former director of the Intelligence Bureau, ought to have assumed charge without delay to take the peace process to its logical conclusion.[66] That did not happen. For the Centre, there were other issues meriting greater attention than talks with rebel groups in the Northeast.

Full Circle in Myanmar

After settling down at a secured hideout in China's southwestern province of Yunnan close to the border with Myanmar, Paresh embarked upon the task of restructuring ULFA, but under vastly changed circumstances. The advantages of operating out of Bangladesh were gone, along with the support of the senior functionaries who had been associated with the outfit from its inception. Only Jibon Moran among the veterans and a dozen-odd experienced middle-ranking functionaries remained with Paresh to sustain the campaign in Assam. Among Paresh's immediate tasks were to erect a mechanism for regular flow of funds to the camps, which was bound to be a major challenge as ULFA's effective area of operation had been constricted to the eastern-most districts of Assam.

No less important for Paresh was the task of identifying a new chairman to replace Rajkhowa. The chairman would have to be chosen from among the tiny crowd of senior and long-standing supporters of the outfit. Sooner or later, his identity would be known, despite his assuming a nom de guerre, which was the norm in ULFA. So the chairman would also have to be based in a location beyond the reach of the Indian government. There weren't too many people in the list to choose from.

In mid-2010, Paresh landed at Taga in Myanmar's Hukawng Valley after ascertaining a safe route to it from his residence in Yunnan. With Paresh came a small consignment of AK-81 assault rifles and ammunition that he had managed to procure from multiple sources in China and Myanmar.[67] Utmost secrecy was maintained about Paresh's arrival, following reports that renewed efforts were being made by the Indian security agencies to nab him in Myanmar. He hardly moved out of the camp, where entry of functionaries from other outfits was also curtailed, except for their leaders.[68]

All the separatist outfits from the Northeast had set up camps and training facilities within a radius of 9-10 km of the council headquarters of the NSCN(K), where its chairman S.S. Khaplang also lived. Sustenance was much easier in Taga than in the hills, with established supply routes ensuring a regular flow of all essential commodities. At least three villages inhabited by the Pangmi Nagas had sprung up near the camps, following their steady migration from the hills from as early as in 1982 and actively encouraged by the NSCN(K). The Nagas cultivated a vast expanse of land by clearing the jungles, which yielded a surplus of rice, pulses and vegetables, which they sold to the camps. Whatever else was required was imported from other destinations, which mostly came by boat on the Chindwin river.[69]

At the camp, Paresh huddled for long hours with Moran and other senior functionaries to prepare the future roadmap. It was resolved to revamp the outfit again for an effective campaign and control over the functionaries. The battalions were to be dismantled and merged into central, eastern and western commands, somewhat similar to the system before Operation All Clear. The entire Brahmaputra valley was divided into east and west zones, consisting of smaller formations called units. There were no zones under the central command, which was to operate from the headquarters and vested with the power to execute operations everywhere. While Drishti Rajkhowa, who had stayed behind in Bangladesh, was to head the western command, Bijoy 'Chinese' Das was placed in charge of the eastern command. There was also to be a moving capital, similar to 'Doi Kao Rong' after ULFA's first committee came into being in 1982.[70]

Further, a new training centre at Lungmak near Taga was to be erected, which would double up as a storage space for surplus weapons, ammunition and explosives. The camp at Taga, the smallest, where most of the senior functionaries lived, was to continue as the council mobile headquarters. In the hills, the eastern command headquarters was to be set up at Hoyat Basti in the Naga-inhabited region of Myanmar, close to the India-Myanmar border. This headquarter was in addition to the Arakan Camp at Papung and the Council Camp at Naimung.[71] With the deliberations on the restructuring of ULFA over, Paresh shifted attention to the ambitious plan of stitching an alliance of all separatist groups in the Northeast and Myanmar's Naga-inhabited region.[72]

Paresh was embarking on a tricky task that had not been successful earlier. After the attempts in 1986 and 1990, in the late 1990s, another proposal was floated among the rebel groups for an alliance at Dhaka. The protagonists were encouraged by the NSCN(IM)'s success in forging a coalition called Self-Defence United Front of the South-East Himalayan Region with the NDFB and National Liberation Front of Tripura (NLFT). The outfits from Manipur's Imphal valley had also begun talks among themselves for a similar endeavour, but they were also eager to join hands with ULFA and NSCN(K). A committee formed in Dhaka with representation from all the rebel outfits resolved to create a unified command and appoint a chairman-in- rotation from all the groups with a fixed tenure. NSCN(K) chairman S.S. Khaplang gave his consent to this too, as it would only mean more benefits to him in terms of cadres and weapons. But Paresh threw a spanner in the works, probably because he was not given importance in the discussions. His opposition was enough to scuttle further efforts at taking the venture to its logical conclusion.[73]

Paresh's new plan envisaged representation from all the seven states in India's Northeast and eventually representation from 'revolutionary groups' from other regions engaged in combat against the Indian state. For Paresh, an alliance among all the outfits was imperative owing to the limited results achieved by ULFA's separatist campaign so far. Some leaders of the other groups agreed with the plan. If the outfits agreed to join hands, the subsequent step would be a government-in-exile appointed for the seven states of India's northeast by the rebels.[74] The matter was discussed in detail at a meeting convened at the Taga camp ahead of Paresh's departure to Yunnan, where the opinions of all the participants were solicited. Except for Khaplang, who was most eager for such an alliance, a majority of the other representatives said the issue would have to be discussed with their colleagues before a decision could be made.[75] There was unanimity among the leaders for enhancing cooperation among the rebel groups and for executing combined operations.[76]

The possibility of a Chinese link to this endeavour towards a new alliance among the groups could not be ruled out, given the backdrop of Paresh's arrival at Yunnan. An uncompromising rebel leader in the grip of the Chinese security agencies would serve a range of interests for Beijing, including keeping a tab on developments in the Northeast and the neighbouring regions. Something as politically significant as a government-in-exile in India's Northeast could certainly not have been conceived by Paresh without the blessings of the Chinese agencies. It might also have been envisioned as the Chinese answer to Dalai Lama's government at Dharamshala in Himachal Pradesh, which was set up decades ago.[77]

China's engagement with militants from the Northeast had been extremely covert and selective and had been through different phases since the late 1960s. Before Paresh floated the proposal for the alliance, there was a buzz among some Manipuri groups that China was willing to revive its policy to offer assistance to the outfits if they were able to form an alliance and garner a force of 20,000 cadres. The rumours came to light after UNLF chairman Sana Yaima disclosed them during his interrogation by Indian intelligence agencies after he was handed over to India by Bangladesh.[78]

In all likelihood, China may have been contemplating greater influence over Myanmar's Sagaing Division, to replicate the power it had in the mountainous Wa-inhabited region of the disturbed Shan State in the country. China's modus operandi in the Wa border zone had been to provide weapons to the United Wa State Army (UWSA) for the erection of a formidable fighting force, which eventually became the largest ethnic armed organization in Myanmar. China has huge strategic and economic interests in Myanmar, including gaining access to the Indian Ocean through the country. This was outlined in an article titled 'Opening to the Southwest: An Expert Opinion', written by former vice minister of communications Pan Qi in the September 1985 edition of the Chinese government's mouthpiece *Beijing Review*.[79] By 2010, a slew of agreements had been finalized between the two neighbours for the construction of natural gas and crude oil pipelines.[80]

Sponsoring rebel outfits in Myanmar is China's strategy to further its interests in the region using a carrot-and-stick policy with the Tatmadaw (Myanmar Armed Forces). Further evidence of Chinese interest in Sagaing Division came only a few months after Paresh departed from Taga after finishing with the meetings. Two middle-ranking Chinese intelligence officers arrived at the ULFA camp, probably to gain first-hand knowledge of the rebel base. They were escorted all the way from the border by a squad of Manipur's PLA up to Taga, in a journey that took close to ten days, along the same route that Paresh had travelled. The two stayed at the ULFA camp for a week, interacted with senior functionaries of other outfits and toured the villages in the region before hitting the return trail.[81]

So, it seems as if Paresh surged ahead with China's approval to forge an alliance of the Northeast rebel groups. According to the plan, Khaplang was to be the chairman, Paresh would assume the dual charge of vice chairman and commander-in-chief of the combined force, and two general secretaries were to be selected from the PLA and UNLF.[82] Paresh was almost confident of sealing the deal by the end of 2011, which also explained why he agreed to give interviews to two journalists from Assam, while making elaborate preparations for them to be escorted from the border all the way to Taga. A series of meetings with the leaders of all the outfits was planned to be convened at the rebel base to give final shape to the plan. Finally, the announcement of ULFA's new executive council with a new chairman and the arrival of a weapons consignment were also timed to coincide with the journalists' sojourn at the camp.[83]

Subsequent developments, however, did not pan out entirely as envisioned by Paresh. The journalists' assignment to Taga was supposed to have been a secret, but it was leaked to the rest of the media even before they reached the destination. The Indian security agencies soon unearthed the information that Paresh was headed to Taga to meet the journalists. He was compelled to defer his visit to the camp by a few weeks for reasons of safety.[84] Details of the ULFA (Independent)'s new sixteen-member executive council that had already been constituted was emailed to the media, fuelling speculation about the identity of the new acting chairman, Dr Abjijit Barman, and a few others whose names were never heard of before. Paresh assumed the dual charge of chief of staff as a major general in the outfit and as vice chairman in place of Pradip Gogoi, who had offered support to the peace process with the government. Moran was promoted to the rank of colonel, heading the finance department as acting finance secretary. Bijoy 'Chinese' Das and Dhristi Rajkhowa were also elevated to the rank of deputy chief of staff.[85]

The identity of Dr Abjijit Barman, alias Dr Abhijit Asom, remained a secret, but only for a couple of months. Soon after ULFA announced the new executive committee, the Indian security agencies zeroed in on three candidates, all of whom were active sympathizers of the outfit, till they were certain that Dr Barman was none other than the UK-based medical practitioner Dr Mukul Hazarika who had been associated with ULFA since the early 1990s. The security agencies had already compiled a dossier on him containing details of his activities at global forums and of his residence in London.[86] Subsequently, all the details found mention in a charge sheet by the National Investigation Agency (NIA), which led the NIA court to declare him and Paresh as absconding.[87] The agency had also firmed up plans to approach the UK government with a request for Hazarika's extradition.[88] Hazarika knew he was safe in the UK and beyond the reach of the Indian government. He even gave an interview over the phone to an Assam-based news channel, where he delved into ULFA's rationale behind the campaign for Assam's sovereignty.[89]

The United Front

The change in Paresh's itinerary led to the cancellation of the crucial meeting at Taga with the other rebel leaders and, predictably, the postponement of a final resolution on the alliance. When he reached the camp a month later, towards the end of 2011, two football matches representing the outfits were organized to mark their solidarity. Paresh exuded confidence about the united front being formed at the earliest, which would be followed by the establishment of the government-in-exile.[90] There was already some buzz in the camp about the possibility of a visit to Taga by the new acting chairman from the UK in the following year. The aim of the meetings he would attend would be to stitch together a united front.[91]

The setback to the plan notwithstanding, Paresh was successful in establishing new routes for the supply of weapons to Taga. Another consignment of weapons, comprising a 100-odd second-hand Heckler & Koch assault rifles (HK33), new 9 mm pistols of European make and ammunition, was ferried to the camp on a tributary of the Chindwin. The new element this time around was that they were not Chinese weapons; nor were they shipped from Yunnan, although the role of Chinese middlemen in the deal could not be ruled out. The weapons supposedly travelled a long distance from the Thailand-Myanmar border via multiple routes, by land and river, and through checkpoints manned by the Myanmar army. The transportation was managed with bribes.[92]

ULFA's revamp, coupled with the availability of weapons, generated hope among the leaders of an intensified campaign in Assam. However, only grenade explosions continued intermittently for the next couple of years, and there were few casualties. The grid erected by the security forces was difficult for ULFA to breach and carry out large-scale strikes. Even more disheartening was the series of unexpected incidents at the camps in Myanmar, beginning with the surrender of east zone commander Bijoy 'Chinese' Das before the government in Assam. The death of Jahnobi Mahanta Rajkonwar, a school teacher who had left her family to join ULFA, at a hideout along the Myanmar-China border led to immense negative publicity for the outfit. ULFA's version that she had died in an accident did not tally with the account of some overground functionaries in Assam, who were of the view that she was hacked to death by two cadres.[93]

There were more killings that rattled the ULFA camps in Myanmar. Early in 2014, a central executive member, Partha Gogoi, was shot dead after being found guilty of conspiring with the Assam police to effect the surrender of a few functionaries who were camping with him in Nagaland.[94] But there might have been other reasons why he was handed the death sentence. Partha was among the few persons in ULFA who knew the details of Paresh's network with Chinese gun dealers and intelligence personnel in Yunnan.[95] In all probability, he was aware of Paresh's future plans, about which he hinted to a senior Special Branch official at a meeting near Kaziranga, just a few days before he died. He revealed his plan to surrender and claimed that there were other ULFA functionaries in Nagaland who were willing to return to the mainstream. The agency offered Partha some money to bring them to a designated spot in Assam. The scheme faltered after Paresh was informed of this on the phone by a cadre in the group who was reluctant to lay down arms.[96] Partha knew too many secrets, and their disclosure could spell serious trouble for Paresh. The former was thus shot dead while asleep and his body dumped at a secluded spot in Mon near the Assam-Nagaland border.[97]

The Special Branch was already in a tizzy about Partha's revelation that Paresh had sent senior ULFA functionaries to Chechnya and Kazakhstan. He had told the police that the visit to Chechnya was for gaining knowhow on chemical weapons but was unable to figure out how the central Asian republic fit into Paresh's scheme of things.[98] Paresh's links in Kazakhstan were already known to an intelligence agency, but the Special Branch was left speculating on the reasons for his links there as it certainly could not have been for business or weapons.[99] Nor would a visit to that country by ULFA functionaries be possible without the knowledge of Paresh's Chinese and Pakistani handlers. There were no clear answers, although the Special Branch officials did not lose sight of the fact that Kazakhstan was one of the world's leading uranium-producing countries.[100] Had Paresh chalked out plans to do something using uranium?

To the security agencies, Partha's death served to convey the impression that dissension was widespread in the ULFA camps. The situation could just be ripe to foment a rebellion similar to when two companies of 28 Battalion had returned to the mainstream six years ago. The Special Branch succeeded in sending over a dozen new recruits in collusion with some overground rebel leaders for an operation at the camps in Myanmar. Their mandate was to motivate as many functionaries as possible to surrender in Assam and target senior functionaries to kill them, if there were opportunities.[101] The task was easier said than done. The plot was unearthed when one of them spilled the beans to a functionary who had been based at a camp for the past several years. Thirteen of the conspirators were put before the firing squad, while two managed to escape.[102]

Moles at the camps had been a recurrent phenomenon in all the outfits. Expulsion of functionaries on suspicion of spying had also not been unknown, and had happened on many occasions in the other rebel outfits as well. More recently, NDFB president I.K. Songbijit was driven out from the organization by a faction led by B. Saoraigwra following a series of meetings at the camp in Taga. Financial hardship compelled the entire rank and file of United People's Party of Kangleipak (UPPK) from Manipur to exit from Myanmar and sign a ceasefire agreement with the government in Manipur.[103] But capital punishment for so many functionaries was an exceptional thing, which certainly did not enhance ULFA's status among the other groups.

The Coordination Committee representing the six Manipuri outfits was still unwilling to accept Paresh's proposal for a united front. They were upset over the rejection of their demand to appoint UNLF's jailed chairman Sana Yaima as the head of the alliance.[104] For Paresh, it was imperative to assign Khaplang to the post as it would serve to convey a wide array of meanings, including the merger of the separatist movements in India's Northeast and Myanmar's Naga domain. Some Manipuri leaders were also unwilling to play second fiddle to Paresh as the military chief of the planned alliance. They suspected that he would impose his own agenda on all the groups. Nonetheless, they resolved to continue with their cooperation, which was already happening among all the other outfits, and even to take part in joint operations against the Indian security forces in the Northeast.[105]

There was no option for Paresh but to extract the optimum from the existing circumstances. He could not report to his Chinese handlers that he had been unsuccessful in his endeavour to forge the alliance. His first task was to sever all links with the pro-talks faction engaged in talks with the government. Chairman Rajkhowa was expelled from the organization after being served a three-month notice to rejoin, resulting in the appointment of Dr Abhijit Barman to the post. Subsequently, Paresh went ahead with the coalition project by bringing the NSCN(K), NDFB and KLO under the banner of United National Liberation Front of Western South East Asia (UNLFWSEA), with Khaplang as the chairman.[106] This development came close on the heels of a series of meetings between the top functionaries of these groups after Paresh's arrival at Taga sometime in the latter half of March 2015.[107]

Concurrent with the birth of the alliance was NSCN(K)'s decision to abrogate the ceasefire with the Indian government that had been on since 2001. This decision triggered the second split in the outfit, with two kilonsers (ministers), Wangtin Naga and P. Tikhak, exiting with a group of functionaries from Nagaland and Arunachal Pradesh to form the NSCN (Reformation). They pinned the blame on Paresh for having convinced Khaplang to repeal the ceasefire with the Indian government, which would not have benefited the outfit.[108]

Khaplang was a veteran rebel leader who could not have been swayed by Paresh to repeal the ceasefire with the Indian government. He could not have been oblivious of the consequences of renewing hostilities with the government troops in the Northeast. He justified the decision, on the rationale that the ceasefire with the Indian government would not further the cause of sovereignty the Nagas.[109] There had been no negotiation between the two sides or submission of demands by the rebel group, as it usually happens in a peace process. New Delhi was reluctant to begin talks with a rebel chief based in Myanmar who was a bitter rival of the NSCN(IM) and with whom there was a possibility of a negotiated settlement.

Khaplang saw greater benefit in maintaining a distance from the Indian government. The chief's decision to end the ceasefire was not sudden. Rather, it was the outcome of a clever strategy that had been devised earlier. By terminating the agreement, NSCN(K) demonstrated its loyalty to Naypyidaw and its commitment to the separatist groups from the Northeast. The unwritten understanding between the NSCN(K) and the Tatmadaw had already been converted into a written agreement on 9 April 2012. This agreement enabled Khaplang to strike a fine balance between the different goals and demands of the NSCN (K) and Naypyidaw. His objectives of ensuring non-interference by the Tatmadaw in the region under his control in Sagaing Division and continuation of close ties with the rebel groups from India's Northeast appear to have been fulfilled with the accord.[110]

Not surprisingly, the NSCN(K) had attended some meetings on the nationwide ceasefire agreement convened by the Myanmar government with other rebel groups in the country.[111] That ties between the two sides had undergone a transformation can be gleaned from the fact that the Myanmar government made arrangements for Khaplang's treatment at a hospital in Yangon when he had fallen sick. A photograph subsequently published in the media showed Aung Min, a top government negotiator, with the insurgent groups, meeting the Naga chief in hospital.[112]

For the Tatmadaw, cordial ties with NSCN(K) were crucial for several reasons. At a time when conflict was on with other rebel groups in Shan, Kachin and Rakhine States, the Tatmadaw would not have liked to wage war with the Nagas. It had not yet been able to establish its authority in the areas controlled by the NSCN(K). Cessation of hostilities, on the other hand, would allow the government to make inroads into the region. Myanmarese teachers were stationed at some villages to teach the language to the children. The country's flag was also now hoisted at some villages, which was unthinkable two decades ago.[113] Gone were the days when the word 'Burma' (meaning the army) struck awe in the hearts of the people and when it only meant raids and destruction. Khaplang himself admitted that people could now sleep in peace without the danger of early morning attacks by the Myanmar army.[114] As a concession to Khaplang, the Tatmadaw had agreed to turn a blind eye for the time being to his close association with the rebel groups from India's Northeast.[115]

Paresh's hope of a government-in-exile suffered a huge setback, although he remained hopeful of the plan being implemented.[116] The unity among the groups was still unbroken, which was amply evidenced by the twin operations in Nagaland and Manipur by joint squads of the rebels between May and June 2015, resulting in the killing of at least twenty-six soldiers from the Assam Rifles and the Indian army.[117] New Delhi was rattled by the devastating strikes. The government authorized the army to carry out a couple of cross-border strikes against mobile camps belonging to the PLA, which only led to the death of about six low-ranking rebel functionaries.[118] But Naypyidaw lost no time in denying any such operation in its territory, in a clear message that it was unhappy over India's conduct. The damage was somewhat controlled after India's NSA Ajit Doval dashed off to Myanmar. Subsequently, both countries agreed to enhance cooperation on security matters.[119]

For New Delhi, there was no option but to accept the grim reality that the Tatmadaw was unwilling to dismantle the rebel camps for the time being. There were not less than sixty big and small camps belonging to the rebel groups in the region under the control of NSCN(K) and in the southern zone of Sagaing Division, contiguous to Manipur.[120] In addition, some Manipuri groups also had a presence at other places in the country, such as Mandalay and Rakhine State, where investments had also been made by them in business concerns.[121] It was more important for the Indian government to ensure Myanmar's cooperation with the ambitious Act East Policy and the Kaladan Multi Modal Transit Transport Project, aimed at providing a maritime outlet to the landlocked Northeast through Mizoram.

In the end, Paresh was thrilled when he embarked upon the return journey to Yunnan, despite his failure to enlist the Manipur groups into the alliance and form the government-in-exile. The lethal ambushes on the Indian security forces proved that he was a potent tool for the Chinese to rake up disturbances along the India-Myanmar border, which could be a cause of friction between the two neighbours. Naypyidaw's burgeoning ties, either with New Delhi or the US, was certainly not in China's interest. It was no surprise that Paresh continued to have an unhindered stay at the shelter in Yunnan.[122] Eventually, and unsurprisingly, the pro-China tilt became more conspicuous in ULFA's press releases and video messages—to the extent that Arunachal Pradesh was even described as being 'illegally occupied' by India, in a press release signed by chairman Dr Abhijit Asom addressed to the Dalai Lama during the latter's visit to the border state in 2017.[123]

Anup Released from Jail

Around the time Paresh landed at Taga for restructuring ULFA, a momentous decision was made by Anup and his two associates who had been languishing in jail since 1997 in Bangladesh. They resolved to participate in the pro-talks faction led by chairman Rajkhowa instead of joining hands with Paresh to continue with the campaign for an independent Assam.[124] With the Awami League sweeping to power in Bangladesh, there was hardly any possibility of Anup landing in Myanmar even if he had wanted to join the anti-talks faction. Moreover, he was convinced that Paresh's dominant role had been a major cause in triggering the downhill trajectory of the outfit as well as its internal strife.[125]

However, unlike the route that chairman Rajkhowa and the rest of the functionaries had traversed to reach India, the return of these three was fraught with complications. The court had sentenced them to different jail terms for the crimes they were charged with—possession of a satellite phone and foreign currency, unlawful entry into the country and the obtaining of passports through illicit means. But the terms were concurrent, which meant that they would be released from jail sometime in 2003. Anup envisaged that he would continue to remain in Bangladesh, like the other ULFA leaders, after walking out of jail with the two associates. He was certain that the BNP-led government would be able to resist India's demands to extradite him, but he was mistaken. Anup received feelers in jail that the government may not be able to defend him as the country was a signatory to the SAARC Regional Convention on Suppression of Terrorism.[126] The Indian government had been keeping a close eye on his jail term and it was an issue that figured frequently in the meetings held between the border forces of the two countries.[127]

So, stepping out of prison was a risk Anup wanted to avoid. A safer option, he inferred, was to apply for political asylum in court, which he did with the assistance of a human rights organization, Bangladesh Manabadhikar Bastabayan Sangstha. It was approved, with a judgment that all the three ULFA functionaries were to continue to remain in jail to avoid being handed over to India. The terms were renewed through subsequent petitions without any hindrance, until Anup decided to approach the court with an appeal in 2013 to allow the government to extradite him and his associates to India.[128] New Delhi was prompted to expedite the process following an extradition treaty that had been signed between the two neighbours earlier in the year.[129] This apart, there were continuous reminders from the pro-talks ULFA faction to the government for extraditing Anup from Bangladesh as his participation would give more weight to the peace process.[130]

Anup's hope of a quick return to Assam was belied when he was informed that the procedure could take as long as a year to complete.[131] It might take longer if New Delhi was slow to reciprocate in the matter of Dhaka's demand of handing over a couple of criminals who had fled to India from Bangladesh. Anup was disappointed, but there was precious little he could do except to instruct his wife and children to begin the process of crossing over in to India after informing the Indian government.[132] It wasn't until two more years that Anup and his associates finally walked out of jail, after the cumbersome procedure of extradition was completed by the two governments.[133]

They landed in India on 11 November 2015, where the CBI was waiting to arrest Anup in connection with a murder in Golaghat, which took place sometime in the late 1980s. He was released from the Guwahati Central Jail a month later, after obtaining bail in all the cases registered against him. The government did not oppose his bail as it was certain about his active participation in the ongoing peace process.[134] This was another blow to the anti-talks faction headed by Paresh, which had voiced its opposition to Anup's extradition.[135] Nor was Anup keen to make efforts to persuade Paresh to join the talks, as he knew it would be a futile endeavour.[136]

However, Anup's arrival could not break the stalemate in the peace process that been in place over the past two years. In the talks held in mid-2016, the home ministry explicitly told the ULFA delegates that the forthcoming agreement ought to be a 'final settlement' on the vexed issue of citizenship in Assam.[137] The cut-off year of 1971 for determining citizenship in the state, which was inserted in Assam Accord, had been challenged in the Supreme Court by many civil society organizations in Assam as being unjustified and discriminatory, since the cut-off of 1951 prevailed in the rest of the country.[138] The ministry preferred to wait for the judgment and prepare an agreement with ULFA that could contribute further towards resolving the matter in the disturbed state.[139] The ministry was not unhappy to defer a decision on the peace process. The BJP leadership was not bothered for the time being as the party and its allies had already swept to power in Assam's assembly polls in mid-2016 after defeating the Congress.

Besides BJP's vacillation on the matter, the fundamental reason for delays in all peace processes in the country is rooted in the drawbacks that have crept into the Indian government establishment. There is a menacing dearth of long-term planning, not only in the home ministry but in all the ministries at the Centre and the state governments. It is the thumb rule for mandarins in the ministries to maintain the status quo to the extent possible, as the likelihood of controversy is always less when such a policy is adopted. Most of the officials at the Centre who are deputed from the state cadres wish to continue staying in the capital, which is particularly true of the bureaucrats from the Northeast.

According to an RTI reply received in 2019 by a media house from the Department of Personnel and Training, of the 370 IAS officers in the rank of Joint Secretary and above with the Central government, as many as 33 were from the Assam and Meghalaya cadre—the maximum for any of the 26 IAS cadres in the country.[140] Therefore, these officials take extra precaution not to annoy their seniors or the political leadership, which could put an end to the chances of their deputation being extended. Added to this are the post-retirement ambitions of a large section of the Secretaries and the intelligence bosses, which certainly necessitate remaining on the right side of the political leadership.

It is not surprising that the peace process with rebel groups had been unpredictable and prolonged in India. Prime minister Rajiv Gandhi expedited the process in the 1980s with the rebel outfits and civil society groups in Assam leading the movement against foreign nationals. There were three agreements for Assam, Mizoram and Tripura drawn up in a brief span of time, but the sincerity displayed during his regime was not discernible in the subsequent governments. An exception was the accord clinched with the different factions of NDFB in Assam early in 2020, creating a record of sorts in the annals of insurgency in the country.[141] The BJP-led government in Assam was on the back foot and trying to wriggle out of the chaos resulting from the intense protests in the state against the Citizenship (Amendment) Act, which grants citizenship to a section of non-Muslim refugees from Bangladesh, Pakistan and Afghanistan. The accord was a tactic by the BJP to divert attention away from this matter and cement its ties with new groups in Assam's Bodo-inhabited region to ensure electoral success in the future. As such, the pace and outcome of the peace processes depend considerably on the political gains from these exercises for the ruling parties.

There were no talks with ULFA until mid-2017, when a former director of the Intelligence Bureau, Dineshwar Sharma, renewed the negotiations with the outfit. Like his predecessor, Sharma was committed to bringing the negotiations to their logical conclusion at the earliest.[142] However, his tenure was too brief for such an errand as he was abruptly relieved from the role after five months. His new assignment was as special representative to Jammu and Kashmir for a 'sustained dialogue' with all stakeholders with an aim to bring peace to the troubled state. In his position for Assam and the Northeast came former special director of R&AW, A.B. Mathur, who had served earlier in the Northeast and had followed ULFA's activities closely in Bangladesh.[143]

Mathur was nominated from the office of the NSA, Ajit Doval, in the same way that former special director of the Intelligence Bureau, R.N. Ravi, was appointed as interlocutor for the Naga peace talks. These were some decisions on interlocutors not appreciated by the home ministry.[144] The ministry, especially, abhors the direct links between the interlocutors and the PMO. It does not like to be kept in the dark on any matter related to the internal security of the country. Consequently, as a result of the turf war that followed, the possibility of an early agreement with the militant outfits in the Northeast further reduced.

Lack of consensus on matters also occasionally resulted in knee-jerk reactions in the negotiations with ULFA. In Shillong, Tribal Affairs minister Jual Oram issued a statement that the government was actively considering grant of scheduled tribe status for six communities in Assam, as demanded by ULFA. He pointed out that a decision had been taken to appoint a committee headed by a special secretary in the home ministry for recommending the modalities for completing the process, which would again be examined by an inter-ministerial group. The minister was also of the opinion that the interests of the existing tribal communities in the state would not be hampered if the six communities were to be included in the category.[145] Nothing more was heard regarding this, either about the committee or about the government's efforts to accept the demand.

False hopes were raised again towards the end of 2018 following Mathur's arrival in Guwahati and his extensive discussions with senior ULFA functionaries and members of the committee constituted by the state government to submit recommendations for the implementation of Clause 6 of Assam Accord, which provides Constitutional safeguards to the indigenous communities of the state.[146] The trigger this time came from the violent protests that erupted in the Northeast against the proposed Citizenship (Amendment) Act. The hill states in the Northeast were apprehensive of being swamped by refugees from Bangladesh. For Assam, there were additional reasons that prompted lakhs of people to hit the streets. The cut-off date in the Act for grant of citizenship to a section of non-Muslims from the neighbouring countries was 31 December 2014, which nullified the date of 25 March 1971 in the Assam Accord. The change also meant grant of citizenship to lakhs of Bangladeshi Hindus excluded from the National Register of Citizens (NRC).

The ruling BJP was concerned about the impending general elections in mid-2019. It expected to win a sizeable number of seats from the Northeast, which was possible only if the agitation subsided and the tie-ups with the regional allies sustained. Before arriving in Guwahati, Mathur had been briefed by prime minister Narendra Modi and home minister Amit Shah on the prospects of an agreement with ULFA, which would also entail an amendment to the Constitution for special rights for Assam, similar to the provisions made for the hill states.[147] The government's gesture appeared to be in sync with the assertion by ULFA that it would not sign any agreement unless scheduled tribe status was granted to the six communities that it had identified, land rights assured for all indigenous groups and seats reserved for them in elected bodies to ensure that political power would not be snatched away by non-indigenous communities.[148]

Mathur's sojourn in Guwahati evoked widespread rumours that the BJP would choose to implement Constitutional safeguards for the indigenous communities through the agreement with ULFA instead of accepting the recommendations of the Clause-6 committee.[149] It was believed that the BJP did not want to give credit to AASU, which had been leading the campaign against the new citizenship law. All this appeared possible, but clearly it was not enough to seal the deal. Many recommendations of the Clause 6 committee and ULFA's charter of demands were similar. The BJP leadership became confident of a marvellous performance in the general elections in the Northeast, even without agreements with any rebel group. Its assessment was proved correct. The BJP and its allies won eighteen of the twenty-five seats in the Northeast. The ULFA leaders were certain that they would not hear again from the government on the agreement till a few months ahead of the assembly elections in Assam in 2021.

Tatmadaw's About-Turn

ULFA's anti-talks faction in Myanmar fared even worse than its overground counterpart in Assam, which was engaged in the peace process. Paresh's efforts to expand the alliance met with limited success as only two small outfits—NLFT and the People's Democratic Council of Karbi Longri (PDCK), formed by expelled NDFB president I.K. Songbijit—agreed to enrol as members of the UNFLWSEA.[150] Nor could the plummeting trend of its campaign be reversed in Assam, which was a clear indication of the upper hand having been gained by the security forces in the state. Still, alternative tactics were continually put into action by the outfit to enlarge its support base.

On its thirty-ninth foundation day, ULFA(I) came out with an elaborate 'roadmap' for a sovereign Assam where indigenous communities and tribes were to get equal rights and control in terms of governance, thus discarding the present 'population-weighted representation' system of governance. Further, the roadmap said the government and administration would be under the control of the indigenous people, which was meant to assuage their anxiety about immigrant communities gaining greater political power as a result of their soaring numbers in Assam. Press releases were also issued, making a fervent case for the banning of Hindi songs during Bihu and for resisting the invasion of Hindi culture in Assam.[151]

The issue snowballed into a major controversy when singing icon Zubeen Garg defied the ban, prompting the outfit to warn him of 'dire consequences'.[152] A frontal organization, ANMMMTA (which stands for Arunachal Pradesh, Nagaland, Mizoram, Manipur, Meghalaya, Tripura and Assam), was founded in Golaghat, with the twin goals of propagating the objectives of the new alliance and bringing about mass mobilization through democratic means and the media, but it had no impact.[153] A renewed drive for recruitment was made, bringing on board people with a technical background, possibly to test the waters of cyber warfare. Close to forty youths were roped in during 2017–18, some of whom were settled along the China-Myanmar border.[154]

Even as these policies were unveiled, a danger was looming on the horizon, concealed from ULFA and the other outfits in Myanmar. The trigger was the demise of NSCN(K) chairman S.S.

Khaplang on 9 June 2017 at the outfit's council headquarters in Taga after weeks of illness. His absence intensified the conflict between the Konyak-Pangmi and Sumi factions in the NSCN(K), which had already been at loggerheads over certain issues for several years. The vice president of GPRN, Khango Konyak, had reportedly blocked some proposals forwarded by army chief Nikki Summi. Both hailed from Nagaland and were also contenders for the top position, although it was almost certain that Khango would be Khaplang's successor.[155]

Khaplang had been a godfather to the Nagas in Myanmar and had assumed a larger-than-life persona, similar to that of Angami Zapu Phizo—who had headed the Naga National Council for many decades from the late 1940s and articulated the demand for Nagaland's secession from India—in Nagaland. It was a role that Khango found incredibly difficult to fulfil as chairman, with the result that his authority was never accepted by many of the senior functionaries. Khaplang's young nephew Yung Aung rallied a large number of Myanmar-based senior functionaries to impeach Khango almost a year later, 'to save the party from further breakdown and confusion'.[156] Konyak returned to Nagaland and offered support to the ongoing peace process between the rebel groups led by NSCN(IM) and the government.[157]

In reality, the root of the conflict in NSCN(K) was again the distrust between the Naga leaders of Myanmar and Nagaland. When clashes broke out in 1988 leading to the split in the NSCN, all the tribes from the eastern districts of Nagaland and Arunachal Pradesh had joined hands with Khaplang to drive out the Isak-Muivah faction from Myanmar. The circumstances were no longer the same three decades later, as many leaders from the Northeast considered it wise to sever their links with Myanmar. NSCN(K) army chief Nikki Summi was no less unhappy with Yung Aung's assumption of the chairman's role. Summi's refusal to attend some meetings at the council headquarters in Taga was the beginning of another clash in the organization, sowing the seeds for another split.[158]

The internal feud in the NSCN(K), coupled with the mounting campaign of another rebel outfit, the Arakan Army in Myanmar's Rakhine and Chin States bordering Mizoram, offered the perfect opportunity for the Indian army and the Tatmadaw to collaborate for coordinated operations against the rebel groups at both the border zones.[159] The Tatmadaw had ignored New Delhi's repeated pleas for action against the Northeast rebels owing to an interplay of many factors. By 2019, the situation had undergone a change, prompting a change in its policies too.

The Tatmadaw had friendly ties with the NSCN(K), but it was also upset over the outfit's refusal to sign the Nationwide Ceasefire Agreement, despite repeated reminders.[160] The Arakan Army's expansion in Myanmar's Rakhine and Chin States, which lay in the region south of Mizoram, was a serious concern for New Delhi as it could delay implementation of the flagship Kaladan Multi-Modal Transit Transport Project. Occasionally, the outfit's functionaries had been crossing over to Mizoram for shelter in the villages inhabited by Rakhine Buddhists to escape from the operations of the Tatmadaw.[161]

For the Tatmadaw, the Arakan Army was a cause for alarm as it had ties with insurgent groups in Kachin and Shan States and with China, which was evidenced by the sophisticated weaponry in its arsenal.[162] Towards the end of 2017, eleven personnel of the Myanmar army were killed in an ambush at Paletwa on the Kaladan river by the rebel group.[163] Possibly, the Tatmadaw was under the impression that efforts would be on by the big neighbour to carve out a zone of influence in the region with the assistance of the Arakan Army, similar to what had happened in the Wa Autonomous Region in Shan State. China has high stakes in Rakhine State, including the construction of a deep-sea port at Kyaukphyu, planned years ago for access to the Indian Ocean.[164]

Rakhine State also merited greater attention from the Tatmadaw as it was already reeling under disturbances following the emergence of another outfit called the Arakan Rohingya Salvation Army (ARSA) in the Rohingya community. On 25 August 2017, Rohingya insurgents and their supporters attacked thirty police outposts and an army base around Maungdaw and Buthidaung in northern Rakhine State, killing twelve members of the security forces.[165] It marked a major escalation in the conflict that had been simmering since the previous year. In fierce retaliation to the attack, the army indulged in 'clearance operations', resulting in many killings and the pushing of over 7 lakh Rohingya settlers into Bangladesh.[166] So the region was a veritable tinder box; things could spin out of the Tatmadaw's control if normalcy was not restored soon.

The agreement arrived at between the Indian army and the Tatmadaw entailed Operation Sunrise (I & II), first at Taga by Myanmarese troops, to be followed by another at certain locations in Chin State, where the Arakan Army had carved out a support base. The Indian army and Assam Rifles were to be deployed along certain stretches of the border in Mizoram to check the influx of rebels and also refugees from Myanmar.[167] In 2017, operations launched by the Tatmadaw against the Arakan Army compelled many citizens from Chin State to take shelter in Mizoram.[168] This was to be followed up by more operations by the Tatmadaw to dismantle the other establishments of the NSCN(K) in Sagaing Division, such as the Second Battalion, general headquarters and council, where other rebel groups from the Northeast had also established camps and training facilities.[169] The understanding arrived at for collaboration between the Indian and Myanmar armed forces was part of a larger deal entailing the transfer of a Russian Kilo-class diesel-electric submarine by India to Myanmar a year later.[170]

On 20 January 2019, around 1,000 Myanmar army personnel arrived at Taga after a long march from Khamti in the Naga-inhabited territory of the Sagaing region and settled in temporary camps, which was considered unusual by the rebel groups.[171] The situation took a drastic turn on 28 January when six functionaries of the NSCN(K) were arrested and the outfit was asked to surrender without delay. The other groups sought to negotiate with the army after they were conveyed the same message, but to no avail. The army was in no mood to talk to the rebels.[172] Sensing the futility of engaging in combat, the rebels vacated the camps by grabbing as many weapons, ammunition and essential stuff as possible and made a dash for the hills, while some functionaries crossed the Taga river in the valley to escape the army. The army's primary targets were the camps of ULFA, the PLA and the UNLF, which were burned after a brief exchange with a few rebel cadres.[173] The operation resulted in the death of six functionaries and capture of around fifty cadres from different groups.[174]

The operation had unfolded almost as per the assessment of the Tatmadaw so the outfits would evacuate the camps without engaging in combat. Their combined strength would have been around 3,000 at Taga, but they knew they were not in a position to challenge Tatmadaw. They did not have the infinite resources that would be needed to sustain the conflict for a long duration.[175] Moreover, the Manipuri groups also have camps in the southern zone of Sagaing Division, which exist through a tacit understanding with a section of Tatmadaw, involving the payment of fixed sums of money at regular intervals by the groups.[176] Provoking the army could only land them in greater danger in Myanmar.

The other components of the operation were executed as per the plan chalked out earlier by the two armies. A month later, the Indian army rushed additional companies to Mizoram to assist the Assam Rifles in enhancing surveillance at certain locations along the southern border of the state, coinciding with an operation by the Tatmadaw in Myanmar's Chin State.[177] The army was withdrawn a couple of months later, only after it was convinced that the Arakan Army would not scout for safe havens in Mizoram.[178]

In the north, most of the rebel functionaries evicted from Taga took shelter at the camps near the Second Battalion, council and the general headquarters, which was closest to the border with India. Almost three months later, barring the camps in the council region, all the establishments came under relentless mortar attack for several days. With these attacks, the Myanmar army columns deployed in the adjacent hills compelled all the outfits to abandon the camps. In the Second Battalion, two cadres of PREPAK were killed when a shell exploded at the hut where they lived.[179] Thirty-six functionaries of the NSCN(K) were detained at the army establishment in Khamti. Weeks later, five among them were jailed for violating the bilateral ceasefire agreement signed in 2012 after they were found assisting Indian insurgent groups. On 27 May 2019, the Naga outfit claimed that a 'war-like situation' had been created in the Naga-inhabited region as a result of the 'joint political and military operation' by Myanmar and India in violation of the ceasefire ground rules. In a press release, it said that the Naga army has exercised 'extreme restraint' and refused to sign the nationwide ceasefire agreement since it was 'alien' to the Nagas.[180]

Following their evacuation from the camps, a severe financial crisis gripped all the outfits. The network of funds and the infrastructure that had sustained the flow of essential commodities to the camps were ruptured. Many functionaries evicted from the camps returned to the remote villages beyond the Tatmadaw's reach, but these settlements did not produce a huge surplus to feed hundreds of cadres for an indefinite period. Subsequently, some functionaries from the Manipuri groups and a squad of the NDFB surreptitiously embarked on a long trek in their attempt to get to safer locations and camps in the southern zone of Sagaing Division.[181] ULFA concentrated most of its cadres at the Arakan Camp in the region near the council, not far from the border of Changlang in Arunachal Pradesh, from where it continued to occasionally engage in operations against the security forces in the Northeast.[182]

The Tatmadaw preferred not to extend the operation to the council region for the time being, given the meagre resources at its disposal and the conflicts raging in other parts of the country. It knew that the Naga separatist movement had been immensely weakened, with negligible chances of revival. The dire situation caused by the operation fuelled the second split in the NSCN(K), when chairman Yung Aung expelled commander-in-chief Nikki Summi and two senior functionaries from the organization on charges of convening 'illegal meetings', misappropriation of funds, encouragement of 'divisive policies' and failure to report at the council headquarters upon being summoned.[183]

Summi had no option but to return to Nagaland with his associates, despite the charge sheet and a reward for his capture announced by the National Investigation Agency for his involvement in ambushing an army convoy in Manipur six years ago.[184] For the time being, NIA agreed to turn a blind eye to the charge sheet as the government attached greater importance to weakening the separatist camp in Myanmar. So, Summi signed a ceasefire agreement with the government after reaching Nagaland with his squad.[185] They joined the other outfits there as part of the peace process, the outcome of which had become increasingly unpredictable, like the government exercises with other rebel groups in the Northeast.

Ceasefire, Revamp and Regrouping

The dissension among the Nagas in Myanmar seemed to have aggravated the gloomy ambience at the ULFA camps.[186] There was no large clique in ULFA parting ways from each other, but the passion to continue with the separatist campaign in the prevailing uncertain conditions was fizzling out among a large chunk of the remaining functionaries in Myanmar. Many of them eventually crossed the border to surrender before the government. Jibon Moran, the senior-most ULFA functionary, who headed the finance department and had been suffering from many ailments for a long time, chose to join the camp of the overground functionaries in Assam. By the end of 2020, only about 170 ULFA cadres were left in Myanmar, including the squad in the hideouts along the country's border with China.[187]

These developments happened against the backdrop of rumours that serious factionalism had gripped the outfit's camps in Myanmar. Almost a year before Moran's exit was the vanishing act of Munna Baruah, alias Rupak Asom, from a hideout along the China-Myanmar border. Rupak, who was also Paresh's nephew, was an engineer whose entry into the outfit had hogged media attention for several days.[188] Close on the heels of these developments came the news about the disappearance of former PCG member Rebati Phukan from Guwahati, who was a childhood buddy and trusted associate of Paresh's.[189] Then, Paresh himself had a narrow escape from an accident somewhere in the hills of Yunnan while travelling on a motorbike, resulting in some fractures in the rib cage.[190] The camps were in dire financial straits as the flow of funds had become erratic owing to the intensified counter-insurgency operations by the security forces in some border districts of Assam and Arunachal Pradesh. Paresh grew anxious at the hostile circumstances, even as he was compelled to look for ways and means to check any further deterioration of the organization.[191]

On 15 May 2021, he declared a unilateral ceasefire for three months citing the COVID-19 pandemic in Assam as the reason for the decision.[192] Ahead of Independence Day on 15 August, the outfit issued a statement renewing the ceasefire for another three months and, for the first time since the late 1980s, asked the people not to boycott the event. Instead, an appeal was made to the people to register their protest by wearing black badges and unfurling black flags.[193]

Paresh's decision to declare a unilateral ceasefire came just five days after the BJP-led government assumed charge in Assam under the leadership of Himanta Biswa Sarma, who had been arrested in 1991 for his alleged involvement with the outfit.[194] Paresh thus may have expected the new government to reciprocate with a ceasefire, too. But it did not. Instead, the government chose to pursue a two-pronged strategy of continuing with the counter-insurgency operations and exploring the possibility of talks with Paresh.[195]

A large section in the security establishment was convinced that the ceasefire was no more than an attempt to create a conducive ambience for the recruitment of more cadres and effect a shake-up in the organization.[196] At the same time, there were officers and leaders in the ruling parties who felt that putting in efforts to convince Paresh for a peace process with the government should not be abandoned.[197] Chief minister Sarma ruled out the possibility of any discussion on Assam's sovereignty, which Paresh had been insisting upon, but stated that efforts were on to find a 'middle ground' to ensure an 'honourable participation' by Paresh in the peace process.[198]

There was no adverse reaction from Paresh on the statement, which served to convey the message that he may no longer insist on Assam's sovereignty as the core issue in negotiations with the government. A senior officer at an intelligence agency who had been speaking to Paresh occasionally scurried to send an emissary to meet the rebel leader in a foreign destination.[199] However, what the rebel leader asserted next proved to be an absolute dampener in the whole exercise. Paresh had no qualms about reiterating his earlier demand that sovereignty must figure in the talks with the government. And the government, he pointed out, must spell out in black and white that it was agreeable to the precondition.[200] All hope of convincing Paresh to sit for talks almost came to an end at this point.

Perhaps it was after the rebuff by Paresh that the government decided to recommence efforts to extradite ULFA chairman Abhijit Asom from the UK. India has an extradition treaty with the UK, which was inked in 1994. Not surprisingly, the chairman was interrogated several times by British security agencies sometime in mid-2021 on the charge sheet prepared by the NIA, which had already been submitted to the UK government.[201] At some point, the Indian government grew confident that the decks would be cleared for Abhijit Asom's extradition. However, the Indian government's efforts to extradite him from the UK was destined to be a tough exercise. The most clinching evidence submitted against Abhijit was a photograph aired by a local TV news channel in Assam showing him delivering a lecture at the ULFA camp in Myanmar's Taga.[202]

Abhijit's lawyers in London got on with the task of defending him arduously. Their primary argument that he was a human rights activist and not the ULFA chairman. They got in touch with a senior lawyer who practised in India's Supreme Court and got him to dispatch a letter to some activists of a human rights organization in Assam soliciting information to be passed on to London. The activists were unfamiliar with ULFA's history and the chairman's role in it. Their efforts to accomplish the task with the assistance of some journalists were futile too.[203]

Nonetheless, the lawyers in London were reported to have argued the case well before the British government. They cited several examples of similar requests for extradition from different countries that had been turned down by the UK government, besides forwarding a convincing plea that Abhijit could face the death penalty in India for waging war against the government.[204] Paresh, on his part, had also plunged headlong into making his own contribution to thwart Abhijit's extradition to India. He knew that Abhijit's presence in India could mean a boost to the peace process by the pro-talks faction led by Rajkhowa. For, in all probability, Abhijit would be compelled by the government to support the ongoing talks in lieu of being released from jail. And all this would only result in Paresh's further marginalization and the irrelevance of his campaign for sovereignty. So, Paresh rejigged the outfit again by excluding Abhijit and declaring him as 'fictitious', nothing more than a creation of the Indian intelligence agencies![205] By doing so, he hoped that the lawyers in London would be armed with more fodder to foil Abhijit's extradition. Finally, the UK government turned down the Indian government's plea for Abhijit's extradition in 2022.[206]

Paresh's faction was transformed into a three-tiered structure comprising the supreme council, the high council and the lower council after the revamp. There was no time to hunt for a new chairman. The possibility of finding somebody suitable for the position was extremely slim, as he would have to be at a safe distance from the Indian government. The absence of a chairman did not make a huge difference since Paresh had been dominating the organization for a long time—a fact that was also one of the reasons for the split in 2009. So, he placed himself at the head of the three-member supreme council while Nayan Asom was tasked to lead the two other councils. The list of members in the councils was a stark indication of the decreasing numbers of senior functionaries with Paresh. Not only were all of them included but there were three retired functionaries who were vested with specific roles.[207]

After these developments, it did not take long for Paresh to decide against extending the unilateral ceasefire, which had been extended twice. Towards the latter part of 2021, he warned that operations would be resumed against the security forces for committing atrocities against innocent civilians.[208] Five months later, a squad of eleven spies sent to an ULFA camp in Myanmar, allegedly by a section of police and army officers, was identified. Two among them were put before the firing squad. Their confessions on camera, in which they named a few officers, were mailed to media houses.[209]

Paresh began to assume an aggressive posture again. He reiterated that there was no possibility of a peace process with the government unless Assam's sovereignty was on the agenda for talks.[210] The uncertain situation that made Paresh jittery for some months was over. The constraints of funds for the camps seem to have been overcome for the time being, after several businessmen in Assam were compelled to open their purse strings.[211] There was a sudden spurt in recruitment, with some women also deciding to hit the trail to the camps in Myanmar.[212] By early 2022, the strength of ULFA's anti-talks faction swelled to over 300 in Myanmar, with at least two batches already having completed their training.[213] They were stationed at the four existing camps, including the new central and general headquarters at Hakhi in the Naga-inhabited region of Myanmar. The biggest establishment was at the Second Battalion, which has been reestablished after it was evacuated during Operation Sunrise.[214]

These developments were facilitated by the changed situation in Myanmar, which provided abundant space for the rebel groups to sustain their presence in the country. On 1 February 2021, the military coup against the civilian government led by Aung San Suu Kyi galvanized a rebellion against the military regime to an unprecedented extent. Chin State and Sagaing Division, which are contiguous with India, are among the hotspots of the resistance movement, where even helicopter gunships had been pressed into service by the regime to attack the strongholds of the resistance squads and People's Defence Forces (PDFs).[215] The PDF's armed campaign is in addition to the battle that is being waged against the military by the Ethnic Armed Organization (EAO) such as the Kachin Independence Army, the Chin National Army and the Karen National Liberation Army. According to some estimates, the Tatmadaw's strength would be 2,50,000–3,00,000 and the numbers of combat soldiers even lower, at 1,00,000–1,20,000.[216] It was in desperate need of allies to crush the resistance movement and of policies to neutralize as many hostile armed groups as possible, similar to the tactics used by the military against the people's uprising in 1988.

There were widespread rumours among a large section of the Myanmarese resistance fighters and refugees in Mizoram and Manipur that the Junta had firmed up a deal with some rebel outfits from the Northeast. They were of the opinion that four outfits from Manipur—the People's Liberation Army (PLA), People's Revolutionary Party of Kangleipak (PREPAK), United National Liberation Front (UNLF), Kanna Yawol Kanna Lup (KYKL) and Zomi Revolutionary Army (ZRA)—were hand-in-glove with the Junta and were also participating in attacks against the resistance groups in Myanmar's Chin State and Sagaing Division.[217] The rebels were reportedly told by the Junta that their camps and investments would be untouched, but they must keep a tab on and engage in operations against the PDFs in Sagaing Division and Chin State.[218] Lending credence to the development were reports of regrouping by the separatist outfits in Myanmar's Naga-inhabited zone, almost two years after they had been evicted in Operation Sunrise.[219] An attack by the Chin National Army, which is at the vanguard of the movement against the military in Chin State, on a camp of the PLA was evidence of the strained relations between these groups.[220]

That an understanding between the Junta and the rebel outfits from Manipur exists is not in doubt. However, what also appears certain is the Junta's ostensible confidence that neither the Nagas nor any outfit from India's Northeast will incite trouble in the zones they reside in. Sometime around mid-2022, the Myanmar troops stationed at Taga in the Naga region were withdrawn for deployment in the hotspots where the military faced a stiff challenge from resistance groups.[221] The Junta is more concerned with groups such as the Chin National Army and the Kachin Independence Army (KIA), affiliated to Myanmar's government-in-exile or the National Unity Government (NUG), that have entrenched themselves at convenient locations very close to the border with India. There were ample indications that functionaries of many of these resistance groups are active in Mizoram.[222] Some of them have also been apprehended on a few occasions in the Indian border state and have been found to be in possession of explosives.[223]

The civil war in Myanmar could be long drawn, dragging on for years on end. The warring parties—the Junta and the underground National Unity Government (NUG) with the PDFs and EAO—are determined to continue the armed campaign against each other, which could intensify as they each have the support of many countries across the globe. The continuation of the conflict in Myanmar and the country's geopolitics will continue to provide space for the Indian rebel outfits to sustain their establishments in the country. In the given circumstances, the Junta is unlikely to adopt a belligerent posture towards them at the behest of the Indian government. So, the battle in the Northeast between the separatist rebels and security forces will continue for some more time, with occasional changes in the standard operating procedures and tactics on both sides.

EPILOGUE

ULFA'S CAMPAIGN FOR Assam's sovereignty and independence has come at a heavy price, with long term implications. According to an estimate by some leaders of the pro-talks faction, around 1,900 functionaries have lost their lives in the movement since the outfit emerged in the early 1980s.[1] More civilians have died in the violence, either as a result of being targeted by the outfit, caught in the crossfire between the rebels and security forces or exterminated by the secret killers.[2] During the same period, not less than 13,000 functionaries surrendered and returned to the mainstream, which could be one of the highest among all insurgent outfits in the country.[3] Among the zones in Assam that have been impacted the most in terms of violence and casualties are the eastern districts of Sivasagar, Charaideo, Dibrugarh and Tinsukia, considered the Assamese heartland, and Nalbari in the west.

ULFA has been a factor in influencing the trajectory of political developments in Assam for a better part of the post-Independence period. But, four decades into the blood-spattered movement, the outfit is nowhere near achieving its goals. Its predicament has been the same as that of other rebel organizations in the Northeast that stay on the back foot despite the aggressive counter-strategies employed by the government. The advantage gained by the security forces can be gleaned from the declining trend of insurgency-related incidents in the region. Data compiled by the government suggests there had been a drop in such incidents by as much as 70 per cent in the span of six years between 2013 and 2019.[4]

Early in 2022, the government felt confident enough to revoke the controversial Armed Forces (Special Powers) Act 1958 from some zones in the three states of Assam, Nagaland and Manipur, on the heels of a similar decision to repeal the law in Tripura and Meghalaya.[5] The change in the situation is also reflected in the fact that the overground rebel groups engaged in the peace process with the government are the largest among the five categories of militants that exist in the Northeast (the other four being the separatists, the Muslim fundamentalist organizations, also called jihadi groups, the Maoists and the small groups that surface from time to time, most apparent in Assam's twin hill districts, Karbi Anglong and Dima Hasao).

Sustaining an armed campaign against a mighty state like India is undeniably a difficult task. ULFA's pro-talks faction continues to nurture the hope that an accord will be clinched with the government, but is in no position to press the government for an early decision. The BJP-led government in Assam, which is likely to stay in power for long, has multiple objectives to fulfil. The agreement will become a reality only if it fits into the party's agenda in the state. The anti-talks ULFA faction, as also the rest of the separatist outfits from Manipur, can hope to be safe in Myanmar as long as the country's Junta maintains a neutral policy towards them. It is difficult to predict the scenario in Bangladesh if the pro-India Awami League were to be defeated in the forthcoming general elections in 2023. Whether the separatist outfits from the Northeast are able to reestablish base in Bangladesh remains to be seen, but the possibility of radical Islamist organizations and terror groups gaining prominence in the country cannot be ruled out, in which case there could be disturbances in Assam and other border states in India.

In any case, ULFA cannot regain the position of strength it had in the late 1980s or in the 1990s, as the space for its existence has shrunk in Assam. War-weariness has set in among the residents of the region, whose aspirations and responses have also transformed over the past several decades. ULFA's failure to anticipate the turnout of events was the consequence of an ethos that enveloped the organization from the late 1980s and could not be eradicated. The rivalry between the armed and political wings stretched to an incredible extent, with constant efforts by the former to dominate the organization. The triumvirate—Rajkhowa, Anup and Paresh—were hardly together at the same place for a long time. Barring a few exceptions, there were not too many occasions when the leaders got together to discuss long-term strategy—a fact that was best illustrated during Operation All Clear in Bhutan. The frequent alteration of the organizational structure—in 1995, 2003, 2011 and 2021—triggered more confusion than addressing the issues in the outfit. It would be difficult to find another rebel group in the region or country that has undergone organizational changes so many times.

A decisive turning point for ULFA came in 1997, when the door for representation at global forums was shut forever, followed by Anup's incarceration in Bangladesh. The void enabled Paresh to tighten his grip on the organization and enforce his agenda. His position was strengthened owing to the vital role he played in the management of finances and weapons. His mindset began to shape the organization's policies and reactions to different situations. Paresh is a tactician par excellence, but he may never be a strategist with a long-term vision. As a result, ULFA's focus remained on short-term goals and continuation of the separatist campaign at any cost.

For Paresh, dialogue with the government was futile unless it meant Assam's complete separation from India. He believes, or is seen to believe, that war between China and India is imminent, and that it would result in the defeat of the latter and separation of the Northeast from it.[6] The Northeast region would then emerge as an independent confederacy of the different communities that live there, in alliance with China. However, it is unlikely that China would wage war with India either at the behest of ULFA or for separating the Northeast from the country. Beijing is more likely to continue pricking India with occasional clashes along the Line of Actual Control (LAC) besides engaging in a serious water war in the future by fiddling with the rivers in Tibet.

Not surprisingly, there was precious little articulated by ULFA on Assam's burning issues, except the colonial thesis of the state being stripped dry of its resources by New Delhi, which was repeated at regular intervals. ULFA was never serious about expanding its support base beyond the mainstream Assamese communities in the Brahmaputra valley. Participation of the tea tribes, one of the biggest communities in the state, was negligible. In course of time, rebel outfits emerged among all the tribal communities in Assam without any links to ULFA (barring the NDFB for a brief span). In this regard, as some former rebel functionaries claimed, the Jatiya Unnayan Parishad (JUP) could have been an ideal tool for ULFA's consolidation in the valley over a period of time, but its significance could not be grasped by the leaders. Nobody was in doubt that the JUP had begun to usher in a sort of revolution in Assam's rural areas in the late 1980s. These functionaries are of the unflinching view that ULFA ought to have embarked on a long-term plan for several decades, in a manner similar to the UNLF in Manipur, which was to form the armed wing more than two decades after the outfit was launched in 1964.

In the same vein, there was no effort by ULFA to gain a deeper understanding of the ills afflicting society and economy in Assam. The state has reeled under continuous turmoil for over 200 years since the Moamoria rebellion in 1769 that shook the Ahom regime. The genocide by the Burmese invaders was followed by ruthless exploitation of the state's resources by the colonial government, through policies that were extremely detrimental to the interests of the indigenous communities. This interfered with the process of jati, or race formation, unique to every society. In Assam, the process was ruptured by the unremitting disorder in the state, which did not diminish even after Independence. More centrifugal tendencies were unleashed, sharpening the divisions among the different communities. What was necessary was 'social engineering', including conscious efforts at cultural blending, where the marginal groups would have been able to retain their identities. Civil society organizations and the intelligentsia could have certainly played a pivotal role in bringing this about, but that never happened. Remedies for a disease can be found only when there is acceptance of the reality, which was and still is missing in the Brahmaputra valley. The reason why there is so much reluctance among Assam's mainstream communities to accept the realities of their state and people is a topic for deep research.

Sadly, it is not surprising that there were no real efforts to find solutions to the burning issues in Assam. And it is also not shocking to observe similarities between ULFA's downhill journey and the decline of the so-called 'Jatiyo Sangathans' (nationalist groups) in Assam, such as the Asom Gana Parishad (AGP) and the All-Assam Students' Union (AASU). The AGP had grown so feeble that it was begging for an alliance with the BJP in the state assembly polls of 2016. Its leaders had no qualms about continuing their association with the party in the government, even after the passage of the controversial Citizenship (Amendment) Act in parliament, which nullified the Assam Accord. The commitment to resolve the issue of illegal immigration, which continues to be a grave threat to the indigenous communities, is no longer discernible among these nationalist groups. The BJP has since surged ahead with its Hindutva agenda, which is alien to Assam and is bound to impact the secular fabric of the state. In this regard, mention must also be made of some Muslim outfits in the state that have embarked on a similar programme of radicalization in some zones inhabited by residents of East Bengal origin.

These failures are reflective of a crisis in society in the Brahmaputra valley, which has been triggering irreversible consequences. Leaders, political parties and civil society organizations are all stark reflections of society. A more conscious society will certainly produce more committed and uncompromising leaders and organizations. Therefore, it is quite unlikely that Assam would embark upon a path of redemption even if it were to secede from India. This apart, the Northeast is landlocked, consists of some of the poorest states in the country and is heavily dependent on the Centre for its financial largesse.

All these drawbacks notwithstanding, ULFA has demonstrated its huge potential to survive against many odds. The government had expected the outfit to crumble after Operation Bajrang, and again after Operation All Clear in Bhutan. ULFA proved them wrong. It not only survived but retaliated with more violence. The situation in the neighbouring countries was favourable for the sustenance of ULFA's bases. When ULFA landed in Bangladesh in the early 1990s, the dictatorial regime of president Hussain Muhammad Ershad had just ended after violent protests; Bhutan was limping back to normalcy after the eviction of the Nepalese settlers from the southern districts, and the occasional raids in Myanmar by the army in the Naga-inhabited regions of the country drew to a close from the mid-1990s. The ULFA leadership seized the opportunity to establish bases in these countries, which it sustained for many years. It displayed an uncanny knack for networking in foreign territory, stretching from Europe to Southeast Asia. Perhaps, in terms of foreign linkages, ULFA could be next only to the Liberation Tigers of Tamil Eelam (LTTE) in south Asia, which waged a long battle for independence for the Tamils in Sri Lanka.

In Assam, there was abundant political space for the growth and sustenance of militancy, which was similar to the situation in

Manipur and Nagaland. That space has reduced, but it has not been eradicated completely. The decrease in insurgency-related incidents in the Northeast does not mean that the issues fuelling militancy have petered out. The government's policies continue to remain focused on short-term goals and winning elections. In the past four decades, Assam has definitely witnessed improvement in infrastructure but has not shown a huge difference in terms of an increase in avenues of employment. This is the reason why ULFA never faced a crisis of cadres in the manner that it suffered from sporadic financial distress. Whenever a batch of functionaries renounced the cult of the gun, there were others to hit the trail to the jungle. While fewer young men and women now join ULFA, the majority continue to be drawn from the low-income groups in rural and semi-rural areas of the eastern districts. ULFA has developed into a concept that cannot be erased easily from the minds of the people of Assam. There will always be a section among the youth for whom the path espoused by the outfit appears justified. An academic aptly remarked that ULFA has been more powerful in Assam as an idea than as a political or military organization.[7]

On the flipside, insurgency has been a major factor in compelling New Delhi to pay greater attention to Assam and the Northeast. ULFA's history, in particular, had been replete with many episodes that necessitated the attention of the highest level of the government. True, a sincere effort to come to grips with the complexities of the region is still missing, but there is certainly more deliberation on the region in the capital and greater allocation of funds for development. The Department of Development of North Eastern Region (DoNER) was created in 1998 and later elevated to a ministry. The non-lapsable Central pool of resources mandated almost all ministries, (barring some like the ministry of defence), to earmark at least 10 per cent of their annual budgets for the region. There is also greater monitoring now of the utilization of funds disbursed to the region.

There were also some inadvertent spin-offs in Assam from the separatist movement. The emergence of the SULFA and its activities caused extreme revulsion among the people for a long time. But it was also from these rowdy gun-wielding activists that many successful businessmen emerged; they began to dabble in domains that had traditionally belonged to the Marwaris. The business concerns they established in Assam, and at far-off locations in the state, blazed a trail for others to follow. By the early 2000s, there were few businesses in the state that did not have the participation of the Assamese, which also meant employment for several thousands of hitherto jobless youths.

The quest to venture into uncharted territory became no less prominent among students and professionals, who began to opt for greener pastures in other states of the country and abroad. The disturbed conditions in the state were one of the reasons that triggered this movement during the 1990s, which has continued vigorously ever since. Only a fraction among them has been found to return home after completion of their studies and assignments. The scope of getting decent jobs is certainly higher in the metropolises and the states that have reaped the benefits of the liberalized Indian economy than in Assam. Thus, the seeds for the transformation of the insular character of society in the Brahmaputra valley were sown, and this transformation has only deepened over the years. Large numbers of people have also migrated out from the other Northeastern states owing to lack of employment avenues there. Therefore, in a manner of speaking, insurgency in the Northeast has been a factor that has bridged the gulf, to some extent, between the frontier region and the mainland, which was never envisaged by the rebel outfits.

Assam stands at the crossroads of multiple phenomena and events whose outcome will certainly leave a permanent imprint on the social, economic and political landscape of the state. No other state in the country is overwhelmed by problems as complex as

Assam is, ranging from the political to the environmental domains. The issues are manifold and interlinked, making the state a tinder box that successive governments, both at the state and Centre, and society have preferred to overlook. Implementing pragmatic strategies is thus imperative, from a long-term perspective, while taking into account the sensitivities of the region. There may not be very many options to choose from, given the existing circumstances in the state. Only salvaging existing efforts on many of the burning issues may prevent further turmoil.

ACKNOWLEDGEMENTS

THIS BOOK ENTAILED a long journey of over a decade involving arduous assignments, detailed interviews and conversations with many people. I am indebted to everybody who assisted me in gathering facts and understanding the intricate issues linked to ULFA.

Firstly, the senior ULFA leaders and functionaries who were willing to be interviewed. Topping the list is the supremo of the anti-talks faction, Paresh Baruah, who not only gave me the opportunity to meet him in Myanmar but also was kind enough to discuss certain issues many a time over the phone, which helped me gain a better understanding of how the outfit functioned and transformed over the years. Chairman of the pro-talks' group Arabinda Rajkhowa and general secretary Anup Chetia furnished me with valuable facts and an analysis of the origin of ULFA and the situations in the neighbouring countries where the outfit had established a presence.

Other functionaries from the overground and surrendered categories who contributed to furthering my research were Shashadhar Choudhury, Mrinal Hazarika, Pradip Gogoi, Antu Choudang, Lohit Deuri, Raktim Sarma, Budheswar Gogoi, Biju

Deka, Chakra Gohain, Diganta Konwar, Ruby Bhuyan, Sunil Nath, Diwakar Moran, Hira Sarania, Jitu Talukdar, Bikash Dutta, Mithinga Daimary, Mrinmoy Hazaria, Pradip Sen Deka, Pranati Deka, Pranjit Saikia, Ramu Mech, Suren Dihingia, Bhupen Borgohain, Satabda Kumar, Elisa Payeng, Moni Hazarika, Suvan Saikia, Munin Nabis, Deep Mishra, Hiranya Saikia, Kamal Barphukan, Kania Hazarika, Mihir Deuri, Kaberi Kachari, Samudra Gogoi, Rathin Talukdar, Jiten Dutta and Mihir Chetia.

Among the NDFB leaders of the different factions were chairman Ranjan Daimary and general secretary Gobinda Basumatary, who provided me information on some lesser-known aspects of the presence of the separatist groups in Bhutan and Bangladesh.

There were scores of people from government departments, civil society groups, the media and the legal profession whose inputs helped expand the narrative. I would like to mention H.N. Das, Nishi Kanta Changkakati, retired brigadier Rumel Dahiya, retired brigadier Ranjit Barthakur, Kamaleswar Gogoi, Suresh Saikia, Ananta Kalita, Santanu Bharali, Rita Choudhury, Arup Borbora, Ajit Bhuyan, Dhruba Jyoti Deka, Abhijit Roy, Lachit Bordoloi, Manoj Kumar Nath and Jayanta Goswami.

Many others disclosed information on the condition of anonymity, including former rebels and government officials belonging to the army, police and the intelligence agencies. Also in this category are a journalist colleague and two superannuated government functionaries in Dhaka who helped fill some gaps in the account of Bangladesh.

I will be forever grateful to professor Sumit Ganguly and former Indian high commissioner to Bangladesh Veena Sikri who took out time to go through the entire manuscript and provide catchy endorsements.

My literary consultant and fellow columnist, Atul Thakur, has been a constant source of encouragement. He motivated me not to take too long in completing the book. I cannot thank him enough.

I owe my gratitude to associate publisher Swati Chopra of HarperCollins India for publishing the book and for her suggestions, which helped plug the loopholes in the narrative.

Finally, I will remain ever obliged to two persons who have profoundly impacted my life. Celebrated author and journalist Bertil Lintner has always inspired me to walk the extra mile to gather information. It was from him that I imbibed the credo of producing original content to the extent possible. The clarity, grit and consistency required to complete gruelling assignments were the results of the spiritual lessons from my guru, Gautam Choudhury. I have always looked up to him for advice in difficult situations. May both always be happy and safe in the times to come.

APPENDICES AND NOTES

Scan this QR code to access the appendices and notes.

ABOUT THE AUTHOR

Rajeev Bhattacharyya is a senior journalist, analyst and author based in Guwahati. He has written three books—*Rendezvous with Rebels* (2014), *Lens and the Guerrilla* (2012), *Paresh Baruahr Sandhanat* (Assamese, 2013)—and five academic papers on ULFA before this. He is a regular columnist on the Northeast for The Diplomat, The Irrawaddy, The Quint, Firstpost and Moneycontrol. Earlier, he worked for *The Times of India*, *The Indian Express*, *Times Now* and *The Telegraph,* and he was the founding executive editor of the *Seven Sisters Post* in Guwahati. He is an alumnus of Hansraj College and the Department of History, University of Delhi. He was a Chevening Fellow (2004–05) at the University of Westminster, London.

BY THE SAME AUTHOR

RENDEZVOUS WITH REBELS: JOURNEY TO MEET INDIA'S MOST WANTED MEN

Rajeev Bhattacharyya walked nearly 800 kilometres, over some of the most hostile terrain and through no man's land. His journey, which took three months and twenty days to complete, is unprecedented in Indian journalism. He visited the rebel bases in Eastern Nagaland, which covers a part of Myanmar's Sagaing Division, stayed in the ULFA camp and interviewed its chief of staff Paresh Baruah, as also chairman of the NSCN (Khaplang), S.S. Khaplang himself. He interacted with rebels from banned outfits like the NDFB, UPPK, PLA and other groups—for many of them, this was their first conversation with an Indian journalist. Bhattacharyya is one of very few journalists in the world to have made this journey, and among the fewer still to have had such intimate access.

Rendezvous with Rebels is the story of that journey. It is as much a travel memoir as it is a hard-hitting political account of the fissures that mark the conflicts in India's Northeast and Myanmar's Sagaing Division. Bhattacharyya analyses the historical and current role of ULFA, NSCN and other rebel forces, and sizes up the current situation in Eastern Nagaland vis-à-vis the changes taking place in Myanmar specifically, and the subcontinent generally. It is, ultimately, an up-close examination of a very thorny conflict.

HarperCollins *Publishers* India

At HarperCollins India, we believe in telling the best stories and finding the widest readership for our books in every format possible. We started publishing in 1992; a great deal has changed since then, but what has remained constant is the passion with which our authors write their books, the love with which readers receive them, and the sheer joy and excitement that we as publishers feel in being a part of the publishing process.

Over the years, we've had the pleasure of publishing some of the finest writing from the subcontinent and around the world, including several award-winning titles and some of the biggest bestsellers in India's publishing history. But nothing has meant more to us than the fact that millions of people have read the books we published, and that somewhere, a book of ours might have made a difference.

As we look to the future, we go back to that one word—a word which has been a driving force for us all these years.

Read.